MARTÍN D.

SOCIAL AND CULTURAL VALUES IN EARLY MODERN EUROPE

Series editor
Paolo L. Rossi
Department of Italian Studies
University of Lancaster

In its exploration of the cultural and social upheavals in early modern Europe, this series crosses traditional disciplinary boundaries. It offers a broad-ranging analysis of the forces which shaped structures of belief and practice at all levels of society,
providing original insights into the mentality of early modern Europeans.

The volumes assess the manner in which central as well as peripheral values, institutions and disciplines evolved and, through this identification of metamorphoses, seek to redefine the mechanics of change and to re-evaluate the meanings of a central or hegemonic culture.

Individual titles address many neglected or emerging subject areas, incorporating the
history of the less studied countries of Eastern Europe. In so doing, the contributors examine a vast range of source material, including literary, historical, scientific,
philosophical and artistic evidence.

MARTÍN DEL RIO
INVESTIGATIONS INTO MAGIC

Edited and translated by
P. G. Maxwell-Stuart

Manchester University Press
Manchester and New York

Published by Manchester University Press
Oxford Road, Manchester M13 9NR, UK
and Room 400, 175 Fifth Avenue, New York, NY 10010, USA
www.manchesteruniversitypress.co.uk

Distributed exclusively in the USA by
Palgrave, 175 Fifth Avenue, New York NY 10010, USA

Distributed exclusively in Canada by
UBC Press, University of British Columbia, 2029 West Mall,
Vancouver, BC, Canada V6T 1Z2

British Library Cataloguing-in-Publication Data
A catalogue record for this book is available from the British Library

Library of Congress Cataloging-in-Publication Data
A catalog record for this book is available from the Library of Congress

ISBN 13: 978 0 7190 8053 1

First published in hardback 2000 by Manchester University Press

This paperback edition first published 2009

Printed by Lightning Source

Contents

	Series editor's foreword	vii
	Acknowledgements	xi
	Introduction	1
	Notes on the editing and translation	24
	Prologue, explaining why this treatise has been difficult to write, but why it was necessary to do so	27
Book 1	Magic in general, and natural and artificial magic in particular	31
Book 2	Magic involving evil spirits	68
Book 3	Harmful magic and superstition	117
Book 4	Divination	148
Book 5	The duty of judges in dealing with workers of harmful magic: or, the judicial process in relation to the crime of magic	189
Book 6	The duty of a confessor	240
	Select bibliography	283
	Index	285

Series editor's foreword

The traditional picture of the early modern European witch-hunt where hundreds of thousands of innocent souls were condemned by both Catholic and Protestant authorities, religious and secular, to a fiery fate has now been radically modified. This does not mean however that beliefs in witchcraft, magic, demons, astrology and other superstitions were any less prevalent or important for the society of that time. From Augustine to Thomas Aquinas and beyond, intellectuals had debated the limits and dangers pertaining to magic, seen as the effecting of preternatural control over nature with the assistance of demons. The Church itself could not deny the existence of demons for to do so it would also have to deny the reality of spirits, both good and bad, upon which so much doctrine relied. There were also significant problems posed by natural magic which could call into question the miracles of Christ. Indeed the Catholic demonologists were also aware that the very ceremonies and sacraments of the Church needed defending as they could be, and were, seen as having strong links with magic.

The early Church had set out the distinctions between white and black magic and had proscribed sanctions for those found guilty of *maleficia*. Pronouncements stressed the dangerous illusions perpetrated by demons in order to turn Christians away from the path of the true faith. The penalties were restricted to confession, repentance and charitable work. In the Middle Ages the war against heresy led to the setting up of the Inquisition and the eventual linking of witchcraft to heresy, with the emphasis on the weakness of women which made them particularly susceptible to such activities. Pope Innocent VIII in 1484 gave authority to prosecutions for witchcraft with the bull *Summis desiderantes affectibus*. Two years later saw the publication, in Cologne, of the *Malleus Maleficarum* (Hammer of Witches), a handbook for inquisitors by Jacob Sprenger and Heinrich Institoris (Kramer). This gave a legal framework linked to demonological theories with a codification of procedures. The reasons for the witch-hunts that followed are complex and did not affect all parts of Europe in the same way.[1]

[1] See: *Witches, Devil and Doctors, in the Renaissance. Johann Weyer, De praestigiis daemonum*, New York, 1991. pp. xlvii–lv. Brian Easlea, *Witch Hunting, Magic and the New Philosophy*, Brighton, 1980. C. Larner, *Witchcraft and Religion. The Politics of Popular Belief*, Oxford, 1984. For the cultural and social dimension see *The Devil, Heresy and Witchcraft in the Middle Ages* ed. Alberto Ferreiro, Leiden, 1998.

The demonologists, both Catholic and Protestant, brought immense erudition to bear on such vexing questions as: what evidence was there that magic existed, what were the limits to the power of demons, from whence did such power come?[2] In order to understand the thought processes involved one cannot investigate these topics in isolation. They must be seen within the wider context of current theories of natural philosophy (science) and as integral, fundamental, and indivisible components of rich theological and philosophical traditions inherited and venerated by early modern thinkers, both religious and secular.[3] With regard to natural magic a number of important studies by Brian P. Copenhaver have pointed out how the philosophical theory of natural magic was part of a larger system of natural philosophy, and that 'to discredit occult qualities required a complete repudiation of traditional physics of its metaphysical context'.[4] There was a close relationship between traditional magic, experimental science, Aristotelianism, and Platonism which gave rise to differing and ever-changing conceptions of nature. The popular Hermetica, the revival of Neoplatonic philosophy in fifteenth century Florence, Marsilio Ficino's translation of the *Corpus Hermeticum* and Giovanni Pico della Mirandola's studies of the Cabala represent a body of writings that provided both physical and metaphysical support for beliefs in magic. Magic played a significant role in the history of science and its importance should be acknowledged and understood rather than passed over in embarrassed silence. Belief in the occult existed at every level of early modern society. It informed learned debate in theology, philosophy, medicine and science and was the basis for many civic rituals and political and dynastic propaganda. It was in no way inconsistent for members of the Royal Society such as Henry More and Joseph Glanvill and even the great Dr Samuel Johnson to accept the notions of the spirit world and witchcraft.[5]

One of the main problems for the demonologists was the debate on the natural and demoniacal character of magic. On how to distinguish natural magic (which was good) from witchcraft and magic of demons (which was evil). This

[2] For the various approaches to demonology see: Stuart Clark, *Thinking with Demons*, Oxford, 1997.

[3] For reasons for beliefs in magic see: Brian P. Copenhaver, 'A tale of two fishes: magical objects in natural history from antiquity through the scientific revolution', *Journal of the History of Ideas*, 52, 1991, pp. 373–98; Id. 'Did science have a Renaissance?' *Isis* 82, 1992, pp. 1–21; Id. 'Natural magic, hermetism, and occultism in early modern science', in *Reappraisals of the Scientific Revolution*, ed. David C. Lindberg and Robert S. Wiseman, Cambridge, 1990, pp. 261–301.

[4] See Copenhaver, 'A tale of two fishes', p. 386.

[5] See A. Rupert Hall, *Henry More, Magic, Religion and Experiment*, Oxford, 1990. For a review of different critical approaches see Patrick Curry, 'Revisions of science and magic', *History of Science*, 23, 1985, pp. 299–325.

translation by P. G. Maxwell-Stuart of the lengthy *Disquisitiones Magicae* written by the Jesuit Martín Del Rio at the end of the sixteenth century makes accessible the most significant Catholic contribution to the debate on witchcraft and magic. The sheer weight of Del Rio's erudition where philosophy, theology and the law are conscripted in battle against Satan and his followers gave his treatise, which deals with both theory and practical matters, great authority. Del Rio took witchcraft seriously and linked all kinds of magic (including witchcraft, astrology, alchemy, divination, and prophecy) to heresy. It represented a turning away from God and an alliance with the forces of evil. As Dr Maxwell-Stuart points out the *Disquisitiones Magicae* is more than a handbook on witchcraft, it is also a polemical religious work which gives an insight into the concerns of the post-Tridentine Church. Though he accepted, without question, the existence of witches, Del Rio called for balanced judgement. He demanded scrutiny of all accusations and evidence lest injustice be done to the innocent.[6]

This judicious selection and translation of Del Rio's writings will no doubt form the basis for further research into the theories of witchcraft, demonology, the distinction between supernatural and preternatural powers and the Catholic/Protestant warnings of the particular perils inherent in following superstitious practices. Although, due to the length of the *Disquisitiones Magicae*, it has not been possible to translate the whole text, the introduction includes a précis of all the topics in the book which allows one to appreciate the structure and subject matter of Del Rio's compendium.

---

[6] The desire for correct procedure can be seen in J. Tedeschi, 'The Roman inquisition and witchcraft. An early seventeenth-century "Instruction" on correct trial procedure', *Revue de l'Histoire des Religions*, 200, 1983, pp. 163–88.

Acknowledgements

I should like to thank the staff of the Rare Books and Manuscripts Department in the University Library of St Andrews for their unfailing courtesy and willingness to be of assistance, Maximilian von Habsburg for answering my questions about Archbishop Ernst of Bavaria, and Professor Stuart Clark and Dr Paolo L. Rossi for their helpful comments.

Introduction

It is a remarkable whim of history that of all the major demonologists of the early modern period Martín Del Rio is the least studied and the one whose work still remains more or less untranslated and therefore increasingly inaccessible. This is not because the *Disquisitiones Magicae* has nothing to say, or says little at tedious or repetitive length. On the contrary, Del Rio's review of astrology, alchemy, magic, divination, superstition, and witchcraft is not only detailed and comprehensive, richly illustrated from an immensely wide reading in history, theology, medicine, law, and demonology itself, and carefully argued (as one might expect from a Jesuit scholar), but the whole is also laced with wit, vituperation, and personal reminiscence with the result that his *magnum opus* provides not only an encyclopaedia of contemporary demonological theory and a reference work for theologians, lawyers, doctors, and scholars – Del Rio's declared audience – but also a work of instruction and entertainment for any other reader who enjoys sufficient command of Latin to be able to benefit from the author's expansive erudition.

Indeed, so attractive was the *Disquisitiones* and so influential, that Del Rio became a major (perhaps the major) Catholic authority on magic and witchcraft as soon as the book appeared. He was praised by Pierre de Lancre who said that of all those who had written about the subject, he had done so 'le plus sainement et le plus iudicieusement,' and that he was 'le plus grand, le plus rare, et le mieux censé qui ait jamais esté sur ce subiet';[1] and his fellow-Jesuits Justus Lipsius and Heribert Rosweyde offered him laudatory poems which were printed at the beginning of Book 1. While he was still alive, his opinion was sought by civil authorities in Germany, and after his death he was quoted and referred to as far afield as Scotland where, for example, Sir George MacKenzie in *Pleadings in Some Remarkable Cases* (1672) and *Laws and Customs of Scotland* (1678) regarded him as a prime source of information on witchcraft, and the defence advocate in the trial of Christian Shaw (1697) used the *Disquisitiones* to

---

[1] *Tableau de l'inconstance des mauvais anges et démons* (Paris 1612), 485. *L'incrédulité et mescreance du sortilège plainement convaincue* (Paris 1622), 527. Protestant theologians also used and quoted from him: for example, Bartholomäus Anhorn (1616–1700) in his *Magiologia*.

support his arguments in favour of his client.[2] Even as late as the mid-eighteenth century his opinions could still be quoted (though with reservations), in J. J. Zedler's *Universal-Lexicon*.[3]

Life

Martín was well connected. His father, Antonio, came from a noble Castilian family and his mother, Eleonora Lopez, from wealthy Aragonese lineage. Antonio, however, spent a good deal of his working life in the Spanish Netherlands and so it was there, in Antwerp, that Martín was born on 17 May 1558. In due time a brother, Jerónimo, followed.

The Del Rio family background was one of political intrigue, violence, bitter personal hostilities, and sudden reversals of fortune. Both Martín's father, and his uncle Luis Del Rio, were caught up in the turbulence which visited the Spanish Netherlands during the period of John of Austria's attempt to re-impose Spanish control over the province, and as loyal supporters of Philip II, both Antonio and Luis suffered arrest and confinement, Luis in 1576 and Antonio the following year. Luis did not long survive the experience, dying of fever in 1578, but Antonio managed to retrieve his fortunes a little and went into a kind of honourable retirement in Portugal until his death in Lisbon in 1586.

For the first 25 years of his life, however, Martín could rely on the comfort and privilege afforded by membership of a rich, influential family and was given an excellent education to fit his evident intellectual abilities. This began at Lierre in Brabant where, in addition to Greek and Latin, he either learned or made rapid progress in Hebrew, Chaldee, Flemish, German, Spanish, Italian, and French. From Lierre he went to Paris where, at the Collège des Trois Langues, he continued his Classical studies under the tutelage of Denis Lambin, Royal Reader in Greek from 1560 to 1572 and famous for his editions of Latin authors, and at the Collège de Clermont (later the Collège de France), where he studied philosophy under the Jesuit Juan Maldonado, Professor of Theology there from 1565 to 1574. One presumes that it was during this period, too, that Del Rio

---

[2] Isabel Adam: *Witch Hunt, the great Scottish witchcraft trials of 1697* (Macmillan 1978), 165–7, 169.

[3] Behringer: *Witchcraft Persecutions in Bavaria*, 259, 300, 322, 331, 344. His fame as a scholar lasted apart from the association of his name with the *Disquisitiones*. At the end of the seventeenth century, André Baillet was happy to include him in his list of 'enfans celebres par leurs etudes', commenting, 'Il faisoit paroître dans ses premières années une vivacité d'esprit admirable, un génie aisé, une conception pénétrante, une humeur docile et très-douce, beaucoup d'amour pour le travail, et d'aptitude pour les Lettres', *Jugemens des savans sur les principaux ouvrages des auteurs*, 2nd edn, 8 vols, published in 17 vols (Amsterdam 1725), 10.182.

learned mathematics from Johann Stadius (1527–1579) about whom he later remarked that the man was given to a quite extraordinary faith in electional astrology, an enthusiasm of which, quite clearly, Del Rio did not approve.[4]

From Paris he went to Douai, founded in 1562 by Philip II, where he met the Flemish philologist and jurisconsult, Louis Carrion, later Rector of the University of Louvain, and it was in Louvain that Del Rio finished this stage of his education by obtaining his bachelor's degree in civil law, and there met two people who were to become both friends and admirers, Justus Lipsius and Pierre Dheure. Here Del Rio studied under Cornelio Wauters [Cornelius Valerius], the Professor of Classical languages, and it is perhaps no accident that his first book, a commentary on the works of the third century AD epitomist Julius Solinus (1572), was a corrected version of a manuscript from Lipsius's library with Del Rio's own notes and comments upon comments thereto by Cornelio Wauters. A similar volume of notes on Claudian, perhaps the last great pagan poet, which he dedicated to his father, was produced in the same year, the text having been published in 1571. But these were not the only fruits of this period, for since 1569 he had been annotating the plays of Seneca, and in 1574 he published the results, dedicating the book to his uncle Luis in gratitude for the royal favour Luis had caused to be shown to the family.[5]

In this year, too, Del Rio obtained his doctorate from the University of Salamanca, and it was during this time in Spain, specifically while he was living and working in Madrid, Del Rio tells us, that he came across manifestations of popular magic. 'I remember in Madrid in 1573 there was a trial of a notorious prostitute. Near her house they found a young donkey with its brains removed, and the woman confessed under torture that she had used them for a magical potion. She was flogged and sent into exile';[6] and in 1575 he met a young *Zahuri*, a water diviner, visiting him more than once. These people claimed to be able to see objects buried deep in the earth, water-channels, deposits of

---

[4] *·Disquisitiones Magicae* (Investigations Into Magic) Book 4, chapter 3, question 1 (p. 294). Stadius was interested in astronomy and published ephemerides for 1554–1570 (Cologne 1556), revised to 1554–1660 (Cologne 1570), as well as a history of astronomy (n.p. 1580). His interest in occult science, however, can be seen in his translation of the medical astrology of Hermes Trismegistus (n.p. 1584). It was probably during this time in Paris that Del Rio saw, in the Church of Saint Médard, a stained glass window depicting the Last Judgement, upon which he commented later, *Disquisitiones* Book 3, question 7, section 1 (p. 223).

[5] He did not altogether abandon his interest in the subject after this, for *A Collection of Notes on Latin Tragedy* appeared in 1593–1594 and this was still being used by at least one Classical scholar at the beginning of the twentieth century. See Nonius Marcellinus: *De compendiosa doctrina*, ed. W. M. Lindsay, 3 vols (Leipzig 1903).

[6] *Disquisitiones* Book 5, section 4, no. 14 (p. 380).

3

precious metals, and corpses beneath their tombstones.[7] Why was Del Rio so interested? Was he indulging his intellectual curiosity, or was he actually consulting the child professionally? He does not say, and although the latter is not out of the question, the former supposition is perhaps the more likely. It was not the first time Del Rio had shown interest in the workings of the occult world, for he and Lipsius used to talk about dreams while they were fellow-students in Louvain, and on one of these occasions Lipsius told him a story about a cobbler's wife in Brussels, whose dreams had a habit of turning out to be true to the last detail.[8]

1576 saw the arrest of his uncle Luis[9] and the following year that of his father. But Martin's legal expertise had caught the eye of Philip II and, after being co-opted on to the Senate of Brabant at the King's instance, in 1577 he was appointed Attorney General and in 1578 Vice-Chancellor and King's Fiscal for Brabant.[10] The death of his family's particular patron, John of Austria, that year, however, inevitably upset his prospects. What is more, he had already suffered a devastating blow in the loss of his own extensive library when rebel soldiers pillaged his father's mansion at Cleydael, a loss which perhaps added a certain edge to his endeavours to save books and manuscripts belonging to Justus Lipsius when these, too, were in danger of pillage after the battle of Gembloux (31 January 1578). It was all too much and, tired and disillusioned, he obtained permission from Alessandro Farnese, the victorious commander, to take an extended leave.[11] Not surprisingly, perhaps, he decided to return to his roots and so made his way back to Spain where he published the fruits of his legal experiences, a collection and interpretation of miscellaneous legal texts. Then, somewhat to his own surprise, it seems, on 9 May 1580 he entered the Jesuit novitiate in Valladolid.[12]

After two years as a novice, however, his studies were by no means over, for the Society required him to study theology and Biblical literature for three more years at Louvain and Mainz and it was during his return to the Spanish Netherlands, while he was laid up ill in the Jesuit house at Bordeaux, that he

---

[7] *Disquisitiones* Book 1, chapter 3, question 4 (pp. 11–12).

[8] *Disquisitiones* Book 4, chapter 3, question 6 (p. 308).

[9] An incident he recalls with some bitterness, *Disquisitiones* Book 1, chapter 3, question 3 (p. 10).

[10] He makes a reference to this period of his life in *Disquisitiones* Book 4, chapter 2, question 6, section 4 (p. 283).

[11] He makes a brief reference to Farnese's siege of Antwerp in 1585, *Disquisitiones* Book 2, question 16, section 5 (p. 134).

[12] Twenty years later he could still write, 'Who would have believed that after twenty years I would happily desert the law courts for the religious life?' *Disquisitiones* Book 5, Introduction (p. 366).

learned of his father's death.[13] This news, allied perhaps to his own weakened state, had a profound effect. From this point until the end of his life, he became progressively more detached from worldly affairs and more devoted to prayer and scholarship – to such an extent, indeed, that he was in danger of losing his sight. Then, in 1591, he was allowed to take up a post as Professor of Theology at Douai, but almost immediately found himself put in charge of the teaching of moral philosophy at Liège where he remained for three years. The results of this period in his life later appeared in *Marian Blossoms* (1598), a collection of his sermons in praise of the Blessed Virgin. After a year in Tournai to complete his third probationary year as a Jesuit novice, he returned to Louvain and it was principally during these early years of the 1590s that he seems to have been gathering material for the *Disquisitiones*, although he went on revising and adding to them until the end of his life.[14]

His growing interest in magic can be glimpsed from various references he and others made to this period. Jean van Helmont, for example, was a student at the Jesuit college in 1594 and met Del Rio with whom he discussed the Kabbalah, although the conversations do not appear, at least in Van Helmont's case, to have been particularly fruitful.[15] Del Rio himself records a conversation with 'a religious man, someone worthy of belief', who told him about a magically induced plague (*fascinaria pestis*) which had started in a village in Western Flanders and spread almost as far as the Oise.[16]

But the event of the period which can be seen to have stimulated most significantly his researches into witchcraft was the trial of Jean del Vaulx, a

[13] It was here, he tells us, that he saw roses blooming in the garden during winter, a sign, according to popular belief, of plague to come. *Disquisitiones* Book 4, chapter 3, question 2 (p. 299). This may also be the time he stayed in Calais, although his reference to it is somewhat puzzling, *Disquisitiones* Book 5, section 3 (p. 373). See also infra, pp. 196–7 and note 7.

[14] The short biography by Rosweyde says that Del Rio did not publish the *Disquisitiones* straight away upon completion, but left the work for three years before beginning to make improvements to it, *Martini Antonii Del Rio Brevi Commentariolo Expressa* (Antwerp 1609), 38. One can see constant evidence of these revisions, too. For example, 'Since I wrote this many years ago, now in 1606 I have come across the following anecdote in *Historica Anatomica* by André du Laurens', *Disquisitiones* Book 2, question 22 (p. 105); the lengthy rebuttal of Tooker's book on the royal gift of healing, which was published in 1597, *Ibid.* Book 1, chapter 3, question 4 (pp. 13–15); or the reference to Torsellino's *History of Loreto*, published in 1600, *Ibid.* Book 6, chapter 2, section 3 (p. 520). But the revising is not simply a question of adding references and further illustrative anecdotes. Del Rio re-wrote large sections of the work, a good example being Book 1, chapter 3, question 3 (pp. 7–10) which in the 1608 edition is almost completely different from that of 1599 as well as being substantially longer.

[15] See *Biographie Nationale de Belgique*, 8.902–3.

[16] *Disquisitiones* Book 2, question 18 (p. 98).

monk in the Benedictine abbey of Stavelot. This took place in 1597, just at the moment when Del Rio himself was staying in Liège on his way back to Louvain overland from Tournai. The events which gave rise to the trial had begun in 1592 when many of the monks fell sick and began to die. The cause was imputed to poison and to magic, and when the elderly prior died suddenly at the beginning of February, the blame for his death and for that of all the others fell upon Jean del Vaulx who was thereupon arrested, shut up in a dungeon, and left there on a diet of bread and water. It was not until three years later, during which the monastery had continued to be troubled by manifestations of witchcraft, that the abbey's administrator, Prince-Archbishop Ernst of Bavaria, was informed of Del Vaulx's imprisonment and sent his vicar-general, Jean Chapeauville, to investigate. Quite unexpectedly, and giving evidence of great emotion, Del Vaulx confessed to everything and related a tale of service to the Devil going back to when he was a child, a confession which evidently warranted further investigation, for the Prince-Archbishop sent a further delegation consisting of a bishop, Jean Chapeauville, and a secretary, to question and re-question the garrulously co-operative monk.

Their investigations were long and protracted, and at one point involved other people, including an old friend of Del Rio's from their days at Louvain, the jurisconsult Pierre Dheure, who was now Deputy Burgomaster of Liège.[17] Del Rio records a curious incident which happened to these investigating officers at the beginning of January 1597 while they were on their way to Stavelot. Their carriage suddenly overturned and broke in two. No one was hurt but when they arrived at the monastery, Del Vaulx indicated to them that he knew they had had an accident because his attendant spirit had told him all about it.[18] It was a strange admission of guilty involvement with diabolical forces, but Del Vaulx was nothing if not co-operative and continued to pour out information about meetings with Satan, orgies, and magical incantations, all interspersed with the names of his companions and accomplices.[19]

On 10 January 1597 Del Vaulx at last came to trial with the judges almost overwhelmed by the quantity of evidence with which they had to cope, and it took until 2 April for judgement to be made and sentence passed. This was that Del Vaulx should be degraded and handed over to the secular arm for punishment, but his two secular judges, Pierre Dheure and Jean Molempeter, decided he should not be burned but, rather, beheaded, a sentence which was carried out forthwith.

---

[17] Or *Petrus Oranus*, as he appears in Del Rio's text.
[18] *Disquisitiones* Book 5, section 7 (pp. 385–6).
[19] *Disquisitiones* Book 2, question 16 (pp. 90–1). 'I have read documents [describing this], written in the hand of a very famous practitioner of harmful magic', says Del Rio, and the likelihood is that he is referring to Jean del Vaulx.

Clearly this case had a remarkable effect in stimulating Del Rio's researches into magic in general and witchcraft in particular. For one thing, Del Vaulx's garrulousness over many months provided him with a wealth of material; secondly, he was able to gain free access to it through his friendship with Pierre Dheure;[20] and thirdly, the reliability of the material was confirmed and proved by the confessions of other magicians and diviners.[21] Moreover, this was not the only case of sorcery in which Pierre Dheure was involved, and therefore the two men were certainly able to discuss the subject to Del Rio's evident advantage.

Del Rio remained for several years in Louvain and there he made his final vows as a Jesuit in 1600.[22] But a new university had opened in Graz in 1586 and to this Del Rio was transferred in 1601 (stopping for a while in Mainz), and taught theology there for three years until his declining health obliged him to seek the warmer climate of Salamanca.[23] This period saw him produce three books – *Commentarios de las alteraciones de los estados de Flandres* (1601);[24] a text of a commentary upon some of the poems of the seventh century English bishop, Saint Aldhelm (1601);[25] and a commentary on the *Song of Songs* (1604) – and take part in a learned debate about witchcraft, which was being conducted between various Catholic universities from *c.* 1601–1604.[26] The occasion was a struggle for power in Munich. Johann Wagenreckh, Ecclesiastical Councillor since 1593, was spokesman for those who were keen that witches be persecuted to the uttermost. As a skilled lawyer and a man of fervent conviction, Wagenreckh

---

[20] Del Rio records extraordinary details, such as the occasion when Pierre Dheure stood behind Del Vaulx, traced the silhouette of a dog in the air with his finger, and watched Del Vaulx suddenly begin to twist and turn in agony, *Disquisitiones* Book 2, question 21 (p. 103).

[21] *Disquisitiones* Book 5, Appendix 1 (p. 425).

[22] He had arrived there at some point in 1597 since one of his personal anecdotes begins, 'this year, here in Louvain', *Disquisitiones* Book 6, chapter 2, section 1, question 1, no. 18 (p. 484).

[23] It was while he was in Graz that he read a detailed manuscript account of a long, difficult exorcism which he describes in *Disquisitiones* Book 6, chapter 2, section 3, question 3 (pp. 513–15); and he makes further references to his time there in Book 4, chapter 1, question 3, section 2 (p. 263), and *Ibid.* section 4 (p. 267). He was in Salamanca by 24 July 1604, as he himself tells us in a note at the end of his second appendix to *Disquisitiones*, Book 5 (p. 466). Not long after this, he will have met the theologian Basilio Ponce de León (1569–1629) who had studied at Salamanca and returned there in 1605. Del Rio speaks highly of his 'elegant erudition', *Disquisitiones* Book 3, part 2, question 4, section 5 (p. 236).

[24] A Spanish translation of the Latin original. The Latin text, written under the pseudonym Roland Mirteus, was not published until 1869.

[25] A work Del Rio completed during his stay in Mainz.

[26] For details, see Behringer: *Witchcraft Persecutions in Bavaria*, 236–66.

was opposing with all the vigour at his command anyone who tried to argue against such persecution, and in the hope that some definitive opinion might emerge from the maelstrom of claim and counter-claim, the two greatest contemporary authorities on witchcraft, Del Rio and Nicholas Rémy, were asked to express their views.[27]

In Spain, Del Rio continued to teach and to write. An epitome of Livy's histories (1606), to which Del Rio contributed only a few pages, was followed by *A Work About Mary* (*Opus Marianum*) and a defence of Dionysius the Areopagite against the animadversions of Scaliger (both 1607). He also put in hand a commentary on *Genesis*, which was published in 1608 along with two other devotional works, a commentary on *Lamentations* and *A Lighthouse of Holy Wisdom* (*Pharus sacrae sapientiae*). But the Society decided to recall him to the Spanish Netherlands and so on 18 August 1608 he set out on what proved to be a long a difficult journey, for he did not arrive in Brussels until two months later. Even then he was allowed no rest and set off at once to Louvain where the Society's Provincial was waiting for him. But this extra jolting along ill-kept roads in public transport turned out to be too much for his fragile health and, having arrived in Louvain on 18 October, he was immediately seen by a doctor, who gave him up for lost. At half past seven the following morning, he received the last sacraments and died later that same day. He was fifty-seven.[28]

The *Disquisitiones Magicae*

Rosweyde's commemorative *Life* tells us that the *Disquisitiones* first appeared in Mainz in 1595 – Del Rio himself remarks that he returned to Spain 'four or five years after the first edition of this work'[29] – and was reprinted at least twenty-four more times, the final edition appearing in Venice in 1747.[30] It is dedicated to the Wittelsbach Prince-Archbishop Ernst of Bavaria, Administrator

---

[27] See *Disquisitiones* Book 5, Appendix 2 (p. 433).

[28] A few more works from his pen, edited and published by his brethren in the Society, continued to appear: another essay directed against Scaliger (1609), a collection of sayings and phrases from the Old and New Testaments (1610), a commentary on recent events in the Spanish Netherlands (1610), and a general *History of Belgium* [i.e. the Spanish Netherlands] (1611).

[29] *Disquisitiones* Book 3, part 1, question 3, section 2 (p. 195). It was here and on this occasion, he says, that someone showed him a book by the Jesuit Martín De Roa (1561–1637), *Singularium locorum ac rerum libri V* (Five Books Dealing With Unusual Places and Subject Matter), which was published in Cordoba in 1600. Rosweyde appears to have been mistaken about the date of the first edition. There seems to be no evidence that the *Disquisitiones* was published anywhere before 1599.

[30] For a study of these, see E. Fischer: *Die 'Disquisitionum Magicarum libri sex' von Martin Delrio als gegenreformatische Exempel-Quelle* (Hanover 1975).

of the monastery of Stavelot, who had taken such a close interest in the Del Vaulx affair, although Del Rio is not so indelicate as to make direct reference to this in his dedicatory letter.[31] Instead, he refers to the rapid spread of superstition which had been happening recently, a plague (as he calls it) diffused by humanity's inborn lust for collecting information. Such a plague, he says, needs a cure and it was the pressing necessity to remove and uproot Satan's poisoned/enchanted herbs (*venenatae herbae*) which were helping to spread it, and to provide a medicine for the disease, which stimulated him to write the *Disquisitiones*. He dedicates it to Ernst, he says, because the Archbishop is a pillar of the Church and a man fervent in zeal for the true religion.[32]

The first edition of the whole work was published in three separate tomes between 1599 and 1600. Volume I (Books 1 and 2) received the approval of Del Rio's superiors on 6 July 1598 and of the censor on 8 February 1599, with Del Rio dating his dedicatory epistle from Louvain on 9 March 1599 and receiving the Archduke's *privilegium* on 17th. Publication took place in Louvain in 1599. Volume II (Books 3 and 4) received its approvals on 8 February and 17 March 1599[33] and was published in 1600. The dates of permissions and *privilegium* for Volume III (Books 5 and 6) were the same as those of Volume II, while its dedicatory epistle to Archbishop Ernst is dated from Louvain, 26 February 1600.[34] The title-page of the 1608 edition makes clear both the subject-matter of the work and the audience at which it is aimed. 'Six Books of Investigations Into Magic, wherein is contained a meticulous refutation of the inquisitive arts and idle superstitions; useful for theologians, jurisconsults, doctors, and scholars; by Martin Del Rio, Priest of the Society of Jesus, Bachelor

---

[31] He includes, later in his work, an anecdote about a Westphalian lycanthrope, told by the Archbishop to Karl Billheus who then passed it on to Del Rio, *Disquisitiones* Book 5, section 9 (p. 388). Archbishop Ernst's interest in the occult sciences was well-known. He kept two astrologers in his palace in Liège, for example, and was very much interested in alchemy.

[32] Dedicatory Epistle to Books 1 and 2. Del Rio uses the same medical terminology in the Dedicatory Epistle to Books 5 and 6. Archbishop Ernst had been appointed to the see of Cologne by Gregory XIII in 1583 after the deposition of its previous abjuring archbishop, Gebhard Truchsess von Walburg. The aim of the appointment was to secure north-west Germany for Catholicism, and since Ernst also held the sees of Liège, Freising, Hildesheim, and Münster and was a leading support of a vigorous Catholic counter-offensive to the spread of Calvinism both in Austrian hereditary lands and elsewhere in Europe, he was clearly an ideal candidate to hold key parts of northern Europe for the Church. Hence Del Rio's enthusiasm.

[33] This second date is printed XXVI Kalend. April, which I take to be an error for XVI.

[34] Making an adjustment for the leap year. On censorship, licensing, and *privilegium*, see L. Voet: *The Golden Compasses*, 2 vols (Vangendt & Co., Amsterdam 1969–1972), 2.255–78, and on production times, *Ibid.*, 302–5.

of Laws, Doctor of Theology, formerly of the University of Graz, now Public Professor of Holy Scripture in the University of Salamanca'.

The emphasis upon people's trying to get to know that which they should not, and the dangerous inadvisability of many quasi-religious or overtly magical practices in fact summarises very well the thrust of the *Disquisitiones*, since Del Rio is concerned to show that magic – the attempt to find out the secrets of creation, which God has kept hidden from humankind, and then to use the powers inherent therein either for one's own advantage or to another's detriment – is in its very nature a perilous subject for study and is best avoided. Should assistance greater than human be required for any purpose, an individual should turn to the Church which is the only repository of aids which are both safe and reliable (not to mention licit). Essentially, therefore, the *Disquisitiones* is a religious work aimed more at wayward Catholics than at heretics, although Del Rio does not hesitate, of course, to point out the latter's erroneous opinions on religion, magic, and other related subjects.

The six Books of the *Disquisitiones* are interrelated; they do not merely constitute six disparate essays on aspects of the same basic material. Del Rio begins with a general survey of magic and then examines its constituent parts: natural, artificial, delusory, and demonic (Books 1 and 2). Next, he discusses the various uses to which these different types of magic may be and indeed are all too often put (Books 3 and 4); and finally, he turns to the question of how to deal with people who practise the arts of magic, and how one may counteract the effects of the magic they have worked (Books 5 and 6). This general plan can be broken down as follows.

Book 1: Etymology of the word *superstitio* according to Isidore of Seville. Its use in various ancient authors and in Scripture. 'Superstition' refers (a) to forms of worship which are superfluous to the requirements of genuine religion, and (b) to expressions of an idolatry which may be explicit or implicit. All types of forbidden magic constitute implicit idolatry. The different branches of magic: that which pertains to nature (natural), that which is wrought by human ingenuity (artificial), and that which involves evil spirits (demonic). Its subdivisions: magic for a particular purpose, divination, malefice, and superstition. Hebrew, Greek, and Latin technical terms for practitioners of magic. *Natural magic*: a range of opinions on whether it is licit or illicit. There are two kinds, operative and divinatory. The influence of the stars and planets upon created things both human and non-human, and whether this contributes to the results obtained by magic. The creation of mental and physical images and the powers these are alleged to possess. A consideration of whether wounds can be treated and diseases cured by means of touch, sight, or the sound of a voice, by kissing, or by the simple application of a cloth. *Artificial magic*: this refers to the production of marvels by human ingenuity. A discussion of whether any magical power resides in written characters, sigils, numbers, or music. Can words or incantations cure the sick or cause extraordinary things to happen? Magical amulets and other objects people hang round their necks. *Alchemy*: the etymology of the word and alchemy's actual capabilities. Is alchemy one of the liberal or mechanical arts, is it a branch of magic, does it work, and is it a lawful or unlawful activity?

Book 2: The origin of the type of magic which involves evil spirits, its various types, and the books which describe or promote it. The basis of this kind of magic is a pact between the practitioner and the evil spirit, a pact which may be explicit or implicit. The means whereby one may recognise the results of such magic and distinguish them from natural effects and miracles, including discussions on the invalidity of Elizabeth Tudor's claim to possess the royal touch for scrofula, and the so-called miracles of Antichrist and the Calvinists. Evil spirits work marvels entirely by moving something from one place to another, by deceiving the senses, or by effecting alterations in different objects. A large number of examples, including illustrations drawn from ancient writers. Magicians cannot go beyond the laws of nature and the established order of creation, but within these bounds they can do a great deal. Further examples of the extent of magicians' real or supposed powers, especially in relation to good luck, enchantment of animals, and the production of mixed species such as half-human, half-animal monsters. Whether sexual intercourse with evil spirits is possible, and whether this can produce offspring or not. The meetings of witches at night and their transvection thither. Can an evil spirit enter a physical body, cause one body to be in two places at once, or two bodies to co-exist in one spot? Can magicians make animals talk intelligibly, and can they understand the language of animals? Whether an evil spirit can render a person insensible for long periods, or change one sex into the other, or make an old person young again. The powers of magic over the soul, the feelings, and the intellect. What power does the Devil exert over a soul which has been separated from its body? The extraordinary things which can happen in cases of ecstasy, or of dead bodies. Whether an evil spirit can cause the spirits of the dead to appear to the living, and why God would allow such a thing to happen. A long section of examples, stretching from the first century to the seventeenth. Contrary arguments resolved. Appearances of evil spirits and the emanations which evil spirits present to human eyes. The various kinds and types of evil spirits, and some opinions about them. Their names in various languages including Hebrew, Greek, Latin, Spanish, French, and Italian. How an evil spirit which by nature is invisible can render itself visible. Whether the Devil can really make a person rise from the dead, and the extent of the power which magicians actually wield over evil spirits.

Book 3: This Book is divided into two parts, the first dealing with harmful magic (*maleficium*) and the second with superstitious practices (*vana observatio*).

Part One begins with a definition of malefice and a survey of its various types, and then discusses each of these: (a) malefice which puts people to sleep and allows workers of harmful magic to steal small children and kill them; (b) love-magic, the abuse of holy things which may play a part in this, and illustrations of its various practices, largely taken from Classical texts; (c) the different malefices one can direct against someone for whom one feels personal enmity – the evil eye (*fascinatio*), and the use of substances which may be poisonous (*venenaria*); (d) abortion, difficult birth, failure of mother's milk; (e) arrows, assassins, and the manufacture of images intended to convey the malefice; (f) various illnesses caused by evil spirits; (g) the extraordinary ingestion and vomiting of large, solid objects; (h) possession by an evil spirit; (i) various ways of causing impotence; (j) how to cause hatred between people; (k) how to set things on fire.

The kinds of people who are likely to fall victim to malefice, why God allows workers of harmful magic to misuse holy things, and why God allows the Devil such licence to roam in search of victims of malefice. The Devil is given his head because in the end his activities redound to the greater glory of God, human beings are given opportunities to increase their virtue, and the malefices act as punishment for their sins. Some of these sins are listed, accompanied by anecdotes to illustrate the relevant point: contempt for God, libidinousness, injustice and cruelty, fighting against what is self-evidently true, apostasy, blasphemy, cursing, usury, callous heartlessness towards the poor, mockery of the sacraments, the ceremonies, and the censures of the Church, plundering churches, deriding holy men and Church festivals, pettiness of spirit, despair, and curiosity. Why the Devil prefers to work through others when he could inflict harm himself.

Part Two defines the various types of superstitious practice, gives examples of when it is a mortal sin, a venial sin, and no sin at all, and indicates how one can tell whether a particular superstitious practice belongs to one of these categories or to another. How to tell whether the effect of a superstitious practice comes from God or not, and once this is decided, the various attendant circumstances which have to be taken into account. Can the effect be attributed to sigils, characters, pictures, or words? What about sacred words and pious actions which are misdirected towards false or futile ends? The divinatory arts known as 'Notory', 'Pauline', and 'Angelic'. Various other methods of divination.

Superstitious practices concerned with curing the sick or keeping illness at bay. A refutation of Felix Haemmerlein's *Two Essays on Exorcism*.[35] Tasteless and unnecessary rites which are not approved by the Church. Various magical formulae using Hebrew words. Snake charmers are not tolerated by the Church. Asking an evil spirit to effect the cure of an illness is not permissible. How can promising to restore health or perform a miracle be reconciled with the Faith? How to deal with situations like this in which there is an element of doubt. In which circumstances can something be illicit and yet not sinful? Examples (a) of forms of words used in superstitious practices, and (b) of the superstitious use of various objects.

Book 4: The vocabulary of divinatory techniques. Various kinds of prophecy, and the remarks of Scripture, Plato and Aristotle on the subject. Does God always use angels to mediate prophecy? The subject-matter of prophecy. Saint Thomas Aquinas on the subject. There are two kinds of prophecy: (a) that which comes from priests, and (b) that which comes from prophets. A discussion of the Urim and Thummim.[36] The oracles delivered by the Prophets, and their division into those which were seen, those which were heard, and those which were dreamed. How to distinguish between a revelation which comes from God and one which comes from the Devil. What one must bear in mind about the person to whom a revelation is given: Catholic or heretic, character, way of life, physical constitution, behaviour, social status, age, gender, and the degree of his or her spiritual experience. Revelations made (a) to women who are not saints, and (b) to virgins and women who have been canonised or were famous for the holiness of their lives. What one should look for in the nature of the revelation itself and in the circumstances attendant upon it. Definition of 'divination'. The secrets which can be revealed by an evil spirit. How to tell the difference between divination and prophecy. The various categories of sin into which divination may fall; the many different kinds of divination, including necromancy. Types of divination in which a pact with an evil spirit is either implicit or latent. Foretelling the future; prognostications from the stars, elements, meteors, plants, trees, and animals; doctors' prognostications; physiognomy, chiromancy, interpretation of dreams, casting lots. Various ways, in ecclesiastical and in common usage, of discovering a person's guilt or innocence, including trial by fire and by water. Criticism of the German test of swimming persons

---

[35] Born 1389. He was a canon in Zürich and, according to Del Rio, was still alive in 1454.
[36] A means of obtaining oracles in ancient Israel. It is not known exactly what the Urim and Thummim were, but they were kept in the breastplate inlaid with twelve precious stones, which the Jewish High Priest wore over his ephod. See further *Jewish Encyclopaedia* 16.8–9.

accused of witchcraft, and a discussion of recent publications on the subject. Other methods in common use of testing someone's innocence.

Book 5: Considerations for judges presiding over trials for malefice. Can the usual criminal procedure be retained when trying this kind of crime? Circumstances which make this crime worse than others. When a judge can increase or diminish the statutory legal penalty, and the kind of consideration he must always bear in mind. A judge must not be restricted by ancient judicial usage but should act according to local custom. Details of the way in which this crime should be investigated, including those points which must be made absolutely clear, how long the investigation ought to last, and what kind of indications of the accused's guilt should precede formal investigation. The role of the ruling Prince in such matters. Who are competent judges of this crime, and what are the powers held by inquisitors in this regard? Can an investigation be instituted in the absence of the accused? A discussion of the best indications which allow a judge to proceed safely, and the nature of indications: (a) slight, (b) serious, (c) very serious. When slight indications are sufficient to warrant torture. The role of witnesses, including partners in crime, confessors, friends of the accused, children, and women. The person who denounces the accused must be questioned about relevant circumstances, the possibility of slander must be taken into account, and the evidence should be consistent and undeviating. The requisite oaths to be taken. Indications which warrant torture. The role of a good or bad reputation and the difficulties of establishing either. How to interpret the accused's running away or issuing threats, and the difference between a genuine threat and showing off.

Lesser indications, such as the accused's telling lies, being unsteady on his or her feet, dithering, or changing expression. Was he or she seen in the relevant spot with an instrument of malefice? How did he or she normally behave, and what were his or her reactions during investigation? Indications such as the bleeding of a corpse in the presence of the accused, his or her depraved parentage, everyday use of blasphemous or scurrilous speech, inability of the accused to shed tears, frequent change of domicile, ostentatious piety, and loss of the mark of baptism.

Denunciation and witnesses: a large number of weak or unreliable indications do not amount to a single, irrefutable indication. What should be done when accomplices retract their evidence after sentence has been pronounced, or when the testimony of witnesses varies. Trials for heresy provide a blueprint. Accusation: how this should be made, and the penalty for slander. Arrest and imprisonment: the circumstances of the accused's arrest and imprisonment, the kind of information which will lead to arrest, denunciation by a witness who is ill, whether the accused can be arrested in a church. Immunity from prosecution. What should be done about unjust imprisonment, and is it a sin for someone unjustly imprisoned to make his or her escape? The judge should be on the look-out for various superstitious practices by the accused, such as having magical objects concealed in his or her clothing. Why the Devil does not rescue the accused from prison.

Rules for the application of torture. Torture should not be used unless it is absolutely necessary. How many times torture may be applied. Should someone already convicted be tortured? The different kinds of people who may be tortured in connection with this crime. The different ways in which the evil spirit tries to ensure the accused stays silent. The usual safeguards a judge can use against malefices. Various points raised by Sprenger. The kind of confession which will condemn an accused. Confession by someone who is deaf and dumb. Confession which admits to working harmful magic but denies evil intention. Different kinds of suspicion, and the difference between 'suspicion', 'intellectual certainty of the accused's guilt', and 'presumption'. How abjuration should be made, under what circumstances, and the formulae of abjuration which may be used. When canonical purgation may be applied; its rites and ceremonies. When and under what circumstances an accused can be acquitted.

What is heretical in cases of sorcery (sortilega), and what is not. A discussion of differences in legal opinion on this point. Magicians who claim to work with astrological spirits are bound to them by a pact. A series of axioms relating to magical practices which smack of heresy. Wier's recommendation that one distinguish between various types of magical operator is mistaken. The appropriate punishments under canon and civil law for sorcerers who are (a) clerics and (b) lay people in cases which (a) involve and (b) do not involve heresy. Those who consult diviners or workers of harmful magic incur the same ecclesiastical penalties as the diviners and *malefici* themselves.[37] Further discussion of specific cases. Can a bishop hand over to the secular arm for punishment people convicted of this crime, who are penitent? Should witches (*lamiae sive striges*) who have not killed anyone be burned? When old age provides a sufficient warrant to lessen the punishment.

The crimes committed by witches (*sagae*) are not fantasies. Theologians, lawyers, physicians, and philosophers who have acknowledged the pact between

---

[37] Cf. the parallels and the differences between this and the 1563 Scottish Witchcraft Act: 'It is statut and ordanit that na maner of persoun nor persounis tak upone hand to use ony maner of witchcraftis, sorsarie, or necromancie; nor that na persoun seik ony help, response, or consultatioun at ony sic usaris or abusaris of witchcraftis, sorsareis, or necromancie under the pane of deid, alsweill to be execute aganis the usar-abusar as the seikar of the response or consultatioun', *Acts of the Parliament of Scotland* 2.539 (adapted and abbreviated).

evil spirits and witches (*lamiae*). Books about magic: who may read them and who may not. The punishments for possessing them. Those who write them or make copies of them. In many places it is not the custom to give the eucharist to those who are about to be executed. When this may be done. Extreme unction should not be given to such people. A discussion on what should happen to the body of the executed person; the case of those who die in prison; people who supply the condemned with the means of committing suicide; those who die before conviction and before sentence has been passed.

Book 6: The duty of a confessor in his capacity as judge. A catalogue of the crimes he should investigate; the seal of confession in this matter; cases when it is permissible to reveal what has been learned during confession. How confession should be made, and the circumstances attendant upon it. Differing opinions on whether it is a sure sign of impenitence that a person cannot shed tears. Who can and cannot give absolution in cases of this crime. The duty of a confessor in his capacity as physician of the soul. Examples of superstitious treatments or magical remedies for bewitchment. How to get witches (*sagae*) to confess by using threats, force, and blows; how they are accustomed to transfer their fate to other people; and how the evil spirit relieves them during their ordeal. Is it permissible to seek a remedy for bewitchment from workers of harmful magic; or to use superstitious methods or silly remedies to lift a malefice; or to consult for this purpose someone who is not the originator of the malefice? Is it permissible to destroy the physical sign or instrument of a malefice in order to stop the Devil from doing harm? Arguments on both sides. Natural remedies against malefices. Supernatural, divine, and ecclesiastical remedies. These include the sacraments of the Church, the prayers of holy people, exorcism, works of reparation and charity, invocation of the name of Jesus and of Mary, invocation of the saints, making the sign of the cross, the relics of the saints, holy water, other things blessed by Catholic ritual, holy amulets hung round the neck, and the sound of church bells. A refutation of remarks by Johann Godelmann. A summary of advice for confessors and penitents.

It is clear from this that Del Rio has several aims in view. He intends to argue that any practice of magic is potentially dangerous and should be avoided; only the Catholic Church can offer people safe and effective answers to their spiritual problems;[38] curiosity is a most perilous emotion and one which Satan is quick to exploit for his own advantage; some people are able to trick others

---

[38] As W. Shumaker says, 'A main reference frame for Delrio's judgement is Catholic theology and ... occultist claims are tested against Christian truths', *Natural Magic and Modern Science*, 90.

into believing they have preternatural powers,[39] whereas they are merely dextrous, agile, or actually in league with an evil spirit; proving that someone has genuinely been able to work harmful magic is difficult and any investigation of such persons must be made with the most rigorous care. In other words, the *Disquisitiones* is a polemical religious work, a weapon (to use the Catholic reformers' own terminology) in the war which the Catholic Church was then waging against Satan who had stirred up virulent opposition to the Church in two principal forms – heretics and witches – and it can scarcely be coincidence that by the 1590s, learned debate on witchcraft had become polarised between those who accepted the elaborated theory of magic in all its aspects, and those who were willing to express a greater or lesser degree of reservation. Such polarisation did not necessarily show itself along confessional lines, of course, for there were both Catholics and Protestants at each end of the spectrum, but it is noticeable that the impulses of a new generation of theologians, lawyers, and philosophers, stirred by the aggressive, confident spirit of Catholic reformation, can be seen mirrored in increasingly bitter confessional conflicts in France, many of the German states, and much of the Low Countries where magical activity was increasingly re-interpreted as criminal witchcraft and therefore open to an increase in prosecution. As Clark puts it, 'Those who took up the attack on 'magic' and 'superstition', who demonised these sins and made them into witchcraft, and then sought to eradicate them, were responding not merely to intellectual but to evangelical imperatives ... Those [Catholics] who added, or preferred, an interest in the witchcraft of the sabbat were ... driven by considerations of purity in danger, the Church besieged by its enemies, and the need for a militant response. Thus Catholic demonology was characteristically a subject for Dominicans and Jesuits'.[40]

Nor must we forget that the end of the sixteenth century witnessed the

---

[39] Del Rio is careful to distinguish between supernatural powers, which belong to God alone, and preternatural powers which produce effects so startling and unexpected that they may be mistaken by the careless viewer for the products of supernatural or miraculous powers, although in fact they belong to the natural order of things. See *Disquisitiones* Book 1, chapter 4, question 3 (p. 25).

[40] S.Clark, *Thinking With Demons*, 539. See also pp. 479–502 wherein Clark discusses Catholic identification of magic with the sin of idolatry. Cf. Behringer, *Witchcraft Persecutions in Bavaria*, 216–18 and R. Po-Chia Hsia, *The World of Catholic Renewal* (Cambridge University Press 1998), 148. It may also be no accident that Del Rio was one of a very large number of Jesuits concentrated in the Catholic Low Countries, for it was there that the religious fight against heretical opponents and the spiritual war against Satan's minions seemed, increasingly after 1595, to call for a concentration of Papal troops, Po-Chia Hsia, *The World of Catholic Renewal*, 64. Cf. W. V. Bangert, 'a martial air hung over the field of theology in the 1590s', *A History of the Society of Jesus* (Institute of Jesuit Sources, St Louis 1972), 140.

spread of a millenarianism which preached the coming of Antichrist, the end of the world, and the establishment of God's kingdom upon earth; listed the signs and portents which, it was said, indicated the imminent or present arrival of the apocalypse; and issued ever more strident calls to repentance. If the Last Judgement was indeed about to happen, if Satan had indeed been loosed from the chains in which Christ had held him bound for so long, then the visible and obvious increase in heresy and operative magic provided unmistakable evidences of that looming dissolution, and both Catholic and Protestant preachers and demonologists were in agreement not only on the essentials of that expectation but also on the signs which proved it valid.[41]

The context of the *Disquisitiones*, therefore, is one of urgent spiritual warfare in which theology, law, and philosophy must unite to repel the forces of Satanic evil. Hence Del Rio's striking remark in his Prologue that he sees the *Disquisitiones* as a study in which theology, law, and philosophy play an equal part rather than a work in which one of them has a particular (and, by implication, superior) role. In writing the *Disquisitiones*, then, Del Rio may have decided to concern himself principally with witches and magic rather than heretics and false doctrine, but he was acutely aware that the two categories of foe were almost certain to overlap.[42] It should be emphasised, too, that he did not address himself to the problem of witchcraft alone. As his title says, he was drawing the attention of his Catholic readership to the perils of magic as a whole, along with those of its attendant related occult sciences, astrology and alchemy, and the practices of divination and prophecy; and he was much concerned with the prevalence of 'superstition', a discussion of which is placed at the beginning of the entire work. Modern interpretation of the word tends to stress the irrationality which informs the various behaviours called 'superstitious'. Del Rio and his contemporaries, however, regarded it with greater concern since by 'superstition' they understood essentially the worship of something or someone in place of God, or the displacement of a proper religious focus upon the person of God in favour of something or someone else. In other words, they looked upon superstition as a form of idolatry, the sin prohibited by the First Commandment.[43] There were, it is true, various degrees of seriousness with which one might regard the different manifestations of superstitious conduct, and the idolatry inherent therein might be implicit

---

[41] See Clark, *Thinking With Demons*, 337–45. Cf. his remarks on the 'general circumstances in which Jesuits could intelligibly deliver sermons devoted to visions of the last days and Dominicans could legitimately expect demoniacs and witches to confirm that they had in fact arrived', *ibid.*, 429–30. See also J. Delumeau: *La peur en Occident* (Paris 1978), 213–25.

[42] As he points out in his *Proloquium*, following the analysis of Juan Maldonado whose lectures he had attended long ago in Paris: 'Magic will always accompany heresy'.

[43] See further Clark: *Thinking With Demons*, 474–9. D. Harmening: *Superstitio* (Erich Schmidt Verlag, Berlin 1979), 33–42.

rather than overt. Nevertheless, idolatry it was at basis and therefore not something to be regarded or treated dismissively as though it were of little import, and indeed one of the aims of the Catholic reformation was to eradicate that pagan substratum which had underlain Christianity since the earliest days of its attempt to convert the various peoples of Europe.[44] Hence the interest of theologians and demonologists in the whole spectrum of magical activity of which witchcraft was simply a part.[45]

By Del Rio's day the crime of witchcraft had long been defined in law. It involved the practice of malefice, paction with an evil spirit, transvection, shape-changing, and sexual intercourse with an evil spirit. But practising harmful magic, even if this depended upon some kind of demonic pact, did not of itself make the practitioner a 'witch', and so Del Rio's careful use of *maleficus* and *veneficus* is one indication among others that he wished to concentrate his readers' attention upon the wider picture, the more extensive peril, and to make it clear that any type of magic must be regarded with the greatest possible suspicion and reserve.

Still, one of his major problems was to defend the Church's use of sacramentals (holy water, signs of the cross, relics, etc.), against the assertions of non-Catholics that these were no better than magical adjuncts and that the consecration of the elements during the Mass was, in essence, an act of magic. He was forced to explain that whereas no hope of effective power can be expected from words, characters, sigils, or planetary influences as such without the attendant efficacy brought to them through the agency of an evil spirit;[46] relics, holy images, Agnus Dei, and extracts from Holy Scripture derived their efficacy from God and were therefore different not only in effect but also in kind from their apparent magical counterparts. As for the words of consecration during the Mass, they were instituted by God for the purpose of changing the wafer and the wine into the body and blood of Jesus, and transubstantiation has long been accepted and believed and taught by the Church relying, not simply upon Biblical authority, but upon that magisterium with which she was endowed by God from the very beginning.[47]

---

[44] A. D. Wright: *The Counter-Reformation* (Weidenfeld & Nicolson, London 1982), 40–83.

[45] It is noticeable that Del Rio uses the terms *maleficus* (worker of harmful magic) and *veneficus* (worker of poisonous magic) much more frequently than *strix*, *saga*, or *lamia* (all common terms for 'witch'), and treating *maleficus* or *veneficus*, even in their feminine forms *malefica* and *venefica* as though they were synonyms of *strix*, etc. is a mistake.

[46] Words, for example, he says are no more than beatings of the air, indistinguishable from animal or percussive noises. When written down, they are inert, and secondary powers derived from the ink and paper with which and on which they are written have nothing to do with them, *Disquisitiones* Book 1, chapter 4, question 3 (p. 26).

[47] See D. P. Walker: *Spiritual and Demonic Magic*, 180–2. For Protestant propaganda, see Johann Wier: *De praestigiis daemonum* Book 5, chapter 9. Scot: *The Discoverie of Witchcraft*

Church miracle and demonic magic are thus two entirely different things. Even so, Del Rio is not as unsophisticated as to present a completely monochrome picture of magic and other practices dependent on occult knowledge. Some magical performances, he points out, consist of mere prestidigitatory deception; some marvels depend upon natural forces for their working and appear marvellous only because poorly educated people do not understand how they have been made to work; some astrology is not necessarily sinful, provided it does not attempt to usurp God's privilege of knowing what the future holds; certain alchemical operations may work, while others may be simple trickery; some people apparently possessed by an evil spirit may be more in need of a doctor than an exorcist; even precognition may have a natural explanation and therefore instances of it need not necessarily be condemned out of hand; and one needs to take a highly sceptical view of the so-called 'swimming' test for witches.[48] Nevertheless, his aim is to condemn, not to approve, and his view is one perfectly consistent with, let us say, that of the various Inquisitions: namely, that much of what passed for magic was either nonsense or delusion, and that one is as wrong to be over-credulous as to be too sceptical.[49]

In connection with this, it is worth noting the use Del Rio makes of medical writers – Codronchi, Gentili (cited as 'Fulginas'), Ferrier, Valles, Du Laurens, Van Ronss, and Gemma are only some of the physicians whose books he uses – for he is acutely aware that many phenomena popularly interpreted or commonly thought to be manifestations of demonic possession or the results of bewitchment were susceptible to other explanations of which, for example, damage to or upset in the balance of the humours could be one. Thus, when he discuss lycanthropy, he takes into account four possibilities: the 'wolf' in question could be (a) an evil spirit masquerading as a real wolf, (b) an evil spirit wearing the likeness of a wolf's body which he has constructed out of air, (c) a human being who has disguised himself as a wolf, and (d) a human being

---

Book 12, chapters 8 and 9. For his part, Del Rio draws his readers' attention to the difference between the divinely-bestowed ability of Catholic sovereigns to heal scrofula by touch, and the fraudulent claims of Elizabeth Tudor to be able to do the same. Her 'cures', he said, either did not work or were dependent upon the pact she had made with an evil spirit, *Disquisitiones* Book 1, chapter 3, question 4 (p. 14).

[48] For example, *Disquisitiones* Book 1, chapter 4 (pp. 16–18); *Ibid*, chapter 3, question 4 (pp. 11–12); Book 4, chapter 3, question 1 (p. 294); Book 1, chapter 5, question 1, section 2 (pp. 31–5); Book 6, chapter 2, section 2 (pp. 501–2); Book 1, chapter 3, question 3 (p. 8); Book 4, chapter 4, question 4, section 4 – question 5, section 3 (pp. 322–39).

[49] '[Certain diabolical] pacts are the fantasies of deluded minds', *Disquisitiones* Book 5, section 16 (p. 398). J. Tedeschi: 'Inquisitorial law and the witch', in B. Ankarloo and G. Henningsen (eds): *Early Modern European Witchcraft* (OUP 1993), 92–4, 101. G. Romeo: *Inquisitori, esorcisti e streghe nell'Italia Controriforma* (Sansoni, Florence 1990), 29. But Romeo's whole chapter (pp. 25–65) should be read.

suffering from a particular medical condition.[50] These he presents as theoretical explanations all of which need to be taken into account without one's automatically being given precedence over the others. Del Rio is therefore no credulous bigot, but an intellectual prepared to weigh possibilities and to acknowledge that nature (which holds secrets unguessed by human beings), as well as diabolical manipulation has a part to play in the production of phenomena which may be extraordinary but are not necessarily inexplicable.

The *Disquisitiones*, then, is self-evidently a learned book written by an erudite man for a learned audience. Del Rio's range of apparent reading is impressive, and he will quote from or draw his readers' attention to a quite remarkable spread of literature, remarkable not only in its chronological span from the ancient world to his contemporary present, but also in the literary genres to which he is happy to make an appeal. (He was not alone in this, of course. Several demonologists of the period indicate a similar kind of range so that, as Shumaker has said, 'in reading a treatise by Delrio or Bodin or Lavater or Rémy one has the impression of following the processes of a mind which is not only … highly intelligent and responsible but also impressively well-read'.[51])

Nevertheless, there are occasional indications that sometimes he has relied upon a limited number of sources to guide his deliberations, the most obvious examples occurring in Book 5 where, as he himself acknowledges, he leans heavily on the jurisconsults Prospero Farinacci and Julio Claro; and it is noticeable that when he wishes to discuss any part of the relationship between magic and medicine, he is inclined to turn to the work of Battista Codronchi. A similar restriction applies, in some measure, to his use of illustrative modern anecdotes, by which I mean references to incidents datable to the 1590s. Most of these come from letters sent from various Jesuit provinces and the Jesuit missions in Peru, with Luis Froes's book on Jesuit missionary work in Japan supplying material relating to the Far East.[52] The majority of the provincial references is to be found in Book 6, suggesting that the sources came into Del Rio's hands quite late during the composition of the *Disquisitiones*; but a study of his working methods has yet to be done.

[50] *Disquisitiones* Book 2, question 18 (p. 98).

[51] *The Occult Sciences in the Renaissance* (University of California Press, Berkeley 1972), 74. See also Clark: *Thinking With Demons*, 276.

[52] E.g. from the provinces: Book 4, chapter 1, question 3, section 5 (p. 269); Book 6, chapter 2, question 3, section 3 (pp. 504–5, 507–8, 509, 522, 524, 525–6). Most of these anecdotes come from letters by Francesco Benci (1542–1594). A convenient résumé of his career may be found in *Dizionario Biografico degli Italiani*, Vol. 8 (Rome 1966), 192–3. From Peru: Book 2, question 11 (pp. 73–4); question 13 (p. 81); question 15 (p. 87); question 26, section 5 (pp. 134–5); Book 4, chapter 3, question 2 (p. 299). From Japan: Book 4, chapter 4, question 4, section 3 (p. 317); Book 6, chapter 2, question 3, section 3 (506–7, 517).

One does note, however, that he is relatively sparing in details relating to his personal experience of magic – meeting a child *Zahurí* in Spain and burning a mandrake root on behalf of others too frightened to do it for themselves are almost the only indications we get[53] – in spite of the fact that we know from our increasing familiarity with the prevalent awareness of interplay between the natural, preternatural, and supernatural worlds which characterised this period, that Del Rio, like his educated contemporaries, must not only have had a theoretical appreciation of this interplay and an intellectual notion of how the occult mechanics of such a process worked and interrelated, but, like all his contemporaries, educated and uneducated, must also have taken for granted the reality of this interpenetration of worlds and grown used from childhood to the multifarious ways in which people sought to negotiate their everyday lives through the perils and pitfalls of such a circumambience. The near-absence of personal observations of such behaviour, therefore, may be thought to say something about the extent to which he had consciously decided to withdraw to the realm of books and direct his polemical fire against superstition from the ramparts of Castle Intellect.[54]

In what way, then, can Del Rio's work be said to make an important contribution to the demonological literature of his time? It is partly the range of his intellectual inquiry, which makes reading the *Disquisitiones* an instructive experience. Here is no simple omnium gatherum of much-repeated cliché and frequently-cited texts. To be sure, all the citations one expects to see do indeed make their appearance sooner or later, but Del Rio is engaged in an inquiry, or rather, a series of inquiries – what is magic? how many kinds are there? what does one mean by alchemy, divination, superstition, vain observance? – and the breadth of his investigations demands and produces evidence of reading and (occasionally) of experience, which take readers by surprise and make them that much more alert to what Del Rio is saying. For Del Rio aims not only to satisfy his readers' legitimate curiosity on these points, but to illuminate each

---

[53] *Disquisitiones* Book 1, chapter 3, question 4 (pp. 11–12); Book 4, chapter 2, question 6, section 4 (p. 283).

[54] Del Rio, it seems, represents the *mens negativa* of the Society of Jesus towards the occult sciences, and indeed under the Generalship of Everard Mercurian there is evidence of a certain hostility towards aspects of Hermeticism and the ideas of Raimund Lull in particular. See Taylor: 'Hermeticism and mystical architecture', 65–6. Nevertheless, the inclination of the Society was not entirely negative. Del Rio himself admits that alchemy was defended by two of its members, Benito Pereira and Gregory of Valencia (*Disquisitiones* Book 1, chapter 5, question 1, section 2, [p. 31]), and a remarkable commentary on *Ezechiel* by Jerónimo Prado and Juan Bautista Villalpando, published between 1596 and 1604, reconstructed the Temple at Jerusalem as a divine archetype to be interpreted according to astrological, Hermetic, and Kabbalistic principles. See Taylor: 'Architecture and magic', 90–3.

stage of the intellectual journey by drawing distinctions, issuing caveats, producing accumulations of evidence to indicate why he is taking a certain line of argument, warning against mistaken opinion and endeavouring to demonstrate why that opinion is misconceived or simply wrong, combatting false logic, and illustrating from appeals to human experience past and present those universal and continuous truths of the human condition, which make people act as they do and give opportunity to the embodiments of evil to do the Devil's bidding and ruin souls. Del Rio's book thus throws open, as no other by any of his contemporaries or near-contemporaries quite manages to do, a window between worlds so that his readers may see for themselves, under his guiding tuition, the hidden workings of the world in which they live and of the other worlds above it and beyond.

But the *Disquisitiones* is also extremely practical. Where the first four Books seek to explain and illuminate, the last two intend to instruct. Having laid bare the occult worlds in such a way that the general reader may understand the complexities of God's creation, Del Rio turns to the specialist reader, the man who has to administer temporal justice, and the man who has both care and cure of souls. Justice must do its duty and in doing so it may not be too lenient nor too severe. A proper understanding of the technicalities of what the law requires in relation to crimes involving magic is therefore what Del Rio aims to give the readers for Book 5; for crimes involving magic are unlike any other type of crime. Murder, theft, treason, rape, and so forth concern themselves with the temporal world alone. Magic, however, extends (or at least may, and in Del Rio's eyes probably does extend) its criminal intention beyond the limits of temporality and seeks to commit offences which have a preternatural dimension. A judge, whether lay or ecclesiastical, therefore requires a knowledge of more than the mere letter of civil legislation, and must be prepared to venture his judgement into areas more usually the preserve of priests and exorcists. Again, in Book 5, Del Rio offers him necessary guidance; and similarly, in Book 6, he tries to provide confessors with a thread to what he depicts as a labyrinth of preternatural evil.

Yet, in the end, the *Disquisitiones* also seeks to tell everyone a very simple message. If human beings turn their attention away from God, they will fall prey to the forces of evil who are constantly waiting to exploit any such lapse, and a certain sign that such a lapse has happened can be seen in a proliferation of superfluous, unnecessary, silly, and at bottom potentially wicked behaviours whose foolishness the Church is here to warn against, whose injurious conse-quences the Church is here to cure, and whose wickedness both Church and State are here to punish. It is no accident, then, that Del Rio begins the whole treatise with a warning against superstition, for that, when all is said and done, is the subject-matter of his book.

Notes on the editing and translation

Del Rio needs a biography, for there are dozens of questions thrown up by the *Disquisitiones*, which cannot be answered in a work such as this because of the necessary constrictions of word-limit. Some I have glanced at earlier, but a biographer would be in a better position to comment in proper detail upon the religious context in which the *Disquisitiones* was written; the role of Jesuits in Catholic reform and Catholic demonology; the relationship between the *Disquisitiones* and Del Rio's other works, and between it and the works of other demonologists of the period; and the idiosyncracies of Renaissance scholarship as illustrated by the *Disquisitiones* in particular. Moreover, since the *Disquisitiones* is a very long work, choosing which parts to translate and which to précis must place the translator in the awkward position of knowing that he will inevitably annoy some readers who would have wished him to translate certain sections he has chosen to resume and to resume others he has chosen to translate. Nevertheless, choices had to be made and my guiding principle was that each aspect of Del Rio's approach to his subject should be represented in at least one translated passage, and that between translation and précis the reader should be able to acquire a fair notion of both the argument and the tone of the work as a whole.

The Louvain edition of 1608 has been used since this was the final edition upon which Del Rio himself worked, and it is to this volume that the relevant page numbers in footnotes refer. Passages appearing in square brackets are translated résumés of the original.

Translating technical terms such as *maleficus*, *veneficium*, and *daemon* present certain problems. Since Latin allows a noun in its masculine form not only to stand for a masculine person/object but also to embrace both masculine and female possibilities, one is not always entitled to assume that only males are meant when, for example, the plural *malefici* appears in the text. On the other hand, one is not entitled to assume that females must be included in the intention of that particular context, either. Hence I have used the phrase 'worker of harmful magic', which is accurate without being gender-specific, and the reader will be able to infer from the context in which the word appears whether Del Rio has males, or females, or both in mind at that juncture.

Veneficium, too frequently regarded as a synonym for 'witchcraft', assumes that herbs or mineral substances are being employed for some purpose, usually curative or hostile, and that such ingredients may turn out to be poisonous in their effects. *Veneficium* may, therefore, refer simply to poisoning or to an action magical in intent, which carries the risk of physical poisoning with it. A *veneficus* or *venefica* is thus 'a worker of poisonous magic' and not 'a witch', since the latter may include the former but the former does not necessarily imply the latter.

The phrase 'evil spirit' has been used instead of 'demon' as a translation of *daemon* in order to avoid conjuring up in the reader's imagination a picture of some hideous imp or monstrous devil, since it was a commonplace of the early modern period that evil spirits could appear to human beings under a variety of guises, many of them human and many of them at least non-threatening in aspect, if not superficially attractive. 'Evil spirit' is thus intended to preserve a certain neutrality towards the word *daemon* so that as much latitude as possible can be afforded to the reader's appreciation of what Del Rio is trying to convey in any given context.

Finally, the range of vocabulary in Latin to describe workers of magic is wide and yet each term is not merely a synonym of the others. To translate each, or even most, as 'witch' would therefore be misleading because the subtleties of each term would have been known to the individual writer, especially a learned Classicist such as Del Rio. This is not to say, of course, that in practice there may not have been a certain amount of overlapping, and there are undoubtedly many contexts in which the word 'witch' seems adequately to represent what Del Rio had in mind. Nevertheless, a more cautious approach to the translation of Latin terms for workers of magic is required, and therefore I have included the Latin in brackets so that the reader may see exactly what Del Rio had in mind in each context.

Prologue, explaining why this treatise has been difficult to write, but why it was necessary to do so

[The pride and malice of God's enemies are increasing. They have a thousand ways of doing harm and use innumerable weapons against humanity, of which magic is the most deadly. Books about magic have, so far and for various reasons, been unsatisfactory. Some have been contrary to faith, morals, and truth, and offensive to read: others, thin in substance or obscure and unmethodical. Philosophers, lawyers, and theologians have written on the subject, but each has tended to address his own specialised audience. I have been involved in all three disciplines for a long time and am thus qualified to use what I have learned to forward the truth. I regard philosophy, law, and theology not as three separate branches of learning but as one. So I have carefully investigated the bases of magic (something others have tended not to do), and by making use of both secular and divine scholarship, I have set myself the task of undermining magic with vigour and at length.

In pursuit of this, I have not dragged in just any example so that I can have the opportunity of refuting it, but have brought to light some of the most abstruse material from the books of the magicians themselves, thus revealing their vanity, their perfidy, and their madness. I have examined the subject methodically and in detail, and have published my work in a way which is easy to read and easy to use, and yet which will not prove perversely attractive.

It shows how widespread magic has become in recent times. Evil spirits are on the loose, seeking to take possession of foolish and deluded souls. Never have there been as many witches as there are today, and the main reason for this is the faintness of and contempt for the Catholic faith. Faith repels all the attacks and wiles of the Devil, as experience past and present can confirm. Idolatry and witchcraft go together, as innumerable Jesuit testimonies from India illustrate. Once the Gospel is received, however, such errors and heresies disappear. Witness the Muslims in Africa and Asia, the heretics of Germany, France, and Britain, and the apathetic Catholics called *politici* in Italy and other places.[1] In these areas, magic is immensely strong. With heretics there can be no question that magic is the handmaid of moral turpitude, just as one's shadow is at the beck and call of one's body. So much is obvious and cannot be denied. The point can be illustrated from Scripture, the Church Fathers, and secular historians.

I have read that, as a result of the Moorish occupation of Spain, the magical arts were virtually the only subjects being taught in Toledo, Seville and Salamanca. When I was living in Salamanca, I was shown a secret vault which had been blocked off with rubble on the orders of Queen Isabella. It was a place where forbidden knowledge used to be taught.[2] Magic followed the Hussites in Bohemia and the Lutherans in Germany. Nothing has spread magic more quickly or more copiously in Scotland, England, France, and Belgium than Calvinism. Before, it was to be found only here and there, but now, as a result of heresy, it has infected even the noble, the well-educated, and the rich. Lambert Daneau, a Calvinist minister, writes of a regular coven of witches in Geneva near the cathedral and says that in the space of three months more than five hundred people were sentenced to death by the magistrates.[3]

Juan de Maldonado, a saintly and learned Jesuit, gives five causes of magic: (i) evil spirits take up residence in heretics; (ii) all heresy is prone to violence at the start, but because it cannot maintain this and cannot return to the truth whence it came, it degenerates into magic or atheism; (iii) magic follows heresy, as plague follows famine; (iv) evil spirits use heretics to deceive humanity; (v) the Church authorities are negligent.[4]

---

[1] Del Rio may have been thinking of the French *politiques*, a party of Catholics urging religious toleration for Calvinists and a strong effective monarchy. They were particularly active in the 1560s and early 1570s. *Politiques* was a derisive term applied to them by more fervent Catholics.

[2] Isabella and Ferdinand wintered in Salamanca in 1486. I can find no reference to any such vault.

[3] Lambert Daneau (1530–1595), born of an ennobled French family, studied law at Orléans and practised there very briefly in 1560. He went to Geneva in the same year to study theology and after a troubled period during which he moved rapidly from place to place, he settled down as a pastor in Geneva in 1574. After six years' residence, during which he played a notable role in Genevan politics, he became Professor of Theology at Leiden. His career, however, continued to be restive until his death. He published a large number of works including one on witchcraft, *De veneficis quos vulgo sortiarios vocant* (1574). Del Rio refers the reader at this point to Pierre Crespet, *De odio Sathanae* (1590), from which he seems to have got the Daneau anecdote. Crespet was a highly respected Celestine monk whose two volumes on the hatred of Satan and evil spirits for humanity were directed specifically against magicians.

[4] Juan de Maldonado (1534–1583), a Spanish exegete and theologian, became a Jesuit in 1562. He was Professor of Theology at Paris between 1565 and 1574. He published his *De angelorum et daemonibus tractatus* in 1606. J. L. Pearl has suggested that the *Disquisitiones* was much indebted to Maldonado's Paris lectures of 1570–1572, *The Crime of Crimes*, 66, 70–1.

We have seen heresy flourishing in Belgium and we see swarms of witches laying waste the whole of the North, like locusts. We see the numbers of atheists and *politici* increasing, while there are few fervent Catholics left. The heretics are strongly opposed by the Jesuits. This book is a weapon in that war.

The *Proloquium* ends with prayers to the Virgin and Saint Michael for help and protection.]

BOOK I

Magic in general and natural and artificial magic in particular

Chapter 1: Superstition and its various forms

[For Lucretius and other pagan writers, religion meant 'fear of God', and since they thought that God played no part in human affairs, they equated religion with superstition, 'superstition', according to Isidore's etymology, being the same as 'superfluousness'. Others associated superstition with the increasing fears and foolishness of old age. For Christians, however, superstition is the wickedness of idolatry. (Compare the Syriac and Greek words and the usage of the Church Fathers.) Lactantius made this distinction: 'religion is worship of that which is true, superstition is worship of that which is false'.

Modern theologians define religion as 'that virtue by which we show true and obligatory worship to the true God', and they say there are two extremes to be avoided. One is being over-religious, the other not being religious enough. The former indulges in superfluities and is thus corrupted. Any form of worship which involves the slightest touch of evil cannot be called religion; and as the very word *superstition* indicates that there is something wrong with the worship, it follows that any worship which is superstitious is not true worship. So all superstition is the worship of that which is false, as Lactantius said.

He was mistaken, however, when he thought that this falsity had a single origin. There are, in fact, two. The principal gives rise to worshipping something . or someone in place of God. The other is worse, often lethal, always harmful: namely, the worship of something to which worship should not be given. The first is generally called *idolatry*. The second has no other term than *superstition*, and I do not propose to discuss it any further. One must, however, differentiate between two forms of idolatry: (a) *overt idolatry* which openly and expressly transfers worship of God to a creature as, for example, the Jews worshipping the golden calf, the Egyptians Anubis, or the Romans Quirinus; and (b) *tacit* or *implicit idolatry*. All forbidden magic is tacit idolatry.]

Chapter 2: Magic, its types, and the different words for 'magician'

Magic can be defined very loosely, and in a way which will be universally acceptable, as 'an art or skill which, by the use of natural not supernatural power, accomplishes extraordinary and unusual things, the manner in which these are done being such as to overwhelm people's emotions and their capacity to comprehend'.

I have used a very broad definition because I notice that eminent men, following Francisco de Vitoria,[1] have made their definitions too narrow and have thus left out artificial and natural magic. I have used the words *art* or *skill* to mean any kind of intellectual and practical activity, whether it produces knowledge by means of convincing argument or not. The activity may be mechanical or scholarly, artificial or free from art, true or fraudulent, superstitious or free from sin. I have used the word *accomplishes* with the implication that the whole mind, spirit, heart, or physical body is involved in the operation. By *power*, I understand something or someone who has been invoked, whether he be human or demonic. I have called this power *natural* and not *supernatural* in order to exclude true miracles which are the work of God alone, and in consequence I have preferred to use the words *extraordinary things* rather than *miracles*. Finally, I have mentioned the *understanding* and the *emotions* because, as a result of the large number of magical operations which are taking place these days, only the wiser sort (who in every age are few) understand what is going on. Magic, then, has to be defined as broadly as this and should also be categorised under the headings 'final' and 'efficient' causes.

Under the heading *efficient cause*, magic is said to be divided into Natural, Artificial, and Diabolic because all its effects are to be ascribed to the innate nature of things, or to human agency, or to the malice of an evil spirit. Under the heading *final cause*, it may be divided into (a) 'good magic', provided this be done with good intention and uses lawful methods, something which applies only to Artificial and Natural Magic; and (b) 'evil magic', whose methods and ultimate aim are both depraved. This refers particularly to forbidden magic which is tacit idolatry and a type of superstition.

This forbidden magic can be described as follows: 'a skill or art by which, as the result of a powerful pact made with evil spirits, certain marvels are performed, thus overwhelming people's emotions and their capacity to comprehend'. I have mentioned a *powerful pact* since the whole power of this type of magic relies upon a pact which is tacit or openly avowed. Theologians call this 'tacit idolatry' because, certainly in the majority of cases, magicians offer

[1] Spanish Dominican and theologian (*c.* 1486–1546). He was Professor of Theology at Salamanca.

their worship to a creature as though it were a god, a generous benefactor, as one might say, from whom they acquire something for themselves.

Because it has several aims in view, this frame of mind gives rise to four types (as it were) of this 'tacit idolatry' or forbidden magic. Sometimes, for example, the practitioners want to find out how to bring off an operation which is nothing less than extraordinary and marvellous. The proper expression for this is *Particular Magic*. Sometimes the magician tries to discover secret and hidden things about the future (or even the past or present). The word for this is *Divination*. Sometimes he wants to be given instruction and help, not so that he may do good, but so that he may do harm to other people or take his revenge. The word for this criminal activity is Harmful Magic (*maleficium*).[2] Finally, sometimes there are those who are permitted, without detriment to others, to benefit themselves or other people by means of this operation, either for use or for pleasure. Under these circumstances, theologians use the term *Trivial* or *Vain Observance*.

The word MECHASSEPHEM comes from the root CHASAPH, meaning anyone who employs harmful magic with intention to deceive, or who uses any kind of wicked magical art.[3] Hence we give such a wide interpretation to *malefici* [workers of harmful magic], *maleficae artes* [maleficent arts], *maleficia* [deeds of harmful magic], or *veneficia* [deeds of venomous magic]. There has not been wanting, however, a certain person, strongly suspected of this offence and an avowed protector of witches [*sagae*], who would try to persuade his readers that this word (at least as far as the law of *Exodus* 22 is concerned) should be restricted to poisoners.[4] But this is easily refuted. For a start, the root CHASAPH

---

[2] I have translated this word throughout as 'harmful magic' rather than 'witchcraft' because, although the word is frequently a technical term for witchcraft, it encompasses more than that. Any magic which is intended to harm someone else is *maleficium*, but someone who performs a *maleficium* is not necessarily a witch. It is usually clear from the context whether Del Rio is discussing witchcraft in particular or harmful magic in general, the latter being by far the more usual case.

[3] *Mekhashefah* refers specifically to a practitioner of harmful magic. It is a feminine singular noun in the Hebrew text. According to the Talmud, such a person was to be put to death by stoning, *Berakoth* 21b. Cf. *Yebamoth* 4a, *Sanhedrin* 67a-b.

[4] Del Rio, as his later, similar attacks make clear, is referring to Johann Wier (1515/16–1588), a Lutheran physician, who published a book on witchcraft and demonology, *De praestigiis daemonum* (The Deceptive Tricks of Evil Spirits), in 1563. In this he maintained that witches tended to be harmless old women and ought not to be burned. He condemned magic even though he had been, for a while, a pupil of the most notorious magician of the period, Cornelius Agrippa, and he also attacked what he saw as demon-worshipping magic in the rites of Catholic exorcism. His arguments were largely repeated in his later book, *De lamiis* (On Witches), 1577. Wier, not surprisingly, was himself accused of being

does not mean 'to kill by poison', as he thinks it does.[5] When it occurs by itself and the context does not require a restricted sense, it embraces every type of magical nonsense (as in *Malachi*, *Nahum*, and the books of the *Apocrypha*.) [6] But if the meaning is restricted by the context, it directs itself to the specific point which is being made, as the particular context demands. Thus, in *Exodus* 7 it is confined to tricksters properly speaking, since it is only these with whom the verse is dealing. In *Jeremiah* it stands for fortune-tellers, and in *Daniel* for interpreters of dreams.[7]

[Del Rio goes on to give further examples and then discusses Greek terminology, after which he turns to Latin.]

a witch. The Biblical reference is to *Exodus* 22.18 (17 in the Hebrew Bible), 'Thou shalt not suffer a witch to live'. The Septuagint *pharmakous* is ambiguous and could refer to poisoners as well as to magicians. The Vulgate *maleficos* is equally ambiguous, meaning 'evil-doers' as well as 'workers of harmful magic'.

[5] *Kshp* is the usual word for magic or sorcery. It means 'to pray', although Robertson Smith said that originally it referred to herbs shredded into a magic brew.

[6] (a) *Malachi* 3.15. 'Siquidem aedificati sunt **facientes impietatem**' (Vulgate). '**They that work wickedness** are set up' (AV). (b) *Nahum* 3.4. 'Propter multitudinem fornicationum metricis speciosae, et gratae, et habentis **maleficia**, quae vendidit gentes in fornicationibus suis, et familias in **maleficiis** suis' (Vulgate). 'Because of the multitude of the whoredoms of the well-favoured harlot, the mistress of **witchcraft**, that selleth nations through her whoredoms, and families through her **witchcrafts**' (AV).

[7] (a) Exodus 7.11. 'Vocavit autem Pharao sapientes et **maleficos**' (Vulgate). 'The Pharaoh also called the wise men and the **sorcerers**' (AV). Hebrew, *mekhashefim*, 'sorcerers'. (b) Jeremiah 27.9. 'Nolite audire prophetas vestros, et divinos, et somniatores, et augures, et **maleficos**' (Vulgate). 'Hearken not ye to your prophets, nor to your diviners, nor to your dreamers, nor to your enchanters, nor to your **sorcerers**' (AV). (c) Daniel 2.27. 'Mysterium, quod rex interrogat, sapientes, magi, **arioli,** et aruspices nequeunt indicare regi' (Vulgate). 'The secret which the King hath demanded cannot the wise men, the astrologers, the **magicians**, the soothsayers shew unto the King'. (AV). Hebrew, *ashafim*, 'enchanters'.

A brief review of the words mentioned by Del Rio, not all of which are included in the translated passage, may be useful. *Aovoth* (modern *havvot*? : *'ov* = 'ghost') means 'injurious utterance, a magical formula'. This and the next term are two of the three words in *Deuteronomy* 18.11, which seem to be related to necromancy. Cf. *Leviticus* 20.27; *Isaiah* 29.4. The Talmud *Sanhedrin* 65a refers *'ov* to the magician who speaks out of his armpit. *Iddeghoni* (modern *yidde'oni*) is a familiar spirit. *Nachas* (modern *nachash*) means 'to practise divination'. *Kisem* (modern *qasam, qasamim*) is an augurer, although this is actually a very general term. *Ghonem* (modern *yonen*) means 'soothsayer'. The word is connected with whispering or crooning. In the 1606 edition of the *Disquisitiones*, Del Rio has *Ghonem* to begin with, but *Yonen* later in the chapter. For some reason this was not repeated in the 1612 edition which has *Ghonem* throughout. *Chabar* (modern *hover hever*) is 'one who uses charms'. *Lachas* (modern *lahash*) means 'whisper, charm'. The word appears as *Lachar* at first mention, but this may be a simple misprint. In the 1606 edition it is printed as *Lachaz* each time.

In Latin, *magus* has both a specific meaning and a general one which stems from it. The word *Magi* was brought into Latin from Persian[8] via Greek, and in the beginning was a term of honour among Persians and Chaldaeans, applied to the priests of their religious rites, the counsellors of their Kings, their philosophers, and their theologians. This later acquired a bad meaning and was used of all the evil arts.

Venefici (now called *venenarii*) originally referred only to those who used to do harm by means of wicked herbal concoctions. Later on the word was employed of enchanters [*incantatores*] and applied to every kind of witch [*Thessalae*].

Arioli, augures, aruspices, Chaldaei, Thessali, and *Genethliaci* are often confused.

Lamiae bring death to children. The name comes either from the famous kidnapper Lamia (on whom see Antonius Liberalis, Diodorus, and others), or from female demons [*succubae*] (see Philostratus), or from savage Libyans (see Dion the Sophist).

Striges, named after an ill-omened night-bird, are believed to bring death to children. (The ancient Romans were told about these women by Apuleius.)

Varatrices claim to be able to foretell the future, like those shits who call themselves 'Egyptians' and are the refuse of all people and nations. Cf. the ancients' verb *verare*, 'to tell the truth'. Ennius, 'Do seers in the whole course of their life tell the truth all that often?'[9] Or perhaps *veraculae*, as a scholar has conjectured from Suetonius's *Life of Vitellius* [14], 'He had absolutely no time for *veraculae* and astrologers (*mathematici*)'. This scholar says the word is related to hostile malefice (something I shall discuss in Book 3). These women were once called *simulatrices*, 'copiers, a kind of priestess' (see Festus); and *fictrices*, 'moulders, fashioners, pretenders' (see Tertullian).

The people of Lombardy use the word *Mascae* in their legislation. Perhaps this is because they hide themselves behind horrible masks[10] during their assemblies or because, owing to a deformity of the face (which most of them have), they look more like evil spirits or masks than women.

Sortilegi was an ancient name for those who sought to foretell the future by a superstitious casting of lots. But later theologians and lawyers confused this with the impious crime committed by witches (*striges*).

I find that the words *sortiarii* and *sortiariae* date from the time of Hincmar, Archbishop of Rheims.[11] These are both poisoners/workers of venomous magic

---

[8] Literally 'from the barbarians', a word regularly used by ancient Greek authors to refer to Persians.

[9] *Annales* fr. 380.

[10] The word here is *larvis* from *larva* which means 'evil spirit, demon', as well as 'grotesque mask'. 'Assemblies' (*conventicula*) is here likely to suggest witches' sabbats.

[11] (c. 805–882). The word does not occur as part of a list of similar terms whose meaning Hincmar is defining, *De divortio Lotharii et Tetbergae*, interrogatio 15 = PL 125.718–19, and I cannot find it elsewhere in his work.

[*venefici*] and vassals of the Devil, so they can also be called *Satanici* and *Venenarii*. (For examples from before Christ, there is the Canidia of Horace, the Erisichto [*sic*] of Lucan, the Martina of Tacitus, and the Thessalian women of Lucian and Apuleius.) [12] The word *sortiarii* is of fairly recent origin. [13]

Chapter 3: Natural magic, or the magic of physical nature

[The Persians especially were dedicated to magic. They had two gods, one of whom was good and the other, evil. From these two gods came two types of magic. One, entirely superstitious, was concerned with the worship of false gods. The other enabled people to gain knowledge of the innermost natures of things. Later came Zoroaster, who is not one person but several. Del Rio lists

[12] Horace: *Epodes* 3.8 (the context is poison); 5.15–24 (emphasis on the poisonous ingredients of a magic brew); 17.7 (chanting). Lucan: *De Bello Civili* 6.507–68 (Erichtho is ugly, old, and digs up corpses for her magic); her spells are poisons [*venefica*] in 580; she raises a corpse to foretell the future, 624–828; there are references to chants and herbs in 822. Tacitus: *Annales* 2.74 and 3.7. Martina is described specifically as a poisoner. Lucian: *Lucius* 4 (female magicians); 54 (anointing with a magic ointment.) Apuleius: *Metamorphoses* 2.21 (female magicians, *sagae mulieres*, bite corpses.)

[13] Again, a brief review of the words mentioned by Del Rio, not all of which are included in the translated passage, may be useful. *Magus*, as Del Rio says, came into Greek and then Latin from Persian where it referred to the priests of Zoroastrianism. *Veneficus* is someone who makes or has to do with poison. *Ariolus*, usually beginning with an *h* in Classical Latin, meant 'soothsayer' or 'diviner'. An *augur* was originally a person who interpreted the will of the gods by observing the flight or behaviour of birds. *Aruspex*, once again spelled with an initial *h* in Classical Latin, referred to an interpreter of the patterns upon the surfaces of the internal organs of recently sacrificed animals. He also explained prodigies and flashes of lightning. *Chaldaeus* – literally 'someone from Southern Assyria' – was an astrologer. *Thessalus* referred to an inhabitant of Thessaly, famous throughout ancient times for its female magicians. *Genethliacus* is borrowed from Greek and means 'someone who draws up horoscopes'. *Lamia*, again borrowed from Greek, was the term for a female monster who used to devour children. *Striges* (plural of Greek *strix*), referred to a type of owl regarded as a bird of ill omen. *Varatrix* is not a Classical Latin word. It may be connected with *verax*, 'telling the truth', or (perhaps more likely) *veratrum*, a class of herbs both medicinal and poisonous. *Veracula* is perhaps a variant, although one should note that the word in the passage of Suetonius quoted by Del Rio is probably a misreading of *vernaculus*, 'buffoon, vulgarian'. *Mathematicus* (Greek) was either a mathematician or an astrologer, the two not being distinguished from each other. *Simulatrix* is a woman who produces copies of something. The usual example is Homer's Circe who turned Odysseus's men into pigs. *Fictrix* is a deceiver (from the verb *fingo* 'I make imitations, sculpt, mould, invent', etc.). *Masca* is a Mediaeval Latin word meaning 'mask' or 'nightmare', perhaps from Arabic *masaka*, 'to grip'. *Sortilegus* means someone who reads lots cast to determine the wishes of the gods or to foretell the future. *Sortiarius* is a thirteenth century variant of this, unless Del Rio is correct, in which case it is a ninth century variant.

them, along with the names of other famous magicians of antiquity. Of all the books he has mentioned, he says, there remains only the *Chaldaica* or *Magica Logia* by 'Zoroaster', a work more obscure than useful, in his opinion.

God bestowed natural, legitimate magic along with other branches of knowledge upon Adam who transmitted it to his posterity. According to Psellus and Proclus, this magic is simply a more precise knowledge of the secrets of nature, such as the movement and influence of the heavens and stars; sympathy and antipathy between particular things; when, where, and how things should be combined, and what extraordinary results can be achieved thereby, things which seem amazing, even miraculous, to the ignorant.

Natural magic is divided into *operative* and *divinatory*. The latter deals with the discovery of things which are secret or lie hidden in the future. The former is about the production of remarkable effects.

Del Rio then gives a list of people who, he says, should be regarded as magicians inspired by the Devil. The list includes Peter of Abano, Cornelius Agrippa, Paracelsus. It is followed by other names of writers who, he says, are largely heretical either in whole or in part, and then by a good many others whose works need to be read with care. These authors include Girolamo Cardano, Giovanni Battista della Porta, Francisco Pico della Mirandola, and Jean Bodin.]

Chapter 3, Question 1: What bearing do heavenly aspects and influences have on magical effects?

[The principal superstition of ancient magic is that higher powers affect those substances which are on earth, and there is an agreement between what is higher and what is lower, especially sublunary. This is explained by recent writers by means of analogies: for example, that an echo is caused by a wall opposite, or that rays collected in a concave mirror first strike a body opposite them and then set it on fire. Thus, they maintain that similarities between images, or numbers or characters have an extraordinary ability to produce effects. This is a very silly idea, says Del Rio, and proceeds to pour scorn on it. The belief that the sky or the stars possess feelings or an intelligent soul has been condemned by the Church and is an opinion full of error and scandal because of its inherent superstition and idolatry. Even those Church Fathers who seem to have supported the idea spoke figuratively and allegorically. The addled analogy between the heavens, the planets, the ages of man, the parts of the body, and states of mind is worthless. There are no celestial influences save those of light and movement which together produce heat. People's mental dispositions are affected by their physical characteristics, not by the stars, and they always retain their free will undiminished. It is the sin of idolatry to imagine that an evil spirit or the constellations are responsible for effects which actually proceed from God alone, and it is blasphemous and superstitious to profane the sacraments and sacred things with such superstitions. The stars have no such influence, neither have amulets any power to sway the stars, change characteristics, or make any basic impression.]

Chapter 3, Question 2: Can magical effects of this kind, which are like miracles, arise from a person's natural temperament?

[People thought this in the past, and still do. But such a proposition is complete nonsense, as well as being impious, and Del Rio refers his reader to Codronchi: *De morbis veneficis* (Diseases Caused by Poison/Venomous Magic), Miguel de Medina, and Leonardo Vairo: *De fascino* (Casting Spells).] [14]

Chapter 3, Question 3: How great is the power of the imagination, and of what kind is it, with respect to these wonderful effects?

Many people have written at length about the power of the imagination [examples given]. They all agree that the power of the imagination is very great, and because it can be considered either in relation to the body of the imaginer himself or to that of another person, each must be investigated separately. The commentators all agree that the imagination has very great power over the actual body of the imaginer himself, and one explains this by appealing to reason and experience.

(a) Reason. The imagination recalls the images of objects which have been perceived by the senses and aroused the appetitive power [15] to fear or shame or anger or sadness. These feelings so affect a person that he swings between heat and cold, turns pale or blushes, is carried away and taken out of himself or grows numb and is cast down, and Saint Thomas [Aquinas] has explained to us very clearly that the imagination has power over the body of the imaginer with respect to all those things which have a natural affinity with the imagination, such as the limited movements of people during sleep, changes caused by cold

---

[14] Giovanni Battista Codronchi (1547–1628), Italian physician. His book was published in Venice in 1595. Miguel de Medina (1489–1578) published *De recta in Deum fide* (The Right Way to Believe in God) in Venice in 1564. Leonardo Vairo (fl. 1587–1603), Bishop of Pozzuoli. His book was composed in Latin, published in French translation in Paris in 1583, and then the Latin version appeared in Venice in 1589.

[15] See Aquinas: *Summa Theologiae*, Prima Pars, question 1, article 1, for a full discussion of this technical term.

and heat, and further change consequent upon these. But it has no power over the other ways in which the body itself is constituted and which do not have a natural affinity with the imagination, such as the shape of one's hand or foot. No one can add a single palm's breadth to his height, and so forth.[16]

(b) Experience. Everyday experience is illustrated by Night Walkers who do extraordinary things while they are asleep. It is generally agreed that these are caused by the imagination once the senses have been overcome by sleep. Andreas Libavius's book gives information about this. Another doctor, André du Laurens, has dealt with this subject more briefly in his *Historia Anatomica* (Anatomical History), question 12, as follows:[17]

'Let us say that sleepers are moved because the very slight power lying hidden in their muscles is aroused by a strong imagination. But while they dream, they do not move unless the imagination (very much as in the case of that of brute beasts) strongly suggests they should; for the imagination of sleepers is similar to that of brute beasts in that their reason offers it no resistance. This is why they are roused to do many things which they would not dare to do while they were in the waking state. They climb the scaffolding of a very high roof and wander over decorative panels in the ceilings. There is nothing they dare not do in their freedom from fear because the imagination has been put to sleep by a dark mist and it knows no danger. While they are asleep they have no sensation because there is no object present to their senses. Movement has its own object, namely the appetite which presents visions[18] to the imagination. When, therefore, the rest of one's animal faculties are borne away in sleep, only the imagination busies itself, generally in such a way that it moves the motor-power and the rest of the inferior faculties as though they were its servants, the animal spirits which have charge of motion being compelled to go to their organs; and these movements happen because of the interior images the sleepers have of things which compel them to act like this. Those who have an excess of foaming blood and a lot of hot spirit are particularly prone to this condition'.[19]

[16] Del Rio gives references to Aquinas: *Summa Theologiae*, Pars Tria, question 13, article 3, reply 3 and *Summa Contra Gentiles* 3, chapter 103.

[17] Libavius (1550–1616) was a physician and later Professor of History and Poetry at Jena. His *Neoparacelsica* was published in Frankfurt in 1594 and his *Rerum Chymicarum Epistolica* in 1595, also at Frankfurt. André du Laurens was at one time physician to Henri IV. His *Historia Anatomica* was published at Frankfurt in 1599. The reference to his book and the quotation from it were added after the 1606 edition of *Disquisitiones*.

[18] *Spectra*, emanations from physical objects giving rise to visual and mental images.

[19] Cited as Book 4, question 12. It is actually in question 11, and the examples from Galen to which Del Rio proceeds come before, not after, this quotation. See *Historia Anatomica*, 117–18.

[Del Rio repeats Du Laurens's examples and adds that he himself does not think that all the senses must be engaged simultaneously to be able to accomplish an act of imagination, nor that the imagination necessarily needs some external stimulation immediately before it starts to work. He does admit, however, that some kind of physical stimulus is required, the imagination being set in motion by sense-impressions, as Aristotle says.]

I do not find it absurd that future events sometimes send out signals in advance of their actually happening. These signals move the surrounding air, its movement sets our senses in motion, and in this way the movement of the senses is a kind of preparation for the imagination itself. This movement of the senses is a necessary preparation for the imagination, and actually we need no other movement of the senses to set the imagination working. Such is certainly the opinion of Saint Isidore, Saint Jerome, and Thomas More. Andrea Cesalpino, in his *Peripateticarum Quaestionum Libri V* (Five Books of Peripatetic Questions), Book 5, final chapter, argues without much success that the imagination can be moved by external objects and not by a movement of the senses.[20]

As far as another person's body is concerned, some people think that the power of the imagination can stretch itself out a very long way to such an extent, indeed, that it can bewitch or cure people who are at a distance, move things from their place, and bring down from the sky flashes of lightning and rain. See Avicenna: *De anima* (On the Soul), section 4, chapter 4.[21] Other writers, however, disagree in their explanations of how this is done. Some think the imagination operates thus by means of rays which are dreamed by the imaginers, e.g. Al-Kindi: *De imaginibus* (On Images).[22] Others say it works through spirits expelled from the body by the force of the imagination, e.g. Paracelsus: *De imaginibus* (On Images); Pomponazzi: *De incantationibus* (On Enchantments); and Andrea Cattaneo: *De mirabilium effectuum causis* (The Causes of Remarkable Effects), chapter 8, question 3.[23] The rest agree with Avicenna and Fulginas that

[20] Italian physician, botanist, and natural philosopher (1519–1603). His *Quaestiones* was first published in Venice in 1571. The last chapter of Book 5 is entitled, 'The imagination can be moved by external objects, not by a movement of the senses', and he argues his case largely from Aristotle, as one might expect. He employs the same texts as Del Rio, but uses others as well. See the Venetian edition of 1593, pp. 141–4.

[21] Arab philosopher and physician (980–1037). His *De anima* first appeared in the West at Pavia in 1490.

[22] One of the greatest of Islamic scholars (c. 804–873). He wrote on virtually every branch of scientific knowledge, combining the doctrines of Aristotle with Neoplatonic and dualistic concepts. His books on magic and planetary influences were particularly popular during the Middle Ages.

[23] Paracelsus = Theophrastus Bombast von Hohenheim (1493–1541), a German physician. He had somewhat unorthodox opinions about medicine and these served to create for

it works only by the power of the soul which is superior to it.[24] Oger Ferrier, *Methodus* (The Proper Method for a Doctor), Book 2, chapter 11, has attributed this power to the power of the imagination, but does not say whether it works by the power of the soul or a stream of mediating spirits. I think, however, he agrees with Avicenna.[25]

But one's first conclusion must be this: *The human soul cannot effect any miracles of this sort upon a body quite unconnected with that of the imaginer, whether by imagination or by any other power, be it mediating rays, spirits, or mental images.*

This is the common conclusion of the theologians Saint Thomas [Aquinas], Silvestri of Ferrara, Medina, Pico, and Vairo, whom I have already cited, and of the medical writers Valles, Codronchi, Bökel, Cesalpino, and others.[26] The point is proved because imagination is latent action and for that reason the soul doing the imagining cannot imprint a real quality upon a separate object, which is what it would have to do. There are no such rays. Such a great power cannot reside in spirits. Mental images have the power of building up a representation to a certain extent, but one person's soul is not naturally in alignment with anyone else's soul or body. So when the charlatan Mirabiliarius Caesarius the Maltese pretended to make certain magical prognostications in Antwerp in 1599, and forced someone to choose an object which he wanted him to choose, claiming that he did this by using the power of his spirit to dominate the other man's spirit, it is obvious he was lying.

Pomponazzi maintains that these spirit-images can give rise to something which is real (presumably he means the thing of which they are a mental image), just as prototypes do in the mind of God. But this is said out of ignorance. Prototypes in the mind of God are real in themselves and not merely

him a rather dubious reputation. His study of the Jewish Kabbalah was regarded with particular suspicion by orthodox medical authorities. Pietro Pomponazzi (1462–1525) taught philosophy at Mantua, Padua, Ferrara, and Bologna. The *De incantationibus* was published in 1520. Del Rio returns to attack him in more detail later. Cattaneo may be assigned to the early sixteenth century. His *Opus de intellectu et de causis mirabilium effectuum* has neither date nor place of publication.

[24] Fulginas = Gentile Gentili (d. 1348?), Italian physician. He was published in the late 15th and early 16th centuries.

[25] Ferrier (1513–1588) was physician to Catherine de' Medici. His *Vera Medenti Methodus* was published in 1557.

[26] Francesco Silvestri of Ferrara (1474–1528) wrote commentaries on Aquinas and Aristotle. 'Medina' is probably Miguel de Medina (1489–1578) who was imprisoned by the Inquisition for some of his ideas. Del Rio refers to him later in this chapter. Francisco de Valles (1524–1592), Spanish Humanist, philosopher, and physician, wrote commentaries on Hippocrates and Galen as well as other medical works. In 1572 he was appointed physician to Philip II. Johann Bökel published a book, *De philtris* (Magic Potions) in Hamburg in 1599. This is probably the book Del Rio has in mind.

attributes of something. They are also of a higher order than these spirits. They do not create anything new in God, nor do they change anything. When it comes to what God has created, no mental picture in the imagination has ever produced something real which looks like itself. For example, the mental image of a horse does not create a real horse, and if I create a mental image of heat I do not warm someone who is naked and feeling the cold when he is at a distance from me. If the power of the imagination could do anything like this, alchemists would long ago have acquired mountains of gold.

A final point: if these spirits do exist, they must be weak because when they are discharged from the imaginer, like a foetus from its mother's womb, they are damaged at once by the surrounding air.

[Those who take the opposite point of view are mistaken. Three additional points: a fowler cannot draw down birds from the air simply by using his imagination; no one can be bewitched simply by someone else's imagination; no one can be cured in this fashion, either.]

Second conclusion: *It is quite likely that, by chance, the imagination can exert power over a body in its vicinity provided (a) they are closely joined and the one is in physical contact with the other (b) the imagination is very strong, and (c) the neighbouring body has a strong affinity with the one next to it.*

[This conclusion enables contrary opinions to be reconciled, one of which denies that the imagination can change bodies outside itself, while the other says it can. In support of the latter opinion, Miguel de Medina, Marsilio Ficino, and Benito Pereira cite examples of extraordinary differences between offspring and parents in the animal world.[27] Del Rio then discusses Jacob's experiments in cross-breeding (*Genesis* 30.32–40) and the opinions on this offered by several authors, ancient and modern. He adds several examples, including the story of an evil spirit which impersonated a certain woman's husband and went to bed with her asserting, as people do when they are drunk, that he wanted to engender a demon. The child born of this intercourse looked like a demon and immediately after its birth began to frolic and jump about.[28] But none of these examples, says Del Rio, is sufficient to prove the point, since they can be attributed to the imagination of the mother.]

[27] Marsilio Ficino (1433–1499), Italian Humanist and leader of the Platonic Academy in Florence. Benito Pereira (*c.* 1535–1610), Spanish exegete, Jesuit.

[28] The story comes from a book by Antonio de Torquemada (called 'Jerome' by Del Rio), a Spanish humanist, floruit 1553–1570. *Jardin de flores curiosas en que tratan algunas materias de Humanidad, Philosophia, Theologia y Geographia, con otros cosas* was published in 1570 and is a compilation of folk-lore, witchcraft, and other occult subject-matter.

I shall now pick out part of a charming poem by Thomas More, addressed to 'Sabinus'.

'Important scholars who direct all their efforts at uncovering the secret effects of nature – important scholars, I say, tell us that whatever image dominates the mother's mind when the child is begotten secretly, in some mysterious way, imposes accurate and indelible traces of itself upon the seed. These marks penetrate deeply and grow with the embryo, and thus the child reflects the image inbred in it from the mother's mind.'[29]

He then goes on to say that four of Sabinus's children did not look like him because his wife did not think of her husband while he was far away. But another son, conceived in adultery, did resemble Sabinus because, during inter-course, his wife was worried in case he should turn up unexpectedly, like the wolf in the fairy-tale. The cause of the former dissimilarity, however, could have been that she was directing her attention and imagination elsewhere during the act of conception. So in my opinion the dissimilarity may have been caused entirely by the woman's imagination, although I should also say that the imaginations of both husband and wife may very well have coincided at the same moment (as Francisco Valles says in his *De sacra philosophia* (On Sacred Philosophy), chapter 11),[30] but neither of them at that moment was acting via the imagination upon the body of the other. The imagination operates simply on the fertile seed which has been a part of the imaginer, and therefore the soul of the imaginer imprints a form on the seed – for example, the colour of the skin or the curliness of the hair – but does not do so by direct action since the seed is not capable of this. But by imprinting the virtue of transferring from the generator and conferring upon the foetus, he is forming those things which are consistent with the generator's soul, so that what was in the soul of the generator spiritually may start to exist physically in the generated body.

[Is the man's imagination alone sufficient to do this? There is a diversity of opinion on this point, because it is not clear what and how much the male and female seed bring to the material and constitution of the foetus. If the father contributes only to the shape and the mother contributes equally to the shape and supplies all the material, it is more likely that the father's imagination alone is not sufficient. In any case, the imagination which operates after conception is more powerful, because we see that offspring already formed in the mother's

---

[29] *Ad Sabinum* vv. 18–33. The poem is no. 205 in Volume 3 of the Yale edition of the *Complete Works*. These lines receive a note on p. 395 of that volume, giving further examples of the same phenomenon.

[30] Published in Turin in 1587.

womb feels the disbursement of the imagination, something to which pregnant women bear witness every day.]

I have read that a citizen of Wittenburg was born with the face of a corpse. This happened because while his mother was carrying him in her womb, she suddenly came face to face with a dead body as she was walking along the road. At Eisenach, a chaste and very beautiful married woman gave birth to a dormouse because one of her neighbours had hung up a little bell for a particular dormouse, with the intention that its sound would drive other dormice away, and this special dormouse ran up to the pregnant woman. She, taken by surprise, was so terrified at the sudden arrival and sight of the dormouse that the foetus in her womb degenerated into the shape of that little beast. During the pontificate of Nicholas III, a woman in one of the palaces in Rome gave birth to a child which looked like a bear. According to the doctors, this was because there were pictures of bears to be seen all over the palace. At Paderborn there was the famous case of a heretic woman, not quite sixteen years old, who gave birth to a son vested and tonsured like an ecclesiastic. Because of her violent hatred of Papists (as they call us), she was always cursing them to people she met while out walking. On the other hand, this may simply have been divine vengeance.

I now give further examples, drawn from other sources. I include cases of both maternal and paternal influence. Here is one relating to the mother. There was at Antwerp a pregnant woman who used to take delight in a monkey. She gave birth to a single daughter who exhibited many simian traits, such as hiding away, mimicking people, and things like that. Here is an example relating to the father. Ludovico Del Rio,[31] a man who enjoyed the highest esteem, faithfully accomplished a task for the King and for that reason was arrested by traitors during a full session of the Senate in Brussels. When his wife, who was pregnant at the time, saw the ring-leaders of the rebels bursting into her house, she was terrified out of her wits. After she had given birth, I baptised the child. Ever since birth that child has had its mother's terror in its panic-stricken eyes and even now, in adolescence, its loss of mind continues. Fernel writes in his *De hominis procreatione* (On Human Procreation) that if you cover a pea-hen with pieces of white cloth while she is sitting on her eggs, she will produce chicks which are entirely white, not varied in colour.[32] Now, surely no one maintains that eggs have nothing to do with the mother's body? So you see hereby the power of the imagination.

---

[31] Martín's uncle.
[32] Jean Fernel (1497–1558), French physician, also interested in mathematics and astronomy.

[Del Rio says he will not discuss the disputed point whether the effectiveness of the relationship between like and like rests solely upon the power of the imagination, or whether the motion of the seed and the power of formation claim part of this for themselves.]

Saint Augustine tells the following story about a certain man. 'Whenever he pleased, he used to utter cries like the sounds of someone in grief, withdraw from his senses, and lie on the ground like a dead man. The effect was so profound that not only did he not feel people pinching and pricking him, but sometimes he did not even feel pain when they applied fire to his body, until afterwards when he became aware of the wound. That his body stayed motionless, not through effort on his part but by lack of sensation, is proved by the fact that he was found to emit no breath, just as in the case of a dead person. He reported afterwards, however, that he heard people's voices, if they were speaking distinctly, as if from far away', *De civitate Dei* (The City of God), Book 14, chapter 23.[33]

The learned [Augustine] presents this as a fact on the grounds that, by the strength of his imagination, the man removed himself from any sense of what was going on around him. But think, reader, whether it is not more likely that the man was a magician [*magus*] and had agreed to be snatched into ecstasy because of a pact he had made with an evil spirit. The effect of this kind of imagination is clearly superior to any other imaginative power, since ecstasy does not depend upon human will.

Chapter 3, Question 4: Can wounds and diseases be treated simply by touch, sight, voice, breath, kiss, or binding with a linen cloth?

No matter how much they differ in detail, apologists for superstition have this argument in common: spirits,[34] they say, trickle from the heart through the arteries and burst out through the sight of the person doing the looking, or the mouth of the person talking, or the pores of the person touching. Then, having been emitted by the more powerful will of the person who is seeing, speaking, or touching, they insinuate themselves into the arteries of the person being seen, listening, or being touched, and from there search out his heart and effectively penetrate it.

First conclusion: *This power cannot be attributed to the voice.* The proof of this is that it is only by chance that the voice can have an effect upon the listener because of the sound or meaning of the words, and so change the listener by

---

[33] Actually 14.24. Del Rio has edited the text slightly, but the difference is not significant.
[34] *Spiritus*, not *daemones*.

the joy, fear, sadness, etc. which it brings him. (See the excellent exposition by Vairo).[35] This is not contradicted by stories about the wonderful effects magicians [magi] produce by means of wicked spells, such as whispering certain words into the ear of a bull which then falls down as if dead, and then whispering other spells which bring it to its feet; or the story that parental curses, too, scarcely ever fail to take effect. But I maintain that these stories about the bull and so on do not contradict my conclusion because they work by means of a pact made with an evil spirit. As for curses, if their effect is swift, this can arise from violent change due to shame or fear or sadness; and if their effect is slow, one should not suppose this is because of the sound of the words. Rather, one should think that God, with his impartial judgement, is punishing the iniquity and impiety of the children. In connection with this, I recall the story of a woman from Westphalia who, by her curses and execrations, restored her son who had been completely unable to move. Other writers have attributed this to the operation of an evil spirit.[36]

Second conclusion: *Neither vision by itself, nor vision linked with bare imagination, is enough to effect such a thing.*

[Various authors prove this point with regard to both enchantment and to healing. Authors who take the contrary view say that the eye sees by sending something out. Du Laurens, however, argues that vision works by absorbing the image presented to it and that if vision does not reach a particular object, that object, in effect, does not exist.]

First thoughts suggest that there are many things which argue against this point of view: love caused by pleasing appearance on both sides, inflammation of the eyes, the spells of old women, defective mirrors, golden orioles,[37] wolves, ostriches, cockerels, and basilisks. Let me deal briefly with these.

Sight is, up to a point, an occasion of the beginning and the increase of love because at the start it offers the imagination an image of the appearance of the form which has been seen. This image – a constantly revolving fantasy – is the reason someone makes up his mind that the object of his love is worthy of being loved and pursued. This is how a person begins to love. Soon love is heated by the presence of the beloved object and grows more powerful. This

---

[35] Del Rio gives marginal references. Vairo: *De fascino* (Casting Spells), Book 2, chapter 11. Similarly, Codronchi: *De morbis veneficis* (Diseases Caused By Poison/Venomous Magic), Book 2, chapter 5.

[36] Marginal note. Giovanni Lorenzo d'Anania (died 1582), Italian antiquarian. After the death of his patron, the Archbishop of Naples, in 1576, he retired to Calabria and devoted himself to the study of magic and the natural sciences. His *De natura daemonum* (The Nature of Evil Spirits) was published in Venice in 1581.

[37] Reading *galguli* for *galgali*. See Pliny: *Naturalis Historia* 30.94.

is not because it sees the love-object with the eyes of the body (for those who are absent are tortured much more by love), but because it thinks about it all the time. It endows the love-object with greater worth than it actually has and, by building up this kind of mental picture for itself, furnishes both kindling and torches for its ardour. Now, if there were not something intrinsically wrong in the notion that love depends upon physical sight of the beloved object, why is it that when several men see the same woman at the same time and are seen by her, one man falls desperately in love while the others could not care less?

Inflammation and indelible spots on mirrors caused by the sight of a menstruating woman do not spread from the sight itself nor from her actual eye, but rather from infected breath bursting out of her mouth and nostrils, or from the hollows next to the eye, and the leakage of contagion from a mixture of spirits.

[Del Rio gives details of how tears, inflammation, and harmful humours and spirits make their way out of the skull through the eye-socket. The sight of an old woman can terrify children because her ugliness disturbs their humours. If the golden oriole looks at someone suffering from jaundice, the bird attracts the disease to itself and so cures the sufferer. This Del Rio attributes to some occult sympathy between the bird and the disease, not to the bird's vision. The sight of wolves deprives people of their speech. There are various explanations for this.]

Thomas of Cantimpré [38] says this happens because the wolf sends out rays from its eyes to the man and thus immediately drains his spirits of vision, and that once these have been dried up, his arteries are drained, and with the instrument of the voice thus hampered and constricted, his voice becomes hoarse, *De apibus* (On Bees), Book 2, chapter 57, page 39. I do not accept this business about rays. I prefer to agree with others who say that when people stumble upon a wolf unexpectedly, they are particularly frightened by its gleaming eyes and formidable appearance. Sudden fear drives the blood towards their heart, all their limbs grow cold, and a sudden change takes place throughout their body. Hence the hoarseness and obstruction in the voice. I do not think this is merely an idle explanation given by hunters. After all, if the wolf sees the man first, it gathers itself together to punish him and inflict harm on him; and to make sure the man cannot call out, the wolf blows upon him a kind

---

[38] Encyclopaedist (1201–1270/72). Del Rio here refers to one of Thomas's most famous books which circulated for a long time in manuscript and was not published until 1472. A good Latin edition appeared in 1597.

[39] *Venenatus sit*, literally, 'he has been poisoned'. But the connection with *veneficium* – 'magical art' as well as 'poisoning' – is essential to the passage.

of vapour. When the man has been bewitched[39] in this manner, the wolf brings the hoarseness on him. But when the wolf sees it has been cornered by the man and has been seen by him, it is afraid and does not think of planning an escape by emitting this vapour.

[Del Rio continues to discuss sight in relation to stories about the ostrich, tortoise, lion, and toad.]

On the gaze of the basilisk (a tale more famous than true), see Nicander: *Theriaca* (Cures for Snake-Bite); Dioscorides, Book 6; Pliny, Book 8; Solinus, chapter 30; Scaliger: *Exercitationes* (Exercises), 24; Mercuriale: *De venenis* (On Poisons), Book 1, chapter 21.[40] These say that if the animal is discovered, it infects the surrounding air with its violent and venomous breath and kills those who stumble across it. (See André du Laurens, question 11.) They add that it dies if it catches sight of itself in pure, clear water. Let me say, in a word, I do not believe it. If spirits did come out of its eyes, they would be of the same substance as the seer and therefore would not kill him. But if these spirits were not part of the basilisk's natural substance before they were enclosed in his eyes, they would have done him harm. So it is ridiculous to say these creatures are infected and poisoned by looking into water.[41]

I shall add to the arguments of Vairo one which seems to me to be more problematical. In Spain there is a group of people known as 'Zahuri' or, as we should say, 'Lyncei'.[42] When I was working in Madrid in 1575, I visited, more than once, a boy belonging to this group. They say these people can see objects which are in the very bowels of the earth, water-channels, treasuries of precious metals, and bodies beneath their tombstones. The belief is very widespread and very well-known. It is not only Pindar, Tzetzes, and other poets who think this can be true. So do philosophers and several people who attribute this power to the Zahuris's melancholic humour and the great strength of their natural spirits. This reasoning would make better sense if people merely thought the Zahuris see things which really are invisible. But the truth is they rely on visible clues, so the story is ridiculous. For example, they know there are channels of water underground because these give off vapour in the morning and in the

---

[40] Nicander reference = 397–410. Dioscorides = *De materia medica* (Things Which Make Medicines), chapter 53. Pliny = *Naturalis Historia*, section 78. Scaliger's book was published in 1557. Girolamo Mercuriale (1530–1606), physician, treated Maximilian II successfully and was honoured and rewarded by him. His book was published in Basel in 1584.

[41] There is a hand-written note beside this paragraph in the margin of the 1606 edition which I am using. It says, 'I have actually seen the flesh of a basilisk. It was killed by the power of a mirror in Siena in 1744 and brought to Freiburg on 29 July 1749'.

[42] *Zahori* (modern Spanish) = 'water diviner'. Lynceus was one of the Argonauts, famous for his keen sight.

evening and thus reveal their locations; they recognise the presence of veins of metal from the types of herbs which usually grow nearby; and when they say they know the location and condition of treasures and corpses, it is my opinion they have them pointed out and revealed by evil spirits. The sharpness of their eyes can cover a very wide area, provided no solid body gets in the way. But the tomb or the earth are so dense, solid, and opaque that no one can see through them. Illumination and transparency are both missing, and both conditions are necessary to one's ability to see anything at all. Moreover, the Zuharis usually restrict their ability to see to certain days (Tuesdays and Fridays) because of the secret pact they have made with evil spirits. A redness of the eyes, which is particularly noticeable among them, does more harm than good to the acuity of their vision.

Third conclusion: *Contact alone is not enough for this purpose.*[43] Both Vairo and Codronchi argue the case for bewitchment (*fascinatio*), but their arguments apply equally to other extraordinary happenings. First, touch (however one defines it) has been given to a human being for the preservation of his own life. It has no power other than the power of touching. If, however, it were to have power to perform wonders, that power would have to be either wholesome or harmful by nature. If wholesome, it would bring safety first of all to its own body; if harmful, it would first kill the person in whom it was present, and yet we see no evidence of either of these things. Secondly, everyone it touches should be affected equally. It ought to cure (or even wound) those whom it does not wish to cure or wound. Finally, no one should need to employ any additional rites or ceremonies, yet we see that things are altogether otherwise.

[Examples of the effects of touch, drawn from nature and music, are now discussed.]

[Sixth example] A corpse pours blood in the presence of its killer on account of the former contact between them. Some people attribute this to a miracle, others to chance whereby occasionally it actually has happened that a corpse has started to bleed in the presence of its murderer. I have reviewed the whole question elsewhere [44] and have not yet come across an argument more convincing than the one which says there is an antipathy springing from the violent hatred of the murdered person for his murderer. This is because a hidden, mysterious quality is imprinted upon the body and remains there after death. See the reference by Lucretius: 'The body seeks that which has wounded the mind with love. For people generally fall towards a wound and the blood spurts out

---

[43] I.e. to effect cures or wonders.
[44] He refers to his commentary on Seneca's *Octavia*, 127.

in the direction of the blow which strikes us: and if he is nearby, the red horror drenches the enemy'.[45] [Further references given.]

[Seventh example] One may cite various kinds of cures which occur with astonishing frequency. First, the daily practical proof offered by soldiers who cure even the most atrocious wounds merely by breathing on them, kissing them, or binding them up with linen cloth. They call this 'the art of Saint Anselm'. In Spain this is known as 'the art of the *Salutatores*';[46] in Italy, as 'the art of the Gentiles' or 'of Saint Catharine' or 'of Saint Paul'; in Belgium, as 'the art of the sons of Good Friday'. All Belgians boast that they are endowed with the gift of curing various diseases. This notion receives support from no less an authority than Pomponazzi in his book *De Incantationibus* (On Enchantments), chapter 3. He says that, just as these powers of healing are found in herbs, stones, and living creatures, there is no reason to suppose that similar powers are not found in the whole human race so that in one person may be the virtue of such and such a stone, and in another the virtue of such and such a plant. What, therefore, this plant or that stone can do, this or that human being will be able to do by the power of nature.

But this business is too complicated to be unravelled by a single proposition. So I say first, *the gift of conferring health or effecting a cure is a supernatural gift and a grace given freely by God*. This should be held as a point of faith – in the words of Saint Paul, 'To one is given through the Spirit the utterance of wisdom, and to another the utterance of knowledge according to the same Spirit; to another, faith by the same Spirit; to another the gifts of healing by the same Spirit; to another the working of miracles, to another prophecy, to another the ability to distinguish between spirits'.[47]

In Flanders, all those born on Good Friday, and a sequence of seven legitimate boys with no females interrupting the line, are thought to have the gift of healing (although this applies only to fevers). This cannot be explained away as due to natural causes, so any such cure is indeed extraordinary and, provided no superstition is involved, agrees with the statement I made earlier. For it is not unlikely that, because of the fearfulness attached to Good Friday, the holiness of its mystery, and the honour of the matrimonial estate, God has granted the cure.

---

[45] *De rerum natura* (The Nature of Things) 4.1048–51. There are one or two minor verbal differences between the text quoted by Del Rio and the generally accepted modern version.

[46] 'Health-givers'. Del Rio later refers to *saludadores*, whose modern translation is 'quack doctors', and *ensalmadores* = 'quacks' or 'bone-setters', from *ensalmo*, 'a spell, charm, incantation'.

[47] 1 *Corinthians* 12.8–10.

[Del Rio now enters upon a long disquisition upon the ability of the Kings of England to cure by touch. In particular, he enters into great critical detail regarding a book published in 1597 by William Tooker, entitled *Charisma, or the Gift of Healing*. Tooker or Tucker (*c.* 1558–1621) became one of Elizabeth Tudor's chaplains in 1588. His book sought to vindicate the power of English kings to touch for the disease known as King's Evil and naturally Elizabeth much approved of his book as she thought it strengthened her claim to be a lawful queen. This, of course, is precisely why Del Rio spends so much time demolishing the argument, especially as Tooker boasted he had Catholic witnesses to the validity of Elizabeth's healing powers. Such a claim clearly needed to be countered as firmly as possible. Miracles, says Del Rio, belong to the Catholic Church alone; they cannot happen in confirmation of a false faith; and the Catholic Church is the Church of the true saints, a Church to which neither Elizabeth nor Tooker belong. If cures do indeed take place after her touch, it is either because the sick were not truly sick, or because of the medicine they have taken, or because an evil spirit is involved.

Next, Del Rio contrasts the real cures resulting from the touch of the Catholic Kings of France. He goes on to admit that people have been and are still cured by touch alone, for examples can be found in the lives of the saints and from everyday experience. The Saludadores of Spain, who claim to cure by touch, cannot be condemned outright; but neither can they be approved without reservation. Del Rio rejects Pomponazzi's argument that certain people are constitutionally or astrologically able to do harm simply by looking at others and thereby casting a spell, and criticises the Saludadores' claims that they can perform all kinds of wonders. As for the supposed cures by soldiers, Del Rio is in no doubt that they rely upon a pact with an evil spirit and are therefore criminal offences.]

Chapter 4: Artificial Magic

This accomplishes remarkable things through human agency. I am speaking now only of operative magic. I shall come back to divination later. Artificial, operative magic is of two kinds, *mathematical* and *deceitful*. I call 'mathematical' that magic which rests upon the principles of geometry, arithmetic, or astronomy: for example, the sphere of Archimedes, about which Cicero wrote and which, according to Claudian, was made of glass; the combustions caused by mirrors during the siege of Syracuse; Archytas's wooden doves which could fly; the Emperor Leo's twittering birds made of gold; the bronze birds of Boethius, which could also fly and sing; bronze serpents which could hiss; and many similar things which have been described in history books. Hero and Pappus call this magic 'thaumaturgy'.[48] Such magic, however, surely cannot achieve anything which runs contrary to nature since it lacks the power of natural causes and the specific movement and dimensions of these when they have been brought into the equation, as is obvious in the case of Archimedes's mirrors, or in modern hydraulics and automata. So, if one is exposed to some effect which transcends the capability of natural causes, one should regard it as an unnatural event, even though human agency has been involved in constructing the instruments whereby the effect is achieved.

[Del Rio now gives further examples of extraordinary artifacts whose effects he says can be explained by reference to hidden human manipulation, human ingenuity, or human dexterity.]

The other type of magic is theatrical and deceptive and can, indeed, be called *deceitful* (which is why the wonders done by magicians were called 'toys' and 'sleights of hand' by the Greeks,[49] and 'games', 'amusements', and 'objects of derision' by the Romans. See Heraldus in Book 1 of Arnobius, page 31.) To this category belong most of the things people believe jugglers, itinerant performers, and tightrope walkers do by means of spells (*incantationes*), but which they actually accomplish because of the agility of their feet and hands, as in the case of the man from Rieti in Pomponazzi's story. In animals, the effects are achieved by training them over a long period of time (see Leo on the ass and the camel);[50] and sometimes through straightforward imposture and hidden passages, as the priests of Bel pretended that food was devoured by a [bronze] snake; or in the case of the famous table of the Sun which the crowd of pilgrims thought supplied food of its own accord, whereas in fact the food was supplied by the inhabitants of a neighbouring city.[51] [Further examples given.]

[48] A marginal note draws attention to various sources which I here give in their modern form. Cicero: *Tusculanae Disputationes* (Discussions at Tusculum) 5.64–6; *De natura deorum* (On the Nature of the Gods) 2.88. Plutarch: *Marcellus* 15. Zonaras: *Annales* 9.4. Aulus Gellius: *Noctes Atticae* (Nights in Athens) 10.12.9–10. Glycas: *Annales*, Part 4 [292D]. Manasses: *Animalia*. Cassiodorus : *Variae Epistulae*. Politian = Angelo Ambrogini Poliziano (1454–1494: *Panepistemon* (All-Knowing). Poliziano was an Italian Humanist, philologist, and poet. His play *Orfeo* is regarded as a landmark in the creation of Italian opera. Hero of Alexandria (floruit second half of the first century AD), was a writer on geometry and mechanics. Pappus of Alexandria (floruit end of the third century AD), was a writer on geometry. Book 8 of his *Synagoge* (Collection) deals with mechanics.

[49] Del Rio uses the words *paignia* = playthings, toys, cheats, games, comic performances, and *kybeia* = games of dice, sleights of hands. The Latin words are *ludi, ludicra,* and *ludibria*.

[50] Leo Africanus = Hasan ibn Muhammad, al-Wazzan, al-Fasi (*c*. 1494–1552). His *Description of Africa* was published in Rome in 1526.

[51] Bel = the *Book of Daniel* 14.6–15 (Vulgate). This chapter does not appear in the *Authorised Version*. Table of the Sun = Herodotus 3.18.

Wonder-working magic, like natural magic, is of itself both good and licit, as all arts of themselves are good. Both, however, may become illicit (a) when they produce an evil result; (b) when they give rise to scandal and people think that these things happen through the agency of evil spirits (and in consequence things of this kind should not be permitted unless the entertainers have public and appropriate attestation of their art from Catholics); and (c) if some spiritual or temporal harm to body or soul threatens the entertainer himself or the spectators (for which reason those who, without necessity or just cause, expose themselves to the danger of death through entertainment are damned.)

[Nevertheless, natural and artificial magic may also be cloaks under which diabolic magic can hide itself, a point to which Del Rio says he will return.]

Now let us turn to certain points about deceitful magic, other aspects of which will be discussed later in Book 2, question 8. Ulrich Molitor, in his *De Phytonicis Mulieribus* (Women Who Prophesy), has wisely observed that the Devil can so arrange matters that one thing seems to be something else.[52] There are plenty of examples of such things done by entertainers, and Satan (says Molitor) is the master of jokes. No one doubts that the Devil can accomplish these things with some degree of subtlety and in this case the pupil is never more learned than his teacher. An example of this can be found in Nider's *Formicarius* (The Ant Heap), in the chapter on workers of harmful magic (*malefici*) and their deceptions.[53]

'At Cologne, a young girl was summoned to appear in court. She had been performing remarkable things, apparently by magic, in front of an audience of the nobility. It was said she had ripped a napkin to pieces and suddenly put it back together again in full view of everyone. She threw a glass at a wall. It broke and instantly she repaired it – and so on and so forth. She was excommunicated but escaped the hands of the Inquisition.'

Bodin[54] notes that they usually mingle one piece of subtility or technical dexterity with ten magical tricks in order to persuade people that whatever they

---

[52] Molitor (died 1492), a Swiss lawyer. His book was published in Constance and Cologne in 1489. *Phytonicis* is another spelling of *Pythonicis*. This refers to 'Pytho' which was the title of the priestess of Apollo's oracle at Delphi in ancient times. The adjective later developed meanings beyond the notion of simple divination and eventually became another term for 'witch'.

[53] Johann Nider (*c.* 1380–1438), a Dominican theologian. His book was written in 1437.

[54] Jean Bodin (1530–1596), writer on politics and witchcraft. His *Daemonomania* (Madness of Magicians) appeared in 1580 and is a digressive collection of stories about witches and sorcerers. Bodin denied the efficacy of many magical operations, accepted certain uses of astrology, and distinguished witchcraft from natural means of getting to know the secrets of nature.

do is managed just short of magical trickery, by dexterity and skill alone, so that whatever witchcraft (*sortilegium*) they mix in may seem to be the result of subtility and agility. Satan loves to provoke others to laugh so that while they are laughing and happy they may imbibe impiousness. This tricksters, jugglers, pranksters, comedians, and itinerant entertainers often enchant their very judges who are enticed into absurd joy and astonishment and account everything mere fun and not something which ought to be punished. There has always been a frequent crop of such things everywhere, and even today the corn, more harmful than garlic or hemlock, can be found in the Courts of certain Princes. In France, for example, in the presence of Charles IX (who was, in other respects, a King who received much praise), Triscalinus, while everyone was watching, charmed rings, one by one, from the collar of a nobleman who was standing some distance away. The rings flew to him and he received them in his hand (or so it seemed), and shortly afterwards people found that in spite of this the collar was whole and quite undamaged. The large gathering said it could not have happened by skill or human action, and that Triscalinus had accomplished all this by the power of the Devil – something he had earlier denied.

[Other examples follow, of what would nowadays be called 'illusions'.]

Chapter 4, question 1: Do [magical] characters, rings, sigils, or images have the kind of power magicians claim for them?

[Del Rio gives several examples of magical practices which use engravings of one kind or another, whose power is meant to be derived astrologically or by reference to angelic names or from magical sympathy and antipathy. Del Rio denies the efficacy of such things, adding, 'There is no greater power to make people credulous than the power of the imagination'. Any such power, he says, depends upon evil spirits. He then criticises Cardinal Cajetan (1469–1534) who was prepared to concede the possibility that certain of these magical propositions might have some truth behind them.]

Chapter 4, question 2: Is there any magical power in arithmetical numbers or numbers in music?

The orthodox Fathers of the Church studied the connection between numbers, but as far as they were concerned numbers were divine mysteries. They did not attribute to them any natural or magical power. Pythagoreans and Platonists were particularly superstitious about this subject. Conclusion: *number, as number, contains no natural or supernatural operative power.*

[There follows a discussion of the significance of the climacteric year, which doctors attribute to the motion of the melancholic humour. Del Rio depends on and indeed summarises the arguments of André du Laurens on the subject.]

From what has been said it follows that if the herb *cinquefoil* has certain effects they should be attributed, not to the number five, but to the substance of the plant's leaves. It is superstitious to believe that one of its leaves cures a one-day fever, three a tertian, and four a quartan. It is also superstitious to believe that three seeds of heliotrope are good for tertian fever and four for a quartan. The same may be said of similar curatives which are tied on with bandages and which continue to be used because of the bad example set by custom and practice. A similar superstition believes that little pills or undiluted potions do more good for an illness with an odd number[55] than they do for one which is even-numbered.

Musical numbers exert great power, not as numbers but by variation of tone and modulation of sound, both of which have a pleasant effect on the mind. It follows from what has been said that those who claim there is some power in certain Psalms (in as much as they have been assembled in a particular order), are foolish and superstitious. Such people also believe there is advantage to be gained from reading the Psalms and that this will set them free from serious dangers. [Del Rio gives examples relating to Psalms 1, 10, and 100, and the power supposedly attached to these numbers.] But neither ten nor a hundred nor any other number has any actual power to do good, for they have no physical or ethical excellence. But they do have an artificial one which proceeds only from the imagination of the person who is counting. This, however, has no effect over the things which are being counted. What is more, in the Hebrew Bible the order of Psalms is different from that in the Vulgate. Therefore a Psalm which is 'lucky' in the Latin version is 'unlucky' in the Hebrew – a quite absurd proposition. Equally ridiculous is the notion that the Hebrew for 'one' is lucky but the Latin is unlucky.

[Del Rio now discusses the attribution of power to musical numbers, an opinion he regards as largely foolish. He says it is possible that the ancient stories about Orpheus's power over living creatures are true because animals endowed with the sense of hearing may well be captivated by musical modes. But when it comes to his power over rocks and stones, Del Rio draws a line. Much of this section is, in fact, detailed criticism of Fabius Paulinus (floruit 1600) who published *Hebdomades* (Seven Books on the Number Seven) in Venice in 1589. Paulinus's argument is based on the proposition that the heavens are

---

[55] I.e. an illness which is supposed to last for an odd number of days, such as tertian fever.

moved by harmony and that the stars and planets affect everything below by means of rays which print each created thing with the signature of the star or planet whence they emanate. Del Rio denies all this and says in addition that medicines are not improved by being mixed according to astrological observations, and that singing cannot be endowed with any celestial power which gives it a particular virtue of its own.]

Let me add, however, another story of the extraordinary effect of music. There is something called the *Tarantula* which takes its name from Tarentum in Apulia. There are two kinds of tarantula which Bustamante in his book *De animalibus sacrae scripturae* (Animals in Holy Scripture), along with other people, does not seem fully to distinguish.[56] One is a kind of lizard, sometimes called a 'gecko'. (The Spanish call it *salamanquesa*, but that is by the way).[57] The other is a type of spinning or venomous spider peculiar to Apulia and unknown, as far as I am aware, in Spain. (See Mattioli: *In Dioscoridem*, Book 2, chapter 57).[58] It wanders about in the fields during summer and creeps out of small holes in the ground and strikes those reapers whose legs are not protected by leggings. Some of those who have been bitten cannot stop singing; others laugh and wail, or jump about, or shout, or fall asleep, or turn insomniac, or are subject to attacks of vomiting, or they sweat, or tremble, or become stricken with fear. Others suffer in other ways and become like lunatics, frenzied people, or maniacs.

'But it is extraordinary', adds Mattioli, 'that the power of music easily soothes anyone suffering from the effects of this poison. As far as I can tell, when sufferers hear the sound of stringed instruments or pipes, they begin to dance and jump about, and continue thus for a very long time. Eventually they either fall to the ground in exhaustion or continue jumping and dancing until the poison leaks out through movements of their skin, or comes out with their sweat and is shaken off. The hired musicians are changed at intervals so that sufferers may continue dancing without intermission and so be cured. While this is being done, people fortify them with antidotes, especially theriac, mithridaticum, and other remedies which counteract poisonous bites'.

To these, he says, may be added music which seems to be of assistance because the poison affects the melancholic and lymphatic parts of the body. [Specific illnesses require specific remedies. Not everything has the required effect.] I have heard people say that if the tarantula which has stung you dies, even in a different location, you will be freed from the illness caused by its

---

[56] Juan Bustamante de la Cámara, a Spanish naturalist (floruit 16th century), appears to have been suspected of practising Judaism in secret.

[57] The word seems to be connected with 'salamander'.

[58] Pierandrea Mattioli (1500–1577), Italian botanist and physician, famous for his *Commentaries on Dioscorides* which were published in Venice in 1554.

sting. If this is true, it is miraculous and I can offer no explanation. For how can there be such an expulsion of poison so far removed from its point of origin? How can it operate at such a distance?

Chapter 4, question 3: Do words or incantations have power to cure the sick or to accomplish wonders?

[All kinds of people, including ancient authors, Arab writers, most of the Kabbalists, recent Jewish writers, and all those writing about magic, appear to subscribe to this notion. But they rest their cases on different premises, and Del Rio carefully distinguishes between different modes of operation which these authors tend to treat as more or less the same.]

God first ordained a certain natural order so that everything might be complete, and he bestowed upon individual things their nature and particular essence, giving each one its own mode or working agreeable with this nature. These modes of working are known as *natural operations* because they have been placed in things in accordance with nature.

Next, God added a supernatural order which can be divided into two parts. First is the *order of grace* or the *miraculous order*. To this order pertain certain operations which go beyond the power of any human or angel. The basis of these operations is not the nature of the individual thing but the grace of God, his absolute will and omnipotence. These are said to be *operations of grace* and, in the strict meaning of the word, *supernatural* or *miraculous operations*.

The second is the *order of marvels*. This order does not go beyond the boundaries of the natural order, but is said simply to go beyond reasonable explanation. People (most people, at any rate) are not aware of this and so they usually call it 'supernatural' too, in the widely accepted meaning of the term. But the more accurate and more meaningful term is *preternatural*. To this order belong many wonderful operations done by good or wicked angels, either by means of localised movement or by a sudden application of natural agencies. Since natural things are not capable of offering resistance to these operations because their power is not the equal of that of the angels, effects obtained thus are, broadly speaking, natural rather than supernatural. Uninformed opinion has it that they surpass the natural order and should be counted as supernatural. But the truth of the matter is, they should be called 'preternatural' or 'amazing' or 'prodigious'. God, then, has instituted three orders: natural, miraculous, and prodigious; or, if you prefer, two: natural and supernatural.

[To these, humanity has added a third, the order of artifice, in which humans seek to adapt or modify nature. When it comes to attempts at curing illnesses, neither words nor incantations have any kind of power at all. 'Mere pronunciation or writing of words confers nothing upon one's health'. Del Rio now deals with Pomponazzi's arguments to the contrary, refutes the claims of Kabbalists to produce wonderful effects by manipulation of the Hebrew alphabet, and denies that names have magical significance.]

Chapter 4, question 4: Amulets and charms

[Some Greek athletes wore strips of cloth on which were written magical signs of words, hoping thereby to ensure victory over opponents who were wearing similar charms. The Romans used to hang amulets round their children's necks in order to ward off the effects of the evil eye. The Jews believed their phylacteries would protect them against evil. This same erroneous way of thinking is attributed to Catholics not only by Wier, but also by Nicolas Rémy whose writings give the impression he is a Catholic.]

First point: The type of amulet which is hung round the neck carries no natural power because it bears words, characters, a single image, or a cluster of images. On the other hand, it may contain a natural power of antipathy or sympathy because of the material of which it happens to be made.

This is the conclusion of all the Catholics, and even of the heretics, I cited in my previous Question, and this conclusion is correct because the property belonging to something one ties on oneself must come from the nature of what is tied on, and has no competence except by reason of the material of which it is made or its subject-matter. So if any effect is produced – the cause of which cannot lie in the *natural* power of the subject-matter – that effect will constitute an unnatural prodigy, and the amulet will be a superstitious object. Costa ben Luca, a Portuguese Jew, has collected together many examples of this kind of thing. One example which is found in his work is the amulet made of lignite, which Spaniards tie round the necks of their children. It bears the image of a hand making a scornful gesture, the thumb stuck between the first two fingers. This amulet is called a *higa* in Spanish.[59]

---

[59] Costa ben Luca was the ninth century author of *De incantatione et adiuratione collique suspensione epistola* (A Letter dealing with Magical Chanting, Exorcism, and Hanging Things round the Neck). This short tract was published by Walter Ryff as one of the addenda to his commentary on Pliny: *Naturalis Historia* 30.1–2 (Würzburg 1548). In a marginal note, Del Rio cites the work as *De ligaturis* (Bindings). This may indicate a different work by Ben Luca on the same subject, but it is more likely that Del Rio was either remembering the title incorrectly or quoting from someone else who had made a mistake. Modern Spanish has the same word referring to the same subject. It is derived from *higo* meaning (a) fig and (b) female pudenda. Latin *ficus*, the etymological source of *higo*, carried both meanings, too.

Second point: Provided one places no reliance on the written words as such, or the number of crosses, or the image, or anything like that, it is pious and holy to wear round one's neck, out of simple reverence, the relics of saints, the wax images of the agnus Dei, the Gospel of Saint John, one of the Psalms of David, and similar quotations from Holy Scripture. The effect proceeding from these, however, will be supernatural and must be attributed to the kindness of God. The practice of tying round one's neck anything else which is not sanctioned by the Catholic Church or does not have medical approval is entirely forbidden.

[So the employment of relics and of similar holy aids is a wholesome, pious custom approved by Holy Church and defended by the Church Fathers and by the saints, whereas the use of aids condemned or disapproved of by the Church is absolutely prohibited, as can be seen from the decrees of the Church Council held in 745 by Pope Zacharias.]

Chapter 5: To what type of magic should one assign the art of making gold, known as 'alchemy'?

[Four things need to be discussed: (i) does alchemy achieve its intention? (ii) is it one of the liberal arts? (iii) to which type of magic does it belong? (iv) is it lawful or unlawful?]

Chapter 5, question 1: Is real gold made by means of this art?

[Other questions have to be asked first.]

Chapter 5, question 1, section 1: What is alchemy, and when was it discovered?

[Some scholars derive the word 'alchemy' from Arabic, but actually both it and the art are older than that. In Del Rio's opinion, the word is Hebrew in origin and 'signifies none other than the art of smelting or liquefying. For in Hebrew, *alchini* means "journeys" or "flowings/fluxes", from *alich*, "to make to walk" or "to flow": hence, the art of liquefying or smelting metals'. Del Rio says he will concentrate on that part of alchemy which deals with gold-making. 'This either increases the amount of gold from the sprinkled shreds of a little gold-dust, or produces gold from something which is not gold. The art which produces from liquefied gold either the same amount of gold, or less but cleaner, does not merit the name of "gold-making"'. A review of early alchemical writings produces the scathing comment that all this is idiocy and that he (Del

Rio) prefers to remain sane. He goes on to survey ancient authors, ending with Zosimus who, he says, preceded Arab alchemical writers who merely copied and improved on his work.]

Chapter 5, question 1, section 2: The effectiveness of alchemy in making gold

The devotees of alchemy consider their art so firmly established that they maintain they nurture and draw forth from their furnaces[60] a gold more perfect than that usually found in nature. Those who hate alchemists are of the opinion that everything of this kind is trickery, deceit, and pure bombast by people who like showing off. I myself think it safest to tread a path between these two extremes. Let us see, briefly, what can be said on both sides of the argument.

In my view there are three opinions: (a) real gold cannot be produced thus; (b) something rather like gold can be produced but should not be mistaken for the real thing, nor sold for the same price as genuine gold, and nor should it be used in medicines; and (c) gold can be produced thus, a gold more perfect and more pure than that which comes from the bowels of the earth. [The first is the opinion of Tostado, Egidio Romano, Averroes, and Abano. The second was really the opinion of Saint Thomas Aquinas who is followed by Cardinal Cajetan and other Thomists.[61] The third is the opinion of all alchemists.] I can add to these a fourth, the Pyrrhonian and Academic opinion of the Sceptics who say that as far as they are concerned there is not sufficient proof. I think this is actually quite a common opinion these days. Among the Jesuits who defend it are Benito Pereira and Gregory of Valencia in *Disputatio*, question 13, point 1.[62] They are doubtful about the excellence and perfection of alchemical gold and suspect that real, perfect gold has never been manufactured by anyone.

---

[60] Technically *athanor*, a self-feeding, digesting furnace capable of maintaining a steady heat for long periods. It is often represented as the 'house of the chick'.

[61] Alonso Tostado (*c.* 1400–1455), Spanish exegete and theologian. Egidio Romano, also Egidio Colonna (*c.* 1247–1316), Italian philosopher and theologian. Averroes = Ibn Rushd (1126–1198), Muslim philosopher, physician, and theologian, was a major influence on Mediaeval Christian philosophers and theologians, especially through his commentaries on Aristotle. Pietro d'Abano (1250–1316), Italian physician and philosopher. He was charged with practising magic and twice brought before the Inquisition, being acquitted on the first occasion and found posthumously guilty on the second. Tommaso de Vio Cajetan (1469–1534), Italian theologian, Master General of the Dominicans, and cardinal.

[62] Pereira (1535–1610): *Adversus fallaces et superstitiosas artes* (Against Deceitful and Superstitious Arts), published in Ingolstadt in 1591. Valencia (1549–1603) became a Jesuit in 1565. The book to which Del Rio is referring is *Disputatio de idolatria contra sectariorum contumelia* (A Discussion of Idolatry, opposing the Insults of Heretics). The details of the citation differ between the 1606, 1608, and 1612 editions. I have given that of 1606.

Valencia also indicates that it cannot be done (or can be done only with difficulty) by human industry and skill.

Axiom 1: *There are no arguments sufficient to convince those who think that real gold cannot be produced by alchemy.*

[The burden of proof rests with those who would argue the contrary. Notice that the art itself is uncertain, and alchemists themselves do not agree either about their terminology or manner of working. Nor do they agree about their basic working material, or even about what they should call the 'Philosophers' Stone'.]

[Nevertheless,] poets have been allowed to conceal the principles of their wisdom by metaphors and fables. Aristotle has been permitted to wrap himself, according to his frequent custom, in obscure sayings and inky darkness. The Holy Scriptures themselves speak in parables. Why, then, do you blame alchemists if they too have amused themselves by using different names? If it is behaviour less than fitting, less than happy, less than pious, make allowances. Look at the subject matter and despise the words. The ineptitude or the childishness of the instructor has never been able to extinguish the truth of something or the effectiveness of an art. Why, then, is it extraordinary that this art also has its impelling attractions[63] for those who disagree with it, since no branch of philosophy, canon law, or Scholastic theology is known to be without them?

[Critics of the art, however, claim that alchemists do not understand the nature of metals because they think that metals are living things and take nourishment; or that they have superior but occult souls; or that metals are the fat and marrow of stones which have been flung off by the stars; or that gold is perfect and all other metals are crude, unformed gold in potential; and that heat is the medium of its perfection. Alchemists, say their critics, do not agree about what gold actually is. Some say it is ash, others vitriol, or sulphur and natural mercury, or arsenic, and it is true that some alchemists make basic mistakes in the reasoning behind their various methods of working. Del Rio calls these 'crude casters of metal, workers at the forge, engineers not scholars'.]

But by no means does it follow (and this is the point which stands in need of proof) that they cannot manufacture gold. For the carpenter does not fail to make a sword because he does not understand the nature of iron, or the proper movement of the sword when employed in fighting and the appropriate manner of brandishing it. The alchemist who introduces into his working other things needed by his art produces no less perfect rose-water, even if he does not understand the essence of the rose, the power of fire, and the principles

---

[63] *Compulsationes*, literally, 'chiming' or 'tolling of bells'.

of distillation. What, therefore, if someone who does not know the nature of metal expertly uses the requisite separation, congelation and all the other stages of alchemy, too? Will the cooking power of his fires be less effective under his bellows?

[A knowledge of the nature of gold is therefore not necessary to its production and in consequence someone who *does* understand the nature of metals will certainly be able to produce it. The rest of the section is devoted to a discussion of what gold actually is and whether substances such as sulphur and mercury can form part of the basic matter out of which gold may be formed by the alchemical art.]

There are essential differences between things, except for human beings, of which we know nothing. So we are compelled to formulate definitions based on accidental differences which can often be common to several things which appear likely to be of different types. For example, if you define a dog, you undoubtedly define it by its hunting property, and yet a hyaena imitates this and is not a dog. The whole argument goes thus: a dog is an animal without reason, has four legs, and is a swift hunter. This applies also to the hyaena. But no one then infers that the word 'dog' is the same as 'hyaena', or that a hyaena is just the same as a dog. Rather, it should be inferred that something is found in a hyaena which is more perfect in a dog.

[By analogy, then, it does not follow that because the same definition applies to gold and to silver they are therefore indistinguishable as two species. But it does follow that they are simply metals. Silver, indeed, is imperfect because it can be perfected, whereas gold is absolutely perfect because it cannot be perfected in relation to its being a metal. Del Rio now turns to technical argument about the composition of animate and inanimate things. He accepts that things are capable of being perfected and that in consequence the alchemical process of gold-making does not run contrary to nature.]

Chapter 5, question 1, section 3: Continuing the same subject

Axiom 2: *It is quite probable that the art of alchemy can achieve its aim and that it can, rather than cannot, transform things into gold.* I say 'quite probable' because in fact the axiom is not proved by logical argument but simply on the basis of probability. According to this, however, the arguments are almost convincing in the moral sense.

[Del Rio reviews examples of the ways in which one thing has been and can be seen to change into another, such as larvae into flying creatures, and pieces of wood into stone if they fall into certain fountains. It is also well-known, he says, that evil spirits can use a natural agent such as putrefaction to produce both inanimate objects and imperfect animals. Therefore one metal can be changed into another by the same process. But the Devil cannot suspend the laws of nature in order to accomplish this. So a human being can learn how to do the same, either by his own industry and application, or at the Devil's instruction.]

Chapter 5, question 1, section 4: Is it established in any literature that gold has been made by this art?

[Opponents of alchemy appeal to experience, a strong argument in their favour, and ask why no one has yet managed to make alchemical gold. Whatever experiments are adduced as proof are based on the testimony of alchemists themselves. These operations may be fraudulent, as in the case of Bragadino of Venice, who was punished in Bavaria in 1591. Yet my conclusion is that in fact it is entirely credible that some people have made real gold through alchemy. I say so because there are so many accounts of its having been done, that it would be impudent to disbelieve them all. Arnald of Villanova is credibly said to have made such gold, and the account is confirmed by the testimony of Ramón Llull who witnessed it for himself.[64] Similarly, Girolamo Cardano testifies to the transmutation of gold in the presence of the Doge and leading patricians of Venice, and three Venetian patricians were witness to a like demonstration in 1550.[65] So witnesses who have put their accounts on paper attest the reality of alchemical operations. Moreover, the fact that princes as well as paupers apply themselves to alchemy is guarantee against every operation's being fraudulent. What is more, alchemy is a complex operation and therefore subject to possible error during the working.]

Chapter 5, question 2: Should gold-making be considered one of the liberal or one of the mechanical arts?

[Nothing in alchemy is mechanical save the operation itself and the application

---

[64] Villanova (c. 1235–1313), alchemist, astrologer, and physician. His works were translated into all the major European languages. He was critical of magic which he thought was influenced by evil spirits. Llull (c. 1235–1315), a Catalan mystic and philosopher. He taught Arabic and philosophy at Miramar and is credited with several works on alchemy.

[65] Girolamo Cardano (1501–1576), Italian, a voluminous writer on mathematics, medicine, and natural magic. He was arrested by the Inquisition in 1570 for having cast a horoscope of Christ.

of fire. Some alchemists are, of course, merely metal-casters, but others claim for themselves, as of right, the honourable title of 'philosopher'; and even if every alchemist uses his hands as well as his intelligence, the same may be said of any workman, or indeed doctors and surgeons.]

Chapter 5, question 3: To which branch of magic does alchemy belong?

[If the result of the alchemical operation is not genuine, it belongs to the magic of trickery. If the result is genuine, it has worked through the power of an evil spirit and therefore belongs to the branch called 'demonic magic'. Del Rio proceeds to illustrate his point by referring to stories from Bodin's *Daemonomania*, Cedrenus, and Gomez Miedes, *De sale* (On Salt), Book 2.] [66]

Chapter 5, question 4: Is alchemy lawful or unlawful?

[Certain authors think alchemy is unlawful, but this is not the opinion of the majority of legal commentators. Indeed, civil law numbers it among the metal-making arts. First conclusion: alchemy does not appear to be condemned by any law in a secular court. But what of Church law? Two canons seem to condemn it, but the first of these actually refers to transformation of humans into animals. The second, which Del Rio quotes at length, is a decree by Pope John XXII directed against alchemy, alchemists, and those who employ their art and its products. But the punishment attached to this decree, says Del Rio, is levied against those who use alchemical material to adulterate the currency, and he refers to another decree by the same Pope on the same subject.]

A two-fold reply to this Canon presents itself to me. First, the decree has not been brought into use, but has not been rescinded, either. For after Pope John's time up to the present day, this art has flourished in Rome itself, particularly under Leo X, scarcely a hundred years later. [67] To him, Aurelio Augurello, the famous poet, dedicated his book, *De chrysopoeia* (On Gold-Making). [68] Among everything else he says this (very arrogantly), about his Philosophers' Stone: 'Were the smallest part of it to be projected through the waves of the sea – the

---

[66] Georgius Cedrenus, Byzantine historian. He wrote a comprehensive history beginning with the creation and ending in 1067. A Latin version of this (*Annales*) was published in Basel in 1566. Bernardino Gómez Miedes (1521–1589), Spanish historian, Bishop of Albaracin. A second edition of his book on salt was published in Valencia in 1579.

[67] The pontificates of these two Popes are actually two hundred years apart: (a) 1316–1334; (b) 1513–1521.

[68] Giovanni Aurelio Augurello (1441–1524), Italian poet and alchemist. His book was published in Venice in 1515.

sea at that time consisting of mercury – the whole immense ocean could be turned into gold'. The book by Pico della Mirandola, entitled *De auro conficiendo* (On Making Gold), deals with this subject.[69]

Reading books of this kind has never been forbidden in Italy since his time. Secondly, the Canon proceeds from the assumption that all alchemical gold is false and that it is therefore especially to be condemned when people turn it into money. So one may assume that those who produce real gold and use it for business and the discharge of their debts are not condemned under this heading, since in fact they indulge themselves in this art out of intellectual curiosity and do not actually want to use it in trade or payment of bills. Therefore it is not the art properly ordered and exercised which is condemned, but the abuse of the art.

Second conclusion: *In the court of conscience, this art is permissible, not to everyone but to carefully selected individuals. For most people, therefore, it should be considered illicit on the grounds that for them it is pernicious.*

The arguments of Angelus[70] and other leading authors prove this conclusion decisively and do not contradict the previous conclusion. It should be noted, too, that whatever is illicit about this art does not spring from its nature which is not in itself evil (in as far as it is an art and imitates the sciences), but good in its own right, just like any other form of speculative knowledge. It springs, rather, from the fault of the circumstances which are usually attendant upon and peculiar to this operation. If these are not present, I do not see what can be reprehensible about it. Still, as they almost always are present, it is rare that there is not some fault or sin for some reason or other. That is why I said, 'For most people it should be considered illicit on the grounds that for them it is pernicious'.

[What are these circumstances? Del Rio distinguishes four: (a) the goal, if it involves greed and the acquisition of money: it is also forbidden to use alchemical gold in medicines, although one may be permitted to make personal adornments out of it; (b) the method, if it involves a pact with an evil spirit.]

Experience tells us that whenever a large number of people practises alchemy, acts of harmful magic (*maleficia*) and witchcraft (*sortilegia*) also flourish, as we ourselves are experiencing in this unhappy age. At such a time there is no lack

---

[69] The book is dubiously attributed to Giovanni. Its full title is *De auro libri tres* (Three Books About Gold) and it was published in Venice in 1586, long after Giovanni's death. *De auro conficiendo* is Book 2 of this work.

[70] Presumably Andreas Angelus (Engel) (1561–1598), German historian, author of *Wider Natur und Wunderbuch* (A Book of the Wonders and Perversities of Nature), published in Frankfurt in 1597.

of people who have recourse to superstitious ceremonies which have no effect whatsoever, such as wearing a tunic of undressed linen on a particular day, abstaining from certain foods, and other nonsense of that kind. If hatred or self-indulgence be added to greed, thence, to an great extent, is created the slippery slope which leads to philtres and poisonous concoctions. Nor is the alchemical tradition of misusing the names and words of Holy Scripture as substitutes for alchemical names and precepts an unimportant sin; and it is no less a sin when alchemists include in their books figures or images which are plainly obscene, or even thoroughly blasphemous because of their abuse of sacred material – something the printer from Basel who published the *Rosarium*[71] has done. Images of the Holy Trinity, Christ the resurrected Lord, the coronation of the Blessed Virgin Mary, which heretics have thrown out of their churches, these he has transferred to alchemical mysteries and transformations. But this is not astonishing, for there are ridiculous Sacramentarians everywhere. Finally, it is a sin for people to engage often in over-curious experiments while they follow now this way of reasoning, now that. Such people never know anything because they are always engaged in the process of learning more.

[(c) the time, if it means using time which would be better spent in prayer or the performance of civic and social duties; and (d) the person, if the practitioner is poor, ill-educated, and not fervent in religious belief and practice.]

This art must be considered illicit for poor people, and it is certainly full of danger for anyone who has no property. This is obvious, because such people are accustomed to direct their attention to material gain and are thus prevented from using their reason. Their intention is to use alchemical gold for commerce, medicines, or money; or, if they themselves are not going to use it, there is a clear danger that their heirs may do so. These people are impoverished by the art they practise. They do not provide necessities for their families and are the reason their wives and daughters are compelled to support themselves by an unworthy trade. Because they lack means and tools (on account of their poverty), they easily progress to superstition, and in particular to pacts with an evil spirit. Alchemical writers have offered sober testimony to this, too. Geber, for example, says, 'This science is not suitable for the poor and needy man, but rather is hostile to him';[72] and the philosopher Politian says it is impossible for a poor man to practise philosophy.

---

[71] Probably a reference to the *Rosarium Philosophorum* (The Rosary or The Rose Garden of the Philosophers), which was first published in Frankfurt in 1550.

[72] 'Geber' was a name used to designate the author of several works on alchemy. Details about who he really was are confused and controversial.

[Del Rio concludes by quoting Geber on the need for an alchemist to be not only very intelligent but also wealthy, the first of which points is confirmed by Arnald of Villanova. Alchemists also require their pupils to be humble, just, pious, and God-fearing, and Del Rio adds that alchemists should communicate everything to their confessors and follow their advice. They must also be careful not to be too curious, as curiosity quickly misleads people into sin. Del Rio approves of an English law which says that alchemy can be practised only under royal licence, and thinks this law should be adopted by other countries. Alchemy is, of course, a licit activity for kings and for wealthy folk, provided they do not neglect their public duties. As Cardinal Cajetan has said, 'This art should be practised either by nobody, or by kings – and then only after they have taken wise men's advice'. For the generality of people, however, the fact that a Roman Pontiff has condemned the art should be warning enough to refrain from practising it.]

BOOK 2

Magic involving evil spirits[1]

This is the most important subject for discussion in my work and in consequence I must break it down unto several chapters or questions so that I can discuss it as lucidly as possible.

Question 1: Is there such a thing as magic involving evil spirits?

Those who follow the Sadducees, Democritus, Aristotle, Averroes, and Simplicius in asserting that evil spirits do not exist also say that this form of magic does not exist. *But this opinion of theirs is impious and heretical.* Evil spirits do exist and so does the magic which involves them. Such a magic is not based upon the industry or inventiveness of human beings, nor does it rely upon natural causes. It rests, rather, on some kind of non-material, separate power (*virtus*). [Holy Scripture, tradition and testimony all prove the point. So do all Catholic theologians and most of the philosophers. Del Rio then gives names.] Finally, we know that, according to tradition, there have existed famous schools of harmful magic right up to the present day at Salamanca and Ioletum in Spain, at Lake Nursia in Italy, and in the cave at Vesaignes-sous-Lafauche.[2]

Question 2: Whence does this magic come? Who invented it?

There are those who say that evil spirits exist but deny that this type of magic is done by means of evil spirits or devils (*diaboli*), attributing its effects either to God operating directly through magicians of this kind, or to God using good angels in order to produce these effects. These people say that certain graces have been given freely (just as, for example, the gifts of language and of health are freely given), and that these gifts are not infrequently granted

---

[1] *De magia daemoniaca.*

[2] For 'harmful magic' here, Del Rio uses the word *goetia*. This, borrowed from Greek, invariably has a negative sense in both Classical and later sources. It is derived from *goes* meaning 'someone who wails', referring, according to Seneca, to the 'uncivilised howling' (*barbaricus ululatus*) in which spells were chanted. A marginal note in Del Rio draws attention to Anania: *De natura daemonum* (The Nature of Evil Spirits), Book 3, folio 104.

to people like Balaam and to other reprobates.[3] I maintain, first, that this opinion is entirely blasphemous since it attributes to the magical arts something which belongs properly to graces freely given, and confuses genuine miracles with acts of trickery. Secondly, it makes the free gifts of God subject to human artifice and certain ridiculous practices. Thirdly, it says that God would unreasonably and malevolently prohibit something which he himself graciously bestows upon human beings as a favour.

The opposite point of view, which may be found in various places in Holy Scripture, proves only that effects such as these happen (up to a point), through magical arts and graces freely granted, and that God sometimes produces miracles by means of wicked people for the propagation of the faith as well as his own divine glory. It has happened that someone who operates through a gift of grace freely given is not restricted to a particular time, occasion, or the use of specific ceremonies, as magicians (*magi*) usually are, people who accomplish nothing if they are found wanting in the least degree. Nor can this kind of gift, freely given by God, be handed on to others by means of training and instruction. Magicians, however, do hand on this magic to their pupils, and those who listen to them, provided they follow their precepts, do the same things as their instructors.

Others say that these effects are produced by good angels whom they call, on account of their pre-eminence, 'spirits' (*spiritus*). This is what the celebrated modern magician, Scotus of Parma, used to boast. (He was the one who sent the apostate Bishop of Ubii, Gebhard Truchesius, mad.) This is also the ancient, fraudulent claim of the Platonist magicians in particular: Iamblichus, Porphyrius, Plotinus, Proclus, and Julian the Apostate. According to their tradition, magic is divided into *white* (which they think is lawful) and *black* (which is unlawful). Hence, they call the 'white' *theurgia* and the 'black' *goetia*. Actually, the Archmagician himself pretty well rejects this *theurgia* which is obviously some kind of fictitious comedy.[4]

---

[3] Del Rio refers the reader to *Numbers* 23 in which Balaam who has been asked by the King of Moab to curse his enemies refuses to do so in obedience to God's private injunction to him.

[4] Heinrich Cornelius Agrippa of Nettesheim (1486–1535), German occultist. Agrippa led a remarkably diverse life, exercising his very varied talents all over Europe. He lectured on the Kabbalah in France, became physician to Louise of Savoy, and then moved to the Netherlands where he practised medicine. For a while he was Imperial archivist and historiographer to Emperor Charles V. His two major occult works are *De occulta philosophia* (The Secret Philosophy) which he expanded and published in 1533, and *De incertitudine et vanitate scientiarum et artium* (The Uncertainty and Uselessness of the Arts and Sciences), published in Antwerp in 1531, in which he repudiated many of the ideas he had propounded in his former book. Del Rio describes the theurgia as *fictitiam* and *palliatam*. This latter

'[Many people think that theurgy is not unlawful on the grounds that it is regulated by good angels and the power of God himself. But] *very often, under the names of God and angels, it is involved with the deceptions of evil spirits,* [even if we suppose that, not only through the powers of nature but also by means of particular rites and ceremonies, we actually do win over and attract to ourselves those celestial and divine powers about which the ancient magicians, in many a book of precepts, have passed on information.] *But the greatest part of* [all] *the ceremonies consists in* [preserving] *cleanliness,* [first] *of mind,* [and then] *of body* [and of those things which are around the body,[5] such as skin, clothing, dwelling-place, vessels, utensils, oblations, offerings, and sacrifices. For their cleanliness administers to intercourse with and contemplation of divine things and is especially demanded in sacred matters, as we may see from the words of Isaiah: 'Wash you, make you clean, put away the evil of your thoughts'.[6] Truly, uncleanness, which frequently taints both air and human beings, disturbs that most clean and celestial influx of divine things, and drives away the clean spirits of God; and there is no doubt that sometimes] *unclean spirits*[7] *and deceiving powers look for this so that they may be venerated and worshipped as gods'.*

[Let such followers of the Devil thus learn from Agrippa, says Del Rio, the truth about their white magic. God does not involve himself in such magical operations either directly or via good angels, so the effects of 'demonic' magic are undoubtedly instituted and brought to fruition by evil angels, and any opinion to the contrary is mistaken. One can prove this from various authorities (to which he then refers), and he quotes from John of Salisbury: 'Long ago the holy Fathers condemned those who practise the more harmful tricks, the magical arts, and various kinds of astrology. They banished them from Court because they knew that these skills, or rather, plague-bearing deeds of harmful magic (*maleficia pestifera*) were produced by a close intimacy between evil spirits and human beings'.][8]

---

word is the name Classical Latin gave to a certain type of comedy. It may also have different meanings in later Latin, such as 'veiled' or 'fancily trimmed', but the context here seems to ask for something closer to Classical usage. The passage from Agrippa which follows is taken from *De incertitudine*, chapter 46. The 1537 edition I have used has no page numbers. Del Rio has mangled the text considerably. I have translated directly from Agrippa and shown what is missing from Del Rio by putting those passages in square brackets and Del Rio's version in italics.

[5] Del Rio abridges what follows to 'externals'.

[6] Agrippa misquotes *Isaiah* 1.16: 'Wash you, make you clean; put away the evil of your doings from before mine eyes; cease to do evil'.

[7] *Spiritus* here and in the phrase at the end of the previous sentence.

[8] Salisbury (*c.* 1115–1180), English diplomatist, Bishop of Chartres. He was secretary to two Archbishops of Canterbury, Theobald and Saint Thomas Becket. The quotation comes from

My point is also proved because for the following reasons one cannot say these spirits (*spiritus*) are good: (a) they command people to worship them and offer them sacrifices as though they were gods: good angels cannot order this; (b) these arts are directed as much to bringing death to others by theft, slaughter, adultery, etc. as to helping them; (c) they mix together many lies and deceptions; (d) the magicians are shown how to exercise command and compulsion over the spirits, especially in connection with things which are quite impossible and plainly ridiculous. None of this can be consistent with good angels, and for this reason I think Glycas should be read with care.[9] He distinguishes magic from *goetia* as follows: while magic may originate with beneficent spirits (*geniorum*) and achieve some kind of good, *goetia* springs from maleficent spirits and produces evil. Not only has Glycas improperly taken over the generic term 'magic' for the specific 'theurgy', he has also slipped into the error of those who support white magic and attribute its administration to good angels.

[Palingenius Stellatus made the same mistake. In his proscribed book, *Zodiacus*, he thinks the air is full of good spirits (*bonis daemonibus*) whom he makes the authors of these arts and whom he calls gods. He is not a bad poet but neither is he a good Christian. Indeed, he is more of a heretic than a Catholic.][10]

The next error belongs to those who are of the opinion that magical effects happen through the agency of the souls of the dead. Catholic theologians have long exposed these people and have done so without difficulty. The reasons which are convincing in the case of good spirits (*spiritus*) are also convincing when it comes to the spirits of the blessed, which are the souls in Purgatory. They do not come thence unless with God's special permission, so that they may seek favours of the living. Now, souls given over to perpetual punishment cannot come forth with any licence or permission of evil spirits because, of course, they have been consigned by God's command to the very worst of prisons. It is therefore perfectly clear that the claims made by necromancers about summoning up souls with the help of a *grimoire* are fraudulent.[11] If they

---

De nugis curialium (The Frivolities of Courtiers), Book 1, chapter 9. 'Frivolities' etc. is the sub-title of the book, whose formal title is *Policraticus*. Chapter 9 is headed, 'The derivation of the word *praestigium* and the originator of the art'. *Praestigium* is the Latin word for a trick or a deceit, often one performed by a juggler, conjuror, or other public entertainer.

[9] Michael Glycas, 12th century Byzantine historian. He wrote a chronicle of events from the Creation to 1118. It includes a polemic against astrology. A Latin version of his *Annales* was published in Basel in 1572.

[10] Marcellus Palingenius Stellatus = Pietro Angelo Manzoli (floruit 1528), Italian poet and, according to conjecture, physician. His book was published in Venice in *c.* 1531.

[11] A grimoire is a magician's manual for invoking or evoking spirits. It is an altered form of the French word *grammaire*. Cf. also *glamour*, originally 'magic, enchantment, spell'.

were to come forth, they would do so at the command of the one God; but there is no reason why God would order or permit this. To think that he would do so because of the prayers and incantations of magicians is impious.[12] Consequently, the overriding efficient cause of these arts is the Devil himself, followed by a natural tendency of human intelligence which has been twisted as the result of the original Fall.

[Del Rio ends by quoting from Celio Calcagnini: *Libellus de amatoria magia* (A Treatise on Magic to Induce Love),[13] and by exhorting himself and the reader to pursue truth with the help of theology.]

Question 3: The types of magic which involve evil spirits, and the books connected with this subject

Since there is no such thing as theurgy or 'white' magic, it follows that all this magic of wonders is nothing other than *goetia* and 'black' magic. This we usually call specialised magic. The Arch-magician [Agrippa] divides it into two types: (a) the one whose practitioners, he says, surrender themselves to an evil spirit, sacrifice to him, and worship him; and (b) the one which he would persuade us is free from a pact with evil spirits but which commands them by nods of the head and, through the power of divine names, summons, adjures, and compels them to obey. The former, he says, is forbidden by human and divine law, is particularly wicked, and should be punished with every type of fire.[14] The latter he says accomplishes what it claims to do, especially with regard to compelling evil spirits (which he goes on to argue is a proper thing to do), although it is exposed to the manifest dangers of illusion.[15]

[Del Rio now reviews the history of magical tradition which, according to some writers, stretches from teachings received by Adam from the angel Raziel and handed down through a sequence of Old Testament figures such as Enoch, Abraham, and Solomon, to the treatises of the Middle Ages and early Renaissance by Albertus Magnus, Johannes Trithemius, and Cornelius Agrippa himself.]

---

[12] Marginal note: Anania: *De natura daemonum* (The Nature of Evil Spirits), Book 3, folio 97. Petrus Thyraeus: *De apparitionibus spirituum* (On the Appearances of Spirits), Book 1, chapter 11, no. 216 and chapter 13, no. 301.

[13] Calcagnini (1479–1541) Italian poet and astronomer. He came from Ferrara and, for a time, was Apostolic Protonotary. The pamphlet to which Del Rio refers appears in Calcagnini's collected works under the title *Amatoriae magiae compendium*. See *Opera Aliquot* (Basel 1544), 497–503.

[14] Presumably fire upon earth and the fires of Hell.

[15] From Agrippa: *De incertitudine*, chapter 45.

Question 4: The basis of this magic, that is to say a pact, explicit or implicit

First conclusion: *All magical operations rest, as on a foundation, upon a pact made between the magician and an evil spirit. Thus, as often as the magician wishes to effect anything, he is constrained explicitly or implicitly by this prop to his art to demand that the evil spirit meet the terms of the agreement.*

This is proved by the authority of the Church Fathers. Saint Cyprian says that magicians have a treaty with an evil spirit. Gratian recalls the words of Saint Augustine in the codex of his *Decretals.* These are as follows: 'All arts of this kind, either of frivolous or harmful superstition, come from a certain established plague-bearing association, like a pact of faithless and deceitful friendship, between individuals and evil spirits'. Secondly, it is proved by Imperial decree: 'Many people use magical arts to disturb the elements. They do not hesitate to undermine the life of children and they dare to summon the spirits of the dead and expose them to the air, so that someone may destroy his enemies by means of their wicked arts. May a deadly plague carry these people off, since they are alien to nature'. Thirdly, one should believe the decree of the Articles of the School of Paris, which runs thus: 'To enter into a pact, tacit or explicit, with evil spirits is not idolatry but a type of idolatry.[16] We maintain that there is an implicit pact in all superstitious observation whose effect one may not reasonably expect to come from God or from nature'. Fourthly, reason persuades us of this pact, for many wicked people wish it and the evil spirit desires it. As the prophet Isaiah tells us, they say: 'We have severed the treaty with death and we have made a pact with Hell'.[17] [Aquinas applied this text to magicians, as did Popes John XXII and Sixtus V. Indeed, Satan dared to offer a pact to Christ himself.]

Now, as I have said, magical effects happen through the action of evil spirits, not by the power of the magicians; and since evil spirits cannot be compelled by human beings to do this, it follows that they rush to help of their own free will. But evil spirits pursue the individual with unsparing hatred, so one must not imagine they rush up out of the goodness of their hearts. Obviously they exact a price in return for their effort; and so from this it is clear that the assembly and association of magician with evil spirit is like that of two brigands. One wanders openly in a wood while the other lurks secretly in ambush. The first attracts the attention of a traveller by means of a hiss or a sign, and the second pierces him through with a treacherous arrow. The first man often does

---

[16] Here, Del Rio adds the word 'error' to his text.

[17] 'And your covenant with death shall be annulled, and your agreement with hell shall not stand', *Isaiah* 28.15.

not see this and does not know which weapon it was that brought death: yet he agrees to the poor wretch's death. The magician is like the first brigand, and the evil spirit like the second. The situation is rather like that in which powerful individuals who are greedy for revenge attach to themselves men who are quick with a dagger. They nod to these men with an agreed signal as an indication of whom they want killed and when.

[Older and more recent theologians are also in accord upon this point and we may notice, too, the common confession and consent of workers of harmful magic (*malefici*) and of witches (*sagae*) at all times throughout Europe. Only Johann Wier seems to disagree.]

Second conclusion: *The evil spirit is at liberty either to fulfil this pact or to fail to carry it out.*

This is proved by experience and reason. Reason tells us that an evil spirit cannot be compelled by a human being to stand by his promises, and experience tells us that he is utterly deceitful and filled with a desire to cheat. Therefore he rarely carries out what he has promised. When he does stand by his promises – which he does, occasionally – he does so not by compulsion but of his own accord with the crafty intention (a) of keeping his hold over the magician he has bound to him, and (b) of enticing others and persuading them that there is power in trifles of this kind.

Third conclusion: *A pact of this kind has two parts, one explicit, the other implicit. One cannot have the same opinion about both in every circumstance.*

This conclusion must be explained rather than proved. The explicit form of such a pact occurs in various kinds of ritual observance during which loyalty and homage are promised to the evil spirit (*cacodaemon*) himself who appears visibly in corporeal form in front of witnesses.[18] [Examples given.] Sometimes the magicians present a book of requests to the Devil. Thus, in our own time, the Mantenses [Norman magicians], wrote a little book which they intended to present to the Wise Women, guardians of necromantic magic.[19]

[Del Rio records five requests contained in this book: the women were to consecrate the magicians' magic books so that the demon the men invoked would appear in the shape of a handsome young man and obey them; the

---

[18] Marginal note: This is described in *Malleus Maleficarum* (The Hammer of Women Who Work Harmful Magic), part 2, question 1, chapter 2; and by Alfonso de Castro: *De iusta haereticorum punitione* (The Just Punishment of Heretics), Book 1, chapter 6. De Castro was a Spanish theologian (1495–1558) whose book was published in Salamanca in 1547.

[19] Del Rio calls them *Sibyllae*. In Classical Latin, the word refers to women who interpreted the messages of a particular deity to human beings who asked him or her questions.

women were to sign the books with a powerful magical sign; the magicians were to be protected from arrest and judgement; they were to succeed in everything they did and make money therefrom; and their enemies were to be powerless against them.]

In return for these things, the magicians promised they would take these wise women as their ladies and rulers for ever and, for as long as they lived, would offer them people's souls every year – i.e. they would kill people and sacrifice them, or at any rate initiate one individual to this same sin of treachery – on this very day of the consecration of the books. But, in fulfilment of their part of the agreement, the wise women would be obliged to furnish them, in good faith, with the things they were demanding. All these men were burned in Paris, along with their books.

[Another very similar method is performed without witnesses, and a third employs a substitute for the evil spirit for fear of what the spirit may look or sound like. All these forms of the pact have in common a renunciation of the Christian faith, at the end of which the spirit 'thrusts his nail into their forehead, making them rub away the oil of baptism and destroy the mark it made'. The spirit then re-baptises them with water, gives them a new name, forces them to deny their Christian god-parents and assigns them others. The new initiates give the Devil some of their cast-off clothing [20] (because he is eager to lay personal claim to something which belongs to them),[21] as well as blood, and perhaps one of their daughters. Next, they swear an oath to the evil spirit at the top of a circle drawn on the ground, and ask that their name be deleted from the Book of Life and inscribed in the Book of Death. They offer sacrifice, 'and witches (*striges*) make certain promises that every month or fortnight they will kill a small child by witchcraft (*strigando*), i.e. by sucking out its life'; and each year they are bound to pay something to their teachers, the evil spirits. The evil spirit imprints his sign or mark upon them: the location varies. Del Rio gives examples of various types of mark, not necessarily connected with witchcraft. Once marked, the initiates make various promises.]

They will never worship the Eucharist. They will always offer injuries and insults to the Blessed Virgin and the rest of the saints, not only in word but in deed also. They will tread underfoot, pollute, break in pieces, and keep themselves at a distance from any relics of the saints, images, the sign of the

---

[20] *Scrutum aliquod vestimenti.* The word *scrutum* literally means 'husk, grout, paunch, tripe'.
[21] Personal contact is one of the principal ways through which occult power is exercised. Witches, therefore, were keen to get hold of something (it did not matter what) belonging to their potential victim.

cross, holy water, blessed salt, wax figures and anything else which has been blessed or consecrated by the Church. They will never give a complete confession to a priest and, in steadfast silence, will keep secret their traffic with the evil spirit. On pre-arranged days they will fly to meetings [of witches], if they can, and there they will always actively accept orders telling them what they must do. Finally, whenever they can, they will add to the numbers of those enslaved to the evil spirit. The Devil promises each one that he will always be in attendance upon them, that he will grant their prayers in this world, and that he will bless them after death.

[This obligation, however, is not mutually binding, for the initiates gain no real power or advantage, and yet sign themselves away to eternal death.]

In these three versions of the pact there occurs the most grave and deadly sin of idolatry, because idolatrous worship is openly offered to creatures which God has made. If magicians cast away faith, they are apostates. If, on the other hand, they do not throw it away entirely, in as much as they believe they owe such worship to the Devil, or that the Devil has power to do things the Catholic faith says he cannot do, then they are heretics. But if they merely pretend to do all this, they are neither apostates nor heretics but mortal and very grave sinners because then they worship the evil spirit of their own accord. Even if they are compelled by the evil spirit to do this out of great fear (as sometimes happens), they commit only a slightly less serious mortal sin.

[Del Rio now illustrates his point about the way a witch's initiation mimics religious ceremonies with an extended quotation from Grillando, based on a witch's confession.] [22]

The implicit pact is of two types. First, when someone knowingly and willingly uses those superstitious signs usually employed by magicians, which he gets either from books or from conversations with magicians or other people. This is a mortal sin, for in no way is it licit knowingly to enter into any fellowship, directly or indirectly, with depraved spirits (*spiritus*), as theologians and canon lawyers agree. If, however, anyone has taken a natural remedy which he has got from the books of or conversations with magicians, that would not be connected with any pact, and so the person may legitimately use a remedy of this kind. The second type of implicit pact is when someone unknowingly

---

[22] Paolo Grillando (floruit early 16th century), Italian priest, auditor of criminal causes in Arezzo, Papal judge in the district of Rome. Del Rio is referring to his *De quaestionibus et tortura tractatus* (Treatise on Methods of Questioning and Torture) which appeared in his *Tractatus de hereticis et sortilegiis* (Treatise on Heretics and Witches), published in Leiden in 1536.

uses magical signs because he does not know they are evil and originate from an evil spirit. This usually happens to those people who, in good faith, read superstitious books, thinking they are by reputable philosophers or physicians. A similar thing happens when they are told about them by people who have the reputation of being good and true to the faith. This is either not a sin at all, or a very slight one in private individuals provided two conditions obtain. (i) If it can be proved they are the kind of people one may assume to be ignorant of such matters, as opposed to ministers of the Church, confessors, heads of monasteries, and Doctors,[23] their ignorance is for the most part passive and stupid and their sin less grave than that of those who knowingly perpetrate such things; and (ii) if the ignorant person is ready to give up superstition of this kind once he has been told about it; because after admonition he is no longer ignorant and persistence then becomes a matter of obstinacy and the magnitude of the offence increases.

[If you ask why the evil spirit chooses to make a pact, the answer seems to be that the evil spirit and the would-be evil doer are alike in malice. Each reacts to the other, with the evil doer being deceived by the evil spirit into thinking he really does have control. It is a very grave sin to make any kind of pact with evil spirits, and Del Rio concludes the chapter with a lengthy section which argues that one cannot make excuses, as some people do, for magicians who use evil spirits for a good intention, even in imitation of Christ and his apostles. Moreover, the Church has been promised power to work miracles in the name of Christ, so why should anyone have recourse to Beelzebub? It is also a vain and foolish thing to do, for the evil spirits do not keep their side of the bargain. 'They are liars and pursue human beings with an irreconcilable hatred which, from the time of their fall, they have never relaxed and never will diminish or relax. If God were to allow it, they would quickly destroy every mortal. But because they see they are not allowed to do so, they labour assiduously for the death of people's souls by using a variety of different allurements to sin so that thus they may constrain human beings to fall from blessedness.' Del Rio now gives examples of how bitter they can be, and shows that to make a pact and become intimate with evil spirits is dangerous and pernicious as well as vain and foolish; and he ends with a long anecdote taken from Rémy's *Daemonolatria*, chapter 9.][24]

---

[23] *Doctores*, i.e. theologians or canon lawyers, not *medici* (physicians).
[24] Nicolas Rémy (1530–1612), French advocate, Attorney General of Lorraine. His *Daemonolatria* (The Worship of Evil Spirits) was published in Lyon in 1595.

Question 5: By what signs can one recognise the workings of magic which is dependent upon a pact from its physical, miraculous, and artificial effects?

[When one cannot find evidence of a miracle or an act of nature or a piece of trickery, then a pact has occurred. Theologians explain the attendant circumstances which lead to such a conclusion: (i) if what is done goes beyond its natural capacity and cannot be ascribed to God or good angels. Valencia and Aquinas agree that marvellous effects cannot be achieved naturally by a cause working from a great distance; (ii) if the operator uses secret words, characters, figures or signs, or sacred words wrenched to alien meanings; (iii) if the effectiveness of the operation is attributed to certain rites and particular observances; and (iv) and if power is attributed to superstitious practices. Any one of these claims should rouse suspicion. Two or three together are evidence that something unnatural is taking place. On the other hand, if wonderful effects happen without any of these attendant circumstances, we may adjudge them natural provided we bear in mind (a) Satan's power to deceive, and (b) our own ignorance about many things in nature. Trickery can be discerned without much trouble.]

Chapter 6: Does this magic produce real effects? How can one recognise what kind of pact lies behind them?

Whoever maintains that every effect is the result of trickery, or believes that every effect is real, should be regarded as a water-melon rather than a human being. Too often the evil spirit deceives us because he is the father of lying, because frequently he affects the eyes or dupes the other senses by casting a vain image in their path. But not infrequently God obstructs him so that he does not really do something which may or can please the magicians; and when Satan sees this, he takes refuge in trickery lest his lack of power be discovered. When the evil spirit wishes to produce a real effect, however, and God allows him to do so, provided the effect does not surpass the powers he has, God undoubtedly does not stop him from producing a real effect. For natural causes do give rise to a real effect; so the Devil can use them and apply active things to passive, and therefore will be able to produce effects which are real. According to the divine author, Dionysius of Athens,[25] the Devil lost none of his natural gifts by sinning and so it follows that he has a natural strength which is very powerful, along with a multiplicity of daily experience and an exact knowledge of the

[25] Pseudo-Dionysius the Areopagite (floruit c. 500 AD): De divinis nominibus (On the Names of God). Del Rio seems to be referring to the passage in which pseudo-Dionysius discusses evil and demons, 724C–725C, especially 725A.

essence and qualities peculiar to each and every thing – so much so that he can very easily produce the genuine effect he wants. This is why the majority of theologians carefully recognise two magical effects: the real and the apparent. On account of these, Tertullian [26] calls magicians entertainers and sophists, and I add to these a third type, that of mixed effects, true and false.

[Examples of magical effects from ancient literature are given, along with the entertaining story of a Bohemian illusionist, taken from the *History of the Kingdom of Bohemia* by Janus Dubravius, Bishop of Olmutz.] [27]

The following are things which (for shame!) certain very credulous but otherwise pious princes, allow to take place in their presence. Iron objects, silver platters and similar things of great weight are put on top of a table and then, without the assistance of a magnet, a cord, a hair, or other means, are pulled from one end of the table to the other, jumping up and down as they go. Someone pulls out a playing-card from the rest of the pack without letting anyone else see it, and then its face is changed three times while the person still has the card in his hand. There are mirrors which seem to show things from far away places. In the space of three hours a real shrub is made to grow a span's length from the table, and trees with leaves and fruit suddenly appear. Lanterns lit with a special flame make all the women present look as though they are naked, and reveal those parts which nature tells us should remain concealed; and while the women are unclothed, they perform a ritual dance as long as a lantern, which is hung up in the middle of the room, continues to burn. (The lantern has certain characters inscribed on it and is filled with hare's fat) – oh, and other stories of the same kind, the sort of thing apprentice entertainers cram into their heads from reading the works of Battista della Porta.) [28] Since neither natural causes nor appropriate artificial causes are advanced to explain such things, they should be ascribed to trickery.

[There follow examples of real effects from Holy Scripture, including (a) the incident of the raising of Samuel by the witch of Endor and (b) the contest between Moses and Pharaoh's magicians, both of which Del Rio discusses at length.]

---

[26] Marginal note: Tertullian: *Apologeticus* (A Man Ready to Defend Himself), chapter 23 (The charge to which Del Rio refers occurs at the start of the chapter.); *De idolatria*, chapter 9.

[27] (1486–c. 1553), Austrian historian and natural philosopher. He also wrote a book on the making and care of fish ponds, which was translated into English in 1599. His *History* was first published in 1552.

[28] Giovanni Battista Della Porta (c. 1535–1615), Italian physician. He wrote several books on occult subjects, including *Magia Naturalis* which was first published in Naples between 1558 and 1561.

My opinion is that the incident relating to the soul of Samuel belongs to the 'mixed' type of magic. It really was Samuel's soul which appeared but the incident contained falsehood and a deception of the senses, since that which was seen by Saul obeyed the voice of the enchantress. Samuel had not brought with him either his real body or his real shroud. The other example, relating to the Egyptian sorcerers, also belongs to the 'mixed' type, provided we follow the opinion of those who do not know that the snakes were introduced by fraud. On the other hand, if we follow Saint Augustine, it belongs to the 'real' type. [Del Rio continues by telling a fabulous story about another contest between two magicians.]

So now it remains for us to discuss how to distinguish genuine effects from counterfeit by looking at the pact involved. Marvels are accomplished, not by the magicians but by the Evil Spirit himself. Therefore magicians will not be able (as some people have written without due caution), to accomplish what the Evil Spirit cannot; but whatever he can do, the magicians can do as well because of the pact. Once this basic point has been made, the following rules may be established: (i) if the magic effect is of the kind which depends upon power exercised by an evil spirit (a power which is reserved to the omnipotence of God alone), then the effect should be considered fraudulent; (ii) but if it is not agreed that the effect is caused by the power of an evil spirit the matter is plainly doubtful and one must then refer oneself to the circumstances. The reason for doubt is that God does not always allow an evil spirit to do whatever he is capable of doing and will stop him from doing it. Moreover, the evil spirit does not always actually want to do what he is permitted to do but, being one who lies to humanity, rejoices in deception.

Question 7: Can a magician perform a real miracle?

[These marvels are not done by the magicians themselves but by an evil spirit, and they will not be able to do anything the evil spirit cannot do. But the magicians will actually accomplish what the spirit is able to do through the pact they have with him. References to Clement of Rome, Porphyrius, and Iamblichus.]

I should like the reader to observe that I do not use the word *miracle* in this discussion to mean 'some extraordinary effect', as secular authors do. I follow the more restricted theological definition which is that of the Greek *to theras*, 'an effect produced only beyond and above the power of created nature' – for example, restoring sight to someone born blind, or resurrecting the dead. But when the effect is consistent with the power of the created individual (for example, the ability to stir up rain and winds, cure fevers, etc.), this is usually known as *to thauma* – not simply 'a miracle', but 'a miracle in accordance with x', or 'as far as we are concerned', or 'a wonder', or 'something extraordinary'. Again, these wonders (*mira*) are divided into (a) 'absolutely wonderful, which refers to something worthy of astonishment of itself and in its own right, even if we know why it is wonderful and how it is done; and (b) 'wonders in accordance with x' or 'wonders as far as we are concerned', which refer to things which astonish us as long as we do not know why they are extraordinary, but will cease to do so once we know the reasons.

It occurs to me that there are various points by which a wonder (*mirum*) may be distinguished from a miracle (*miraculum*). (1) If, as I said, the effect surpasses the power both of the created individual and of nature, it will be a miracle. (2) If the proposed aim of the effect is not good (e.g. spiritual or physical welfare) but merely bad (e.g. curiosity, something alien to good morals, or repugnant to the true faith), it is not a miracle. Thus, the prodigies and 'miracles' of Antichrist will not be true miracles, as Saint Paul wrote to the Thessalonians; and it is obvious from this what we must think about the cure of swollen glands done by the princess Elizabeth, Queen of the English, if, as Tooker claims, she does it in confirmation of her faith. (3) The wonders of evil spirits are often deficient in the smallest details, whereas miracles are perfect because they are works of God. See *Exodus* 8 on the contest between the magicians and Moses. (4) The wonders of evil spirits vanish in the face of miracles, as the rods of the magicians were devoured by the rod of Moses, and the oracles of evil spirits are dumb in the presence of saintly people. (5) Finally, miracles happen by means of open, sober invocation of God. The wonders of magicians always happen by means of a mixture of discordant, secret, vain, ridiculous, or superstitious prayers or signs.

First conclusion: *No magicians can produce miracles in the proper sense of the word.* [The power to work miracles is reserved to God alone. The power of his creatures is limited by natural boundaries. The Church is able to perform miracles because of God's grace, and God may sometimes permit individuals to work miracles in confirmation of the true faith. But he cannot give confirmation of a false faith through miracles. Therefore one cannot say, 'X has performed a miracle, therefore his faith is true'. One must be careful how one uses the word 'miracle'. Second conclusion: *Magicians cannot work perfect wonders, either.* Something which is quite extraordinary is not the same thing as a miracle. Third conclusion: Magicians can work many wonders according to whether they are helped by an evil spirit or are permitted to do so by God. The Devil understands many wonderful secrets of nature and can produce his effects naturally and very quickly, and it is difficult for us to appreciate how extensive this power of Satan is.]

Question 8: By what kind of pact with the Devil do magicians work these wonders?

All evil spirits operate either by immediate action through local motion or by mediated action; and this is done in two ways, either by a deception of the senses or by application of active things to passive through a genuine alteration. This is the teaching common to all theologians. So the spirits operate *by local motion, by alteration, and by delusion.*

(1) Local motion. Inferior bodies obey the angels to such an extent that they can rotate the heavens, although whether in fact there are such movers of the spheres must be discussed elsewhere. Given that they can move them, however, it follows that there is no body so huge that evil spirits cannot move it from its place by some hefty shove – provided, however, they do not thereby disturb the order of the universe. So they will not have the power to move a whole element from its place (and it is with this limitation in mind that one should understand Firmilianus when he wrote to Saint Cyprian that effects arising from a local or partial movement of the earth will not be genuine), and nor will they be able to change the way the heavens move in their ordained orbit. But an evil spirit can move bodies very forcibly by *local* motion and this is what makes us see the heavens move very rapidly. So this is how the spirit can remove something from one's view and substitute something else so instantaneously that the he deceives the minds and eyes of the onlookers, and persuades them that the change of the one thing into another is genuine. [Examples given.]

(2) The application of active things to passive. By this alteration or change of things, he often creates wonders whose causes are natural but unknown to us, although very well known to himself. For he sees the substances of all natural things and has studied the particular properties of each. He knows the right times for application, and there is scarcely any clever device or contrivance he does not know. For what has he not achieved by daily assiduous experience and observation? In particular, he knows everything good angels have accomplished since the beginning of the world, what people have thought, and the very many things revealed to Satan by means of good angels at God's command, things which the good angels have learned from God. Therefore, very often many things are done which the operation of nature alone could never have done, unless evil spirits had helped her by this unnatural application.

[Evil spirits thus use natural agents as instruments to accomplish their intentions. Del Rio discusses what he means by 'instruments' and gives examples of what they can do. Natural agents achieve their effects without the Devil's adding anything to their innate power. A cook, for example, confers nothing upon the fire he uses to prepare a meal. Therefore the cook is, in this case, the principal cause of the final effect, and the fire is the instrumental cause.]

(3) I shall now review operation by delusion. When neither local movement nor the type of working I have been discussing is sufficiently effective, magicians usually take refuge in travelling showmen's tricks, and by means of false appearances so play upon people's senses that even the least thing magicians do may be considered done by deception. (I am expanding the word 'deception' to include 'trickery, 'deception', and 'error' even though these are normally kept distinct.) The Devil has three particular ways of deceiving people: by changing the object, by changing the intermediate air, or by changing the sense-organ itself.

[Del Rio now says he will follow the explanations given by Molina.[29] These largely give an account of the tricks of the street entertainers' trade, and Del Rio supports these by references to early Christian literature and later theologians and chroniclers. He then quotes a story from the Polish historian Martin Bielski,[30] and ends with a series of references to tricks played by the Devil.]

Question 9: How remarkable were the effects attributed by the ancients to magicians?

[This section consists mainly of references to and extended quotations from ancient literature, especially Ovid, Tibullus, Lucan, Seneca, and Claudian, relating to the deeds of magicians and sorceresses.]

Question 10: What powers do magicians have over the natural order and the laws of the universe?

[Magic boasts that nature obeys her and that she is superior to all the laws of the universe. This is false. Such supremacy is reserved to God alone. Magicians cannot produce any substantial or accidental form; they cannot create anything either from nothing or from anything in nature. They cannot produce substantial forms unless alterations and arrangements of matter have taken place first. They cannot insert a vacuum in nature, or restore anything once it has been taken away, or change or overthrow the natural order of things, transfer a body from

---

[29] Luis de Molina (1535–1600), a Spanish Jesuit. He wrote a book on free will, which is likely to have been Del Rio's source at this point. It was published at Antwerp in 1588–1589.

[30] (c. 1495–1575). He published a *Kronika Swiata* (History of the World) in Cracow between 1550 and 1564, and a *Kronika Polska* (History of Poland) in Cracow in 1597.

one extreme to another, move it some distance from themselves, or move it instantaneously or with any speed at all. They cannot eliminate the connection between things or the subordination of one thing to another; nor can they interfere with the action of a natural agent, although such a thing is possible in the case of doctors who use the agent indirectly as a medium of cure. Del Rio now gives references to ancient writers whose anecdotes show how the Devil deceived pagans into thinking they were witnessing marvels, whereas in fact the 'marvels' were simply natural events such as *ignes fatui* or sudden outbursts of fire – although 'if there is evidence of some agency extrinsic to what follows, then that agency is certainly not natural, but demonic'. Nevertheless, we should not run to marvels as the immediate explanation for everything which strikes us as unusual. Del Rio directs his readers' attention to the well-known *Commentary on Genesis*, chapter 9, by the 'astrologer' Luther,[31] who ascribes aerial phenomena to the work of demons. Del Rio dismisses his arguments and points instead to genuine examples of demonic activity given by Nicholas Rémy. He ends with further references from early Christian literature and an extraordinary anecdote about religious obedience.]

Question 11: What power do magicians have over heavenly bodies, the stars, and the elements?

[(a) Magicians cannot control the movements of the heavens or of the stars; neither can they reverse their fixed orbits. Examples. (b) They cannot transfer one element from its natural place to another. References to early Christian and pagan authors. (c) They can, however, calm tempests, rouse thunder and lightning, hailstorms, showers of rain, or any other manifestations of the weather, and send these down upon any fields they wish. Many examples from both Scripture and demonological literature, including this anecdote about rain-makers in Peru.]

The Indians procure rain by means of the a ridiculous ceremony which is described in letters, dated 1590 and 1591, from our Jesuit brethren in Peru. Gaspar Stitillius gives the following extract. 'When they need rain, one of their magicians cries out in a loud, impassioned voice, at greater and greater speed, that everyone must go to the mountain and that when they have all arrived there, they must abstain from food according to custom. (Their "fast", however, refers merely to salt, pepper, and food which has been cooked.) When the period of fasting is over, they call earnestly upon the stars at the tops of their voices and pray for water. Then they turn towards their fields and their castle and,

---

[31] *Mathaeologus Lutherus.* The passage occurs during Luther's discussion of the rainbow.

taking a drink offered to them by a young woman of noble birth, they drink it down. This causes them to lose their senses and their reason, and they look like dead men. After they have recovered, however, they mingle honey with water and maize and sprinkle the mixture towards the clouds. On the next day a noble old man, or at any rate someone of good reputation who is held in honour, is laid on a couch under which they light a slow fire. When the old man begins to sweat, the magician catches the sweat in a jar, mixes it with goose-blood and the juice from a crushed root, and again throws this liquid into the air as if to soak the clouds. He asks that, by means of the sweat, the blood, and the water, the rain they desire be bestowed upon them, and if by chance it rains on the day they work their superstitious ceremonies, they give thanks to the stars and carry the magician shoulder high and honour him with many gifts'.

[(d) An example of Tartar magicians' causing darkness to fall. (e) Magicians can corrupt the air and water in certain places and render them both decayed and lethal. Examples given. (f) They can prevent fire from burning, so that someone can walk through it and not be harmed. Examples given. (g) They can affect the weather by using certain minerals, with results which seem marvellous but are, in fact, due to natural causes.]

Question 12: What power do magicians have over external things or the good things one owes to fortune?

[Evil spirits, and through them magicians, have wide-ranging powers over property. (1) They destroy flocks and herds. Example. (2) They alienate corn and fruit crops. Examples. (3) They can destroy crops and render the land infertile. Example. Rémy says magicians usually do this by scattering powder they have received from an evil spirit, and this creates various kinds of caterpillars and locusts. Sometimes the evil spirits send gadflies and sometimes wolves to destroy farm animals. Additional modern examples. (4) They burn down houses. Example. (5) They can destroy reputations. Examples. (6) They can conjure up banquets which are no more than illusions. Examples. (7) With God's permission, they can snatch captives from imprisonment. For example, an evil spirit sent by a magician offered to liberate Frederick, Duke of Austria, from captivity, but the Duke made the sign of the cross and the spirit vanished. This happened in 1533. Further ancient examples. (8) Del Rio says he has no doubt that magic can be worked through the agency of evil spirits. Examples, drawn largely from Mediaeval chronicles. (9) Many people are persuaded that men have been elevated to dignities and honours by magical means. Examples of certain Popes slandered in this fashion. Del Rio answers the charges with a vigorous defence.

(10) The same explanation may be offered about those who acquire great wealth, as Psellus says. By applying active things to passive, the Devil can produce what passes for good coinage. Del Rio thinks that the Devil is merely the instrument whereby good angels, with God's permission, actually effect the creation of money. The Devil knows where treasure is hidden and can produce it when he wishes. Examples given from Rémy. Faustus and Agrippa are credited with creating money which, after a few days, turned into worthless rubbish. Other examples of the search for treasure, including an anecdote from 1520. The section closes with praise for the Emperor Charles V who had exiled Agrippa and other nobles from his Court and Empire because they had promised to find him treasure through their magical arts.]

Question 13: Do magicians have the power to cast a spell on brute beasts?

[This section consists of quotations from and references to Holy Scripture and ancient and modern literature to show that magicians do indeed possess this power.]

Question 14: Can they use their art to produce or bring into being anything which is of more than one kind and, in particular, capable of feeling?

[Saint Augustine said that imperfect creatures such as flies, worms, and frogs which are born from putrefying matter, can be produced by applying active things to passive. Magicians do the same thing through their pact with an evil spirit, as when the Devil gives witches (sagae) some powder and they throw it into the air and all kinds of insects are born therefrom at once. Magicians can produce other forms of imperfect creatures too (examples given), but Del Rio thinks they cannot produce perfect creatures. An evil spirit, however, can do so. Examples.]

Evil spirits can also produce strange monsters, unless one is going to argue that these are born from the wicked congress of humans and animals – undoubtedly the origin of most monsters. One is example is the monster from Brazil which was seventeen palms high, covered in lizard-skin, with swollen breasts, lion's limbs, and staring, flame-coloured, glittering eyes, and a flame-coloured tongue – something like the monsters with semi-human faces which were captured in the forests of Saxony in 1240. Similarly, at the time of the Marsian War,[32] Alcippe gave birth to an elephant; in 1278 an Helvetian woman bore a lion; in 1470 a woman from Pavia produced a cat; and in 1531 a woman from

---

[32] 90–89 BC. The Marsians were renowned for their magicians, who specialised in curing diseases.

Augsburg, in one and the same birth, produced a human head wrapped in membranes, a two-footed snake, and a complete pig. One can read other things of this kind in modern authors.

One example which caps the rest, extraordinary though they may be, is the one reported by Castanneda in his *Annales Lusitaniae* [History of Portugal].[33] On account of some crime or other, a woman was transported to a desert island and there abandoned. A large number of monkeys, which were numerous in the area, stood round her, growling, and then one, bigger than the rest, arrived on the scene, took her by the hand, and coaxed her into a huge cave. He set before her, himself, and everyone else, plenty of apples, nuts and various roots, and invited her to eat. Then the animal forced her to have sexual intercourse with him, an outrage which was repeated for many days, and as a result of which she gave birth to two children.

The unhappy woman, who would have found death infinitely preferable, continued in this fashion for several years until God in his mercy sent thither a ship from Portugal. The soldiers disembarked at a spot watered by a spring which emerged from the ground right next to the cave, and by good fortune, the monkey was not there. The woman rushed up to the first human beings she had seen for a long time, threw herself at their feet, and begged them to take her away from the outrage and appalling slavery she was suffering. They took pity on her misfortune and agreed to take her on board with them. But lo, the monkey bore down upon them, and with clumsy gestures and deep roaring summoned back his wife (who was, of course, not a wife), when he saw the sails spread to the winds. He ran forward and drew the mother's attention to one of her children; he issued threats and, far from retreating, seemed on the verge of hurling himself into the sea, and none of this did he do with any half measures. Having made his threat, he dashed back to the cave and, just as quickly, returned to the shore and showed her the other child. Then he renewed his threats and plunged into the water, pursuing them closely, raging all the time, and swimming after the ship as long as he could until the waves proved too strong for him.

The whole of Portugal can bear witness to this very famous incident. The King condemned the woman to be burned at Lisbon but, at the prayers of certain people who begged for her life, he commuted the death-sentence to perpetual imprisonment.

[Is the reader astonished? Del Rio gives examples of peoples descended from animals.]

---

[33] Fernão Lopes de Castanheda (died 1559). A French translation of his work appeared in 1581.

Actually, I do not put much faith in these tales because I am sure that a real human being cannot be born from intercourse between a human and an animal. An animal's semen lacks that perfection which is required to house a noble human soul, so if anything is produced by intercourse of this kind, it will be a monster, not a human. For it is the composition of the inferior semen which determines the kind of foetus which will follow, and therefore at best it will produce only something which looks like a human, and I cannot believe that a brute creature of this type, with parents of different species, can be considered perfect (for example, the children born to the Portuguese woman were neither monkeys nor humans). It is, rather, a monster of a mixed and imperfect type, such as a mule which comes from a horse and an ass, or a *thos* [34] which comes from a hyena and a wolf.

[Del Rio adds further examples from a *History of Peru* by Petrus Chieza, and then points out that the condition of the semen and the humours of the womb have their part to play, and that intercourse between witches and evil spirits may result in extraordinary births.]

To these I add an absolutely true story. Here in Belgium a certain criminal individual had sexual intercourse with a cow. It was noted that the cow became pregnant, and after a few months she gave birth to a male offspring – not a calf, but a boy. Several people were present and witnessed him falling from the womb of his mother, the cow. They then picked him up from the ground and handed him over to a nurse. The boy grew up, and was baptised and instructed in the precepts of the Christian religion; and, because of what his father had done, he applied himself to works of piety and penitence. The boy was perfectly human, but his mind had bovine leanings which made him want to graze in the fields and ruminate his cud. What should one think about this? That he was not a human being? Such is certainly my belief. Nevertheless, I deny that his mother was the cow. What, then? The Devil knew about his father's sin: indeed, he instigated it. Shortly afterwards he made it look as though the cow was pregnant and then, at a time of his choosing, produced an infant he had stolen from someone else and placed him under the cow while she was heavy in womb and on the point of giving birth. This is how she appeared to drop the boy. In consequence, a piece of fantasy was born, and the boy was persuaded he was the son of a cow. His imagination got to work and in consequence he thought he had imbibed certain propensities from his supposed mother. To think that he was a real human being, born from the material of bovine semen, and that the fully-formed organic arrangement of a human body was perfected in the womb of a cow by means of the heat and power of a

[34] Greek = a short-legged carnivorous animal of unknown species.

bovine spirit is something which I think all philosophers will agree with me should be reckoned as impossible.

[Del Rio ends the section with further examples, mainly from ancient and Mediaeval sources.]

Question 15: Do *incubi* and *succubae* really exist? Can there be issue from intercourse with such spirits?

Axiom 1: It is common for workers of harmful magic (*malefici*) and witches (*lamiae*) to perform the sexual act with evil spirits. The former do it with *succubae*, the latter with *incubi*. Several heretics – indeed, the majority of them – incorrectly deny this proposition. So do some Catholics, but not very many. [Del Rio gives names from both communions, and references to early Christian literature.] Evil spirits can assume the bodies of dead people, or construct for themselves from air and the other elements bodies which feel like flesh to the touch. These they can move as they wish and make them warm. By artifice they can make show of a sexuality they do not possess by nature, and abuse men by appearing to them as a woman, and women by appearing to them as a man. They lie down and spread themselves out underneath the woman, and can bring along real semen taken from someone else, and so imitate natural emission. Therefore they are able to do everything posited by the first axiom, and since they can do so, and experience tells us that they do, there is no reason why we should doubt it.

Axiom 2: Offspring can be born from such an intercourse with an *incubus*. [The Devil can take semen from someone else (for example, from a man while he is asleep), and carry it off while preserving its heat; and just when a woman is ready to conceive, he places it in her womb to mingle with her female semen.]

Axiom 3: Evil spirits cannot, as living creatures do, generate life by their own power and from their own substance. [Evil spirits do not multiply among themselves, nor do they have any kind of body. (References given.) Evil spirits are insubstantial and therefore cannot produce semen from themselves. 'So my opinion is that intercourse between an incubus and a woman sometimes produces offspring, and that in these circumstances the real father of the child is not the evil spirit but the man whose semen the evil spirit has misused'. Del Rio now cites authorities for and against this proposition, along with examples from ancient and modern times. The arguments of those who deny it, he says, are very flimsy, especially those of Rémy whose objections Del Rio now proceeds to answer.]

First: he says that an evil spirit and a human being are different species. Therefore there cannot be offspring from such a copulation. I answer: While it is true that mules, *thoes*, leopards, panthers, and other hybrids are born from intercourse between different species of animal, it is a non sequitur to apply that example here because in this case generation is not attributable to an evil spirit but to the man whose semen it is, as Saint Thomas [Aquinas] rightly says. [Reference given.]

Second: he says that an evil spirit knows nothing of how life and death begin. Therefore he cannot be the author and origin of the process of giving life. I answer: The vital spirit is not in the evil spirit but in the semen itself, just as the power of warming is not in the drinking-cup or the spout of the wine-jug, but in the wine itself. (See Aquinas and Sprenger.)

Third: he tells us that witches (*sagae*) say that the semen ejaculated by the evil spirit is cold and brings consternation rather than pleasure, and that therefore it will not be possible for generation to follow. This was the argument of Marcus of Ephesus, as quoted by Psellus. Rémy confirms it by the confession of witches who said that all sense of pleasure is absent from such a copulation which is extremely painful. I reply: I am compelled by the futility of this argument to spend more time than I might wish on refuting something which is both inane and filthy. Certainly it seems that when an evil spirit wishes to deceive by taking the appearance of a particular man and does not wish anyone to know he is an evil spirit, he can give a most exact imitation of whatever is required in copulation between a real man and a real woman; and therefore of necessity he takes care, if he wants generation to follow, to use what is necessary for this purpose. Generation, however, is something which very rarely happens. He cannot ever, of himself, cause generation because he cannot procreate anything like himself. But sometimes he attempts generation from someone else's semen collected by a *succuba* who does this for him as a favour. Therefore he seeks out a great quantity of semen, and when he has found it he preserves it and brings it back so quickly that its vital spirit does not evaporate. Then he pours out the necessary quantity whenever it is required.

[When the evil spirit does not intend to generate, he pours out something which resembles semen and is hot (to avoid any suspicion of fraud), but controls the body he has assumed in case contact with *him* give rise to fear and horror. On the other hand, when he does not need to disguise himself, his semen is both unreal and cold, and there can be no generation of children thereby. He asks *succubae* if they want to become pregnant and if they do, he uses real semen. (See Sprenger.) Del Rio goes on to discuss the presence or absence of pleasure in these encounters, citing modern authorities in support of what he is saying.]

Fourth: Rémy says that one cannot believe that God agrees with this kind of act or gives a soul to a body born of this type of coition, thereby adding the final touch to the evil spirit's imperfect work. I reply: The evil spirit, as far as the operation of nature is concerned, is in this case merely the instrument which applies the principal agent – the real human semen.

[God therefore concurs in the formation of a human body born from this human semen. The sin in the birth belongs to the witch (*saga*) and the evil spirit. The argument that although the natural order of things is preserved in fornication, adultery, and incest, it is not so preserved in the case of intercourse with an evil spirit is simply frivolous. The natural order *is* preserved in this case because male semen is mixed with female semen and therefore a child may be born as a consequence. A further argument by Molitor is refuted. Del Rio does not believe, however, that children can be born of intercourse between an *incubus* and a *succuba*, for which he gives physiological reasons. He discusses variations upon this theme, with references to ancient and Mediaeval literature. Can evil spirits make a virgin conceive in the absence of male semen? Del Rio thinks they can, and gives references to Mediaeval authors. Do evil spirits sometimes have intercourse with witches the wrong way round?[35] Del Rio refers the reader to several witchcraft treatises and demonologies. His final question is, can giants or pigmies be born by the exercise of magical power? He discusses this at length, with reference to Holy Scripture, ancient, and Mediaeval literature.]

Question 16: The nocturnal meetings of witches (*sagae*). Are witches really transported from one place to another?

[Protestant writers, such as Luther and Melanchthon, believe that both transportation and meetings alike are delusions, and so do many Catholic authors. (Del Rio gives a list.) Their arguments, however, are not very convincing. Although witches can be deceived, it does not follow that they always are deceived. Sometimes their souls do not leave their bodies. Often their bodies are so deep in sleep that the women believe they are awake and see and hear images, whereas in reality they do nothing of the kind. Del Rio says he knows several examples of this. He dismisses the argument that because women are sometimes found lying motionless they do not ever fly. He says this merely shows that sometimes the women are mistaken. He refers to Alciati[36] who asks, can we say that the women go to a meeting and leave an evil spirit next to their husband in the bed? Experience, authority, and the confessions of credible

---

[35] *Praeposteram libidinem.* This may mean (a) with the woman on top of the man (b) with entry from the rear, or (c) anal intercourse.

[36] Probably Andrea Alciati (1492–1550), an Italian lawyer who published several works on the law. Del Rio refers to 'Book 8', but does not give his source a title.

witches confirm the possibility, says Del Rio. When the witch (*strix*) sets out, her husband is made to sleep deeply, and something resembling his wife is put in her place. (Examples from Rémy.)

Del Rio discusses various aspects of the *Canon Episcopi*[37] and then returns to Alciati who argues that at the name of Jesus all those attending a witches' meeting disappear, which proves they must have been merely phantasms. Del Rio says that the witches (*sagae*) do not vanish, but their attendant evil spirits carry them off very quickly while the eyes of onlookers are closed.

Evidence says that when witches anoint themselves, sometimes they are not carried off but are found lying in the place where they anointed themselves. Del Rio says there are various explanations for this. Sometimes the evil spirit prefers to deceive the witches and not move them, so that he may persuade judges and princes that the witch is lying and so preserve her from execution. In this way, he keeps his pact with her, to the greater danger of the human race. Sometimes God allows this to happen, sometimes he does not. Del Rio accepts that witches (*sagae*) are sometimes transported by an evil spirit from one place to another on a goat or some other animal, or on a reed or stick, and that they are physically present at their meetings. (References given, including both Catholic and Protestant authors.) He illustrates the point with anecdotes taken from both Mediaeval and ancient historians. The stick, he says, is usually smeared with an ointment which contains the fat of dead children, and this is why witches practise infanticide.]

Once they have anointed themselves in this way, they are usually carried away sitting on a staff, a pitch-fork, or a distaff; or they stand on one leg in a basket; or they sit on brooms or a reed, or a bull, a pig, a male goat, or a dog. [Examples from Rémy.] So this is how they are normally borne off to the meeting, 'the sport of good fellowship', as they call it in Italy. There, on most occasions, once a foul, disgusting fire has been lit, an evil spirit sits on a throne as president of the assembly. His appearance is terrifying, almost always that of a male goat or a dog. The witches come forward to worship him in different ways. Sometimes they supplicate him on bended knee; sometimes they stand with their back turned to him; sometimes they even throw their legs in the air and hold their head, not forwards but tilted right back so that their chin points up to the sky. They offer candles made of pitch or a child's umbilical cord, and kiss him on the anal orifice as a sign of homage. What more can

---

[37] A legal document issued in about 900. It dismissed the notion of the physical reality of witchcraft and suggested that those who believed in it were weak in their faith. The Canon became one of the key documents of witchcraft literature and was quoted or referred to by most of the demonological writers who followed.

one say? Sometimes they imitate the sacrifice of the Mass (the greatest of all their crimes), as well as purifying with water and similar Catholic ceremonies. [Del Rio says that in Book 3 he will offer evidence that they also sacrifice children to the Devil, and retain the Host from communion and offer it for desecration at their meetings.]

Once they have committed these and similar atrocious and execrable abominations, they sit down at table and start to enjoy food supplied by the evil spirit or brought by themselves. Sometimes they perform a ritual dance before the feast, sometimes after. Usually, there are various tables – three or four of them – loaded with food which is sometimes very dainty and sometimes quite tasteless and unsalted. Each witch has his or her place allotted according to station or wealth. The evil spirit attached to each of these workers of harmful magic (malefici) sits near him:[38] sometimes on one side of him, sometimes opposite. Nor do they omit to use a grace worthy of such a gathering, using words which are always openly blasphemous and in which Beelzebub himself is declared to be the creator, giver, and preserver of all things. (This information comes from a list of graces, which they stick underneath the tables placed at their disposal. I have read a copy of these formulae written in the hand of a very famous worker of evil magic.)

Sometimes they take part in this feast with their face covered by a mask, a linen cloth, or some other veil or facial representation.[39] Usually they are masked. After the feast, each evil spirit takes by the hand the disciple of whom he has charge, and so that they may do everything with the most absurd kind of ritual, each person bends over backwards, joins hands in a circle, and tosses his head as frenzied fanatics do. Then they begin to dance. Sometimes they hold lighted candles in their hands, with which they worship the evil spirit, and exchange kisses in his presence. They sing very obscene songs in his honour, or jump up and down to a drum or a pipe which is played by someone sitting in the fork of a tree. They behave ridiculously in every way, and in every way contrary to accepted custom. Then their demon-lovers copulate with them in the most repulsive fashion.

When they sacrifice, they usually start with an act of adoration; but they often make sacrifices outwith the sabbat. Finally, we are told, each person gives an

---

[38] This and the following adjectives are masculine in Latin. One is led to presume from the majority of other writers on the subject that most of the people present at such gatherings were women. Del Rio's use of the masculine form of words both here and elsewhere in this section merely indicates that the company is mixed, in accordance with the usual Latin practice of using the masculine form of adjectives and pronouns to cover both the sexes.

[39] 'Mask' = larva, which is both an evil spirit and a mask. 'Facial representation' = persona, once again a mask whose likeness is that of a human face. The word 'masked' in the next sentence is personati and is, again, masculine.

account of the wicked deeds he has done since the last meeting. The more serious these are and the more detestable, the more they are praised with ever greater fulsomeness. But if they have done nothing, or if their deeds are not dreadful enough, the sluggish witches are given an appalling beating by the evil spirit or by some senior worker of harmful magic (*maleficus*). Finally, they receive powders – which some writers say are the ashes of the he-goat whose shape had been taken by the evil spirit whom they worship, and which has suddenly been consumed by fire in front of their eyes – or else they receive some other poisonous substances. Often they are given the task of harming someone, and then is pronounced the decree of the evil spirit Pseudotheus:[40] 'Avenge yourselves, otherwise you will die'. (This, as you will appreciate, is contrary to the law of charity.)

Each person then goes home. If they live nearby, they go on foot. If they live further away, since they are transported to the meetings, they come, as far as is possible, either in the silence of midnight when the power of darkness is strong, or at midday: which reminds us of what the Psalmist says about 'the destruction that wasteth at noonday'.[41] Abenezra writes that magicians observe certain days and hours.[42] Our witches (*striges*) seem to have different appointed days in different districts. In Italy, they gather on the night before Friday at about midnight [references given]; whereas in Lotharingia, they meet on the nights before Thursday and Sunday, as Rémy says. Others, I have read, meet on the night before Tuesday.

The evil spirit can transport them without the use of an ointment, as I have said, and sometimes does so; but for various reasons he prefers to use one. Sometimes the witches (*sagi*)[43] are too timid to make the venture or too weak to bear the horrible contact with Satan via the body he assumes. Sometimes he stupefies their senses by means of the ointment and persuades the poor wretches that its power is very great. On other occasions he mimicks the holy sacraments instituted by God, and by these quasi-rituals imports a degree of reverence and veneration into his orgies. The power of the ointment adds nothing to the transportation. Hence, it is obvious that even if those who wish, out of curiosity, to take part in the meeting at the appointed time, and anoint themselves, and are thereby transported through the air – something which, as has been proved on many occasions, God permits to punish this rash, self-indulgent curiosity – if anyone firm in the faith and armed with charity were

---

[40] 'False god'.

[41] *Psalm* 90, verse 6 (Vulgate).

[42] I.e. Abraham ben Meir ibn Ezra (1092–1167), a Jewish Biblical exegete from Toledo. He also wrote works on grammar, mathematics, astrology, and astronomy.

[43] Masculine form of the word.

to anoint himself with this unguent with the intention of conquering the evil spirit's deception and confirming the true faith, there can be no doubt (as Binsfeld rightly says)[44] that no transportation would follow. The reason is that such a person refrains from entering into a pact with an evil spirit and will not have been permitted by God to enter one. Moreover, when witches (*sagae*) anoint themselves outwith the appointed time of a meeting, they do not fly away and nor are they carried off, because this is not part of their contract. They know this, and so they do not anoint themselves unless they hear the signal for a meeting.

[That witches can indeed be transported in body is proved because (a) it is well within the Devil's power to do this (see Augustine and Aquinas), and (b) God permits such a thing to happen. (Examples given.) There is also a large number of examples taken from experience. (Reference and examples given, including lengthy anecdotes from Grillando, Spina, Rémy, and the following anecdote which comes from the *Medical Letters* of Baudouin van Ronss.][45]

In the village of Oostbrouck not far from Maastricht, there was a widow who found herself obliged to take in a servant as a lodger in order to help with her domestic expenses. With the usual nosiness of servants, he often used to look through the netting[46] and see his landlady come into the stable where she would make her way to a specific place and then reach out her hands and grasp hold of the hay-trough next to the horse's stall. Wondering what on earth this behaviour signified, he decided to take a risk and do the same thing, once, without his landlady's knowledge. So after she had gone through her customary procedure and seemed to have disappeared, he made his way to the same spot, checked it was the right place, and then, following his landlady's example, seized hold of the hay-trough.

Immediately he was caught up into the air and carried off to the town of Wyck and into a hidden, subterranean cave where he found the scum who are workers of harmful magic,[47] discussing their acts of malefice. His landlady and

---

[44] Pierre Binsfeld (1545/6–1598), German theologian, Bishop of Trier. His *Tractatus de confessionibus maleficorum et sagarum* (Treatise on the confessions of workers of harmful magic and witches), was published in Trier in 1579.

[45] Bartolommeo della Spina (*c.* 1475–1546), Italian philosopher, Dominican, author of *Quaestio de strigibus* (An Investigation Into Witches), published in Rome in 1576. Baudouin van Ronss (died 1596), Belgian physician. He wrote several works on medicine. His *Epistolae Medicinales* were published in Leiden in 1590.

[46] *Transenna.* Here it must be referring to some kind of screen over the stable window.

[47] *Coenum maleficarum.* 'Coenum' means scum or filth, and carries a sense of moral degradation as well. 'Maleficarum' is specifically feminine and is here clearly meant to refer to witches.

her friends were astonished by the servant's unexpected appearance. She asked him how he had managed to come thither so suddenly and what trick he had used to do so, and he told her, step by step, how he had done it. She immediately became indignant and turned very angry, afraid that now their secret, nocturnal meetings would be revealed. So she decided to talk to her partners in crime and ask them what they thought should be done in this difficult situation, and they came to the conclusion that they would accept his presence amicably, but would make him swear to remain silent and not communicate or reveal to anyone those secrets which he – beyond either his merit or his comprehension – had happened to see. He for his part made no such promise, but spoke to them in soothing tones and, with a view to getting them to behave with greater mildness, pretended that he prayed they would allow him (at some future date) to become a member of their witches' guild (*collegium sortilegarum*).

But while they were discussing this, the minutes glided by and it was time to go. Doubt now set in, and his landlady badgered the rest to decide whether he should be sent back home, which might prove a danger to everyone who had attended the meeting, or whether he should be killed for the general good. In the end they all chose the more merciful of the two and decided to send him back once they had exacted from him an oath of silence, and his landlady said that once he had given his word she would carry him home on her shoulders. So the two of them got into position and were then borne swiftly through the air by a wind from the East. But now, listen to this! They had covered a good part of their journey when there came into view a huge lake covered in reeds. This provided the maleficent old woman (*malefica anus*) with an opportunity and, fearful lest the youth repent of his initiation into their frenzied rites, she saw a way of getting rid of him. So she suddenly shot forward and threw him off her back, hoping, one must suppose, that the violence of the fall would kill him and that he would be swallowed up in the depths of the lake.

Ah, but how very merciful is God, who does not seek the death of a sinner, but rather that he be converted and live! For God put a stop to the mad woman's intention and did not allow the innocent youth to be drowned. Indeed, he countered it and let the young man live right up to the present day. You see, as chance and good luck would have it, the man was not dealt a fatal blow by falling into the lake, and the violent impetus of his descent was somehow broken by the reeds. Dawn was beginning to break. The poor man's body was tortured by a thousand agonising pains and the only part of it which still worked was his tongue. So with laboured breath he started to groan and kept it up until some huntsmen who were passing by gathered round him, extremely surprised by the unexpected sound of wailing, and there in front of them they found a man who had dislocated both his hips. They asked where he had come

96

from and what kind of an accident had brought him thither, and he told them everything, just as it had happened. Then they brought him in a carriage to Utrecht where Master Johannes Culemborg, the mayor, struck by the strangeness of what had happened to him, asked a good many questions about every astonishing detail and then ordered his men to track down[48] the landlady-witch (*fascinatrix era*), arrest her, and put her in chains. The moment she came into the mayor's hands, she confessed absolutely everything".

[This last, says Del Rio, is enough to contradict the Protestants Wier, Godelmann,[49] Luther, and Melanchthon who would explain witches' flights by referring to medical conditions such as melancholia. So when witches anoint themselves and say they are transported, it is no figment of their imagination. They[50] take careful note of their surroundings, unless they are masked (*larvati*), and of what they do and whom they meet. They are often seen by other, perfectly sane Catholics, going to and returning from their meetings. Sometimes they have been seen and arrested without any clothes on; or they have fallen from the sky; or they have been badly wounded. When they get home, they are so tired they sleep for three days. (See Rémy.) They all confess the same thing with corroborative details.

Nor is such a flight to be explained by reference to dreams. Those who offer such an explanation commit a sin, 'For the Catholic Church does not punish crimes unless they are certain and manifest; nor does she consider people heretics unless they have quite clearly been taken in heresy'. (Del Rio gives references to pertinent literature.) Why does the evil spirit hold such meetings? So that the witches may enjoy the association; to aggravate their sinfulness; to increase numbers by initiating new witches there; to make them bolder in wickedness; to provide them with illicit sensual pleasure; and to harden them to wicked behaviour. (See Spina.)

Del Rio concludes with further references to Holy Scripture and to modern demonologists, and raises one last point. Since an angel has no body, can he move a physical object? Various answers given by other authorities, says Del Rio,

---

[48] Van Ronss's narrative is carefully constructed. He uses the word *indago* = 'a ring of huntsmen or nets thrown round a particular location to prevent the escape of game' to refer (a) to the men who discover the injured servant in the reed-bed, and (b) to the men sent out to arrest the witch. A parallel between the two situations is thus created. The contribution of literary style to demonological and witchcraft literature is an aspect of the subject which needs close study.

[49] Johann Godelmann (1559–1611), German lawyer and diplomatist. His book *De magis, veneficis, et lamiis recte cognoscendis et puniendis* (The Proper Way to Recognise and Punish Magicians, Workers of Venomous Magic, and Witches) was published in Rostock in 1584.

[50] *Sortiarii*, literally 'diviners', generally used of witches. Again, it appears in the masculine form, but without necessarily excluding women.

are mistaken. In his opinion, an angel cannot move anything beyond his own power or the nature of the object to be moved. But when he assumes a body, he can use the natural ability of that body to move another body.]

Question 17: Can an evil spirit change the size of bodies in such a way that he will be able to penetrate their various parts; and can he locate one body in two different places, or two bodies in one and the same place by penetrating them?

Briefly, I think that the answer to all these points is No, because they are all contrary to the principles of natural science and the way in which nature is ordered.

[The rest of the section gives reasons for this opinion and references to the relevant literature.]

Question 18: Can magicians transform the bodies of one species into those of another?

[Del Rio says he is not talking about ancient fables, or natural changes in imperfect animals, but about magical transformations brought about with the help of an evil spirit. (References given, including the belief of the Nicaraguans that witches [striges] can change themselves into cats, monkeys, and pigs.) But a human soul cannot inform the body of an animal, nor can an animal soul inform the body of a human being; and when Circe changed Odysseus's companions into pigs, they did not lose the rational part of their soul.]

The soul is immortal and cannot be damaged or wounded by an evil spirit. So those people who think they have been transformed into something else are always labouring under an illusion, just as those who think they are seeing something they are not in fact seeing at all are often deluded, too. The sensible person who does not wish to be deceived must distinguish the transformation from its attendant effects (and if Jean de Sponde had done this, he would not have given us so much useless, puerile drivel on the subject in his *Commentaries on Homer*).[51] So one may conclude that whereas the transformation itself is delusory, many of its concomitant effects are perfectly real.

For example, both human beings and their livestock can be destroyed by an evil spirit using a body made of air, or the body of a wolf, or by human

[51] Jean de Sponde (1557–1595), French Classicist, poet, and Catholic apologist. His edition of Homer's works, together with the commentaries to which Del Rio is referring, was published in Basel in 1583.

beings in the guise of wolves (a point I shall clarify later), or by humans without such a guise who have worked themselves into an animal frame of mind. These last may be suffering from a fault in the humours and an excess of black bile, which has caused their mind to be taken over by by a kind of wolfishness so that they are possessed by a hatred for livestock and humans, and a desire to attack them, tear them in pieces, and devour them. There are several medical terms for this condition, including *lykaon* or *lycanthropy*, Arabic *chatrab*, and Latin *melancholia* or *insania lupina*.[52] A similar disorder makes people think they are dogs, lions, or other animals. Those who are simply suffering from an illness of this kind are not magicians (*magi*), and although they believe they are wolves and imitate the savage behaviour of a wolf, to other people they seem to be what they actually are – just human beings. [Examples given.] But when others, too, imagine these people are wolves, dogs, cats, or some other animal – like the woman in Palladius's Life of Macarius who seemed to be a mare, or the Neuri in Herodotus and Mela, or (to give a modern example from the second part of Camden's *Hibernia*), popular belief about what happens to certain of the Irish every year – this is magic and cannot proceed from illness alone.[53]

It is the Devil's habit to deceive in a number of different ways. Sometimes, for example, he substitutes one body for another. He puts a person to sleep and while he or she is off in some secret place, he takes the body of a wolf or manufactures one out of air, and wraps himself in it, like a garment. Consequently people believe that the things he does are done by the poor wretch who is actually somewhere else, fast asleep. [Reference to a story by

---

[52] *Lykaon* is a technical term found in the seventh century Greek medical writer, Paul of Aegina whose work Del Rio cites at this point. Both it and lycanthropy were said by Greek doctors to be a form of madness in which the patient had a ravenous appetite and exhibited other wolf-like qualities. The Arabic term may be based on the verb *shatara* = to rip or tear. *Melancholia*, a medical term borrowed from Greek, refers to a condition involving black bile, and *insania lupina* simply means 'wolfish madness'.

[53] Palladius: *Historia Lausiaca*, chapter 19 = *Patrologia Graeca* 34.1044. The relevant part of the story says that a man fell in love with a respectable married woman who was too modest and chaste to be seduced by him, so he consulted a magician who made anyone who looked at her think she was a horse. The Neuri were a tribe living north of Scythia. Herodotus (4.105) says that it was rumoured they practised a dangerous form of magic by turning themselves into wolves for a few days every year. This is more or less repeated by the geographer Pomponius Mela: *Chorographia* 2.14. Camden's information, however, is not of the same kind. The Irish, he says, claim they have wolves for their fathers. They call them 'Beloved of Christ', pray for them, make diligent supplication for them, and are therefore not afraid that wolves will be hostile, *Britannia* (Frankfurt 1590), 716. 'Beloved of Christ', which is a translation of Camden's Latin, should perhaps be 'Friends of Christ' if Camden's *chari* is meant to represent Irish Gaelic.

Guillaume de Paris.][54] Sometimes (and this is a fact derived from a number of people's confessions), he wraps actual people very tightly in genuine animal skins, and in this case he gives them a wolf's pelt which they are supposed to keep hidden in the hollow of a tree. Sometimes, in accordance with the pact he has made with them, he manufactures from air the likeness of an animal, surrounding the magicians (*magi*) with it, and builds the copy round each part of their body, fitting head to head, mouth to mouth, belly to belly, foot to foot, and arm to arm. He usually does this when the magicians apply certain ointments to themselves with a view to effecting this change (as in the case of Dolanus the lycanthrope, which has been published in judicial records), or when they merely use the words they have learned from him. [Examples given.]

Once the real body has been removed, the Devil wounds it in the same place he knows has been wounded in the animal body, and Bartolommeo della Spina gives us a contemporary illustration of this in chapter 16 of his *Quaestio de strigibus* (An Investigation into Witches).

'Another witness of this apparent transformation of witches (*striges*) into cats, an artisan from Ferrara by the name of Filippo, made the following declaration to me earlier this year in court under oath. Three months previously, he said, a certain witch (*strix*) had undertaken to cure his son of a bewitchment (for which, incidentally, she herself may have been responsible), and made him agree that he would not stop her from coming to his son if he were to see any cats[55] fawning around him or behaving in a playful fashion. Well now, that same day, an hour after she had left the house, Filippo and his wife noticed a large female cat they had never seen before, trotting towards the boy. This frightened them and they made several attempts to drive it away, but were distressed to see she kept coming back, until finally they lost both their patience and their temper. So they closed the door and, while the cat raced round, looking all over the place for a way of escape, Filippo threw his spear at her. It took him more than one attempt, but at last he landed her a very heavy blow which finally forced her to hurl herself out of a window high up in the wall. The result was that her body appeared to have been completely flattened. Now, from that very moment, the elderly witch I mentioned[56] was confined to her bed for a good long time, since every bone in her body had been broken, something which made the parents more or less certain (where before they had been merely suspicious) that the woman was indeed a witch and had subjected their

---

[54] Dominican inquisitor, died *c.* 1312. His principal work was *Postilla super epistolas et evangelia* (Notes on the Epistles and Gospels).
[55] The text makes it clear these are female.
[56] *Strix illa vetula.* Strictly speaking, *vetula* refers to an age less than *vetus* = 'old'. In Classical Latin, it tends to imply what we would call 'middle-aged'.

son to the enchantment which was draining him of his strength. For the marks of the heavy blows the cat had received, looking like the marks one finds on the bodies of those who are sick, were found on the elderly woman.'

Not quite five years ago, in a village in the west of Flanders, not far from Diksmuide, very near the confluence of the Iperlae and the IJzer, while a magical plague was expanding in remarkable fashion,[57] I happened to hear the following story from a devoutly religious man, well worthy of belief, who was in the neighbourhood at the time.

A peasant and his son were drinking in an ale-house and the man noticed, out of the corner of his eye, that the trollop[58] was chalking up double the amount of ale when (as is their custom) he drank a toast to her. He pretended not to notice, but when he and his son had had enough, he summoned the taverner, asked her for his bill, and was charged the sum marked up in chalk. He refused to pay and the two of them exchanged blows; then, flinging down on the table the amount he knew was correct, he left. Boiling with indignation, the woman called out, 'You will not have the power to reach your house today, or I am not the woman I am!' But he paid no heed to her threats and went on his way.

When he reached the stream where he had left his boat, however, neither he nor his son (who was pretty strong), could shift it from the bank, even though they leaned on their poles with all their strength. It was as though it had been nailed down in the mud. Now, it so happened that two or three soldiers were marching past, so the peasant hailed them. 'Come and help us get this boat off the bank, mates.[59] I'll pay you for it and you can have a big drink on me'. They answered his call, came along, and pushed as hard as they could; but for a long time they pushed in vain. Then one of them, sweating and gasping for breath, said, 'Why don't we unload all this stuff from the boat? Perhaps we'll find it easier to get it down to the water if it's empty'. So they emptied the boat of its load. But then (mark this!) they saw a huge sallow toad in the bottom of the boat, looking at them with glittering eyes. One of the soldiers, rather than pick up the toad, drilled a hole in it with the point of his sword, as far as its swollen throat, and threw it into the water. There, apparently

---

[57] *Fascinaria pestis mire gliscit.* 'Fascinaria' indicates that the plague had been caused by magical means, through the evil eye in particular. The verb *glisco* means (a) distend, swell, and (b) increase in power or violence. Del Rio seems to have chosen the verb because of its association with buboes, the inflamed swellings symptomatic of one type of plague.

[58] *Copa.* In Classical Latin this refers to a woman who provides entertainment in drinking places. Hence her reputation was tainted.

[59] *Contubernales boni.* A 'contubernalis' was actually someone who shared a tent, a comrade-in-arms, or one of two cohabiting slaves.

dead, it rolled over on to its back, belly upwards. The other soldiers wounded it still further while it floated, and suddenly the boat came free.

The peasant was very pleased and brought his helpers back to the same tavern he had left earlier, asked for a drink, and was served by a waitress. He asked after the taverner and was told she had become very ill and was in bed, dying. 'Stupid woman!' I said. 'Do you think I'm drunk? I left her standing over there scarcely half an hour ago, and she was in good health and a nasty frame of mind, just like yourself. I'm going to go and see what's going on'. He went into the bedroom and found that the woman had died of wounds which had slashed and ripped open her neck and stomach. 'How did she get these wounds?' he exclaimed. The waitress insisted she did not know and was sure the woman had not set foot outwith the house.

The case went before a magistrate who came to the conclusion that the wounds had been caused by both slashing and stabbing blows, and that they had appeared in the very same places where the soldiers had struck the toad. The toad itself was nowhere to be found.

Question 19: Can magicians make animals speak, and can they understand what animals are saying?

[This section is largely given over to citations from and references to ancient and Mediaeval literature.]

Scripture shows that animals can sometimes speak if God gives them the power to do so. But for the most part I think the phenomenon takes place with the assistance of angels who speak via the animals, except in the case of magpies, crows, and parrots, etc. which can speak by nature. When it comes to voices from fire, air, water, dead bodies, severed heads, statues, and trees, however, the speech is the work of an angel. (Examples.) Sometimes, with God's permission, the Devil works a pseudo-miraculous trick. As for whether magicians understand animal speech, one must suppose they do so with the help of an evil spirit, not an angel, although they may also be able to interpret the movements of animals.

Question 20: Can an evil spirit bestow upon animals the ability to reason?

[This depends on whether they are endowed with such a faculty in the first place. If they are, the evil spirit can easily make them understand something. If they are not, he cannot. Del Rio then discusses the matter and concludes that none of the best authorities credit animals with endowment of the power to reason and (following Girolamo Fracastoro)[60] that animals do what they do largely by instinct.]

Question 21: Can evil spirits deprive a person of feeling, or make him sleep for a very long time, or do without food?

[With regard to the first part, the question is not whether an evil spirit can deprive a body of its power to feel, but whether he can deprive of feeling something which is naturally able to feel: for example, the body of someone undergoing torture. (Examples from both ancient and later literature discussed.) 'Every day, workers of evil magic (*malefici*) make light of the severity of the pains they suffer on the rack. They overcome them all with laughter or sleep or silence'. (Examples, including an incident of 1599 related to Del Rio by the Jesuit Provincial in Belgium.) Some people attribute this to the witches' ointment; others to a miracle. Others take it to be a sign of their innocence; others to unusual strength of mind and body, and others to the use of narcotic substances. Most people, however, attribute it to magic worked with the help of an evil spirit. (Examples given.) But narcotics can also be used to make people sleep for a long time. (Examples.) As for the ability to go without food, there is no doubt that an evil spirit can make this happen. (Examples.)]

Question 22: Can magical arts operating with the help of evil spirits change one sex into the other?

[References to and examples from ancient and more recent literature, tending to show that this kind of thing can happen naturally.]

Question 23: Can an evil spirit give an old man back his youth?

[The ancient stories of such a thing are false and repugnant to nature, since they involve the preliminary sacrifice of the old man. (Example.) But there are texts from the Scriptures, which suggest that rejuvenation is possible. Certain aspects of youthfulness can be restored. (Examples from recent literature.) A counter-argument is that human life has a term fixed by God. This, however, varies from person to person and God may permit wide variations. (Examples.) A stronger argument says that human life depends on a natural humidity which is maintained by food but diminishes over the years. It can be restored, but doctors do not think this can be done by their art or by nature. Del Rio replies

[60] Italian physician and poet (1483–1533). His complete works were published in Venice in 1574.

that if doctors do not know how to do this, it does not follow that an evil spirit is equally ignorant or has not the power to effect it, if God gives him permission. Moreover, if life can be extended by years, in theory, at least, it could be extended to eternity. But nature could not cope with this, and such a thing would be sinful.]

Question 24: What power does magic or an evil spirit have over a soul which is joined to a body and animates it?

[(1) An evil spirit can deceive the senses. (2) He can use the imagination to create fantasies of various kinds. (References given, and a quotation from Mattioli.) (3) He disturbs the senses and humours in order to cause sinful thoughts. (References to Protestant literature.) (4) He assists the memory to retain sinful thoughts. (References to Holy Scripture, ancient, and later literature.) (5) One can restore one's intellect and the rest of one's constitution to a more desirable working order by various means, including medicines and purges.]

These evil spirits (*mali isti daemones*) love to pour darkness into human minds by making the humours dense and the spirits (*spiritus*) few, stupid, and impure. They bestow upon their followers wicked potions (*pharmaca*) by means of which they cast down people from their right mind, something which often happens to those who have been besieged by evil spirits.[61] They lead people astray with misguided and wicked suggestions, persuading them of various things, quite incorrectly: at one time saying something is illicit, and at another that in fact it is allowed; or that something is a grave sin when in reality it is venial (the intention here being to torture people with scruples); or they drive home the idea that things which are contrary to right and law are actually just; or they say that things are contemptible and trivial when in fact they are lethal and ought to be feared strongly (this being done with a view to rendering the conscience lax and wanton.)

[Can an evil spirit teach the arts and sciences? He certainly can if he wishes and has God's permission to do so. He may appear in visible form or speak internally. Such instruction is either illumination or illusion. Modern Anabaptists, for example, eat and drink Holy Scripture and yet continue to think they are right to persist in their errors. Who teaches them, unless it be the Devil? (Quotations from Nider, with Del Rio's comments on them.) The Devil tried

---

[61] *Spiritus* here refers to those subtle highly-refined substances or fluids which were believed to permeate the blood and principal organs of the body. *Pharmaca* is a word borrowed from Greek and refers both to herbal remedies and, by extension, to some form of magical spell.

to deceive Saint Ignatius of Loyola, but failed. (Quotation from Saint Ignatius.) Now, if he could try to deceive such a saintly person, how much more easily would he have succeeded in teaching falsities to pagan minds? (References given.)]

Here are further examples of teaching received from the Devil. In March this year, 1600, in accordance with a decision made by the Inquisitors of the Faith, the bones of a certain Roman Ramirez, together with a statue, were burned to ashes at Toledo. Ramirez had died in prison while awaiting trial. He was accused among other things of having received knowledge of medicine from an evil spirit, and since this criminal united in his person several aspects of magic, I shall make it my business to translate the accusation faithfully from Spanish into Latin. He said he had already been accused once and abjured the Muslim error, but added that he had relapsed (as is the wont of dregs such as he), and returned to his vomit. For many years he had kept the great fast they call *Ramadan*, and observed the rites and ceremonies of Muhammad by first saying *guadoc* and *zála*, washing his whole body, putting on a clean outer garment, reciting the *azoras* (i.e. prayers) of that sect with his face turned to *al-quibla* (i.e. the East), raising and lowering his head and bowing himself down to the ground, extending his palms upwards to the sky while he was saying *Alaqueur* (i.e. 'God is great'), and rising before daybreak to celebrate the fast Zahor.[62] This absolved him of his sins and then he solemnly celebrated the feast[63] of *Ramadan* itself for three days. This he did by abstaining from all labour and servile work, especially on the first day, by putting on a clean outer garment, and by making the declaration *guadoc* and *zála*, along with many other Muslim rites and ceremonies. Then, adding crime to crime and sin to sin, he revived a pact or treaty, which he had made with an evil spirit many years before, with the intention of undertaking a wicked exploit. He worshipped this spirit, did him homage, and dedicated his soul to him on condition that the spirit assist him with favour and advice as often as he might be needed or asked in connection with anything at all. So Ramirez requested and obtained from the evil spirit a knowledge of and expertise in the cure of many secret, hidden (*occultae*) illnesses by means of herbs, fumigations, and superstitious incantations; and as a matter of fact he restored not a few people to health this way.

At the same time he persuaded people that he had a wide and detailed

---

[62] 'Guadoc' is probably a reference to the *shadah*, the declaration that there is no God but God and that Muhammad is his prophet. 'Zala' = *sala*, the five daily prayers of the devout Muslim. 'Azoras' = *ashurah*, readings from the Koran. 'Al-quibla' = *al-Qibla*, the direction faced by a Muslim while praying, i.e. towards the Ka'ba in Mecca. 'Alaqueur' = *Allah w'Akbar*, God is great. Zahor = *Zuhr*, actually the name of the midday prayer.

[63] Del Rio calls it 'Pascha', using the usual Latin word for Passover or Easter.

knowledge of both sacred and profane literature, and that he had a very good memory (since he plainly had no skill in reading or writing.) So he used to recite to others, word for word from memory (and quite openly for money), stories which were recited to him as if he were reading from a book open in front of him – something he did with the help of the evil spirit. In this way he amassed not a little power because of the money he was given by his audiences; and when someone asked him how he had acquired so reliable a memory, he replied that someone who had a very close association with him, a man highly skilled in the nature of herbs and who enjoyed the familiarity of an evil spirit, had given him some kind of drink. He also said that on one occasion, when this same person wanted to set out for Saragossa which was fifteen leagues away, he made a conjuration (*de bon y varon*, as they say),[64] and suddenly acquired a horse. They both mounted it and very soon arrived at the gates of the city where they left the horse and removed its bridle. Then they did the business for which they had set out, turned back to the gate, threw the harness on the horse again, and were brought back home almost at once.

Similarly, there was an incident which took place in the town of Deza. A woman was going to bed (angry, as it happened), and commended herself to an evil spirit. Suddenly, someone (she did not know who) removed her from that place. Her husband came to Ramirez and asked him for his help. Ramirez replied that the man should not be downcast and that he would restore his wife to him. He gave him a letter, telling him to go to a certain place among the vineyards, where he should make a circle, stand in the middle of it and when he heard a crowd of people passing through, he was to ask, 'Where will the King be?' If he was told that the King was crossing by that route, he should throw the letter to the ground in front of him. The man did as he was told and his wife was returned to him. But he did not see who brought her back or how it was done.

The procurator fiscal added that Ramirez used to say a good many very obscure things, including some which touched upon places very far away about which he could not have known anything except through his pact with an evil spirit.

[While Ramirez was away, someone came to ask for his help in freeing his daughter from an evil spirit. She had begun to show symptoms of possession on her wedding day, and seemed to hate both her parents and her new husband. A priest was called to exorcise her and the evil spirit told him that 101 spirits beside himself had infested the woman, but that they were now gone to Deza

---

[64] A phrase perhaps related to *buen varón*, 'a man who can be trusted, a man of good judgement, education, and experience'.

to meet Roman Ramirez. It was only he, the spirit said, who could order all the spirits to leave the woman. At this point, the parents summoned Ramirez to cure their daughter.]

The moment he entered the house, the woman began to say and do extraordinary things, crying out that she knew he had arrived, but did not know why he had come. Then, as he entered the room, she lost consciousness, her face became contorted, and she remained like this for three days without food or drink, having no power to move at all. The magician drenched her with a strong suffumigation of sandalwood, juniper oil, and other things, summoned her back from her fainting fit, and then addressed the spirit which had invested her.

'Leave her alone. Leave her alone and depart. Flee, unless you want me to repeat the suffumigation'.

The evil spirit was unwilling to reply, so Ramirez told everyone to leave the room and, thinking no one could hear him, he questioned the spirit and protested, 'Why don't you answer me? The spirit which attended my grandfather had more humility. What have I done for you to disdain to speak to me? Isn't it enough that I have sacrificed to you for such a long time? Now make this woman sleep so that she doesn't hear anything we say'.

[Ramirez went on to complain that he was in debt and needed money to pay for a garden he had contracted to have made and asked the spirits to leave the woman's body for fifteen days and leave her well and safe during that time, so that he could get paid by a grateful family. It was in the spirits' interest, he added, that he should continue to have a great reputation as an exorcising magician. They could possess the woman again later on, if they wished to do so.

But when Ramirez noticed that this conversation had been overheard, he threatened the spirit with violence unless he left, so the spirit departed. The woman's parents, however, did not pay him as much as he was expecting, so he threatened them with a return of the evil spirit and ordered other spirits to come and possess the woman's husband. This they did and afflicted him horribly. Summoned a second time, Ramirez then expelled these spirits by means of suffumigations, and here the anecdote ends.

Del Rio closes by adding a sixth point to those with which he began Question 24. The power of magic and evil spirits over the will, he says, is quite restricted and the spirits can succeed in overcoming it only by presenting it with constant enticements which inflame the imagination and the passions. They cannot force anyone to do anything against his will, and no one can sin unless he has consented to do so. Therefore Satan (unless God prevents him) works to engender this consent. God allows people to be tempted, but not beyond their capacity to resist. (References to Holy Scripture, early Mediaeval and later literature, with a long quotation from *The Life of Saint Angela de Foligno*.)] [65]

Question 25: What power does the Devil have over a soul which is to be separated from the body, and over the separation itself? Ecstasy, and extraordinary things which happen to dead bodies.

[The Devil can cause ecstasy by binding or loosing the exterior senses in one of two ways: (a) he blocks the paths by which the sensitive spirits reach the exterior senses, or (b) he attracts the spirits to the external organs of sense and then holds them there, unable to descend. This is a natural cause of rapture, easily within the Devil's power. This is how witches (*sagae*) and magicians (*magi*) fall into ecstasy, deceived by Satan into thinking they travel far and wide while actually they lie asleep. (Quotation from Olaus Magnus).[66] It is a mistake to think that people throw themselves into a magical trance. It is done through a pact with an evil spirit. (References to ancient and more modern literature are given and discussed.)

Death is a separation of the soul from the body. If this separation takes place, the person dies. Only God can separate the soul from the body by means of a trance and still keep the body alive. (References given and discussed, especially a work by the sixteenth century Marco Antonio Mocenigo, *De transitu hominis in Deum* [The Passage of Humankind to God]). The second type of separation of body and soul is death, which the Devil cannot effect save with God's permission. But when death has taken place, although the Devil cannot touch the soul, he does have power over the body. He can assume a corpse and appear in it. He can work wonders thereby, which astonish the ignorant: for example, making blood flow in the presence of the corpse's murderer.

Corpses may be preserved from decay by natural means (references), but the evil spirit knows how to do this, too. He can also keep both living and dead bodies from burning, and cause the hair and nails of a corpse to grow. (References.)

---

[65] Italian mystic (1248–1309). She is actually 'Blessed', not 'Saint'.

[66] (1490–1558). Swedish historian, Archbishop of Uppsala. His book, *Historia de gentibus septentrionalibus* (History of the Peoples of the North) was published in Rome in 1555.

Question 26: Can the power of evil spirits cause the souls or spirits of the dead to appear to the living?

Section 1

First conclusion: That the souls of the dead can and sometimes do appear to the living by virtue of God's power, you know is consistent with the tenets both of the Catholic faith and of genuine philosophy. [Proof: this was the common opinion among ancient writers.]

Section 2

[Those who believe nothing unless they see it, and in consequence believe nothing at all, are contradicted by the fact of God's power to make souls visible. Apparitions may be of three kinds: (a) *intellectual*, when separated beings appear only in one's mind, and appear as themselves, not under some other guise; (b) *imaginary* or *spiritual*, when separated souls appear to our inward senses under other forms which are recognisable to us; (c) *corporal*, when they appear to our external senses as physical images.]

Section 3

[It is appropriate and useful that God should sometimes allow this to happen.]

Section 4

[Authority, divine and human, tells us that such a thing can and does happen.]

Section 5

[The conclusions of Church Councils, the Fathers, and historians. Examples drawn in sequence from the first to the sixteenth centuries.]

Section 6

[Objections quickly reviewed.] [67]

Section 7

Second conclusion: Magicians make use of the power of evil spirits to show us the real souls of the dead.

---

[67] These four sections are quite long, but space prevents a detailed account of their argumentation.

Question 27: The appearances of evil spirits or the spectral images which evil spirits throw in our path

Section 1

[There are various causes of illusions, and there are various types of evil spirits. Many things are considered to be spectral images when in fact they are quite natural or the result of contrivance, and are caused by impairment of one's senses or one's physical weakness. *Ignes fatui* are natural, but frequently deceive people. So are islands which move from place to place. (Examples.) Vapours seem to take different shapes; places and objects produce noises. (Examples.) All these are either natural or artificial, but may be mistaken for evidence of spectral presence or activity. Compare, too, the remarkable automata of the ancient world (examples), and the artificial spectres created by illusionists (examples). An alteration or impairment in the sense-organs is also not an infrequent cause of 'apparitions' (references). The Devil is accustomed to make use of such natural frailties and abuse people's tendency to be credulous.]

Section 2

[There are various kinds of evil spirit and they have different desires and different ways of working. (References.) Psellus divides these spirits into six *genera*, which are here repeated with additional examples and comment: (1) belonging to fire; (2) belonging to air; (3) belonging to earth; (4) belonging to water; (5) belonging underground; (6) avoiding the light. Del Rio now describes eighteen of the different kinds of spirit, with references to Hebrew, Greek, and Latin, and accompanies his references with a large number of examples drawn from a very wide range of literature. The eighteen include *incubi*; frightening apparitions whose names are used by nurses to quieten children; those which manifest themselves as an animal such as a goat or a snake, or as soldiers grouped in platoons or lined up ready for battle; those which appear in the form of girls or women in woods or other pleasant places; those through whom God sometimes gives warning of plague or war; or who cause trouble because of the amount of noise they make; and those who are the guardians of hidden treasure.]

Question 28: How can an evil spirit make itself visible to eye of the flesh when it has no body?

[It is generally agreed that a spirit cannot do this unless he assumes a body. He either makes one from the elements or gets inside a corpse and uses that.]

Section 1

Sometimes, then, they assume the dead body of a human being or an animal and make it move. This they do, not by a motion which confers life upon it (vital motion), but only by a motion restricted in its area of operation (local motion) – the kind of motion whereby they can stir the air; and I think that if God permits it, they can so make adjustments to this body (especially one which is not too far decayed) that they can completely deceive the sense of touch, and I see nothing put forward in argument by any learned or pious person which persuades me otherwise. Take, for example, what the Lord says in Saint Luke [24.39] where he proves he really is in body and is not a spirit of the imagination. 'Handle me, and see; for a spirit has not flesh and bones as you see that I have'.

Now, this does not add much to our discussion, and certainly does not move it forward. The Lord merely wished to prove that they could feel him and distinguish him by touch; that their eyes were not deceiving them; that he actually did have a body which was real because it could be touched; and that it was not an unburied ghost clothed with a fictitious body. There was no question in this case of a body's having been assumed. It is clear he had flesh and bones, and by this Christ proved that he was not a spirit – something the disciples believed because they saw he had entered through closed doors, which a body cannot do, be it alive or dead; and because they could recognise by touch only that it *was* a body but not *whose* body it was, he told them to use their eyes and *see* – (this is the correct sense, as the text indicates) – his hands and feet; and from the wounds which were still there they were quite certain that this was the man who had been crucified three days before. So from this it is clear that the words of the Lord are true and credible, even if we were to say that the body had been assumed by an evil spirit and could be so modified by him that the sense of touch was deceived.

Well now, I ask you: does not the evil spirit do things every day far more astonishing than simulating the softness of flesh, the hardness of bones, the warmth and gentle heat and all the other qualities associated with touch which one notices when touching a body? I say he can *simulate* these qualities. He cannot produce real ones, those real vital characteristics which belong to a living body and proceed from its informing soul. Simulated characteristics, and those which approximate to the real thing, do not require an informing soul and can be constructed from the substance of the intellect, to the extent that they appear real to the external senses.

[I agree with those who say that even in a corpse so recently dead that it is still warm, the vital heat is missing and rigor mortis has begun to set in. But I do not agree with their conclusion regarding an evil spirit's ability to assume such a corpse. I think that in the case of such an assumption, the evil spirit is inside the corpse, *simulating* the signs of life. It is easier to do that than create real signs. So it does not follow that because a corpse, still warm, cannot furnish its own vital signs, therefore the evil spirit inside it cannot simulate those signs sufficiently to deceive the sense of touch. (References and examples.)]

Section 2

Sometimes the Devil surrounds himself with a body made from the elements, and once it has been formed by the power he has to do such a thing, he makes it one with him, just as a lifeless body capable of being moved is united to the mover existing inside it. I doubt whether he can choose his material simply from the air, and I do not think he can condense air alone to the point where he produces something solid. But whether he can or cannot, he usually finds it easy to mingle parts of air (the element he uses most), earth, water, cloud, vapour, and exhalations with the result that he easily produces colours from this mixture and easily condenses them into parts of a body and makes them stick together. [References given from Scripture, and ancient and modern literature.]

At this point one must make a distinction. When evil spirits appear in a real corpse, they cannot surround that corpse with a second, living body and neither can they assume any other body when they are wearing a dead one. Physical laws are against it because the spirits cannot penetrate those dimensions which govern size. But when they appear in an elemental body, either they cannot assume another corpse or body at all, or they can do so only with very great difficulty. (I incline to the former opinion.) However, they can surround a real, living body with this elemental body so that it seems to be a human body, or an animal bigger and more gigantic than the real one. I see no reason why this cannot be so, for the argument that air has the ability to expand and become less solid, or to thicken and become dense is persuasive.

[Very occasionally, evil spirits may also manifest themselves in small statues. (Quotation from Thomas of Cantimpré.)]

Section 3

It is popularly believed that there is always something about the appearance of the bodies which have been assumed by evil spirits, which indicates that they constitute a demonic apparition, and I would be quite prepared to believe that this is true. But I think that if the evil spirits are not stopped by a greater power, they can appear in whatever shape they wish and manifest a perfect human form, handsome – indeed, beautiful in every detail.

[The rest of the section gives examples from a wide variety of sources.]

Section 4

Finally, to perform ceremonies intended to make evil spirits appear to us or to show us the souls of the dead (something they cannot actually do) is in no way permissible and, indeed, is a mortal sin. [References.]

Question 29: Can the Devil really make a man rise from the dead?

Section 1

[References to ancient and modern literature refer to ways in which the dead can be revived.]

(1) I think that animals which are born from putrefying matter can, once they are dead, be revived by an evil spirit using natural remedies. [References to relevant literature.]

(2) I think that an evil spirit cannot restore to life the more perfect living beings which are not born from decaying matter. This is because these require certain more perfect arrangements of their material and a more careful preparation of each organ, which cannot be achieved except by the natural power of semen. [References.]

(3) I think that an evil spirit cannot make the soul of a dumb animal animate another body. This is because individual souls of this kind produced from the potentiality of matter die if you separate them from their own matter. But what about a human being?

(4) I think that an evil spirit has very little or no power to do such a thing. He cannot make a person rise from the dead. He cannot make a person's soul enter its own body and give it life and shape.

[He himself cannot inform the body, nor can he direct into it for this purpose a human soul which has been separated from its body. Only God can do such a thing. But an evil spirit can, with God's permission, introduce a damned soul into the body to move it and make it perform certain actions. Because of the pact they have made with evil spirits, magicians (*magi*) can use superior demons to compel inferior demons to do their bidding, with the intention of making them enter a body and cause it to move. (Example from Agrippa.)]

Section 2

[This section consists largely of references to ancient literature on the subject of resuscitation, and then a long quotation from Rémy.]

From these examples of the evil spirit's fraudulent work is born a particularly ridiculous belief among witches (*striges*). They hold that sometimes the oxen or the rams which they have killed, boiled or roasted, and then eaten are sometimes brought back to life afterwards in the twinkling of an eye by the evil spirit. It is not difficult to discover the various ways the evil spirit is able to do this.

First, he can close the eyes of witnesses by sending into them a humour or some other sense-impression, or by agitating the spirits in the imaginative faculty and bringing them in this state to the senses in general and to the organs of the external senses, whither images and semblances impressed thereon by agitation of the spirits and the object of the sense-impression, normally descend. There, these semblances are usually held back, and when the process of apprehending them has once started, it is shifted about so often that the exterior sense thinks it is equally affected and genuinely altered as though by an external object. It is the kind of thing which usually happens to a sleeper in his dreams, but the Devil can make it happen to people while they are awake, because the physical organs obey incorporeal substances as far as local motion is concerned. (See Saint Thomas Aquinas.)

Secondly, he can do this by substituting one thing for another. For what prevents the evil spirit from taking away the dead ox, along with its skin and bones, and putting a live ox in its place, and doing this so quickly that the speed of the exchange is not seen by the bystanders? Meanwhile, as he is taking away the corpse and replacing it with another ox, he can interpose a cloud or some other piece of trickery so that the bystanders do not see that the place is empty and the ox has been taken away.

Thirdly (as Spina says is confessed by several witches [*striges*]), he can bring it about that when the King or Queen of the journey or assembly[68] takes a stick and strikes the pelt in which the bones have been collected and piled up, all of a sudden some evil spirit gets underneath the skin, joins everything together, assembles the pieces, alters the skin so that it assumes the shape of the ox, lifts it up in the air, and then guides its movements so that it looks as though the original ox has been resuscitated.

Fourthly, he can form a complete ox's body from air, with new skin and new bones; or he can put together another body from air along with the remaining bones and attach it to the rest of the skin, and when it is required he can keep it intact under the skin, move it, and make it walk and low. When necessary he can also withdraw from it, and then it will look as though the ox has collapsed and died. 'This is why', says Spina, 'witches (*striges*) maintain, as a group, that after such oxen (which they believe have been resuscitated) are brought back to their masters' byres by command of the Lord or Mistress of the journey, they die within three days, as if some wasting disease were shrivelling

---

[68] I.e. the leader of the witches during their transvection or at the sabbat.

them up in a matter of hours, and that after a while what seemed to be quivering flesh quickly breaks up into the material it was before'. (*Quaestio de strigibus*, chapter 7).

[A final word on miraculous resuscitations.]

Question 30: What power does magic have over the evil spirits (*cacodaemones*) themselves?

Section 1

[Ancient books on this subject have perished. In the case of good spirits or angels, Del Rio thinks they have some natural power to coerce, or at any rate restrain wicked spirits. But they cannot do this indiscriminately in the case of demons inferior to themselves, and when it comes to demons of equal or superior rank, they can act only upon God's command or with his permission. The same can be said of the power wielded by one set of evil spirits over another. (References.) But whereas good angels submit to their superiors, evil spirits do not submit to theirs except perforce and with ill grace because, although there is rank and degree among them, it lacks that formal structure which allows an efficient, effective chain of command to operate. (References.) Magicians who wage magical war against each other in an attempt to damage or destroy each other rely upon the power of evil spirits, and their battles are similar to those waged between such spirits. (Illustrative anecdotes follow.)]

Section 2

Holy people have very often received from God an extraordinary power to keep evil spirits under control, as is attested by innumerable miracles whereby they have conquered and crushed them. The same power has always invested the sacraments, sacramentals, and exorcisms of the Catholic Church.

[The rest of the section illustrates these points with reference to a wide variety of literature.]

Section 3

There is no physical thing which has the power directly and of itself to coerce an evil spirit to appear, come, depart, do anything, or cease doing something. For no physical thing can equal the strength of substances which are both spiritual and separate. Therefore evil spirits cannot suffer anything from these naturally, although they can do so supernaturally. Hence I do not agree with magicians when they talk about various natural remedies against evil spirits, as Hermes [Trismegistus] does when he tells us that evil spirits are brought together by means of a suffumigation of aloe wood or whale-sperm, or made to flee by a suffumigation of sulphur. (See also Porphyrius and Proclus who pass on many similar pieces of nonsense, and someone quoted by Hippocrates, who records even more inane foolishness.) I do not agree with heretics who say that exorcisms and consecrated objects have no supernatural power, and make a great fuss about them.

But neither can one approve of the credulousness and superstitious behaviour of certain Catholics who ascribe supernatural power to things which have not been consecrated, such as *hypericum*,[69] rue, horn, goat's dung, baths, and whippings, and think that if they use these the evil spirit is adversely affected and thus he is annoyed or driven away. Whipping the body in this fashion may well cause, and intensify, an illness; so someone who is sick will just make himself worse. What is more, anger and sadness serve to increase those states of melancholia, which the evil spirit wishes to encourage. So while stupid people want to harm the evil spirit by doing things like this, they actually give him help.

[There is nothing in any of these 'remedies' which can distress an evil spirit. When the saints flogged themselves, they had an effect because they were permitted to work a miracle. Baths may help because they purge the melancholic humour. Rue and *hypericum* are extremely useful for treating wind. Dung and goat's horn dispel wind, too, because their smoke is acrid. Evil spirits often possess people who have too much black bile. Consequently certain mineral or herbal remedies may have an effect. (Examples and references.) The Biblical story of David's calming Saul by playing the harp does not provide a precedent. The music soothed the agitation of Saul's humours and thus rendered him a less suitable object for demonic possession. Nor can evil spirits be caught and trapped in bottles or rings, as poets would have us believe. (References.) Del Rio then quotes Alonso Tostado to the effect that evil spirits cannot be coerced by human beings into doing anything, the only exception to this being ecclesiastical exorcisms, and the section ends with quotations and references designed to illustrate these points.]

[69] The name of various species of St John's wort.

BOOK 3

Harmful magic and superstition

Part 1: Harmful magic

Question 1: What is harmful magic, and how many different kinds are there?

I am not arguing about whether it exists or not. I take for granted that it does. Those who deny this are contradicted by the precepts of Holy Scripture, canon and civil law, and by historians, poets, common belief, and the testimony of all past ages. No branch of magic delights the evil spirit more because, as Synesius says, 'the disasters of humankind are food and drink to evil spirits'. By the word *malefice*,[1] however, I do not mean just any kind of injury or sin, but rather a magical, superstitious sign or effect. The person who employs malefice is called *maleficus*, and the person who is injured by it is called *maleficiatus*. So it can be described as follows: 'Malefice is a type of magic by which an evil spirit intends to harm another individual'.

I have said 'a type of magic' in order to restrict what is rather a broad term to this kind of harmful activity, and I have added 'by which some evil spirit' because if a pact or a treaty with the evil spirit were lacking, there would be no point in the subject's appearing in this treatise, any more than murder, rape of a virgin, theft, or larceny. Malefice can be subsumed under two headings: 'Intention' and 'Efficient Cause'. By 'efficient cause', I do not mean 'the permission granted by God', or 'the evil spirit who carries it out', or 'the depraved free will of the evil magician who agrees to receive help from an evil spirit and co-operates with him', because these three things always go together in every act of malefice. For not a hair of one's head can fall with God's permission; nor can an evil spirit do more harm than God allows; nor can he bring to a conclusion what he is allowed to do unless the worker of harmful

---

[1] This technical term will now be employed instead of 'harmful magic'. It translates the word *maleficium* which is often employed for 'witchcraft' as, indeed, Del Rio very frequently employs it here. But since he is discussing magic as a whole, I have preferred to use a technical term which includes witchcraft but also permits the reader to refer it also to the wider concept of harmful magic.

magic (*maleficus*) consents to the malefice. This last point is manifestly in sacrilegious imitation of Almighty God who requires the consent of the minister so that he can grant salvation through the ministration of the sacraments. That such an intention on the part of the worker of harmful magic is a prerequisite is shown by the fact that we see that the touch or powders of witches (*striges*) harm only those the witches wish to harm, as many examples from Rémy demonstrate; and indeed this is certainly true of the instruments of magic (*maleficia*) which are not composed of natural poisons. So, by 'efficient causes' I mean the instruments and material whereby people may be injured, which act together to harm without the need for an intermediary.

1) Witches do harm by means of certain very fine powders which they mix in food or drink, or rub on a naked body, or scatter over clothes. The powders which kill are black; those which simply cause illness are ash-coloured (or sometimes reddish-brown), whereas the powder which removes a spell and acts as a medicine is exceptionally white. The virtue of these powders, however, does not come from their colour or from any other quality, but is entirely dependent on a pact made with an evil spirit. The colours merely serve to clarify the intentions of those who attend the sabbats, so that the witches (*striges*) may not make any mistake about which one should be used for which purpose ('what for what', as the saying goes). Hence one may conclude that the white powder used by one witch as medicine often proves lethal in the hands of a second, and the ash-coloured powder used by one to bring disease brings death when employed by another. What is more, one and the same witch (*saga*) may use the powder to bring death on one occasion and to cure illness on another. It all depends on the way the evil spirit is pleased to change its signification. [References.]

2) They work malefice with herbs, pieces of straw, and other rubbish such as that. This they do by throwing them on the ground, and when the person against whom they wish to work malefice walks over them, he will most certainly fall sick or die.

3) They use white or dull red ointments which have the consistency of tar. Droplets of white and bright yellow metal are mixed in with these ointments, which causes them to shine, and if you throw the ointment on the fire, it sparks and crackles, and emits a strong smell which is unlike anything else. Many witches always have some of it smeared on their hands so that no opportunity of doing harm may slip past them. The ointment is lethal if it rubs off on you or if it touches your outer garments.

4) They poison people merely by breathing or blowing on them. This is how they are accustomed to cause miscarriages, as well as very great danger to life. [References.]

5) They cause immense harm with words alone, as Lucan says: 'Even when the mind has not been polluted by any poisonous oozing, it dies after it has been enchanted'. Vergil says: 'They have mingled herbs and words which are not without harmful intention'. There can be no doubt this is what the evil spirit has taught them. Therefore Ovid refers to the incantations of Hecate: 'At once she pounded together herbs well-known to cause harm and juices which inspire terror, and when she had blended these together she added the incantations of Hecate'. Seneca lists a good many poisons in his *Medea*: 'To the poisons she adds words which are to be feared no less than they'.[2] The extraordinary thing is that sometimes they harm people by means of threats alone, or with loud, violent complaining – although I believe that this was not the way of the pagans. They used to wear a wreath round their heads while they caroused in order to counteract this particular evil. No, the practice belongs to our age, as experience has proved. Nevertheless, I maintain (and I emphasise) that all these things are accomplished, not by any power in the words, but by the operation of the Devil as a sign of his agreement and approval.

6) They do not hesitate to use sacred things. For example, a witch touched the holy water sprinkler with her powders, aspersed another woman with holy water, and thereby made her ill. (See Rémy.)

Finally, some witches proceed more openly, and with the help of an evil spirit cause someone to be strangled or to drop down dead. They suffocate very small children during the night by smothering them with the mattress; or they kill them by thrusting a needle behind their ear, as the midwife Helvetia did, according to Sprenger's account.[3] They snatch children from the cradle and rend them in pieces; or they use them to make their ointments, as I have said elsewhere; or they eat them, a food they find very pleasing. [Examples from Classical and early Christian literature.] Sometimes they drop poison upon the children, and this either makes them die at once or causes them to waste away after a little while. Sometimes, too, they suck out their blood. This is the origin of the ancient belief about a bird, also known as the *strix*, which gnashes its teeth. For example, Quintus Serenus: 'Moreover, if the dark *strix* presses down upon little children, squirting rank milk from its teats on the lips which are turned towards it'; while Ovid, in the following verses, accepts another theory: 'They fly at night, seeking children without a nurse, and despoil their bodies

---

[2] Lucan: *De Bello Civili* 6.457–8. Vergil: *Georgics* 3.283. Ovid: *Metamorphoses* 14.43–44. Seneca: *Medea* 738–9. Seneca's word for poison, *venenum*, also carries the implication of 'magical herb'.

[3] Jakob Sprenger (floruit 1500), German Dominican, Inquisitor of Cologne. He is credited with being part-author, along with Heinrich Krämer (Institoris), of *Malleus Maleficarum* (The Hammer of Women Who Work Harmful Magic), first published in *c.* 1485/6.

after snatching them from their cradles. They are said to pluck the entrails out of the sucklings with their beaks, and their throats are filled with the blood they drink'.[4]

[Del Rio now gives more examples drawn from ancient literature, followed by a brief discussion of Hebrew words for this type of witch, and further points about the passage quoted from Ovid.]

These days they do not so much pretend to be nurses as take the appearance of wild animals and attack those children who are left unguarded and suck out their lives along with their blood while they are asleep; or they kill them with a poison which makes them waste away.

Question 2: Malefices which cause sleep

[This question deals with the various ways in which someone can be put to sleep by a potion, or incantation, or rituals designed for that purpose. Witches do this so that they can poison people, steal infants, kill them, or steal, or rape, or commit adultery. Magicians (*magi*) may use natural soporifics (examples given); but for the most part they employ magical methods. Examples taken from a wide variety of literature are then given. Del Rio describes a particular magical device, 'the hand of glory', which consists of a hand removed from a corpse, whose fingers are rubbed with fat and then set alight, and then he ends with further accounts of magical activities, taken from Binsfeld and Rémy.]

Question 3: Malefices which cause love

Section 1

[Del Rio begins with philtres and discusses the various names they are given by Classical and Mediaeval authors. He then turns to 'contemporary malefices of this kind', and gives a long quotation from Paolo Grillando's book on witchcraft.[5] In this Grillando describes three kinds of love-magic. (1) Philtres, which consist of mixtures of various substances such as the Host, consecrated or unconsecrated, menstrual fluid, semen, human dung, herbs, leaves, roots, human hair, nail-clippings, and pieces of material which have touched the body of the person to be bewitched. Where possible, these are reduced to powder and introduced into the person's food or drink. (2) Ligatures, which may be put in the intended victim's clothing, or concealed under a pillow, the threshold

---

[4] Serenus = Serenus Sammonicus, *Liber Medicinalis*, 1035–6. Ovid: *Fasti* 6.135–8.

[5] *Tractatus de hereticis et sortilegiis omnifariam coitu eorumque penis* [Treatise on heretics and witches, their presence everywhere, and the punishments they should receive], Lyons 1536.

of a doorway – anywhere, in fact, over which the intended victim, male or female, is likely to pass. Other objects mentioned as suitable for this purpose are water from the font, holy oil, blessed olive or palm branches, candles, an Agnus Dei, incense, Paschal wax, relics, sacred vestments, or altar cloths. (3) Images of various kinds. These are addressed with invocations and prayers to the Devil. (Illustrative passages from John of Salisbury, Vergil, and Ovid are added at this point.) This magic is of two kinds: that which intends to kill the victim, and that which is intended to provoke love. (Examples from Classical and modern literature, and a quotation from the Oratorian, Thomas Bossius.)]

Section 2

First: these philtres cannot bend the will of anyone to love a person he does not want to love. But the imagination can certainly be stirred up, the humours excited, and the whole interior of the body set, as it were, on fire to such an extent that, while the evil spirit strives to gain the upper hand by means of various alluring temptations, the body is troubled by a frenzy of lust and is thus forcefully dragged towards the desire for sexual intercourse with someone or other; and if at that moment a lover comes along, armed with maleficent magic, and uses the arts by which silly women are usually captivated, he may press hard his attack on her at once; or the evil spirit may take such pains to stir her memory and fantasy with regard to that special man – pointing out to her the particular reasons he ought to be deemed worthy of love, and removing from her other reasons which might make her think him unworthy – that the prey falls into the trap.

So this is how and why the Devil can deceive people by means of this type of magic. The man or woman in the street, however, cannot distinguish between the actions of the will, the movements of lust, and the impulses of their lower nature. Consequently one need not believe those people, male or female, who offer as an excuse that their will has been coerced, that they really do not want to do such a thing and that they would like to abstain, when actually they want to commit the sin. [Literary references given.]

Secondly, there are many drugs which have a natural power to stir up the humours, excite the semen, and heat the whole body. But if he cannot find any of these, the evil spirit can use anything he likes and then, according to the pact he has made, he can without any external assistance induce in the body turmoil, flatulence, itching, and heat; and at the same time he can expel from a woman's imagination any suggestion that she is worthy to be loved (if it comes from a woman whose suit he does not approve), and bend her imagination to love someone else. But he can bend only someone who is willing to be swayed; for the evil spirit has no jurisdiction over the will, and cannot compel it, because of the freedom granted to human beings to make their own decisions.

[There are many examples of this type of magic both in ancient and Patristic literature. (References.) Del Rio also refers to Scripture, Herodotus from whom he quotes in a Latin version, Vergil, and other Classical authors; and the rest of the section discusses the harm which such philtres can do to the human mind and body, his comments being supported by many references to and quotations from Classical, Patristic, and later literature.]

Section 3

[This section is devoted to a discussion of remedies to counter the effects of such magic, many of which are ineffectual. Del Rio quotes from and refers to a very wide range of relevant literature from Classical times to the modern period.]

Question 4: Hostile malefice

By 'hostile', one means anything which damages the properties of the mind, the body, or circumstances of life, or is likely to damage them, or has been provided by a worker of harmful magic (*maleficus*) for that purpose, such a malefice being hostile in act, in power, and in intention. The things which are used in this magic are for the most part, cold, bitter, harmful, and opposed to human nature and salvation.[6] This is why Grillando calls them *mala venena*, 'wicked poisons/spells'. He thinks it is the opposite in amatory magic whose principal ingredients (he says) are hot, sweet, and pleasant to humankind, assist natural heat and the power to fornicate, and in consequence are known in law as *bona* not *mala venena*, 'good poisons/spells, not bad ones', because they are not intended to kill people. Those who have read the previous Question carefully will easily be persuaded that this is not always true.

Section 1: Enchantment (*Fascinatio*) [7]

[Del Rio says that the concept should be seen as having three different meanings: (a) the poetic or popular (b) the philosophical, and (c) the magical.]

---

[6] Or 'personal safety'. The word is *salus* which can refer to either. The ambiguity should be noted in view of Del Rio's reference during the next two sentences to *venenum* which may mean 'herb used in magic', 'poison', or 'spell'.

[7] The Latin word means 'an evil spell' and 'a phallic talisman'. It may be compared with the Greek *baskanos* which is related to notions of slander and bewitching by means of the evil eye. Ancient writers linked the two words (although there does not appear to be any actual etymological connection), and Del Rio follows their example later in this section.

The first is particularly open to argument. According to this usage, people are said to be enchanted by the sight or the active aspect of the enchanter, or even by some malevolent individual who praises them, the enchantment happening simply because he glances at them in a malignant or malicious way, or praises someone else with whom the first individual is at odds. This opinion has spawned a good many others. For example, they say that this danger threatens those who are beautiful rather than those who are ugly, and children rather than adults. Secondly, they say that the danger is removed by use of certain auspicious words, especially if these are addressed, in accordance with required ceremony, to those on whom the enchanters look with praise and admiration. The danger may also be removed, they say, if children wear some kind of rather indecent object round their necks – which is why the word *fascinum*, 'spell', has been applied to the penis, because little pendants such as these are worn to ward off enchantment. This custom has been modified so that the children wear something slightly more respectable – an amulet made of lignite, ivory, or silver, and depicting two fingers with the thumb stuck in between in such a way as to express more or less the original idea. You can see it today in Spain, where it is called a *higa*;[8] and if someone points his fingers in this fashion at a person who is getting up very early in the morning, people think this takes the place of the amulet. If you bind your forehead with *baccar*,[9] or if you spit three times into your chest, or if, while you are scoffing expensive food, you hold out some of it to anyone who is staring at you, you will be acting with a view to averting any bad luck and to make sure no one will be able to enchant you.

[References to and quotations from ancient literature. Del Rio goes on to condemn as ridiculous various attempts which have been made to explain how such enchantment works, and cites ancient authorities, Plutarch in particular, to illustrate his points.]

So with reference to this particular form of enchantment which I have called 'poetic' or 'popular' and which is supposed to take place through an alliance of sight and an ill-willing imagination (as the Greek word for it indicates),[10] then I say it is something not natural but incredible and superstitious. [Supporting references.]

Second conclusion: philosophical or natural enchantment cannot really be called 'enchantment'. It is, rather, 'contagion' or 'infection'.

---

[8] I.e. a rude sign or gesture.
[9] An unidentified aromatic plant, possibly a kind of cyclamen.
[10] I.e. *baskanos*.

[Del Rio now discusses inflammation of the eyes, which is said to be spread simply by the exchange of looks, and he quotes Ovid and Plutarch in support, adding his own comments to long quotations from Plutarch. 'To him this kind of enchantment is like a series of injuries caused by contact and rubbing – in other words, a kind of natural contagion'. A quotation (in Latin translation) from a novel by the third century AD Greek writer Heliodorus underlines the point. Del Rio then turns to philosophers, theologians, and doctors, but expresses one or two reservations about what they say. In the case of menstruating women's contaminating mirrors, for example, he asks, when spirits (*spiritus*) or vapours convey contagion to the mirror, are these virulent spirits emitted by the eyeball itself? Or do they carry contagion via the cavities and angles of the eye, through which eye-infections exude? Del Rio inclines to the latter explanation. His remarks include references to Valesius, Pliny, and Richardus.[11] Women may be dangerous to men, he adds, because they seduce them by means of their conversation, their looks, or wanton behaviour. He then discusses Abulensis,[12] with whose judgements he largely agrees, on the subject of popular notions of enchantment; for example, that so-called 'popular' enchantment has a physical basis and is grounded in the mistaken Platonic notion that sight happens through the emission of rays from the eyes; and that certain creatures are naturally endowed with the power to hurt others, including humans, who do harm only when the requisite agencies operate together. Del Rio gives references to writers on 'philosophical' enchantments and then turns to the question, 'Should one call the harmful power which is gathered by the spirits (*spiritus*) from a corrupted humour "enchantment"?' which is followed by a discussion of the etymology of the word 'enchantment (*fascinatio*), relating it to the Greek *boskanos*.]

Third conclusion: a third and more frequent type of enchantment depends on the malefice of an evil spirit co-operating with a witch (*strix*) or a sorcerer (*sortiarius*) who wishes to do harm, and has made a pact with him. It can be defined as a pernicious characteristic produced by the skill of an evil spirit because of a tacit or overt pact made between a human being and an evil spirit.

[A wide range of literature is cited and quoted to support this point. Eyes which have the power to bewitch may have double pupils, or the likeness of

---

[11] Valesius = Francisco de Vallés (1525–1592), Spanish physician. Del Rio later refers to his *Sacra Philosophia* (Sacred Philosophy) which was published in Frankfurt in 1600. Ricardus Anglicus (floruit 13th century), English doctor and alchemist. He wrote a book on anatomy (*Anatomia*) between c. 1242 and 1252, but this was not published until long after his death.
[12] Abulensis (adjective meaning 'from Avila') = Alfonso de Madrigal Tostado de Rivera (died 1455), Spanish theologian and historian, Bishop of Avila.

a horse or a dog can be seen in them – marks which show that Satan has signed the enchanter as one of his own. Women arrested in recent times have had in their eyes the mark of a bitch's paw or a toad's foot.]

It is a common notion that all magical trickery should, by way of metaphor, be called 'enchantment'. This is the sense of the title of Jacquier's book, *Flagellum Fasciniorum* (The Scourge of the Enchanters),[13] and of the saying that judges are 'enchanted' by witches (*striges*). On this point, German inquisitors[14] write as follows: 'There are women who work harmful magic (*maleficae*) who know how to bewitch judges simply by looking at them with a single glance of their eyes. But they cannot do them any harm'. [This is followed by a second quotation from the same source.] In my opinion, however, God does not allow this to happen to faithful judges who proceed according to proper form and in accordance with justice. Those judges, however, who are unjust, not strong in their faith, or curious, may be affected.

It now remains to be seen whence comes the common idea that enchantment springs from a person's eyesight because of someone is being praised. I like Francisco de Vallés's idea that perhaps it happens because men and women usually take more notice of children who are somewhat plumper than usual, have a healthier sheen to their faces, and are prettier than normal. People praise such children, and stroke them, handle them, and cradle them in their arms. [Quotations from Hippocrates and Celsus.] So when, as often happens, these children (who have hitherto given every appearance of being in the best of health), happen to fall into some great misfortune of life, the common people do not understand the reason for such a sudden change and, because they do not understand, suspect some evil-doing and throw the blame for it upon the eyes and words of those who look at the children and praise them. Every day plump, pretty little children attract such looks and praises, and since it is easy to find some wrinkled, misshapen old woman among their admirers, and since this kind of person is physically offensive, morose, and hateful, the harm is attributed to her rather than to anyone else.

Section 2: Malefices involving poisons

[Del Rio, with the help of a large number of references and quotations, discusses *veneficia*, methods by which witches can do harm with the help of poisons applied in a variety of ways.]

---

[13] Nicholas Jacquier (floruit 16th century), French Dominican. His book was published in Frankfurt in 1581.
[14] He means Sprenger and Krämer, authors of the *Malleus Maleficarum*.

Section 3: Abortion, difficult birth, drying up of milk

[References to and quotations from literature dealing with these manifestations of witchcraft. Del Rio includes two passages from Johann Beetz's *Commentary on the Ten Commandments*,[15] the first of which runs: 'An old woman, full of wicked days, wishing out of envy to stop the milk of her neighbour's cow, took a knife, went to the opening of the byre where the cow was and, facing away from the moonlight, said,

"Hier snydick een spaen in mollekens ghevvaen,
Ende een ander daer toe, so neem ick het milck van deserkoe."[16]

The owner of the cow heard these words, snatched up a stick and ran after the woman, and while he beat her, he said,

"Hier slaen ick eenen slach, ende eenen anderen als ick mach,
Ende den derden daer toe, soo behoudick d'melck metter koe."[17]

This was the best remedy.'

Further examples given.]

Section 4: The arrows of the Assassins, and the maleficent makers of images

[Del Rio describes a class of workers of harmful magic, known as *sagittarii* (archers) or *balistarii* (slingers), anathematised by Innocent III. He refers the reader to Sprenger, Binsfeld, Olaus Magnus, and other sources for details. Similar to the *sagittarii*, he says, are the makers of certain images. 'They stick pins in them, or melt them in the fire, or break them in pieces, and this makes sure that those people represented by the images waste away or suffer some other kind of death'. Girolamo Cardano accepts none of it, but he is refuted by many authors. (References and examples drawn from a very wide range of literature.)]

Section 5: Various illnesses caused by evil spirits

[This section consists largely of anecdotal evidence and long quotations from Sprenger and Cornelius Gemma,[18] and shorter ones from a *Life of Saint Angela of Foligno* and Mattioli's *Commentary on Dioscorides*.]

---

[15] (Louvain 1486). Del Rio tells us that Beetz was a learned Carmelite 'who lived about 130 years ago'.

[16] Here I cut a nick in her plumpness, and add another one to it. Thus I take this cow's milk.

[17] Here I give you a blow, and I give another one like it, and I add a third to them. Thus I preserve my cow's milk.

[18] Cornelius Gemma (1535–1577), Belgian physician. He wrote several books on astronomico-astrological topics, including a study of the divine characteristics of nature (Antwerp 1575), a description and discussion of the comet of 1572 (Antwerp 1573), and a similar study of the comet of 1577 (Antwerp 1578).

I must now explain by what pact an evil spirit inflicts illnesses. Francisco de Vallés has given an accurate account of this. The evil spirit is certainly the external cause in as much as he comes from outwith the body to take up residence in it and to bring illnesses to it. If the illnesses need a physical basis, he triggers internal causes. This is how he starts melancholic diseases. First he stirs up the black bile which is within the body, and drives black specks [19] into the brain and the cells of the internal sense-organs. Then he increases the amount of black bile by moving to it agents which dry it up with excessive heat, or he retains it so that it cannot be expelled. He also causes epilepsy, paralysis, and similar injuries by bringing down fluid which is somewhat too thick, which he does by blocking one of the ventricles of the brain, or by obstructing the roots of the nerves. He is the cause of blindness or deafness by gathering harmful matter in the ears or eyes, and often, in order to induce hate, love, or other disturbances of the mind, he produces images with a view to making these emotions lodge themselves firmly in the imaginative faculty. He picks out a spiritual substance from the blood to arouse physical affections, separating it and purging it of material grossness. Then he uses these spirits (spiritus), as the nearest instrument to the soul, to work with remarkable effectiveness and speed. It is my contention that he elicits from things which are very poisonous some fifth essence, as it were (as alchemists are accustomed to do from gems and gold), steeps those vital spirits in it, and so imbues someone with a magical illness (maleficus morbus), as Cesalpino, who has a practical grasp of these things, has remarked in his Liber de daemonum investigatione (Inquiry Into Evil Spirits), chapter 16.

[When the evil spirit has done this, it is difficult for human beings to find effective remedies. Illnesses caused by some external instruments of malefice, such as ointments, signs, bits of dead body, and so forth, have no natural power to work venomous magic (veneficium), but are simply signs that there is a pact whereby an evil spirit is doing the work. (See Cesalpino and Rémy.)]

Section 6: Extraordinary ingestion and vomiting of large solid objects

There is a large number of extraordinary diseases caused by malefice, but in my opinion the most extraordinary of all occurs when the sick person ejects from the mouth or the back of the throat, thorns, bones, pieces of wood, pebbles, pieces of glass, needles, knives and other iron objects, balls of hair, scraps of cloth, fishing lines, the tip of an oil-lamp, and so forth, which it seems impossible to believe can be introduced into the body by eating or any other means. [Illustrative stories from Sprenger, and Gaufrido's Life of Saint Peter of Tarentaise.]

---

[19] Literally, 'soot'.

My first comment is that certain things from corrupted humours commonly combine in human bodies; for example, porous stones, pebbles, hairs, shells, thorns, balls of hair, and such-like things which the evil spirit has been able to create in the bowels or appropriate extremities of parts of the body – something which can also happen naturally, as both ancient and modern doctors agree. Many people besides myself know the son of a Count who, almost nineteen years ago, in Luxemburg, used to pass rather large pieces of brick in his urine; and although quite a number of people attributed this to his adulterous wife's venomous magic (*veneficium*), it could still have happened naturally because of a corruption of his humours and a fault in his kidneys. His wife was enslaved to the sect of Calvin, and more friendly with the minister than was necessary. So the common suspicion was not unconnected with her morals and her doctrine.

Secondly, I think that there is no natural way in which any putrefaction can engender in the human body needles, knives, scissors, and metallic artefacts of this kind. It is unlikely that natural heat can give rise to metallic objects in the body, except over the space of a good many years; and it is even less likely that such different humours can coalesce by accident into this particular amalgam and artificial arrangement, unless we return to the nonsense of Democritus and Epicurus who say that everything is made of an accidental concurrence of atoms. I have not read anything so far which attributes this power to nature.

Thirdly, in my opinion evil spirits can effect all these things in a variety of ways by means of workers of evil magic (*malefici*). First, they can so delude the senses that someone may think these things are being introduced into his body or being disgorged therefrom, whereas actually it is merely the evil spirit who is making (a) real knives appear along with the rest of the artificial stuff the patient is vomiting, none of which has ever been in his body at all, or (b) the humours themselves, which are now being vomited forth. The spirit can also condense and colour air for the same purpose, and the result is very life-like, since the objects appear to be solid and dense. Not long after one sees them, however, they vanish away. But the spirit can, without going as far as illusion, introduce this kind of thing secretly into the mouth whence the objects are quickly ejected, and he can also insert and hide them in other parts of the body. Wier (a man with no brain) denies this. I do not see why he does so, because trustworthy doctors and surgeons (and he himself praises several of them) testify that they have seen such things come out of bodies, or that they have cut them out and held them in their hands.

[Del Rio concludes by discussing three theories which have been formulated to explain this phenomenon. (1) The evil spirit puts someone into a deep sleep, removes his or her sense of pain, and then personally introduces the material into the body without leaving any trace of his entry. (2) The evil spirit reduces solid objects to a very fine powder and then reunites them at such speed that the eye cannot see it happening. Thus, people think the solid objects really are coming out of the body. Del Rio is willing to accept these two theories, but he does not like a third, although it is a popular explanation. (3) The evil spirit opens and stretches the pores of the body in such a way that objects can be thrown into it in the same way a stone is thrown into water.]

Section 7: Malefice resulting from prayer

[Catholics accept that demoniacs are often invaded and possessed, or besieged by evil spirits which enter their bodies and simultaneously receive power to vex and afflict them. (References and an anecdote.) The anecdote produces comments. (1) It describes obsession not possession. (2) Theologians make a distinction between the two. In the case of possession, the evil spirit enters a body just as he used to enter the statues of pagan idols. The heavy breathing of demoniacs, along with many other signs, gives an indication of this. The spiritual essence of an evil spirit, however, is so opposed to the physical substance of the body he enters that he often destroys the body by the simple act of entering it. (3) The soul of a demoniac is not always as unconscious as it might appear, because often demoniacs remember everything which has happened to them. (4) Theologians have always been of the opinion that an evil spirit enters a body to use it as an instrument of his will. (References and examples.)]

In 1581, in the town of Annonay near Viviers, there was a female worker of harmful magic (*malefica*) by the name of Boyarona who sent evil spirits to harry several different people in a number of different ways. Among her victims were her son and daughter. They had been gathering nuts for each other but, as children do, ate them while they were bringing them home. So the woman handed over both children to be possessed by three evil spirits. (Similar examples.) The fact that magicians can send evil spirits into other people does not arise from any ability they have to compel the spirits' obedience, because magicians possess no such power. Either the spirits invade a demoniac of their own free will as part of a pact and pretend to be submissive, or they force inferior demons to do so who, by doing as they are told, oblige the wish of the superior demon in this act of malefice. In either case, God's permission is required, because without that the invasion cannot take place. God usually permits this only because of some grave sin on the part of the demoniac, although He frequently permits it in answer to the prayers of angry parents. (Example.) Experience has shown that today most witches (*striges*) have formed a pact with an evil spirit so that they can pray to him for vengeance upon someone, either by suddenly inflicting some slow, wasting death on a beast or a human, or by rescuing someone suddenly from the jaws of death. (Reference.)

Section 8: Malefice by binding

[Del Rio begins, 'There is no malefice so common these days', and goes on to describe how men are often prevented by malefice from performing the sexual act. He appeals to the testimony of theologians to prove the truth of this. Certain causes, such as castration, rupture, desiccation, cooling, and such-like may produce the same effect naturally, and the evil spirit can make use of this. Often a man cannot have sex with one particular woman although he is potent with any other, and when the ligature is removed, he is cured. In this case, the cause of impotence is not natural but supernatural or preternatural. As the affliction does not come from God, it must come from angels; and as it does not come from good angels, it must come from bad. The Devil employs an almost infinite number of ways to produce this effect, and Bodin says that he himself had found more than fifty of them.]

Certain magicians (*magi*) simply tie knots in a cord and say certain words, and meanwhile the evil spirit carries out the malefice and the man or woman is rendered impotent (because this can happen to women as well as men.) But observation tells us that it is easier (and more common) for this evil to creep up on men, perhaps because any defect and impediment happens more easily in cases where greater effort or several agencies are required: or because when there are more female workers of harmful magic (*maleficae*) than male (*malefici*), it is men who are more commonly harmed. Most people maintain that the binding can last for a day, a year, for ever, or until the knot has been untied.

[Del Rio says that in the works of those scholars he has consulted, he has found seven causes of impotence. (1) The married couple hate each other either because of some false accusation or suspicion, or because some disease makes its appearance. (Examples). (2) The two people are separated by some mental block. (Examples, including a quotation from Vincent de Beauvais.[20]) (3) The vital spirits (*spiritus*) are prevented from reaching the sexual organs. (4) The semen dries up and will not come. (5) The man's penis remains flaccid when he wishes to have intercourse. (Quotations from Ovid and Petronius). (6) Natural medicaments are applied, which prevent the person from reaching a climax. (7) The woman's pudenda are too narrow, or the man's genitals are retracted, hidden from view, or actually removed. This cause is not so common. (See Sprenger

---

[20] (c. 1190–1264), French scholar and encyclopaedist, Dominican. His principal work is *Speculum Maius* (The Greater Mirror), a compilation of the universal knowledge of his time, arranged systematically.

and Rémy.) Del Rio says that retraction and hiding from view might happen naturally, although he doubts it, but that removal is something quite extraordinary. In the case of men, therefore, this cause is preternatural. In the case of women, the narrowness may have a natural or a demonic cause. Del Rio then comments further on the causes of impotence and gives many references to a wide range of supportive literature.]

Section 9: The malefice of hatred

[Del Rio begins with references to literature on the subject, including Andrea Cesalpino: *De investigatione daemonum*.] He writes that female workers of harmful magic are accustomed to bury the heads and skins of snakes under the threshold or in the corners of a house, with a view to gratifying their hatred. These pieces of rubbish, however, are merely signs of an agreed pact, because the source of a malefice of hatred is an evil spirit. Natural drugs have no other power than to cause someone to be affected by black, turbid blood and a serious melancholy, to overheat the humours, or to make them cold, much to their detriment. Hence there may arise aggressiveness, captiousness, cruelty, and a general misanthropy such as is found in those who labour under the delusion that they are werewolves. The evil spirit directs all this hatred against a particular person by presenting to the magician's imagination all kinds of images relating to hatred, raising them in front of the eyes, so to speak, and reviving them in the memory. [There follows an illustrative quotation from Codronchi.]

Section 10: Malefice which causes fire

[This section consists largely of quotations from Seneca, Rémy, and Erasmus to illustrate the point that witches 'do not merely set fire to the mind, but to bodies and houses and towns as well'. Del Rio concludes with an anecdote. A few years previously, some fire-raisers had crossed the Rhine and left behind in some of the local houses objects such as swords and spears which do not usually catch fire. Yet a few hours later, flame burst from them as though they were fire-darts and the buildings were consumed.]

Question 5: Who can be harmed by workers of harmful magic (*malefici*)?

[Satan cannot harm anyone without God's permission. (Quotations from Saint Leo and references to Holy Scripture.)]

My first point is that, with God's permission – and this I take for granted in what follows – the confederate of an inferior demon can harm the confederate of a superior demon, not by his own power but by force of the licence he has received: for the superior demon cannot resist God's will. Otherwise, if

God allows them to act according to the normal rule, the confederates of a superior demon can harm only their inferiors or their equals, since the normal rule is that God allows them to work against each other according to the amount of power they have. So the strength and power of workers of harmful magic depends on the power of an evil spirit and the pact they have made with him. [Reference to Sprenger.]

Second point. Very often they can harm small children, which God permits because the children are thus preserved from many sins and are taken up happy to Heaven, secure because wickedness will not change their intellect. God allows this either as a punishment or as a test of the parents. (See Saint Augustine.) God often allows children to be killed before they have been baptised, so that they do not incur a graver punishment because of the sins he foresees they would have committed had they lived; and God is neither cruel nor unjust in this, since they merited death on account of original sin alone. Certainly we see that very frequently evil spirits lay traps for those who have not yet been cleansed by the water of baptism and rejoice in their destruction; for in this case the workers of harmful magic who kill them sin much more grievously and offend God more dreadfully. The reason is that they destroy those who are plainly innocent and harmless both in soul and body, and this is especially so if these workers of magic kill their own children and offer them to the evil spirit, as witches (*striges*) are accustomed to do. [Examples from Scripture and later literature.]

Third point. Undoubtedly when they use natural poisons they can, with God's permission, harm both good and bad people. But in fact they harm evil-doers and sinners more often than they harm the just and the good. God more frequently extends the harsh authority of the law to slaves than to the sons and friends of God, although sometimes he allows harm to be done to them as well because of the great good which comes to those who suffer.

One must make a special point of asking whether workers of harmful magic are able to do harm to judges and those who administer justice. This opinion which has enchanted the common people,[21] and has even been accepted by many of the learned, is that by reason of a special privilege accorded to them, judges cannot be so harmed. Two reasons are given for this. One is based on experience and observation of what actually happens in the end; but these are neither constantly the same, nor are they the same for everyone, and so the opinion based upon them is sometimes open to error. The second says that if workers of harmful magic could do harm to judges, it would look as though

---

[21] Del Rio uses *decantata* which refers (a) to chanting or reeling off a lesson which has been learned (with the implication that it has not been properly understood), or (b) intoning a spell, bewitching, or enchanting. It is impossible in English to convey both senses, although it is clear Del Rio intended that this should be done.

they had some authority over God himself since they would have authority over those who discharge an office which belongs to God.

[Del Rio criticises this second notion on the grounds that the power of workers of evil magic is not absolute but limited by the necessity for God's permission, and he illustrates his point with a quotation from Nider and references to other literature. In Del Rio's opinion, the privilege of not being harmed extends only to judges who are dutiful, firm in their faith, and eager to do justice.]

One should also add that not only are evil spirits quite prepared to hand over these vile slaves of theirs to the fires of execution, but that they often deliver them into the hands of the judges. So why should a judge be harmed when he has decided to condemn a guilty person to death? Whence has this unreliable opinion arisen? Here we are speaking of two kinds of malefice. One, which is frequently used, has no natural power to do harm. The other has an innate power to inflict death, and this God does not allow witches (*sagae*) to employ against judges since they are acting in the place of God. If he does allow this type of malefice to be employed, he makes sure that the former kind overrides it, or that the witches misuse their natural powers and thus the deadly malefice becomes ineffectual. More often than not, when they have been put to the test, the women confess that they cannot harm judges; yet they would be able to do so unless God were to stop them, or unless he were to restrain their attack of malefices.

Question 6: Why does God allow workers of harmful magic to abuse sacred things in the way they do?

[Del Rio refers the reader to Grillando for the answer. He himself thinks it is part of God's plan to punish people for their sins.]

Question 7: Why does God allow an evil spirit to run riot through acts of malefice?

[Del Rio agrees with the observations made on this point by Trithemius[22] and Jacquier, and proceeds to divide his comments into two sections.]

---

[22] Johann Trithemius (1462–1516), German historian, Benedictine. His occult works include a book on sorcery, *Antipalus maleficiorum* (Wrestling Against Workers of Harmful Magic), published in Ingolstadt in 1555, and a treatise on secret or angelic writing, *Steganographia*, published in Frankfurt in 1606. Del Rio refers here to his *Libri octo quaestionum ad Maximilianum Caesarem* (Eight Books of Inquiries Addressed to the Emperor Maximilian), published in Oppenheim in 1515.

Section 1

[God's glory is increased because when we suffer malefice, certain divine attributes are manifested to us: namely, the pleasantness with which he governs us; his clemency towards humankind; his wisdom (since the Devil, for all his natural power, is conquered by mere feeble humans); his power whereby he demonstrates that he controls the Devil; and his justice which punishes people's crimes even in this life. Secondly, affliction by the malefice of an evil spirit is useful for human beings. (a) They are required thereby to exercise patience; their constancy is strengthened, their merits are increased, and they are recalled to penitence and the sacraments of the Church; (b) It reveals those who do not love God (they take refuge in forbidden practices), and those who do (they suffer the affliction patiently.) (c) It also confers true humility. (Example.) (d) It enables people to build a road to every kind of virtue. (Example.) (e) It confirms them in the Catholic faith and confounds those who say there are no spirits or angels, such as Calvinists in whom atheism once again puts forth shoots. Our faith is strengthened against modern heretics when we see the fraud of evil spirits condemned out of the magicians' own mouths. Del Rio then refers to *Acts* 19.13 where a man possessed by an evil spirit attacks seven Jewish exorcists who have come to cure him and drives them away naked and wounded.]

It was an evil spirit from Wittenburg which drove Luther into very great distress through diarrhoea. The story comes from an eye-witness who was a close observer of Luther at the time.[23] In 1582 in Birgelli, a Lutheran parishioner was disdainfully knocked to the ground by an evil spirit which was then successfully exorcised by a Franciscan. This story comes from Bredenbach's book. Before that, in 1563, in Augsburg, Doctor Simon, a Catholic priest, liberated a demoniac after several Protestant ministers[24] had tried in vain to do so. Bredenbach testifies to this as well. An evil spirit speaking through the mouth of a female demoniac in Laons in 1566, mocked the Calvinists in the hearing of everyone else who was present, and cried out that there was nothing to fear from them because they were his friends and confederates. The incident is so notorious in the whole of Picardy that it cannot be denied. It has also

---

[23] A marginal note by Del Rio says, 'Staphylus in *Complete Response to Smidelinus*. Anyone who does not have Smidelinus's book may read Staphylus's story in Lindanus: *Three Tentative Books*, dialogue 3, chapter 1, or in Bredenbach's book, Book 7, chapter 40.' 'Smidelinus' or 'Schmidlein' seems to have been the pen-name of Jakob Andreae (1528–1590). His book, *Absoluta responsio D. F. Staphyli in defensionem apologiae suae*, was published in Cologne in 1562. Lindanus = Willem van der Lindt (1525–1588) whose book was published in Cologne in 1565. Matthias Bredenbach (c. 1490–1559) wrote *A Defence of Luther's Critics*, published in Antwerp in 1558.

[24] Del Rio calls them 'ministers of the Confession of Augsburg'.

been well observed that in Geila in Brabant, when Luther died, evil spirits flew from those they had possessed to Luther's funeral; and when, in 1566, Belgium was being subjected to image-breakers, evil spirits once again deserted their victims and were present in Geila, in Amsterdam, and in Gex. The Calvinists, in a spirit of gratitude, chose to leave alone a red-coloured demon in a glass window containing a scene of the Last Judgement in the Church of Saint Médard in Paris. (I have seen this myself.) In Saint Paul's in London there is a single statue of the Devil being trodden underfoot by Saint Michael. I have seen, in Antwerp Cathedral, the only remaining statue of the Devil, situated to the left of the impenitent thief. In Roermond there is a likeness of an evil spirit carrying a little bag, such as one usually sees in pictures of Saint Geneviève; and finally, on one occasion in Leiden, when people made a sortie with a view to destroying a Franciscan monastery in the suburbs, they carried before them an image of the Devil in place of a standard. It was fixed to the end of a long spear shaft to make it look as though they would be fighting under him as his hired militia.

Every day we see that evil spirits, workers of harmful magic, and heretics,[25] as if to vent their common anger and hatred, bring to bear upon Catholics the most relentless assaults and injuries which magicians and the Devil can perform; and we see that these are either rendered ineffectual or that they are completely destroyed through Catholic prayers, benedictions, holy objects, and the sacraments.

Section 2

I have said that the cause of God's giving his permission is to punish sin. This is very common. Sometimes God punishes the sins of another in this way, although he does not do this very often.

[References to works by Saint Gregory. Del Rio then devotes the rest of the section to discussion of twelve sins which may bring down God's particular punishment. (1) Defiance arising from pride. (References to the Old Testament and quotations from John the Archpresbyter and Saint Augustine.) (2) Hatred or envy of someone close to you. (3) Carnal lust and intemperance in the marriage-bed. (References to Scripture and Saint Jerome.)]

A clean heart has been promised a clear vision of God. An impure heart merits the sight and company of an evil spirit. Human obscenity is a great delight to an evil spirit. All female workers of harmful magic are slaves to Venus and there is not a virgin among them, just as there are none among Calvinists and other heretic haters of celibacy. Hence it appears that there is a close link between magic, heresy, and lust.

[25] *Novatores*, literally, 'innovators'.

[Del Rio now gives a recent example from Flanders, but prefers to keep to himself the names of the particular people and places involved. (4) Cruel and unjust oppression or murder of just men. (Examples from Mediaeval and Patristic literature.) (5) Attacking a recognised truth, and apostasy. (6) Blasphemy, 'these days, alas, extremely common'. (Quotations from Thomas Netter[26] and Sophronius.) (7) Cursing and swearing, 'no less common'. (Quotations from Nider, George Godelmann, and Thomas of Cantimpré.) These are followed by an anecdote involving a Spanish soldier in Belgium about 22 years previously. Del Rio then quotes at length further anecdotes from an author designated only by the initials I. C.[27] (8) Usury. 'Witches (sagae) confess that they can inflict no malefice on those who give their time to works of charity'. Del Rio then quotes the Mediaeval author Lambert von Hersfeld.[28] (9) Harshness and lack of pity towards the poor (followed by a quotation from Pietro Bizzarri.)[29] 'Someone has observed that if witches (sagae), on whom Satan has always imposed the necessity of doing harm, lack enemies on whom they may wreak vengeance, they beg for alms and if anyone who has the ability to pay and does not realise they are witches should refuse them, he falls into great danger. Thus, in Poitiers, in 1567, two magicians (magi) confessed that one day they demanded money at the door of a very rich householder, and when he refused they cast a spell with the result that all his servants fell ill of a frenzy and died raving'. (10) Mockery of the sacred mysteries, and abuse of and contempt for the ceremonies and sacraments of the Catholic Church. (Examples are given from a variety of sources both modern and Mediaeval, along with quotations from Gregory of Tours and Bredenbach, and a reference to the story of Saint Hugh of Lincoln.) (11) Plundering and pillaging churches, and removing holy objects therefrom. (Lengthy examples drawn from Mediaeval literature including Peter of Cluny and Pietro Damiani.)[30] (12) Weakness of mind and desperation when overcome by grief. 'These people either do not seek God's help or they do not believe they can pull themselves out of their troubles. Therefore most of them put themselves under the control of the evil spirit as one who can give them aid'. (Examples taken from ancient literature, quoted in the Latin version of Pietro Damiani.)

---

[26] (1375–c. 1430), English theologian and historian.

[27] These initials refer to an anonymous author against whom Del Rio argues later in the *Disquisitiones*.

[28] German historian of the eleventh century.

[29] Italian historian, c. 1530–1590.

[30] Peter of Cluny (c. 1115–1183), French Cluniac, Bishop of Chartres. Pietro Damiani (1007–1072), Saint, Italian theologian, Benedictine, Cardinal.

Question 8: Why does the Devil prefer to use the agency of workers of evil magic when he can, for the most part, do these damnable things himself?

My researches suggest there are two reasons. First, he believes that by means of the pact he does God a greater injury, since he can abuse creatures endowed with reason, washed clean by baptism, and anointed with the chrism, and thus show contempt for the Creator himself, and deprive him of his authority. This is how he does harm to a large number of people, because they do not shrink from familiarity and close fellowship with workers of harmful magic and do not detest the company of the Devil. (For if the evil spirit were always openly to push himself forward, many people would pull back from striking a bargain with him and practising the arts of harmful magic.) So the result is, he draws in more partners in crime and then he ruins them.

Secondly, he can achieve certain things with the help of human beings, which he either cannot manage at all or cannot manage so readily without an intermediary. [Examples from Scripture.] Likewise, if sacred things are abused, as very often happens in malefices, since these are abused by human beings the Devil reaps a handsome dividend in souls and so leads more people into mischief. For (a) he increases the contempt felt by those who despise sacred things, and (b) he falsely persuades those who reverence them that these malefices come from God and not from an evil spirit. Thus he draws on many people to defend workers of evil magic and so forces a sin upon them. The consequence is that people add sacrilege to the superstition of magic, and God is more and more offended, and allows the princes of darkness to practise more every day against wretched mortals. Sometimes, however, the Devil prefers to accomplish by his own efforts something he could do by using human beings. This he does in order to win their favourable regard, remove from them any suspicion that any harm may be involved, and so demonstrate his own power. (See Rémy.)

Part 2: Vain observance

Question 1: What is vain observance?

Saint Thomas Aquinas discusses this. [Reference.] It can be defined as follows. *Vain observance is superstitious magic by means of which one hopes to get an advantage from something which does not possess that advantage supernaturally and which it cannot provide naturally.* One says *vain* because either the intended effect does not happen subsequently or, if it does happen, it brings more harm than advantage. The person who uses vain observance merely perceives the utility in physical or temporal things and this brings harm to the soul. I said *not supernaturally* because those who wait for an effect from God by using means displeasing to God do so in vain.

Question 2: What kind of a sin is it?

Sometimes mortal, sometimes venial. It will be mortal (a) if it stems from a clearly defined pact with an evil spirit, and (b) if someone is aware that there is a tacit pact underlying it, or if he is not willing to desist after he has been warned to do so.

It is venial as long as the person does not know of such a pact with an evil spirit, if he is considered not to know, and if he has not been warned about it (by which I mean he has not consulted those who are skilled in these matters.) Someone may be considered not to know because of his job or position, but when he begins to have doubts it is understood he will seek the counsel of learned men. If he does not do this he is negligent, for he could have got to know about it, and so is not invincibly ignorant.

It is not a sin when someone is merely having a thoughtless practical joke and does not put himself or someone else in danger. The case is the same if someone is suffering from invincible ignorance and uses methods which are either good or indifferent.

Question 3: How many kinds are there?

If you bear in mind the final cause, vain observance can be reduced to four types, so to speak. (1) When one expects to receive some benefit in relation to one's external situation or luck: for example, with one's animals, corn, vines, or having good weather, etc. (2) When one expects some benefit in relation to one's body, such as health, freedom from imprisonment, enemies, sword, fire, water, and things of that kind, with the idea that one will thereby be free from harm. (3) When one expects some natural good in relation to one's soul: for example, a skill, or some kind of knowledge. (4) When one expects supernatural benefits, such as remission of sins by using certain forms of prayer or certain verses of the Psalms or some other part of Holy Scripture, or other things of this kind, which have not been authorised by the Church or by God.

Question 4: How one can know when there is vain observance of this kind.

Section 1

I shall discuss this briefly. First, if it is agreed that the effect of the vain observance is one which goes beyond the power of nature, one must take note whether, from one's reading of Holy Scripture, or according to the definition or approved tradition of the Church, the effect is attributable to God; or (which amounts to the same thing) whether, according to such testimony, one may agree that the effect comes from God. If there is no such evidence, the effect must be attributed to a pact made with an evil spirit and accordingly it must be regarded at the very least as the magical superstition of vain observance. The effects of this kind which someone may be looking for are remitting mortal sins outwith the sacraments, and remitting venial faults outwith sacramentals.[31] A similar kind of observance is foretelling future events and influencing or directing their courses (which actually depend on freedom of the will.)

Secondly, if it is agreed that the thing to which the effect is attributed has this power from God or from nature, it is not vain observance as far as the effect is concerned, but could be vain observance because of some sinful attendant circumstance: for example, a hair shirt, a scourge, or fasting. These afflict and torment the body and have been given power to restrain concupiscent urges which sprout from the strength of the flesh and too luxuriant clothing for the body. But it will be vain observance if you add silly circumstances to these, ones not ordained by nature, God, or the Church, such as observing a particular hour, using a definite number which cannot be more or less, depending on the presence of certain individuals, or prescribing one hand or the other to wield a silken scourge, etc.

The following rules indicate that something is vain observance.

Section 2

1) If the person to be cured must have faith that the effect produces this result: i.e. he believes it can cure him.

2) If the effect is attributable, not to God but to magical images, figures, sigils, or characters, and to these actual things, or to their sound, or to contact with them.

---

[31] I.e. rites or ceremonies such as blessing with holy water, anointing with chrism, or making the sign of the cross. Del Rio is suggesting that if anyone hopes to obtain remission of his sins without having recourse to the sacraments or sacramentals of the Church, but uses superfluous ceremonies which fall into the category of 'vain observance', he or she is committing a grave error.

3) If someone uses particular prayers or sacred sentences or does pious works, and directs them, not directly or indirectly towards the worship and honour of God, but towards things which are of no importance.

[Del Rio explains what he means by 'indirectly', namely, when the practice involves things which are not vain in themselves but may be useful (for example, to the health of oneself, one's family, or one's neighbours). In such a case, any credit for a cure must be given to God alone. (Quotation from Cajetan: '*The fourth superstition is observance in respect of words, carrying sacred things, and saying or using them in circumstances which are not evil but which are irrational; for example, the case of those suffering from nervous spasms, who use the first carlin[32] offered to Christ's cross on Good Friday as a remedy, by making a ring out of it, and so forth. In any such situation, superstition occurs because the attendant circumstances are vain unless people intend and expect that the effect should come from God, and think that God has inspired some holy man to make use of this particular situation, in which case I do not venture to condemn this, as it seems tolerable to me*'. Del Rio says he agrees up to a point, the point being that if anyone asked his advice, he would recommend that he or she avoid such practices.]

4) There is vain observance in particular fasts, in certain prayers contained in books which have been condemned by Pope Pius V, in dubious indulgences and remissions of sins, and in expecting or seeking a desired situation to follow from them. Indeed, using particular fasts and prayers without human effort, and acquiring knowledge by having it poured into one according to the principles of a certain art belongs to the first type of magic, because it arises from an overt pact with an evil spirit and is a mortal sin. The art in question is known as 'the notory art'. [This has been condemned by a number of authorities, including Cirvelo with whose opinion Del Rio concurs.[33] He then describes the procedure to be followed.]

The most usual method is as follows. First of all the pupil is told to wash away the stains of his whole life by a general confession, to communicate frequently, and whenever he falls into sin to confess it at once that same day. He is to observe diligently the fasts ordained by the Church, and add other days of his own accord, especially Saturday when he will take nothing but bread and water. Every day he is to recite the Seven Penitential Psalms and offer certain prayers; and all this he must do to the letter for seven weeks

---

[32] A Sicilian coin.

[33] Pedro Cirvelo (*c.* 1470–1560), Spanish astrologer and mathematician. A second edition of his *Reprovaciõ de las supersticiões y hezicherias* (Objection to Superstition and Witchcraft) was published in Salamanca in 1538. (The first edition has neither place nor date attached to it.)

during which he must abstain completely from all thought for or involvement in worldly affairs. When he has completed this stage, my source prescribes certain other formulae for prayers which he must devise and recite, and it illustrates certain figures he is supposed to worship. It fixes certain hours when he must say these prayers and perform these acts of veneration: these are especially sunrise every day during the first week of a new moon.

He carries out these rites three times in the space of three new moons. Next he must fix for himself a day on which his devotion will be very intense and when he will be the more ready to receive inspiration. Then, at the third hour, he must situate himself all alone in a church or chapel, or kneel on the ground in the middle of a field, raise his hands and eyes to Heaven, and recite three times the first verse of *Come, Holy Spirit*. When he has done this, suddenly he will be filled with all knowledge (just as was Solomon, the prophet and Apostle) to such an extent that he will be struck dumb at the sudden change in himself, as if he had turned into an angel or some other person. There you have all the mysteries of this art.

[Del Rio now makes his disapproval clear and says that it is not God or an angel who floods the practitioner with knowledge, but the Devil. He then mentions ramifications of the notory art, including 'the Pauline art', also known as 'spiritual' or 'angelic'. This can be divided into two types called 'obscure' and 'clear'. The former works by making the practitioner fall into ecstasies; the latter makes angels appear in physical form. This, he says, is nothing more than the *goetia* or the white magic (*magia alba*) which he discussed in Book 1, and the angels are merely evil spirits. He refers the reader to Segni's *De vero studio Christiano* (The True Study for a Christian).] [34]

Section 3

5) It is also vain observance when someone wears relics or the Gospel of Saint John or verses of the Psalms, not simply out of devotion but with useless attendant circumstances such as, for example, believing that the writings or relics must be kept in a triangular or round container; attributing power to the shape of the box, or the material on which the words are written; believing that the words must be written on virgin parchment. He or she may also suffer from superstition relating to time (the words must be written at sunrise), or relating to a person (the person who ties the container must be without corruption), or relating to method (the container has to be tied with a certain number of threads or threads of a certain kind.) No, such a box must have on it no figure

---

[34] Giovanni Battista Segni (died 1610). Italian, Professor of Theology at Ferrara and Urbino. His book was published at Ferrara in 1592.

except the sign of the cross, no image except that of Christ, the Blessed Virgin, some famous saint, or a good angel depicted in the usual fashion; it must bear no barbarous or unknown names of God or of angels; and there must be nothing else which is useless or open to misinterpretation.

[Del Rio then draws attention to condemnations of superstitious uses of legitimate signs and symbols, made by Saint Thomas Aquinas, Martin of Arles, and Saint Augustine.]

Section 4

6) [Del Rio refers the reader to Saint John Chrysostom's condemnation of paying serious attention to omens. To this he adds quotations from Saint Augustine, and other quotations from and references to various Classical authors.]

Section 5

7) It can sometimes be vain observance to come into contact with the lucky gifts which are given on New Year's Day. Pagans used to celebrate this with great solemnity in honour of Janus on 1 January (as Suetonius and Ovid tell us.) Among other things, they used to give each other lucky gifts as an omen or prayer that they would be prosperous and enjoy a good year, or that much else would accrue to them.

[Because of these superstitious beliefs, lucky gifts and similar New Year practices have been condemned by various authorities. If anyone were to observe these customs in honour of Janus, he would be guilty of idolatry. Del Rio then draws attention to New Year superstitions described by Burchard,[35] and condemns them.]

Section 6

8) The eighth superstition involves people who are bothered about time, the observance of days, months, or years – not with a view to the worship of God, but so that they can direct the course of their own affairs. For example, people who collect herbs at certain times, or who cut wood to build houses or ships, are not superstitious if they do so because they are motivated to do so by a natural observation of the movements and influence of the heavens, knowing that at certain times the power of herbs is more effective and wood is less likely to rot or will be better to use. But this practice will become superstition

---

[35] Johann Burchard (1450–1506), German Bishop of Orta and Cività Castellana, and Papal Master of Ceremonies. His best known book is his *Diary* which diligently records the ceremonial in use at the Papal Courts of Innocent VIII, Alexander VI, Pius III, and Julius II.

if they observe one particular week, or day of the month, or hour of the day, and if their observance of such an hour or day is accompanied by useless circumstances or superfluous and unauthorised prayers.

[Del Rio gives a large number of further illustrations, including quotations drawn from Saint Ambrose, Saint Augustine, and Saint Anselm.]

There are also people who touch their brooms with holy oil on certain days so that they may not be harmed by gnats, caterpillars of various kinds, or other insects. There are those who are unwilling to cut their nails on a Friday, or swim on the Sabbath (although they do not abstain, in honour of the Mother of God, from any other ignoble occupation). There are those who believe that there is a greater power in holy water on the Sundays after Ember Days than on other days, if they want to achieve certain specific results; and there are those who keep for a whole year the eggs which hens lay on Good Friday, because they believe that, if they throw these eggs on a fire, they have the power to put it out. [Del Rio objects that all this is absurd and superstitious.]

Section 7

9) Ninth come those various vain observances directed to driving off evil and curing diseases. For example, someone makes an offering from alms he has received, believing that the consequence of his giving from these will have a greater effect. Someone believes that a cross which he has bought or had made and paid for with money he has received as alms is more holy or more efficacious as a result. People offer to the saints wax, or some other material in which they have mixed the hair of the sick person or sick animal. They tie knots so that their cow's milk may not fail. They urinate through a betrothal ring to set themselves free from a malefice. They try to cure headaches and similar illnesses by resting their necks on a pig's feeding or drinking-trough. They measure the sick person's belt while reciting *In the name of the Father*, etc. accompanied by other forbidden ceremonies, in order to find out which saint they should ask for a cure. They split straw with an axe to cure warts on their hands or fingers. In the case of certain diseases of cattle, they make a fire from various kinds of wood and drive the animals into it, or lead them round in a circle and offer to · the saints whatever there is at the first place the animals stop. They knead a cake of Saint Lupus (which, according to this particular rite, they make triangular on the pretext of honouring the most Holy Trinity), cook it, and press into it five holes in memory of the wounds of Christ – this is how they justify what they are doing – and then, in honour of Saint Lupus, they give the cake as alms to the first beggar they meet, not choosing him deliberately, but quite by chance, without knowing who he is; and they think that because they have done this,

their flocks and herds cannot be attacked by wolves (*lupi*) while they are alone at pasture. This is a frequent practice in villages near Thisnes and Louvain.

[Del Rio briefly discusses the superstition inherent in these examples, and gives references to relevant literature. He then quotes from Burchard on the subject of collecting herbs.]

There is a form of prayer in use among Spanish soldiers, wherewith (they claim) certain *salutatores* who live holy lives cure anyone free of charge, simply by the use of bandages and the recitation of certain words. The formula is Spanish, but I shall translate it into Latin.

'Through Christ and with Christ and in Christ is all honour and glory to you God, the Father almighty, in the unity of the Holy Spirit, for ever and ever, Amen. Let us pray. Advised by salutary precepts and instructed by divine institution, we dare to say, Our Father (etc.) Amen. May Jesus, the Power of the Father, the Wisdom of the Son, the Virtue of the Holy Spirit, cure this wound of all evil, Amen. Jesus, my Lord Jesus Christ, I believe that on the night of Holy Thursday, at dinner, after you had washed the feet of your holy disciples, you took bread in your most holy hands, blessed it, broke it, and gave it to your holy disciples, saying, "Take and eat. This is my body". Likewise, you took the cup in your most holy hands, gave thanks, and gave it to them, saying, "Take and drink, because this is my blood of the new testament, which will be shed for many for the remission of sins. As often as you do this, do it in memory of me". I beg you, my Lord Jesus Christ, by these most holy words, by their power, and by the merit of your most holy passion, let this wound and this evil be healed. Amen. Jesus. In the name of the Father, and of the Son, and of the Holy Spirit, Amen. Jesus'.

A question was raised about this formula at Ypres last year, especially because it did not involve recourse to any natural remedy. The Very Reverend Bishop of Ypres, Simon, and his advisers judged this whole treatment superstitious and illicit and forbade anyone to use it.

[Various reasons are given. (1) One should not tempt God by demanding a miracle. (2) Holy people do not use prescribed formulae, but are inspired by the Holy Spirit. (3) The holiness of the practice and its practitioners has not been proven, but rests upon the judgement of soldiers. (4) Those who receive from God the blessing of a cure do not receive it on condition that such and such words be used. Formulae such as the one described here conceal a hidden pact with an evil spirit. (5) Private individuals are not allowed to misuse sacred words in this fashion, especially words from the Canon of the Mass. (6) The words of consecration are applied to something for which they were not instituted, and this is not permissible. Indeed, such a misuse of them is offensive to

Catholics, whereas the Devil and workers of harmful magic willingly and frequently misapply them for their own sacrilegious purposes.]

Section 8

[In this section, Del Rio says he will summarise propositions made by Felix Malleolus of Zurich [36] in his *Two Tracts on Exorcism* in order to warn his readers against them. He deals with seventeen propositions in which Malleolus seeks to defend the use of sacred words and actions in magical operations, or the employment of magic or even evil spirits to counter hostile magic or effect cures, provided the intentions of the person employing them are good and wholesome. Then Del Rio closes the section by commenting on the Emperor Constantine's regulations about workers of evil magic, and astrologers, and by giving a series of quotations from ancient and Mediaeval sources condemning those who seek to cure diseases by magical means.]

Section 9

[Here, Del Rio records instances of popular magic. He says that for the sake of brevity, he will note only the beginnings and ends of the formulae.]

1. To cure horses. They ask, 'What colour is the horse?' and if you say, 'Chestnut', they exclaim, 'Chestnut! If you are suffering from such and such a disease, you will soon be cured, as Joseph and Nicodemus,' etc.

2. Before equals before, equals before before, etc., as the Virgin Mary gave birth.

3. Bind the horse to the shoot of a tree which has never borne fruit, and leave it there for three hours.

4. For any kind of disease, bind a woollen cord round your arm, 'In the name of God', etc., and at the name of the patron saint of your disease, the cord will tighten and become shorter, etc.

5. Say, 'It is finished', and dash the horse's foot strongly on the ground. Then add another verse from the Lord's Prayer, and remove the nail.

6. To cure an animal's disease, fill a glass vial with clear water, nine grains of barley, etc.

7. Drag a thread through chrism, or hide an image made of earth under the altar-cloth.

8. At the time of Mass, touch your teeth while saying a particular verse of the Passion from the Gospel.

9. Together with the patient, before fever has set in, wash your hands and say

---

[36] Felix Haemmerlein (1389–1461/4), Swiss historian. His tracts were published along with other opuscula in Strasbourg in *c.* 1493–1500.

under your breath a certain verse from the Psalms; or take the sufferer's hand and say, 'May this fever be likewise easy for you', etc.

10. Take three Hosts and write on one, 'Of what kind is the Father', etc.; on the other, etc.; on the third, etc.; and give these Hosts to the person suffering from fever.

11. On a Friday, and for the next three days, before sunrise, make the sick person face East. Stand there in the form of a cross, with your hands raised towards the sun, and say, 'Today is the day on which the Lord God came to the cross', etc. Finally, recite nine times the three Sunday prayers and the three salutations of the angel.

12. Write on one of the bed-sheets this saying of Africanus, 'Taste and see that the Lord is good'.

13. Pour into a wine-ladle of cold water a certain number of drops of fresh blood, and between each one recite 'Our Father', etc. Then give it to the patient to drink. Ask him certain questions. Write a certain verse in blood on his forehead. To stop a flow of blood, say, 'Blood, stop in you', etc. 'Blood, stay still', etc. Say this three times. [Further examples given.]

14. For three days, sit on your horse before sunrise, and say, 'In the name of the Father, the Son, and the Holy Spirit, I exorcise you, maggot, by God the Father (etc.) that you eat neither the flesh nor the bones of this horse', etc.
Then recite the *Our Father* and *Hail Mary* a certain number of times. Finally, whisper four words into the horse's right ear and at the same time make several signs of the cross.

15. (a) To find a thief. Sign a glass with the sign of the cross in olive oil, and under the cross write, 'Saint Helena'. Then make a chaste, legitimate ten year old boy hold the glass. Kneel down behind him and say three times the prayer to Saint Helena, 'I pray you, Saint Helena, mother of the Emperor Constantine (etc.), Amen', and when the boy sees an angel in the glass, ask him what your client wants to know. (b) To catch a thief. Go to flowing water and from it collect as many pebbles as you have suspects. Take the pebbles home and put them into the fire on your hearth. Dig a hole in your threshold and, using certain rituals, put the pebbles into some shallow dishes full of water. When you say the name of the thief, his pebble will make the water bubble. (c) Read the Seven Penitential Psalms, along with the Litany. Next comes a terrible prayer to God the Father, etc. and then an exorcism of the thief. Finally, draw a circle and add to it barbarous names, paint an eye in the centre and then, using a hammer made of cypress wood, drive a bronze nail of a certain size into the eye and say a certain verse from the Psalms. (d) Some people cut a hazel branch before dawn on the Sabbath, saying, 'I cut you, this summer's branch', etc. They spread a cloth on the table, saying these words (etc.) three

times. (e) Others employ an exorcism or an anathema which they blasphemously attribute to Saint Adelbert. It begins, 'By the authority of Almighty God', and ends, 'Let everyone say, Amen'. Afterwards they chant, 'In the midst of life we are in death', etc. I very much suspect that this ritual belongs to that heretic Adelbert who called himself a saint and was condemned by Pope Zacharias. You will find his history, and an impious magical prayer belonging to him in Book 2 of *The Life of Saint Boniface, Apostle of Germany*. (f) Other people read Psalm 108 and divide up the verses in a particular way.

16. To cure someone who has been bewitched (*maleficiatus*). Take three measures of violet oil, stand facing the place where the sun will rise, utter the name of the injured party, his mother, and the angels of glory who stand in the sixth grade. Do this for six days, three times a day. On the seventh day, place the man naked, etc. Then the names of the angels should be inscribed on a lamen, etc.[37] On the twentieth day of the month, he will be cured.

17. For the same purpose. (a) Write down the names of the Three Kings, along with three particular verses; or write words which are clearly unknown and absurd, such as these (taken from ancient sources): *Danata darios*, etc; and these (from modern authors): *Abrac Amon*, etc; or these, written on bread: *Frioni, Khiriori*, etc. (b) Or this, *Hax, pax, max*, etc. which is for use against the bite of rabid dogs. (c) For toothache: *Sirigiles Falcesque*, etc; or another, *Galbu*, etc. *Galdes*, etc. (d) *Gibel, Got*, etc. (e) To catch fish (taken from the *Geoponica* of Constantine): *Iao Sabaoth*. [Further references given.]

18. Join two parallel rods in the middle by the power of certain words. Tie them in the form of a cross. Hang them round your neck, or bind a round piece of wood to your chest, while whispering certain formulae, as the Turks do. [Further examples given.] Not long ago I came across two other examples in fairly frequent use here in Brabant. (a) To find out whether a sick person is going to die, they put salt in his hand without his knowing it and wait to see if it melts or not. This is also done in the case of divinations. (b) If someone is suffering from a fever, they tell him to remove his clothes and face the rising sun while reciting a certain number of times the Lord's Prayer and the angelic salutations. By doing this, the patient should be set free from the illness. Even virgins often do this.

[Del Rio closes the section with literary references to further superstitious practices, and ends: 'The Lord hates those who carry out vacuous inanities. By contrast, blessed is the man whose hope is in the Lord, and who pays no heed to vanities and false delusions'.]

---

[37] A lamen is a thin plate, often of metal, used as a charm or amulet, on which are engraved or written magical or astrological signs or characters.

BOOK 4

Divination

There are certain nouns which are tend to be confused in general usage: namely, divination (*divinatio*), prediction (*vaticinium*), precognition (*praenotio*), prophecy (*prophetia*), prognostication (*coniectatio*), and foretelling (*praedictio*). In my title I have used the word 'divination' to cover all these different senses, but if I look at each term more closely, I am aware that they are not the same thing. 'Precognition' and 'foretelling' always include the other four, but foretelling denotes possession of knowledge of a sequence of events and action external to oneself, whereas in precognition the possession of knowledge is entirely internal. 'Prediction' is a word related to both divination and prophecy, but its use is normally restricted to an oracle which comes from the living voice of a human being, whereas 'divination' has a broader meaning than that.

[Del Rio now illustrates his points by reference to Scripture, ancient, and Mediaeval literature.]

Prognostication proceeds from the consideration of causes or signs, and so one has to ask whether one has genuinely understood these or whether one is jumping to foolish conclusions. In consequence, some prognostication is licit and some illicit. From now on, I shall restrict the word 'divination' simply to that which is illicit. Divination differs from prognostication because it does not proceed from signs or argument, as prognostication does. Henceforth, I shall use 'precognition' as a general noun. It will have three parts (like the component parts of the body); (1) Divine Precognition which emanates from God. This will be called 'prophecy', and to it belong certain miraculous or divine portents and marvels. (2) Demonic Precognition, which derives from a tacit or open pact with evil spirits, and will be called 'divination'. (3) Natural Precognition, which arises from signs or natural causes. This I shall call 'presentiment' or 'prognostication', in the strict sense of the words.

Chapter 1: Divine precognition or 'prophecy'

Question 1: The nature of prophecy. The word 'prophecy'

[Del Rio says that 'prophecy' can be understood in six different ways, and he illustrates these with references to Scripture. He discusses the etymology of the word and comments at length on a definition given by Cassiodorus.]

Question 2: The types of prophecy

[Del Rio says there are two: that given by priests, and that by prophets.]

Section 1: The breastplate, the Urim and Thummim

[In this section, Del Rio discusses sacerdotal prophecy in relation to the clothing worn by the Jewish High Priest, especially his breastplate, with the precious stones set into it.]

Section 2: Oracles of the prophets

[Here Del Rio reviews prophecies by sight, by word, and by dreams, with reference to a large number of examples drawn from Scripture.]

Question 3: What is the nature of the pact which distinguishes prophecy or divine revelation from divination or diabolical revelation?

[This is a difficult, though necessary, question to answer, says Del Rio, and he lists some of the authorities who have written on the subject.[1] There are three essential questions to be considered: (a) who is giving the opinion? (b) who has received the revelation? (c) what is the revelation and what are its attendant circumstances?]

Section 1: What one needs to come to an opinion about a revelation

[Anyone who wishes to interpret a revelation, whether his own or someone else's, must ask God for the gift of discrimination so that he can distinguish divine revelation from diabolical. Del Rio then describes various ways in which revelation can be received and uses, as an authority with whose opinions he

---

[1] These include Saint Vincente Ferrer (1350–c. 1419), Spanish Dominican. Jean Gerson (1363–1429), French theologian, Chancellor of the University of Paris. Cardinal Juan de Torquemada (1388–1468), Spanish theologian, Dominican. Heinrich von Vrimaria (died c. 1334), German Augustinian. Pedro de Ribadeneyra (1526–1611), Spanish Jesuit, and Francisco de Ribera (born 1537), Spanish Jesuit.

agrees, Jean Gerson's *Treatise on the Proof of Spirits*, and other passages from Gerson's works, adding thereto a commentary of his own. [2]]

Section 2: The type of person to whom a revelation is made.

[He or she must be a devout Catholic. Del Rio illustrates the problems caused by those who give too easy credence to prophets and their prophecies, with references to ancient literature, and to Mediaeval and modern figures. The person must also have integrity of life and morals, and be free of sins and notable imperfections. Again Del Rio illustrates his points with references to ancient and Mediaeval literature and a range of heretical figures. The person must be healthy because otherwise an evil spirit may use imbalances in the body to create delusions. The person must be neither too old nor too young. Women, he says, present specific problems which will be dealt with in the next section. Finally, the person must be experienced in spiritual exercises so that he or she may not be liable to be deceived by the Devil.]

Section 3: The revelations of women who are not saints

[Women are much more likely than men to believe that natural or diabolical answers to questions actually come from God. Women tend to make much of dreams. This is partly because of women's physical composition which makes them prone to accept imaginings more quickly and more easily than men and thus be the more easily deceived by evil spirits. (Examples from Scripture and Tertullian, followed by modern anecdotes involving women from Peru, Spain, and Belgium, all of whom deceived others by seeming to have the gift of prophecy.) Gerson points out the dangers to confessors in their dealings even with pious women. Le Loyer places the revelations of virgins above those of widows, and those of widows above those of married women.[3] Del Rio demurs, saying that it is better to believe a holy married woman than a lascivious widow or a virgin anxious to find a husband.]

Section 4: The prophecies or revelations of virgins or women who have been canonised and were famous for their sanctity

[Del Rio begins by listing a number of such women, and goes on to reject the arguments of those, including Giovanni Pico della Mirandola, who have expressed reservations about prophecies in these cases, especially those of Saint Birgit of Sweden and Saint Catherine of Siena.]

---

[2] The treatise was published in Rouen in *c.* 1490. It appears in his complete works, Vol. I (Antwerp 1706), 37–43.

[3] Pierre Le Loyer (1550–1634), French scholar. Del Rio is referring to his book, *Quatre Livres des Spectres*, published in Angers in 1586.

Section 5: Signs one should look for in the nature of the revelation itself

[There are six things to be considered. (1) What kind of a revelation is it? Del Rio illustrates his point with a good many Mediaeval references and quotations. (2) If a vision or revelation urges good and pious things upon us, we must give careful thought to whether or not impious, vain, and useless things are being recommended at the same time. Lengthy quotations from Jacques de Vitry and Symeon Metaphrastes illustrate the point.[4] (3) (Taken from Gerson). Could someone have thought of what has been revealed, simply by using human intelligence without the need for revelation? If so, the revelation should be regarded as suspect. Even if the revelation seems to be beyond the wit of human intelligence or demonic knowledge, it is still difficult to judge its worth until time shows whether the prediction was true or not. (4) Is the revelation consonant with Scripture and the teaching and example of the saints? (5) Is the revelation confirmed by other revelations of whose authenticity there is no doubt? (Examples.) (6) If different revelations about the same thing are at odds with one another, both should be considered suspect. But sometimes the Devil tries to undermine true revelations by offering their opposites.]

Section 6: Indications to look for in the circumstances attendant upon revelations

[(1) What is the person's motive for telling others about his or her revelation? (Examples.) (2) What kind of thoughts did one have either before or after receiving the revelation? (Example.) (3) It is very useful to make the sign of the cross in the face of the vision or revelation, and so give oneself protection. (Example.) (4) How did the spirit (*spiritus*) conduct itself? (Quotation from Saint Ignatius of Loyola's *Spiritual Exercises*). (5) Is the mind of the person who receives the revelation happy at first, and does it later give way to disturbance and horror? Does the person who suffers horror from the start remain constant in mind throughout the experience? (Examples.) (6) Are the revelations grafted on to real miracles? (Examples.) (7) Did the revelation foretell something unconditionally? If the opposite happened, or the prophecy was not fulfilled, the revelation was false and did not come from Heaven. (A large number of examples, including a quotation from Nicholas Sanders on the prophecies of Elizabeth Barton relating to the English King, Henry VIII, and his daughter, Mary Tudor.)[5] (8) Is there anything in the revelation which is morally repugnant? (References).]

[4] Jacques de Vitry (*c.* 1160/70–1240), French Augustinian, later Cardinal. Symeon Metaphrastes (*c.* 900–post 984), Byzantine hagiographer.

[5] Nicolas Sanders (*c.* 1530–1581), English historian. His book, *De origine ac progressu schismatis Anglicani* (The Origin and Progress of the English Schism) was continued, after 1558, by Edward Rushton and printed in Cologne in 1585.

Chapter 2: Divination

Where the preceding type was true, this is false. I have given it priority of consideration over 'prognostication' which is of a mixed type.

Question 1: What is divination?

General opinion (or the testimony of Cicero whose two books on the subject are still extant), agrees that it is nothing other than the outward expression of hidden things (*occulta*) arising from pacts made with an evil spirit. I use the phrase 'outward expression' because divination is not achieved by operation of the intellect or by careful study alone. It makes use of signs and spoken words as well and thus differs from an opinion which has been arrived at through vain observance. Divination, however, deals with things in the past and present as much as with things in the future (in as much as they are hidden), and so it is far beyond the reach of human understanding. Consequently I have preferred to refer to 'hidden things' rather than to 'future things'. Prophecy and divination make use of the same material, but when you add things arising from a pact with an evil spirit, these separate divination from prophecy and from natural prognostication. This last comes from systematic training and human observation, while prophecy is poured into someone from on high by God; and however important divination may be, it depends on the operation of an evil spirit who puts on a show of being divine by stealing the art of divination – hence the saying, 'divination is a kind of imitation of divinity'.

It follows that divination cannot go further than the evil spirit's knowledge extends, and in consequence divination cannot be perfected either by art or by nature. Magicians (*magi*) use various aids to assist their divinations. These people have an overt pact with an evil spirit because they know that nothing is more pleasing to him than when humans fall into idolatrous worship. Magicians frequently introduce sacrifice into the process, set up an altar, offer prayers, burn incense, and wear vestments like those of Catholic priests. This is not, however, their invariable practice. Sometimes they do not bother, either because they do not have sufficient time for all that, or because the form of divination they are using does not require it. There are many different types of divination, as I shall explain later. Magicians who have a tacit pact use various observances consonant with the nature of their crime. They do not offer sacrifices, but they do what they do and say, knowingly or unknowingly, in honour of the evil spirit.

Question 2: What hidden things can an evil spirit reveal?

They can do some things, but not everything, because they do not know everything. [This is generally accepted theological opinion. Del Rio then quotes from Mark the Deacon's *Life of Saint Porphyrio of Gaza*, which he proceeds to interpret.] He means that evil spirits lie but are able, if they wish, to tell the truth sometimes, although they usually phrase it in such a way that they deceive by means of this very truth. They can also predict, from the knowledge they have, several things which are not outwith the range of knowledge available to created beings, and this they do in accordance with the following points I shall now proceed to explain.

1) An evil spirit cannot predict with certitude those things which belong entirely and without restriction to the future: and by 'future' I mean first, those things which depend absolutely on the will of God, such as supernatural mysteries, and the government and changes in government of kingdoms and republics, the hearts of princes being in the hand of God who alone changes them as he wishes; secondly, those things which depend on the free will of human beings, such as what I may do or think tomorrow; and thirdly, those things which, provided they do not have a particular and designated cause, are entirely and properly future contingencies.

2) An evil spirit can predict many things, but only with a degree of probability and by making a prognostication based upon things he does not know for certain. First, he makes a comparison based on his very great experience and his daily observation; then he makes full use of his angelic perspicacity and intelligence – and he has an excellent knowledge of the faculties of natural things and what they may be good for; and thirdly, he knows how to bend everyone's will and temperament and disposition, by playing upon the desires aroused by their senses; and he knows which of these three usually works. Consequently it happens that often he predicts as accurately as a carpenter's rule what people are going to do and when they are going to do it. He may even predict that God is going to punish this or that group of people, that such and such an army is going to suffer sword or famine or plague, that X is going to kill Y, or that a prince is going to be expelled from his throne. This last he is able to deduce from seeing how hard the conspirators work, how much they may be trusted, how little attention is paid to them, how sluggish are the precautions taken against such an eventuality, or the pains to drive the conspirators from court. [Example from Nicetas, a Byzantine historian.]

3) The Devil can accurately predict whatever proceeds from necessary causes and cannot be impeded by other natural causes (for example, earthquakes, eclipses, planetary conjunctions, and so forth). He can accurately predict things

which are not inevitable but do very frequently happen and can be impeded by natural causes (for example, showers of rain, clouds, storms accompanied by thunder, and other things of this kind). This sort of thing he discovers by prognostication and predicts it only with some degree of probability. He can also predict accurately those things he knows he will do with God's permission. For example, if God permits, the Devil starts and spreads a plague. He knows when that plague will cease because he knows that the power of the evil will stop on a certain day; and this is even more certain if, according to the terms of this compact, the disease comes to a halt when a certain sign which has been concealed somewhere, or has been pre-arranged, is cancelled.[6] Thus he will be able accurately to predict the end of the evil. [Example.] Likewise, what the evil spirit has understood through revelation, whether they are contained in Scripture or elsewhere, will have been revealed to him by God. It is by this compact, too, that malign spirits once predicted so many things about the mysteries of the faith, Christ's birth and miracles, the abandonment of idolatry, and so forth. [Examples.]

4) There should be no doubt that an evil spirit remembers everything which has happened in the past. This knowledge he has received either by means of a revelation from elsewhere, or he was an eye-witness of those events and his conscious realisation that they were happening left a mental impression which he later remembers as though it were an event taking place in the present.

5) There is no mystery when it comes to events in the present. Evil spirits are well aware of whatever has been revealed to them by some exterior action – secret thefts, things which have been lost, buried treasure, subterranean metals which escape human discovery. There is an argument about whether an evil spirit can discover a person's unexpressed thoughts. Experience has frequently proved that the spirit does not lie when he reveals what these are, but it tells us that he pins them down with spears of infamy – the people he has possessed, the demoniacs. [References to relevant literature and contemporary examples.]

6) Now note some of the remaining frauds of the Devil. When he is ignorant of something in the future, if he finds himself in the presence of people who are rather clever and rather learned, he answers their questions ambiguously in a very low voice, or so enigmatically and obscurely that his audience can scarcely understand him. [Examples.]

7) Evil spirits possess great speed and are able to give advance knowledge of things which are being done in areas far away so quickly that the ignorant think they have predicted them a long time before they happened. [Examples.]

---

[6] I.e. when a magical object of some kind, which is a sign of malefice, is removed from its hiding-place and destroyed.

Question 3: How is divination to be distinguished from prophecy and prognostication?

When the pact is overt, there is no difficulty at all in coming to an opinion. When the pact is tacit, however, there is. There are three things one should note: (1) the main thrust of the inquiry relating to the future and the reason for the making the inquiry; (2) the nature of the matter concerning which inquiry is being made; and (3) the intention of the person making the inquiry.

(a) If the process of inquiry is simply one of deducing one fact from another, this is not divination and an investigation of such a kind should not be condemned. (b) One should not ask that the information one obtains be certain, infallible, or more reliable than one may reasonably hope it will be, because one must consider human free will and other things of that kind. If certainty and so on are asked for, there will be reason to think that a tacit pact exists. This is why one has very strong suspicions in the case of astrologers, interpreters of dreams, and so forth, since these people claim to make absolutely reliable predictions about the future. Astrologers and interpreters of dreams who merely offer probabilities based on observations of the heavens and physical characteristics, however, may be excused. (c) If someone wishes to make a serious inquiry about things which are hidden and tries to do so by using vain means (and only vain means), without any reference to God, then it may be presumed that there is a tacit pact underlying the business. In this third case, however, the person will be acquitted of divinatory superstition (i) if he practises this divination simply by way of a joke, knowing it to be useless – no one is going to judge a person superstitious if he looks for an emerald in the brain of a hen, or a penis on a monkey's back, for example, because he knows he will not find one there – and (ii) if he knows that the business he is carrying out according to this method is inefficacious by its nature, and if he makes his inquiry of God by using prayers and requests. [Examples.]

Question 4: What kind of a sin is divination?

1) It is illicit and superstitious, and it smacks of heresy when discovery of things unknown is sought of the evil spirit himself. It is illicit, superstitious, and manifestly heretical when worship (meaning either adoration or veneration) is paid to the evil spirit; or images or books are baptised; or children re-baptised; or abuse of sacred things takes place. It is not superstitious, but merely illicit, when one makes an inquiry which is not beyond the range of the evil spirit's knowledge.

2) An explicit pact is always a mortal sin, whether the evil spirit be invoked

by word or deed. Nor is there any place among the faithful for ignorance on this point. [Quotation from Saint Alcimus Avitus, and references to Scripture.] Divination is also a mortal sin when it is conjoined with an implicit or tacit invocation, or (which is the same thing), with a pact. But it is venial under the following circumstances: (a) Ignorance, provided this is so great that it is difficult to overcome – i.e. the person is not pretending to be ignorant, or he is particularly stupid, or he has made no effort to get requisite knowledge; (b) Although treating divination lightly is not usually a valid excuse because divination seeks to usurp to itself knowledge which is reserved for God alone, and therefore divination is, in itself, serious even if the manner of its practice be not so: nevertheless, when it is obvious that the practitioner's mind and intention are free from superstition – for example, because he has wanted to achieve knowledge in this rather silly way simply to amuse himself by way of a joke – it will be the venial sin of vanity, and there may even be occasions when a joke of this kind will be free from any kind of fault. [Example.]

Question 5: How many kinds of divination are there?

From Saint Augustine and Saint Thomas Aquinas we learn that the foundation of all divination is an implicit or explicit pact with an evil spirit. It is considered implicit when someone asks for knowledge reserved to God alone, or from someone other than God, and does this by means he should not employ, that is, which have not been instituted by divine providence for this purpose at all. Whoever concerns himself with these vanities and false madnesses undoubtedly wishes to be instructed by the evil spirit who is the author of inquisitiveness of this kind, and is quite willing to involve himself in the process required to make such an inquiry. The explicit pact or invocation is of two kinds. Either it uses verbal formulae such as are used by enchanters (*incantatores*) who conjure by means of illicit formulae appointed for the purpose by the evil spirit: or it makes use of an action or a performance in the full knowledge that the evil spirit has designated this as a sign or marker of his own power and influence.

Theologians such as Grillando reduce all explicit divinations to necromancy, and implicit to witchcraft (*sortilegium*) and augury. They use these words very loosely and incorrectly, in spite of the fact that these words have a fairly restricted sense which does not embrace just any type of divination ('divination' being a word which includes almost countless numbers of different types of divinatory operation.)

[Del Rio now says he will discuss these types under two headings: (a) those which are based on an explicit pact, and (b) the rest.]

Question 6: The types of divination in which invocation is openly used

There are two main types: oracles or demonomancy, and magical trickery.[7] These include a lot of prognostication and little bits of prophecy.[8] As the true oracle of the liar puts it, 'Many are casters of lots, but few give prophecies'. Oracles, prophecies, oracular responses, oracular revelations, demonomancy: all these can be understood to refer to the same thing, because they have something in common, namely that in them the Devil has tried to imitate theomancy or true prophecy by giving petitioners responses from caves or statues or people.

[The rest of the section is devoted to examples ranging from ancient to modern times.]

Section 2: Various ways in which magical trickery is done, starting with necromancy

[This section consists largely of quotations from Classical Roman poets relating to necromancy, along with Del Rio's own marginal notes on Seneca and references to other relevant literature.]

Section 3: Hydromancy

[Del Rio says he will discuss this separately because no method of divination lends itself better to imposters. He quotes the Byzantine Nicetas Choniates, in a Latin translation, and continues] I find there are various types of hydromancy. (1) You suspend a ring over water and it strikes the sides of the vessel a specified number of knocks. (2) You throw three pebbles into standing water and observe the circles which spread around the pebbles, noting how each of the three intertwines with the others in turn. (3) This notes the different ways in which the sea moves. Sicilians and Euboeans used to do this in the old days and many sailors make such observations in modern times. Hence comes the well-known superstition of certain Eastern Christians who baptise the sea every year, as though it were a living creature. Another custom, distantly connected with this, is when the Doge of Venice betrothes himself to the Adriatic each year by throwing a ring into the sea, although this is a symbol of domination and not of magic.

---

[7] Del Rio uses the word *mangania* which is Greek and refers to (a) the magical arts, (b) the wiles of the Devil or of evil spirits in tempting human beings, (c) meretricious arts or heretical opinions, and (d) spells.

[8] *Prophetiuncula*, a dismissive diminutive which Del Rio seems to have coined for the occasion.

[A further example from the reign of Pope Alexander III.] (4) This looks at the colour of the water and the images which appear in it. [References given.] (5) They set upright a pot full of water, whisper some words, and then look closely to see whether the water boils up and spills over. (6) This procedure comes from Fez. There they put water into a glass bowl, mix a drop of oil with it, and think they can make out extraordinary things in the water, as if it were a mirror. (7) This comes from Clement of Alexandria. He writes that German women used to note the sound, eddies, and swirling of streams, and thence predict the future. (8) Finally, there are people today in Italy who are prepared to use hydromancy to uncover the identity of thieves. They write the names of three suspects on three little balls and throw them into water. Those who use holy water for this purpose commit a greater wickedness. [Del Rio ends with a quotation from Saint Bernard of Siena.]

Section 4: Other kinds of magical trickery

[(1) Lecanomancy (*divining by means of a dish*).[9] Ancient references given.] Today it is used by the Turks. Into a shallow bowl full of water they throw precious stones engraved with various characters, and thin plates of gold and silver. They hear a response coming from the bottom of the dish.

[(2) Gastrymancy (*divining by means of the stomach*).] This was done by filling belly-shaped glass jars full of water and then getting a virgin boy or a pregnant woman to look into them. Certain shapes and images used to appear by way of response.

[(3) Catoptromancy (*divining with a mirror*).] Shapes of the things requested appear in polished mirrors. [Quotations from ancient literature.] More recent authors record of Pythagoras that he used to write letters in human blood on a concave mirror, hold the mirror up to the moon, and so make his divination.

[(4) Similar to the above, crystallomancy (*divination in a crystal*), except that they use pieces of crystal set in a ring and pretend that an evil spirit resides in it.] They say that in 1530, someone from Nuremberg saw treasure in a crystal, shown to him by an evil spirit. Later he, with one of his close friends acting as a witness, looked for the treasure which was buried in a certain spot in front of the city, and both of them saw a box in the hole they had dug. Lying next to it was a black dog. The magician (*magus*) approached the hole to open the box and drive off the dog, but he had not brought with him the bone of Cerberus. So he rummaged round the top of the hollow. But the structure collapsed on top of the wretched man and the hole filled up with earth. [Another

---

[9] Del Rio gives the Greek names of the methods of divination he discusses in this section. Most of his examples come from ancient times.

story, quoted in Latin, from Plutarch, and a third concerning Del Rio's personal experience with a glass bottle said to contain an evil spirit.] [10]

[(5) Dactylomancy (*divination from the finger*) uses a ring made or enchanted when the heavens are in a particular position. One observes the movements of the ring while it is suspended over a tripod and while one is chanting certain words. (References given.)

(6) Onymancy or onychomancy (*divination from the finger-nail*). [11]

(7) Aeromancy (divination from the air). This is called 'augury' if it deals with thunder, lightning, or the flight of birds, and 'astrology' if it refers to unusual images in the air, such as horsemen, etc. References given.

(8) One can use the word 'pharmacy' [12] for the incantations used by enchanters who divine by relying on their traffic with an evil spirit and use nothing except an incantation, as certain lesbians do in Fez, not to mention Egyptians as well. [13] References given.

(9) Coscinomancy (*divining with a sieve*). This is a means of divining the names of thieves. They hold a sieve with some tongs and then pronounce the names of the suspects. The sieve will begin to shake at the name of the guilty party.]

[(10) Axinomancy (*divination with an axe*). This is the same kind of method as the former. The axe moves at the sound of the thief's name.] But when they wanted to find out about the future, they put a piece of lignite on top of the axe. [References].

[(11) Cephalomancy (*divining by means of a head*). The Germans used to do this with an ass's head roasted over hot coals. In later times, the people of Lombardy used a goat's head, to which they paid divine honours. Del Rio thinks that some such practice explains the stories about the ancient Egyptians' worship of animals.

(12) Cleidomancy (*divining by a key*). They used to write the name of a suspect round a chart, tied a key to a copy of Holy Scripture. This was held by a virgin who whispered certain words, and then the chart would move and turn at the name of the guilty person.

(13) Anecdote quoted from an anonymous source whom Del Rio designates I. C.] These days, a thief is found out from close scrutiny of an eye. First they read the Psalms and the Litany. Then comes a frightening prayer to God the

---

[10] I have translated this in *The Occult in Early Modern Europe*, 42.

[11] See *The Occult in Early Modern Europe*, 29.

[12] The Greek word covers more or less the same range as the Latin *veneficium*, on which see supra, 24–5.

[13] I.e. gipsies.

Father, and Christ. Then an exorcism is pronounced against the thief. Next, they draw a circular figure in the form of an eye, marked off with barbarous names, and in the middle they put a bronze triangular key which has been consecrated with certain covenants. This they strike with a hammer made of cypress wood and say, 'Thou art just, O Lord', etc. [Then the thief will be discovered. A story about the discovery of a thief in Rostock, and anecdotes of a similar kind end the section.]

Question 7: Types of magical trickery in which there is no explicit pact, or in which it is completely hidden

Those types having an implicit pact can be discussed under three headings: (1) prophesying (*ariolatio*) or divining from signs (*haruspicina*), (2) augury (*augurium*), and (3) casting lots (*sortes*).

Section 1: Divining from signs or prophesying

[Once more, Del Rio gives a list of different types of divination, supported by references to and quotations from ancient literature, since most of his examples come from the ancient world.

(1) *Ariolatio*, originally involving worship of idols, and *haruspicina*, whose etymology is disputed and which involves divining from certain parts of sacrificed animals. References and quotation from Seneca.

(2) Extispicy (*divination from the entrails of sacrificed animals*).[14] References and quotations from Seneca and Juvenal.

(3) Pyroscopy (*divining from fire*). Sometimes vegetable pitch was scattered over a fire; sometimes torches dipped in pitch were set on fire and marked with certain characters, etc. The Lithuanians use this today. If someone is sick they put him opposite a fire, and if his shadow falls towards it, he will have a good chance of recovering; but if it falls away from the fire, they cry out in despair. Further examples given.

(4) Capnomancy (*divination from smoke*). Examples given.

(5) Libanomancy (*divining from incense*). Quotation from Dio Cassius.]

[(6) Tephramancy or spondonomancy (*divining from ashes or libations*). References given.] Today a trace of this superstition still flourishes. The question for which divination is required is written in ash on a finger or a small stick. They throw the ash into the pure air and then examine closely any letters which appear in the disturbed ash. Likewise, they tell someone to think of three people he might wish to marry, or between whom he might wish to effect a marriage. They

---

[14] Again, most of the technical terms are given in Greek.

draw three furrows in ash, tell him to choose one of them, and then stand with his back turned so that he cannot see the furrows. Then a second person points at the furrows until he chooses one of them three times, and that furrow determines the woman who will become his wife.

[(7) Hydromancy (*divination from water*). Quotations from Vergil and Seneca.

(8) Critomancy (*divination from barley*); aleuromancy (*divination from wheat-flour*); alphitomancy (*divination from barley-meal*).]

[(9) Cyromancy (*divining from wax*).] This is used today by the Turks as well. They melt wax, pour it drop by drop into water, and observe the shapes it forms. Old women in Alsace have invented another way of doing this. When someone falls sick, they light as many wax candles as they say there are saints who send disease. To each wax candle they assign a saint, and the one whose candle first melts completely is declared to be the source of the disease and the one who is doing the harm.

[(10) Anthropomancy (*divination by human beings*). This is done by examining the entrails of slaughtered humans. References given.

(11) Daphnomancy (*divination by laurel*). References given.

(12) Bostanomancy (*divination from plants*). References given, and a quotation from Caelius Rhodoginus.] [15]

[(13) Omphalomancy (divination from the navel).] Associated particularly with midwives. They conjecture from nodules on the umbilical cord and the after-birth how often the new mother may give birth in future.

[(14) This is a new superstition from the same school of midwives – amniomancy (*divination from the membrane around the foetus*). The foetus is wrapped in three membranes while it is in the mother's womb. Two of them sometimes emerge with the new-born child, covering its head like a helmet. Old women predict the child's fortune from the colours they see on this membrane. References given.]

(15) This is an equally ridiculous means of divination used by the Jews. It was done by *Ieduim*, mention of which, according to Rabbinical invention, was made by Moses. They have it that there was an animal called a *Iedua* which was human in shape and had a rope hanging from the middle of its navel. It used this to attach itself to the ground, in the manner of a gourd, and would graze on all the produce of the earth around it, as far as its rope would allow. It could not be captured by hunters unless its rope was first cut through by an arrow. Thereupon it died at once. By carrying the bones around in their mouths and using a certain ritual, people acquired the gift of prophecy and were known,

[15] Lodovico Ricchieri (1450–1520), Italian Humanist. Del Rio is quoting from his *Antiquarum lectionum commentarii* (Commentaries on Readings from Ancient Authors), first published in Paris in 1517.

from their manner of acquiring it, as *Iddegonim*.[16] [Del Rio dismisses the tale with contempt and continues] Had they not attributed a human shape to this creature, we could suspect that they were alluding to a certain animal with the appearance of a lamb, which they say is born and joined to the earth in just such a fashion, browsing upon the grass near it as far as its rope allows: and once there is no more food, it pines away. It can be found in the neighbourhood of Moscow. [References given.]

[(16) Lithanomancy (*divination by a stone*). References given.

(17) Rhabdomancy (*divination by a rod*). Quotations from Caelius Rhodoginus and Cranzius follow,[17] and references to Classical and Mediaeval literature.

(18) Lampadomancy (*divining by a lamp*). References given.

(19) Omphalomancy (*divining by the navel*). There are two types, intended to find out whether a girl is a virgin or not. References given. Del Rio finishes by observing that all these types of divination have been condemned by theologians and canon lawyers, and he gives references to their works.]

Section 2: Augury and auspicy

[This section is devoted to listing more types of divination, most of them relating to Classical models and accompanied by references to relevant literature. Number 5, 'omens', contains the following observations.][18]

It sometimes happens in monasteries that when a monk is about to die, he is seen without his head in the church where he has his stall; and in certain noble families, it is a sign that there is definitely going to be a death if a spring which is naturally very clear becomes turbid because of some maggot. In another family, it is a sign of impending death if the ground near the castle collapses into a deep hole. In Bohemia, before the wife of the Lord dies, it is usual for a woman's ghost in mourning dress to appear in the castle which belongs to the noble family. [References] Monsters are mockeries of nature produced when she departs from her usual course and gives birth to inanimate objects; and we give the names 'manifestations' and 'prodigies' to various dreadful and unusual apparitions in the air and the other elements, and to sounds or effects such as showers of blood, battle-lines of soldiers seen in the sky, and things such as that.

---

[16] Del Rio has already glanced at these diviners in Book 1, chapter 2 (supra, 34, note 7). The verb *yoda'* means 'to know' and is the root of *yedde'oni* which refers to diviners and sorcerers.

[17] Albert Krantz (died 1517), German historian.

[18] Del Rio has taken them from Philippus Camerarius (Philip the Chancellor), French theologian, *c.* 1160/85–1236.

Section 3: Illicit kinds of divination

[Again, Del Rio lists eleven more ways of predicting the future. Most are to be found in ancient or Mediaeval literature, and are accompanied by appropriate references and quotations.]

Section 4: What kind of sin is there in these activities?

The following conclusions should be noted in connection with means of foretelling the future and the other types of augury.

(1) It is a serious sin to investigate hidden offences by interpreting signs of one kind and another, or by using methods of divination because one cannot find out things such as these without the help of an evil spirit. So when a certain person tried to find out a secret thief by measuring the stars, even though he had no intention of invoking an evil spirit, he committed a sin so serious that he was suspended from the priesthood for a year – and this by grace and dispensation since, according to the law, he should have been suspended permanently.

(2) It is equally a mortal sin to try to predict what may happen in the future by using augury or casting lots. Clerics are subject to a sentence of excommunication for this.

(3) Although it is not a mortal sin to make observations of this kind[19] (unless the observer actually believes in them), it is always extremely dangerous for him to direct his actions according to such observations, even if he does not believe in them at all. The reason is that God, with perfect justice, usually allows such people to make a bad death. The Devil often lures them into greater sins by sins of this kind and deceives them in matters of greater importance. At the very least, the observer acquires thereby a very bad character which disposes him very much to a loss of faith. [Examples given.]

(4) These days the same must be said about consulting diviners to find out what we should do and what we should think about something. The proof of this is that one is not permitted to make inquiries of this kind except of God. But God does not want us to trap his will in a net by means of divination. Rather, we are to seek it from the Church's teaching, Holy Scripture, our superiors, and other learned and pious men. It is, however, a mortal sin when some superstitious element is added, and one believes that the divination is accurate. But if neither of these factors is present and, without any superstition, someone inquires the will of God by divination, believing that the divination merely has a degree of probability in it, then the sin is venial.

---

[19] Del Rio has just used the word *auguria* which, strictly speaking, refers to observation of the flight of birds and the use of this to predict the future. But here he seems to be saying that simply looking at signs in nature does not, in itself, constitute a mortal sin.

Chapter 3: Prognostication

So far I have discussed licit precognition (Chapter 1) and illicit precognition (Chapter 2). Now I am going to discuss precognition which is sometimes licit and sometimes illicit. This I have called 'prognostication'. It is either (a) 'physical' or 'natural', or (b) 'political' or 'civil', and for this I have retained the word 'sortilegy'.[20]

Question 1: Prognostication from the stars[21]

When I refer to 'drawing inferences from nature', I mean any inferences which actually depend on natural causes or at any rate are advanced with some degree of probability. Inferences of this kind are made by farmers, shepherds, sailors, architects, doctors, physiognomists, palmists, astrologers, and interpreters of dreams. Now let me point out the differences. With regard to prognostication or judicial divination from the stars, one can establish two kinds, the first licit, the second illicit. The first is astronomy which rests upon universal, true, and unchangeable principles and aims at a knowledge of what is going to happen, e.g. the revolution of the years, the course of the stars and the differences between them, the nature of the sun and the planets, eclipses, fixed and retrograde motions, aspects, conjunctions, oppositions, and correspondences. Tycho Brahe, a noble Dane, has already published useful observations on this subject and even more is expected of him.

The second type of prognostication, astrology, is as different from the first as is a flirt from a lawful wife. It rests upon general, variable principles and predicts the effects of future events which are not unavoidable in themselves but contingent upon other factors, such as some kind of enforced dependence on the stars. It was the Chaldaeans who finally turned astronomy into astrology and, according to Diodorus Siculus (*Bibliotheca*, Book 2), the Babylonians called their priests 'Chaldaeans' because the Chaldaeans were pre-eminent in this field. Later on, 'Chaldaean' simply became a word for astrologer, just as 'Arab' became robber and 'Jew' became merchant. (See *Daniel* 2.2; Juvenal 6; Aulus Gellius: *Attic Nights* 1.9).

There are four parts to astrology. The first deals more or less with *Revolutions* and foretells the vicissitudes of war and peace for a whole year, the wholesomeness of the air, the price of food, the diseases of living things, etc. The second deals with the *Governance of Nativities*. It tells us by signs what may befall a person

---

[20] Del Rio uses the word *sors* which, strictly speaking, refers to divination by casting lots.
[21] The first part of this question has already appeared in *The Occult in Early Modern Europe*, 68–70.

throughout his whole life. The third is called *Electional Astrology*. This instructs individuals in what they should deliberately and usefully do, what they should not do, when they should build, when I should take a sea-journey or go by horse, when one should set out on one's travels or stay at home, and when and where specific actions should be taken so that they may turn out fortunately. Long ago, my mathematics teacher, Johann Stadius, used to glory in this form of divination in a quite extraordinary way. But if you removed from his results those things which sometimes turned out to be true because of trickery, everything used to come out very badly and very unhappily for him. The fourth type is the *Tracing of Images*, which is obviously a deceit and something I have already disproved in Book 1. None of the first three is able to predict with certainty, but the further it departs from the general canons of astrology and deals with particular, individual events, the further it recedes from science and certitude and the closer it gets to lying and vanity.

So – First Conclusion: *The astrologer who does not depart from general principles and those guiding premises which are immediately relevant can, in accordance with the canons of his art, predict with accuracy general events many years, perhaps, before they happen unless either his calculations or his instruments deceive him.*

This is what produced the almanacs [22] which are carried round by the common people. I think no one will be able to deny this conclusion because the subject exists on its own terms and has to be interpreted by its own rules. Events such as the ones I have mentioned are determined and certain; therefore they can be known for certain. By the same reasoning, the astronomer will be able to predict, with some degree of probability, future changes in the weather by observing the changing colour of the moon and the sun and other phenomena of wind, rain, or clear sky. The reason is that, for the most part, these things actually do happen (although they are sometimes prevented from happening because of certain causes peculiar to them.) The poems of Aratus, Cicero, Hesiod, Vergil, and Germanicus's *Phaenomena* deal with this.

Second Conclusion: *The first type of astrology is not superstitious if it merely expresses an opinion together with a fear that the opposite may also be true.*

For example. 'The stars are threatening a lack of food. There may be a difficulty in getting food. I am afraid it may not', etc. The second is not superstitious if it expresses merely a suspicion. For example, 'There is a suspicion that this boy will turn out to be such and such. He will be inclined to do this. His horoscope indicates things of this nature', etc. The third is not superstitious if it says only that its assessment is that something will turn out well and if it does not think more than it says – a point which should be

---

[22] *Ephemerides*. In astrological terms, these refer to tables showing the predicted positions of heavenly bodies for every day during a given period.

noted in all three cases. [Reference given.] The reason is that when we take into consideration events which have certain things in common, we may note that the arrangement of the stars in one case bears a striking similarity to the arrangement of stars in another, and in consequence we may calculate or suspect or fear that the outcomes of these disparate events may also turn out to be similar. There is no sin in a cautious observation of this kind, which errs on the side of prudence and so, in accordance with its own rules, is a good observation.

Third Conclusion: *Astrology which goes further than these three types and predicts that something is bound to happen is definitely illicit and superstitious. All divination of this kind is uncertain and useless and unworthy to be called an 'art'.*

[Del Rio now discusses Cajetan's remark that there are usually three mortal sins involved in astrology: (a) when Christians subordinate the mysteries of the faith to the stars and are drawn away from faith by the influence or position of the stars (references); (b) when they think that future contingencies can be known in advance for certain from the stars. This interferes with human free will; and (c) when questions and choices are subjected to these heavenly bodies as though to some tribunal whose decrees have the force of law. This sets people at odds with the grace of God, divine law, and human intelligence. All this can be proved from reason and from authority. Reason says that events do not exist by necessity and therefore cannot be predicted with certainty. Nor do they lie within the competence of the stars. (Here Del Rio directs the reader to the Bull of Sixtus V and to the astrological studies of Giovanni Pico della Mirandola.) Various authorities have pronounced against astrology: Scripture, Councils of the Church, canon and Roman law, Fathers of the Church, theologians, Sixtus van Hemminga,[23] philosophers and physicians, Cornelius Agrippa, historians and poets. Del Rio accompanies all these with relevant references or quotations.]

But astrologers do not lack arguments. In the first place, they cite *Genesis* 1.14 on the lights of Heaven. 'And let them be for signs, for seasons, for days, and for years'. Consequently even some theologians infer that, even though the stars are not causes, they are dependable signs of everything in the future. Julius Sirenius attributes this opinion not only to Plotinus and Porphyry, but also to Origen, Eusebius, and even to Augustine.[24] He also accepts this and confirms

---

[23] A Frisian astrologer (1533–1586) who, as Del Rio says, published *Astrologiae ratione et experientia refutatae liber* (A Refutation of Astrology According to Reason and Experience) in Antwerp in 1583.

[24] Julius Sirenius (floruit 16th century), Italian philosopher. He published his *De fato libri novem* (Nine Books on Fate) in Venice in 1563.

it from the words of Isaiah [34.4]: 'The heavens will be rolled up like a book'. By 'heavens' many people understand 'the firmament', and say that the firmament is called a book in as much as the stars in the sky are like the letters in a book and are signs of the future which may be read thereby.

[Del Rio objects that the stars are not dependable signs of everything in the future, and deals with the authorities cited above, adding more references of his own in contradiction both of them and of Sirenius.]

Secondly, astrologers refer to *Judges* 5.20: 'From heaven the stars fought against them. The stars remaining in their ordained place and course fought against Sisera'. What was the reason they agreed to fight, ask the astrologers, unless the course of the stars and position of the planets was favourable to the Jews and unfavourable to Sisera? So if Sisera perished because this disposition of stars was against him, it could have been foreseen through astrology, feared, and avoided.

[Del Rio replies that (a) according to Josephus, it was a heavy storm which prevented the Canaanites from being able to use their weapons, and (b) that the help sent from heaven refers to angels posted to defend the Israelites, and that the order and disposition were those of the angelic army under the command of the archangel Michael. (References given.)

Thirdly, astrologers turn to Psalm 18.2: 'The firmament proclaims the works of his hands', and say that this means it foretells what God is going to do. Del Rio denies that this is the meaning of the passage, and gives references to relevant literature.

Fourthly, astrologers use history to show that predictions often come true. (Examples and references.) But Del Rio warns that one should beware when astrologers say anything true because that is a clear sign they have made a pact with an evil spirit, and he refers his readers to a wide variety of literature in support. When God has permitted and does permit astrologers to predict correctly, he does so to punish those who listen to them.] What Aristotle said of dreams is absolutely true of this type of divination, too: that it may be true by accident, just as when someone who regularly throws dice or bones claims he can get the result he wants. [Further references to ancient and modern instances, with quotations from Girolamo Cardano and Mariana.[25]]

Fourth Conclusion: *Those physicians who make diagnoses according to the position of the moon and the other planets in the signs of the zodiac (e.g. which sickness will happen to someone, and which arrangement of stars will enable a cure to be found), even if they are not superstitious are certainly harmful to the patients. So are surgeons*

[25] Cardano: *Commentary on Ptolemy on Judicial Astrology*, Book 1, text 14. Juan de Mariana (1536–1624), Spanish Jesuit. He published a history of Spain in Toledo in 1599.

who examine wounds in the same way and take into account the day on which the wound was made and the stars which preside over them (with names such as Centel, Neus, Dibergibel, Lachadiel, Sapissa, Elebra, and so forth), and thus pronounce the wound either mortal or curable. Conrad Wimpina describes all this at length.[26]

[One also finds astrologers who specify on which day the body should be purged by drugs or bleeding or cupping. All this is suspect, because the stars do not have such a great influence on things here below. A doctor's diagnosis should depend more on the constitution of the patient and the known seasons and symptoms of the disease than upon the course and position of the stars, as Hippocrates and Galen have said. Some astrologer-doctors take their dependence on the stars even further and ignore physical symptoms entirely. Del Rio then gives references to relevant literature.]

Fifth Conclusion: *The kind of divination which inquires particularly into secret matters (occultae), such as thefts, treasure, virginity, etc. is pernicious and plainly forbidden under any kind of law.* [References to and quotations from Scripture and legal codes.] Astrologers are often tolerated in public affairs, but this sets a very bad example and is a public evil.

Question 2: Prognostication from the elements, meteors, plants, trees, and wild animals

Next to the stars and the heavens, there is most agreement about the element air. It is very likely that there is no sphere proper to fire – an opinion which is very old and is strenuously defended by certain fairly recent authors. Ausonius recorded it in his *Riddle on the Number Three*: 'Three Graces, three Fates, three tones of voice, three elements'.[27]

In the mid-region of the air there occur a good many meteorological phenomena. An abundance of exhalations gives rise to large and small fires with extremely different appearances because of the diverse forms of the exhalations themselves. These sometimes look like flames or columns or lances or stars

---

[26] Wimpina = Konrad Koch (1460–1531), German theologian. He wrote several tracts on astrology. Del Rio does not specify which one he is using here.

[27] Ausonius was a poet of the fourth century AD. In the margin, Del Rio lists several modern authors who are clearly the 'fairly recent' he had in mind. They include Cardano; Scipione Capece (died *c.* 1551) whose book *De principiis rerum* (Basic Principles) to which Del Rio refers here was published in Venice in 1546; Francesco Patrizi (1529–1597) who published *Discussionum peripateticarum tomi IV* (Four Books Refuting the Peripatetics) in Venice in 1571, a work also listed here by Del Rio; Francisco de Vallés; and 'Villalpando', by whom Del Rio may here mean Cardinal Gaspar Cardillo de Villalpando (1527–1581). Del Rio adds 'and others' to his list but without further specification.

jumping up and down, running all over the place, falling and rising. Sometimes there are comets of different shapes, but I have not the time to discuss these here. All of them, however, denote a long spell of dry weather, and they are also signs of daily violent winds. What is also absolutely true about comets is that if they occur frequently, they foretell barrenness, famine, and plague, because the power of the comet uses up all the humidity of vapours and exhalations: and in consequence they threaten with death people who have an excess of bile and those who are of a somewhat fiery nature – mainly princes and great landowners. The same dryness disposes them to wars and seditions.

[Additions to these points made by astrologers and Squarcialupi [28] are meaningless and wrong. Del Rio maintains that what he himself has said seems to accord with what one finds in nature. But it often turns out that the cause of comets is God's particular wish to warn people about an imminent public catastrophe, or the death of kings or princes, so that they may turn quickly to repentance and amend their behaviour. In this case, comets are classed as portents and admirably commend to us the charity of God who does not strike unless he warns us first. (References to and quotations from modern literature.) Winds and vapours also enable people to make predictions, especially about health and fertility.

Del Rio now offers six illustrations of prognostication from nature. First, peasants are able to make prognostications from ordinary showers of rain, and when these showers turn out to be extraordinary, they may be natural warnings about the weather at that particular season, or they may be supernatural warnings of the anger of God.

Secondly, Del Rio describes how a volcano in the neighbourhood of Arequipa in Peru erupted on 18th February 1600.]

After about a month it stopped and, according to the account of the Jesuits who live there, there was a brief intermission. But people remained afraid that there would be worse to come, and the fear produced a great change for the better in their behaviour. Everyone fell down at the feet of the priests, so much so that they gave them no peace and burst into their bedrooms in order to make their confessions. In this way, God gained the profit of many souls. But Satan did not neglect his opportunity. For the pagan Indians who lived next to the fires went to their magicians (*magi*) in accordance with their usual superstitious practice and they in turn hurried to the volcano. There they performed their wicked chants and made their wicked sacrifices. But the flames devoured the magicians and some of the people standing next to them. Everyone

---

[28] Marcello Squarcialupi (16th century), Italian astronomer and physician. His *De cometis dissertationes novae clarissimae* (New, Easy To Understand Essays On Comets) was published in Basel in 1580.

else suffered condign punishment too, some, filled with despair, hanging themselves and others committing suicide in other ways.

[Del Rio says he has excerpted this narrative from a letter written by one of the Jesuits in Arequipa, and adds further references to other literature.]

Thirdly, the swelling of the sea and rising of the wind and unaccustomed floods of rivers are forewarnings of plague. Earthquakes signify the same thing, too, as Ammianus, Proclus, and others bear witness.

Fourthly, images which occur near vapours and exhalations because the light is being reflected (such as rainbow, halo, coronae, perhelion, and 'rods')[29] can be thought of as prognostications derived from warnings given by nature (for example, fissures and those things which are known as 'pits' and 'windows').[30] There are also those traces of flame known as *ignes fatui* (I am here describing different effects), which arise either from vapour which overflows and overwhelms things in its way, or sometimes from light which has been overcome and crushed.[31]

Fifthly (let us return to terrestrial things), one may gather prognostications from the growth of trees. [Example from Cicero.] A large number of bitter almonds indicates an abundance of corn, and the three-leafed clover shivers and raises its leaves against a storm. Although they have no ears, the sportive leaves of trees, the soft hairs and down of poplars, flying through the air or swimming upon water, give advance notice of a storm. If roses or violets flower a second time at the onset of autumn, plague is imminent. In Bordeaux, during the winter which preceded the great plague there, some roses appeared in the garden of the Jesuit house there: I saw them myself.

One thing which some people have recorded does not seem to be without superstition. At the beginning of autumn, they say, one should gather two or three nuts and cut them open with a knife. In one of them you will usually find a fly, a worm, or a spider. The fly denotes that there will be discords during that year; the worm signifies fertility; and the spider, death.

[Sixthly, Del Rio records further examples of prognostications in Aratus and Hesiod, as recorded by Cicero and Vergil, and finishes with a reference to remarks on the same subject by Pico della Mirandola.]

[29] Perhelion = *Parelus*, which I take to be a variant upon the word. 'Rods' = *virgae*. This word may refer to stripes of colour and here probably indicates an aerial phenomenon such as an imperfect rainbow.

[30] These seem to refer to shapes or gaps in the atmospheric fires. Seneca calls attention to such phenomena, calling them 'wells' and 'deep holes', *Natural Questions* 1.14.1.

[31] In other words, the *ignes* are either formed from the vapour itself or are traces of light which are occasionally visible through the surrounding miasma.

Question 3: Medical prognostication

[Having dealt with false, illicit, and ridiculous forms of prognostication, Del Rio says he will now turn to those which may be taken seriously, as recorded by recent learned writers.] Those signs which are justified by natural principles and genuine experiences are morally honest. Any others are vacuous and alien to the art of medicine. [Of the trustworthy signs, some testify to good health, others to the onset of illness; some show that the patient is becoming ill, others that he has already succumbed to illness; some indicate that he is recovering and is well on the mend, others are ambiguous. None is infallible.]

Question 4: Foretelling from physiognomy [32]

The physiognomist thinks that from the colour of a person's hair and the outward appearance of parts of his body, their proportion, their mixture of qualities, and the person's state of health, he can deduce something about his mode of behaviour, his intelligence, and his mental state. He gives particular consideration to the expression and the face because this is usually the mirror of the intellectual virtues. Hence is derived the term 'metoposcopy'.[33] [References to ancient literature on the subject.] The art has various fundamental principles. First, one looks for a certain likeness to living creatures; for example, those with small eyes are considered to be envious because of their similarity to monkeys. People with big eyes are stupid, the reason being that they resemble cattle and donkeys. [Further examples of the same kind.] Secondly, it bases itself on racial and territorial characteristics. Generally, these depend on a certain physical make-up rather than intelligence and behaviour. For example, physiognomists define dark-skinned people as stupid and obstinate because North Africans are like that. Thirdly, one looks at the sex. Because women for the most part have pale, soft skin and are timid and weak, the physiognomist therefore thinks that men with white, soft skin are going to behave in a similar way.

The second and third principles are based on complexion,[34] for physiognomists think that the same temperament is the cause of both skin-colouring and behaviour. Whoever has a skin of such and such a kind will have a similar sort

---

[32] Parts of this section have already appeared in *The Occult in Early Modern Europe*, 22–3.
[33] Del Rio gives the Greek word which means 'looking at the forehead'.
[34] This refers to the way qualities such as hot and dry, cold and moist are combined in certain proportions so as to produce a particular kind or 'nature' of body and temperament. 'Temperament' here means a blend of humours, qualities, and substances in appropriate proportions.

of temperament, and such and such a temperament will be expected to produce an analogous type of behaviour. Fourthly, they come to a judgement about a person's mental state by looking at the movement of his limbs and his general physical condition. Compare Hippocrates: 'Eyes which do not blink are liable to anger because angry people look with fixed and unmoving eyes'. Solomon was of the opinion that 'a naughty person, a wicked man, walketh with froward mouth. He winketh with his eyes, he speaketh with his feet: he teacheth with his fingers: frowardness is in his heart, he deviseth mischief continually' (*Proverbs* 6.12–14). And Isaiah: 'The shew of their countenance doth witness against them' (*Isaiah* 3.9): that is, their outward appearance hid the secrets of their heart. [Quotation from Martial, 12.54.]

I have heard that Matthias Corvinus, the King of Hungary, a prince whom no one has praised, was far too fond of divination, to such an extent, in fact, that he used to undertake nothing unless he had first consulted his astrologers; and he had such an enthusiasm for divination by physiognomy that from his first sight of the lines on a person's face, he would judge most cleverly what that person was like. This he did in order to show off his mastery of this type of magic to anyone who might try to rival him.

Fifthly, physiognomists seek to find a principle of their art by combining one sign with another and thence deriving still more; for example, jealousy from a tendency to anger, to which they add sadness and corruption of the mind.

One's conclusion, then, is that physiognomy which goes no further than the boundaries of natural philosophy is licit and has some chance of being correct.

[Del Rio now offers proofs of this conclusion, based upon Scripture, law, and philosophy, and goes on to draw inferences from these proofs.]

An opinion based upon observation of animals is more certain than one based on observation of humans because animals are motivated by inclination alone, whereas a human reins in his inclination with his will. So a physiognomist cannot give an opinion about what someone has done, or the actual life of a person, and say that it is such and such. He can talk only of propensity and inclination, as Proclus quite rightly thought: for example he can say only that such and such a person has a propensity for avarice, women, and wine, etc. So he cannot judge what a person can do in accordance with the gifts God has freely given him, because God has distributed his gifts to each person as he wills. The physiognomist cannot come to a judgement about things which are external to a person, such as violent death, wealth, honours, and other good or bad things which fortune brings; nor can he pass an opinion on marriage, rank, and other occupations in which people are free to make their own choices. (The book *De nevis* [Blemishes] by Melampus is full of nonsense such as this.)[35] The reason is that none of these things depends on physical characteristics or bodily constitution. God certainly allows some divinations to be proved right by the way they turn out, but at the same time he allows physiognomists to make mistakes in those matters which are essential to their case.

[Del Rio ends with an illustrative quotation from the *Elogia* of Paolo Giovio and a further reference to *A Treatise on True and False Prophecy* by Covarrubias y Horozco][36]

Question 5: Chiromancy

Chiromancy is divided into (a) physical and (b) astrological.

First conclusion: *Physical chiromancy is licit and is part of physiognomy. So one's opinion about the former is the same as one's opinion about the latter.*

It belongs to physiognomy because it considers the body's temperament from the lines and parts of the hand and then, from the temperament, it tracks down, with some degree of probability, the propensities of the soul. [References given.]

Second conclusion: *Astrological chiromancy is absolutely vacuous, and illicit, and does not deserve the name of 'science'.*

[Del Rio now cites Antoine du Verdier,[37] Sixtus V, and Francisco de Vallés who have argued against this type of chiromancy, and then lists a large number of people who have supported it.]

This art divides the palm of the hand into certain hillocks, small open spaces, and lines. It ascribes individual planets to the spaces and certain stars to the lines. Then it attributes to those spaces and lines planetary and stellar effects which are popularly believed to be true, as Wimpina briefly demonstrates, adding that he does not approve of all this and is doing no more than giving an account of it. [Other references given.] The people who usually make a profession of this vanity are the wives (if they can actually be called 'wives') of that pig-swill which wanders round the whole of Europe, and whose members are

---

[35] Melampus may have been a writer of the third century BC. An edition of his treatise was published in Venice in 1522.

[36] Paolo Giovio (1483–1552), Italian historian, Bishop of Nocera. *Gli elogi vite brevemente scritte d'huomini illustri di guerra, antichi e moderni* (Brief Praises of Men of War, both Ancient and Modern) was published in Fiorenza in 1554.

[37] (1544–1600), French bibliographer. Del Rio refers to his *Diverses Leçons* (Various Readings) which was published in Lyon in 1580. Horozco = Juan Covarrubias y Horozco (floruit 1589–1608), Spanish canon, whose *Tratado de la verdadera y falsa profecia* was published in Segovia in 1588. Del Rio earlier refers to Francisco de Ribera's citations from this book and says that he himself acquired a copy only in 1605 in Valladolid.

popularly known as 'Zingari' or 'Egyptians'. [References given and a quotation on the origin of gipsies from Münster's book on geography.[38] Del Rio follows these with further denunciation of gipsies, and literary references.] Experience tells is that this kind of thing is connected with harmful magic; for if someone gives them a single coin from a bag or a box, quite often all the coins in that bag or box are found to have shifted to join the original single coin – an overt example of malefice. As far as their divinations are concerned, they cannot be excused from superstition or heresy (supposing people like that think in these terms), or scandalous imposture.

[Countries should not allow gipsies to congregate inside their borders, but should keep them under control by means of suitable punishments. (References, and a quotation from Athenaeus.) Del Rio then continues his tirade against gipsies, and explains how dangerous they can be by referring to an incident which happened in Spain at the Feast of Corpus Christi in 1584. The leader of a huge number of gipsies openly boasted about his detailed knowledge of every city in the state, its people, their personal wealth, and the various overland routes and mountain-passes into the country. Del Rio thinks there should be control over the inquisitiveness which has led to such a comprehensive knowledge, and refers approvingly to Charles V's legislation against gipsies and similar travellers. He concludes by saying that Holy Scripture cannot be used to undermine his objections to chiromancy, and that anecdotes in books on the subject by people such as Cocles carry no more conviction.]

Question 6: Prognostication from dreams

[Del Rio begins with a brief review of earlier literature on the subject.]

First Conclusion: *Certain dreams accurately foretell an event. Some make no prediction or make one which is illusory. Therefore one may legitimately take note of some, but not of others.*

[In support of this conclusion, Del Rio quotes from a hymn attributed to Prudentius, and comments that it agrees neither with the Epicureans who rejected the notion that dreams are meaningful, nor the Stoics who maintained that they must be taken seriously. He goes on to quote *Ecclesiastes* 5.6: 'When dreams are many, vanities are very many, and words innumerable. But make sure you fear God'; and *Ecclesiasticus* 34.1: 'Dreams raise up foolish people. He who gives

---

[38] Sebastian Münster (1489–1552), German geographer, mathematician, and Hebrew scholar. His *Cosmographia Universalis* (Geography of the World) was published in Basel in 1550.

attention to lying visions is like one who catches at a shadow and follows the wind at its heels'. Scripture does not support the Epicurean view, since it provides so many examples of dreams sent by God, along with their interpretation. Homer and Vergil were right when they said that there were two gates through which dreams come, and that one emitted false dreams and the other, true.]

Second Conclusion: *Dreams are as reliable as their cause. If the cause definitely produces an indisputable outcome, the prediction of that outcome, derived from dreams, will also be indisputable. If the cause produces an outcome which has some degree of probability, then the prediction of that outcome will also have a degree of probability. If the cause produces an outcome by chance, the prediction of that outcome will also depend on chance and will be deceptive.*

[Del Rio discusses what Classical and early Christian authors have had to say about the cause or causes of dreams.]

Later theologians have divided these causes into (a) divine, (b) natural, and (c) demonic. Natural causes present particular difficulties. They proceed either from a cause internal to the sleeper, or from an external cause. Some internal causes arise particularly in the soul. Such a cause is then called 'animate' or (according to some people) 'moral'. Some causes arise especially from the body, and this type is called 'physical' (although some people call it 'natural' in the strict sense of the word.) The internal animate cause is when dreams arise from things to which the person paid particular attention while he was awake: as Solomon says, 'Dreams follow many anxieties' [*Ecclesiasticus* 5.2. This is followed by another quotation and further references.] The internal physical cause arises from the existing composition and disposition of the body which is unwell either because it is exhausted by starvation, replete with the after-effects of drinking alcohol, or from some over-predominance of one of the humours: or because it is suffering from some other internal problem.

From these causes are born peaceful or shameful dreams, or dreams of many different kinds. Those who have too great a supply of blood dream of scarlet roses, the crocus, gardens, feasts, dances, sexual intercourse, air, flying, and anything which is happy. Phlegmatics dream of the sea, waters, baths, sea-journeys, sinkings, heavy burdens, and slowly running away from harmful things while being hindered in the attempt. Cholerics dream of the colours in the yellow-red range, noisy quarrels, fights, and outbreaks of fires. Melancholics dreams of smoke, fog, darkness, roaming through deserted places, aimless wanderings at night, horrible ghosts, deaths, and anything which is sad. Those whose bladder is full of humour dream of lakes, rivers, and showers, and while they are asleep they sometimes wet the sheets. Those in whom pure, wholesome juices predominate dream that they are rolling round among sweet-smelling, delightful little flowers; whereas, by contrast, those in whose body are imprisoned stinking, corrupt humours dream that they are rolling in filth, slime, sewers, and dead bodies. Those who have the back of their head affected and obstructed by a sticky humour dream they are being crushed and suffocated. The name for this disease in Greek is *ephialtes;* in Latin, *incubus;* in Spanish, *la pesadilla;* and in French, *la coquemare.*[39]

A natural external cause of dreams is when the imagination of the sleeper is moved by an external agent, and there are two kinds of such an agent. One is the surrounding air and the other is an imprinting by or influx from the heavenly bodies; and just as heavenly bodies influence physical matter and so create different forms of stones, metals, and plants, so it cannot be denied that by pouring their influence into the faculty of creating images, which is found deep in physical organs, celestial bodies can produce distinctive visions to which they give shape, and effects which flow therefrom.

Third Conclusion: *Taking notice of dreams derived from natural causes, and interpreting them, is licit in as far as those natural causes correspond to the effects which are associated with what has caused those causes.*

[Hippocrates, Galen, and theologians are in accord over this.] When the cause is internal and animate, we can take notice of a dream so that later on we may organise our studies and our life for the better and with greater freedom from anxiety. But what sort of person is it whose reading and thinking during the day befouls him at night with filthy visions? Let him be as open as possible about the anxiety which causes thoughts like these. Do frequent dreams frighten someone into cowardice and desperation, or drive him to some other sin? Let him investigate the causes of these dreams and procure remedies which will set him free of them. On the other hand, do dreams press someone else towards something which is good, such as religion, celibacy, or penitence? Let him regard such dreams as good, for surely they seem to be sent by God. Interpretation of this kind of dream depends on experience, mental agility, and a knowledge of each individual's intellectual activities, morals, and propensities.

When the internal cause is physical, a person can be afraid of diseases and arm himself against them. Galen writes that when he dreamed that one of his legs had turned to stone, not long afterwards he became paralysed in that part of his body. [Further example given.] When the natural cause is external, we should see whether its effect is founded on something in us. Is there something

---

[39] The basic meanings of these words is as follows. *Ephialtes* = someone who leaps on top of you. *Incubus* = someone who is lying down or sleeping next to you, leaning or hanging over you, keeping watch over you. *Pesadilla* = something small, heavy, and tedious: modern Spanish, nightmare. *Coquemar* = modern French *cauchemar,* 'nightmare'. The basis of the word refers to a nocturnal phantom which presses down upon one.

in the sleeper himself which is the cause of his suffering (for example, if I dream I am about to go to Rome, or go into battle)?

[Del Rio develops this theme, and then turns to demonic dreams.] There are diabolical dreams which evil spirits (*mali spiritus*) treacherously send to sleepers, either to set in motion mental turbulence such as lust, anger, hatred, or desperation: or as a sign of hidden or future things. [Examples follow, drawn from ancient and modern literature.]

Fourth Conclusion: *It is permissible to take notice of demonic dreams in order to beware of the duplicity of the evil spirit. It is not permissible, and neither is it useful, to take note of occult knowledge or future events.*

[Interpretation of things hidden or future events is not possible, this side of a miracle, except through a pact with an evil spirit, and attempts to find out such things are over-inquisitive and superstitious.]

Fifth Conclusion: *Taking notice of dreams sent by God is licit, but interpretation of them is suitable only for those to whom God has revealed the proper way to interpret them.*

[Quotation of *Daniel* 2.27, and a reference to a Mediaeval dream.] The ability to tell a demonic dream from those sent by God belongs to confessors, who provide a cure for the soul and are endowed with the gift of spiritual discernment. [Del Rio says he has commented on this in Book 1.]

To sum up: It should be observed that if one agrees the dream has arisen not from an animate nor from a physical cause, it will be safest to reserve one's opinion about whether it comes from God or from the Devil. If it has been sent by the Devil, one should be careful and spurn it. [References to Scripture and Classical literature.]

I would have finished this section on dreams had I not remembered my regular (and to me most gratifying) friendship with Justus Lipsius while I was living in Louvain. He and I often used to have conversations which I found especially agreeable about matters suited to both our characters, i.e. the way literature and morals should be shaped. The loss of this exchange of ideas I now find distressing and painful. One day we happened to be talking about predictive dreams and he told me the following story. There was once in Brussels a cobbler's wife and for twenty years she made a large number of predictions to various people, which had turned out to be true to the last detail. She said that Spellius – he was the person in charge of the roads: in Brabant such a man is known as *de Koyroe* – would be executed; Requesenius, the Governor, would soon die of disease; the King's High Council would be subject to violence and most of the councillors thrown in gaol, and many other things of a similar kind. Lipsius said he had seen and heard her on a number of occasions. She used to say that a spirit (*spiritus*) used to talk to her in dreams. He appeared as a diffuse, white body whose outlines could not be discerned. She learned everything from him, she said, and when he appeared she was struck with such a great and unremitting terror that she felt as though she would faint. Afterwards the spirit forced her, for fear of her life, to tell other people what she had learned in her dreams and he did not allow her any peace until she had done as she was told. The woman was in other respects of little consequence, somewhat simple, and did not have a particularly bad reputation. On the other hand, she was not of proven sanctity, either.

Various considerations are suggested by this anecdote. I have my doubts whether these dreams were supernatural. Did they come from God or from an evil spirit? Dreams from God usually happen to women just as often as they do to men, and neither the usefulness of the individual to society, nor his or her poverty stands in the way of this. It usually happens, too, that dread accompanies apparitions sent by God, and the person feels compelled to say what he or she has seen. Now, there are several points in Lipsius's story which make me suspect that the dreams came from a black rather than a white spirit. First, there is the appearance of a diffused whiteness, always without shape, and the constant horror which came with it, a horror which did not bring subsequent joy and tranquillity of mind. This is a fairly clear indication that the whiteness of the source was a deception. Its suspect sex and status merely serve to point out the lack of accompanying sanctity, wisdom, devotion, or other signs of that kind. The woman did not get any money or profit from the spirit, but was often given blows, and almost always received abuse. This is what normally happens to witches (*sagae*): this is the payment the evil spirit gives to his people.

Secondly, the things the woman used to predict concerned public matters. But the public scarcely needed telling about these, and the predictions were being made at a time when the public could hardly have had enough time to take precautions against them. Indeed, she would predict things only a few days before they actually happened, so the prediction was made in vain, and people put a trust in her, which they would not have given to a man who knew what he was talking about. This is not how God usually indicates what he wants people to know in advance and what he wants them to be on their guard against, a manner of prediction shorn of anything which may persuade people that the predictions are true.

Thirdly, I am of the opinion that the things she predicted might just as well come under the heading of 'human wisdom and conjecture' as under the heading 'evil spirit'. Take Spellius's execution: the evil spirit knew he was guilty and that an earnest, painstaking inquiry into Spellius's life and actions was being made because of the frequency with which his name turned up in secret denunciations of wrongdoing. Ludovic Requesenius's disease: in his body he had a bloated boil which was absolutely full of bile. Who could not foresee he was going to die? Doctors make a judgement from external signs. Cannot Aesculapius, who was struck by lightning, do the same when the inside of the body lies open to his inspection?[40] Extreme dissatisfaction with the Council of State had been simmering for a long time already, and the person who was stirring it up was not unaware of how bold Hesius was and how much he was exerting himself. Satan knew who among the councillors was more unpopular, and who was less. He kept his eye on everything. He saw the conspirators on the alert: he saw that some people did not trust them or despised them or were powerless against them. So it did not require any great or supernatural sagacity to sniff out what was going to happen and, by using similar premises (as logicians say), what would be the consequence.

Chapter 4: Political prognostication, or ways of foretelling the future

[By this, Del Rio says, he means tests conducted according to universal and human law, designed to discover the truth about something. He lists divining by lots (*sors divorsia*), lottery (*loteriae*), canonical purgation, and popular purgation.]

Question 1: Divining by lots

[This section deals with the Greek and Roman method of divination by casting lots into an urn. Whether this is permissible or not depends on the type of question which is asked. To avoid sin, the questioner must abide by four conditions: (1) he must await the outcome from God, not from fate or the stars, and should invoke God as he casts the lots; (2) the casting should not be attended by any superstitious practices, or misuse of sacred things or Holy Scripture; (3) the questioner must not cheat; (4) his principal intention in casting the lots must not be to search out God's will in an irregular or improper fashion, but to remove discords, jealousies, and quarrels. Del Rio quotes Scripture and the Venerable Bede in support of his contentions.]

Question 2: The divining contract known as 'the lottery'

[This is used when dice are thrown to decide who is going to get a particular object which several people want to have. Del Rio says (a) that this is licit,

---

[40] Aesculapius was the Greek god of medicine, killed by lightning as a punishment for bringing the dead back to life. 'Aesculapius' here, of course, stands for 'evil spirit'.

and produces arguments used by Jean Briand[41] to support his reasons for saying so; and (b) consideration must be given to the fairness with which money is divided amongst those involved in the contract. Del Rio then discusses the way in which lotteries, whether private or public, should be run and the pitfalls which may await the unwary.]

Question 3: Canonical purgation

[This describes two methods used in accordance with Church regulations to determine a person's guilt or innocence of a given offence. The first is by oath, the second by taking the holy sacrament. Del Rio refers to and quotes from Mediaeval historians and Saint Thomas Aquinas.]

Question 4: Purgations in use among the common people

[These attempts to decide innocence or guilt are tainted with superstition and are expressly forbidden by canon law, since such purgations demand that God work a miracle.]

Section 1: Calling on God's judgement

It often happens that those who think they have been injured by others see that they cannot rely on human defence or aid, so they betake themselves to God. This they do, not in the expectation that he will rescue them from those who have done them harm, but so that they may take revenge on their persecutors, and so that God may thus reveal to everyone else that they have been unworthy targets of an injurious act. Sometimes these people are told to present themselves at God's tribunal within a certain time, but sometimes they are given no time at all. This is known as 'a citation to appear before God as judge'. Many people quite rightly do not know what to make of this. Are they to be afraid of such a citation or not? Is the person issuing the citation acting lawfully or unlawfully?

[Del Rio comes to three conclusions. (1) If the person who cites another does so, not out of hatred, desire for revenge, impatience, anger, desperation, vanity, or from any other sinful motive, but because he has been subjected to an injustice and wants to prove his innocence, clear his family's name, or deliver the world from a tyrant, then his action may be regarded as licit. Scripture and other literature is cited in support of this opinion, along with an illustrative

---

[41] Jean Briand (died 1520), Vicechancellor of the University of Louvain. Del Rio refers to his *Quodlibeticae Quaestiones* (Various Inquiries) which appeared in Leipzig in 1519.

anecdote from Thomas of Cantimpré. (2) It is dangerous for people of unproven holiness of life to copy others in issuing these citations. (3) Those who knowingly cite others unjustly commit a mortal sin. Del Rio then refers the reader to Mediaeval historians to illustrate the points he has just been making.]

Section 2: Purgation by single combat

[This section consists largely of illustrative references drawn from Mediaeval and modern literature. The Church has condemned this kind of purgation, and Del Rio quotes part of Gregory XIII's Bull against it, issued in December 1582, and adds his comments upon the text.]

Section 3: The popular method of purgation by fire

[This section consists largely of anecdotes drawn from a wide range of literature in illustration of the practice. The opening remarks and anecdote give a fair idea of the whole.]

In the past, this kind of purgation was done in three ways: by using a pyre, by using live coals, and by using a piece of red-hot metal such as a ploughshare, a brick, spikes,[42] or mailed gloves. Innocence was proved if the person came away unscathed. If he did not, he was considered to be guilty. My researches tell me that sometimes this method was undertaken willingly, but sometimes it was imposed on someone who was challenged to undergo this proof.

Testing by means of red-hot metal is still in use today in Japan, as we learn from a letter, written by one of our Jesuit brethren, Father Luis Froes, in 1595. In it he tells us about an amazing miracle which happened at Omura.

'A Christian who was living among the natives was accused of theft, a crime which is punished very severely in Japan. Now, if someone has been convicted of this offence, no matter how flimsy the evidence may be, he will be condemned to death with no hope of reprieve. But they found it difficult to prove this Christian guilty. So not long afterwards the natives started pestering him, and although they could not do anything else to him, they compelled him, quite improperly, to take an oath according to their usual practice. What happens is that the accused writes on a sheet of paper the oath he is to swear and signs it. Then he puts the paper in the palm of his hand and a piece of red-hot metal on top of that. He has to close his hand and call down upon his head the vengeance and anger of Cham if he is guilty of the crime laid to his charge. If it happens that his hand is burned, they say this proves he is guilty of the offence. But if he and the sheet of paper remain unharmed, he is innocent.

[42] *Conticulae.* The word does not appear in dictionaries, but I have treated it as though it were a diminutive of *contus* = spear, lance, pike.

So when the Christian I mentioned was brought to this pass, he either had to swear the oath or refuse to do so. But if he refused, he would make himself guilty and thus cause his own death. So, confident of his innocence, the man said it was not right for him, as a Christian, to swear by the false god Cham and he could swear only by the true God. The natives agreed he could swear by his own God, so he made the sign of the cross over the paper, put the red-hot metal on top of it (since he was compelled to do so), and with great self-control closed his hand about the metal. An extraordinary thing! Neither his hand nor the paper was burned. So not only was he set free from the punishment with which the natives had threatened him, he was freed from the blame they had falsely attached to him as well'.[43]

Section 4: Popular purgation by water

[Again, Del Rio gives illustrations from Patristic and Mediaeval literature and then includes the texts of two rites of exorcism, the first for hot water, the second for cold. In the first case, the accused plunged his or her hand into boiling water. Innocence was proved if the hand sustained no injury. In the second case, if the hand were burned when it was placed in cold water, God was indicating that the accused was guilty. Another test involving cold water required that the accused be immersed in it completely.]

Here, Reader, you have the whole rite of this type of proof by cold water which was once in use but is now forbidden by Papal decree – not because of the words or the solemn ceremonies (most of which were pious even if they contained some blemishes), but because of their content and because little by little the common people were giving their approval to these ceremonies, even though the Roman Pontiffs objected to them. For the Popes quite rightly condemned this rash tempting of God, as if it were some Jewish demand for a miracle; and it is worth noting that gradually the Papal prohibition gained ground everywhere. First the rite was used in connection with other criminal offences, then, after the time of Saint Bernard, it was used as a test for heresy, and finally this abuse was employed only in cases of malefice (*maleficium*) or magic (*magia*).

Indeed, so closely associated with this crime has it become that, without any invocation of God or the use of any other religious ceremony, judges in certain places misuse this proof, as though they were playing some kind of game. Today, in many places in Germany, and especially the area round Westphalia, they use this proof to track down workers of harmful magic (*maleficii*). These

---

[43] Del Rio says this letter was published in Latin in Mainz in 1598. Luis Froes (1528–1597) was a Portuguese Jesuit missionary who wrote extensively on the customs and history of Japan.

people are regarded as suspicious because of their reputation or because they have been denounced by other women. Then straight away, without further investigation, they are arrested, brought outwith the city where their right hand ·is tied to their left foot and their left hand to their right foot, and thrown into cold water. If the women float, they are very strongly suspected of being workers of venomous magic (*veneficae*) and are thereupon subjected to severer questioning. But if they sink, they are believed to be innocent.

This kind of purgation, or 'proof', has been illegal up till now for Catholics for whom the authority of Papal canons remains undiminished. But reformers who have defected from the Church have fought wonderfully on its behalf, and the mordant philosopher from Marburg, Arnold[44] Scribonius, has defended it as licit.

[Del Rio ends this section by saying he is going to discuss Scribonius's opinions on the matter and points out the large number of authors, cited by Godelmann in his book on witches, who have declared the practice illicit.]

Question 5: The proof (as they call it) of cold water, which some people use in Germany to put witches (*striges*) to the test

Section 1: A discussion of the opinion and explanations offered by Adolf Scribonius.[45]

Wilhelm Adolf Scribonius is a very keen defender of this judicial opinion and practice. He tries to establish it partly on physical, partly on non-physical grounds. On the physical side, he speaks about the lightness of the evil spirit bearing up the witches' (*sagae*) weight on top of the water. On the theological side, he speaks about the hatred and antipathy which exists between the water and the witches.

[Del Rio now says he will quote Scribonius directly so as not to be accused of misrepresenting his arguments, although actually he is relying on someone else's book to provide him with Scribonius's text.]

He says that the ability of witches to float comes from a Satanic lightness which is its efficient cause; for Satan is by nature very light, and has more in common with air (as one might expect) than with water. In consequence, he can hold the witches up on top of the water. He has two ways of doing this.

---

[44] 'Arnold' is a misprint for 'Adolf'.

[45] German physician (floruit 16th century). His *De examine et purgatione sagarum per aquam frigidam epistola* (A Letter Concerning the Examination and Purgation of Witches by Cold Water) was published in Herborn (?) in 1583.

Either he himself supports them and raises them on his back, so to speak; or he unites himself with them and pours himself into their whole body, thus occupying it and taking possession of it – not by a hypostatic union or an internal union which mixes body with body, but by joining his lightness to them in some fashion, and giving and communicating it to them by means of his presence. 'Therefore', he says, 'the Evil Spirit (*cacodaemon*) diffuses himself substantially within the witches (*sagae*) and remains in occupation of them; and by "substantially" I mean it is his spirit which inhabits them (although without his essential being), not the substance of the physical body of the witch. So one is not talking about a lightness which comes without the help of an intermediary simply from the way the body is composed, but a lightness which comes to it from outside and is received from elsewhere'.

[This, says Del Rio, is both obscure and false.] Who believes that all witches (*sagae*) have been taken over by an evil spirit in the same way as those who are possessed, or demoniacs, and as happened to the Gadarene swine? The witches themselves deny this and experience argues against it. If the spirit takes possession of them, how is it he seems to come to them from outside? Is he in two places at once? Does he really come and go as he pleases? I believe he *could* do this, but I do not believe he actually does so. Secondly, if his lightness has this effect, why are not other possessed individuals equally light? Why do they sink in water? Why did the Gadarene swine sink? Because the spirit did not want to hold them up? So it is not the lightness of the evil spirit's nature, but his will which makes this happen. This is the truth, and a further point made by Scribonius underlines it when he says that Satan in the role of God's officer holds them up, and that because an officer is not allowed to go beyond what a judge has laid down as a rule, therefore the evil spirit cannot cause the guilty to drown nor the innocent to be upheld so that the innocent are exposed to danger and the guilty escape unpunished.

[Now Del Rio offers arguments against Scribonius's point about the non-physical way in which the guilt or innocence of witches may be tested in this fashion.]

Next, Scribonius takes refuge in the will of God and predestination. He says, 'What if I were to say that God himself endows with a peculiar and specific lightness the bodies of witches whom he knows are actually guilty, whereby they are borne up on top of the water? It would certainly not follow from this that God had ceased to play a part in the works of his creation;[46] for he could have pre-arranged things so that somehow those who were going to turn into

---

[46] Omitting a 'not' in front of 'had ceased', which does not seem to make sense in the context.

witches would not sink in the water at all. Can this be said to be contrary to God's omnipotence or to God's will, simply because it is not expressly mentioned in Holy Scripture? Certainly not'.

Well now, I say that God *can* do so when he pleases. But I doubt whether he would ever wish to do so and I have found no indications why we should believe he has wished to do so. [Del Rio says he awaits proof of what Scribonius says here.] He adds that the water itself cannot bear up witches. Why does he think this? 'Because', he says, 'Almighty God in his most wise and most just judgement throughout every age has predestined the element water as a saving purification for humankind so that they may be washed free of their sins and use baptism as their entry into Christ's Church; and by these means people are made new, as if we who had been rejected before now entered the kingdom of Christ through a doorway. So in my opinion, water accuses them with a kind of jesting hatred and rejects them. It is very much as though people are testing how strong the witches are, and yet the witches cannot be made to sink'.

So there you have it, Reader. The efficient cause is not to be sought in the evil spirit but in the nature of water which has an inbuilt hatred for witches (*maleficae*), inbuilt by the Creator of nature who knew everything in advance while he was creating the water and had already instituted water as the future instrument of our salvation. He sowed in the water a hatred of these women who are the haters and violators of their own salvation and that of other people.

[Del Rio now quotes from Scribonius a passage which elaborates on the part water plays in baptism, and the reasons for the hatred which water shows towards witches. Del Rio says that much of this is true but not very aptly applied, and then turns to the opinion of heretics such as Luther, Chemnitz,[47] and Calvin. He says that Scribonius's 'jesting hatred' of water for witches must be understood in a metaphorical sense, elaborates this point, and then finishes the section by saying that if any element can feel hatred for witches it will be fire.]

Section 2: The strong opinion and vigorous reasoning of I. C., a Catholic

I. C., whose name I shall keep to myself, rejects Scribonius's first point about the Devil's holding up witches. He thinks nothing like that has happened in this case – no ministration, no operation by an evil spirit. It is, rather, an act of Almighty God alone, working through his good, ministering angels.

[Quotation from I. C. Del Rio hopes that I. C. will pay heed to the common opinion of Catholic theological and legal authorities (as he himself does), rather

---

[47] Martin Chemnitz (1522–1586), German Lutheran theologian.

than to the notions of the reformers. Then he returns to further criticisms of I. C.'s book.]

In the first place, he presumes that most judges these days use this proof. I know this is not true, unless he happens to be talking only about Germany. In Italy and Spain (where the authority of the canons is undiminished) no one uses it at all. Nor does anyone use it in France and Belgium – or so few that they do not count, and those merely ignorant, rustic judges. In Germany itself the more educated have begun to repudiate this usage and those who still continue to use it do so with scrupulous, painstaking care and in fear of making a mistake. This is made clear in a letter sent to Godelmann from Westphalia, which he includes in his book, and which says that most Germans testify to its gradual disappearance in many places.

[There follows a second quotation from I. C.] 'When there are sufficient indications to warrant arrest, an arrest should be made'. (That is undoubtedly true.) 'When there are fairly strong presumptions (even the appearance of fact) against a prisoner, such as can generally be sufficient to warrant torture, the accused should not be tortured at once. This water-test should be employed first in order to provide greater weight to the preceding indications. Nor should the test be administered to prove the person's guilt, but to prepare the way for torture and give it greater justification and to underline the importance of what is being done'.

[Del Rio disagrees. This test is not a necessary adjunct to judicial torture. If the indications are sufficient, there is no need to use the test. If the indications were enough to have someone arrested, there is no call to make him or her undergo the test. 'Either they sink or they do not. If they do sink, why are they not released as innocent? Why go any further? If the woman has been cleared when God is her judge, has she not been cleared sufficiently?' He then quotes a story about a woman who would not sink, in spite of the efforts of the executioner to hold her down, and offers his comments on it. I. C. claims that there is a distinction to be made between workers of harmful magic (*malefici*) and other criminals, and says that since malefices are difficult to prove, judges should be allowed a greater licence in their investigative methods.

Panormitanus,[48] followed by other writers, was of the opinion that supernatation is a sign of innocence and that only in this crime of malefice is the contrary true. In this, however, he is mistaken. There are grave difficulties attendant on any test in relation to this crime which is a difficult one to prove. Witches

---

[48]   This is likely to be Niccolò de' Tudeschi (1386–1445), Italian canon lawyer, Archbishop of Palermo (hence 'Panormitanus'). But there is also a Girolamo Panormitano, a Sicilian Dominican, who died in 1570.

(*sagae*) very often do not feel the effects of torture because they go to sleep or they become insensible to pain; and before they are subjected to torture, one may find much stronger indications of their guilt than one does in cases of adultery or other sexual offences. This is because several people may have been involved, witchcraft being no more secret a crime (*occultius*) than crimes involving sex. The supposed difference between malefice and other crimes has not been proved: neither is it true.

Del Rio now turns to other specific points made by I. C. and deals with them in turn.

I. C.   Judges can and should use the test. Witches are very afraid of it.

D. R.   Why would witches (*lamiae*) fear the water-test more than the rack? They very often present themselves to be tested in this fashion.

I. C.   Denunciations by friends and accomplices are unreliable and deceptive, so the judge should put the accused to this test.

D. R.   Indications of guilt can be proved by other, legitimate means. It would be better to let a guilty person go free than to find him or her guilty by indications which are not legally admissible and an illegitimate test.

I. C.   Binsfeld says that, just as the bleeding of a corpse in the presence of its murderer seems to be a miracle, so is the floating of witches (*sagae*).

D. R.   There is no suspicion of a pact with an evil spirit in the former.

I. C.   Workers of harmful magic (*malefici*) cannot harm or impede judges while the judges are engaged in their judicial duties. 'Witches (*maleficae*), like the evil spirit, wish to harm and exterminate all judges; but they cannot do so because God does not allow it'.

D. R.   Judges and other officials who administer justice do not always avoid impediment or harm.

I. C.   Consultatory divination is permitted under certain conditions. The water-test is of such a kind and fulfils the conditions. The *Malleus Maleficarum* says that it is permissible to use superstitious means to remove a malefice.

D. R.   We are not dealing with a malefice but with a test to see whether someone is guilty of malefice or not. Besides, it is not permissible to use one act of malefice to flush out another.

I. C.   Everything one does should be judged according to its intention.

D. R.   Someone may have a good intention and yet still commit a sin. It is better that a hundred guilty witches (*sagae*) go free than that one innocent woman be condemned or brought into danger by this kind of test. It is a mortal sin not to obey the Church which has universally prohibited popular methods of putting people to the test.

Del Rio concludes by arguing that I. C. has misapplied certain words of Saint Bernard in his argument.]

Section 3: A correct opinion against the water-test, proposed and proved

[Del Rio offers the following proofs of his case. (a) The test is forbidden by canon law and by Papal decrees. (b) Tempting God is a sin. The test should not be considered as a miracle from God but as a magical pact with an evil spirit. (Del Rio illustrates his point with references to Scripture and quotations from Mediaeval history and Saint Augustine.) (c) Disobedience to the Pope in spiritual matters is the same as disobedience to God. (d) A judge who makes an incorrect judgement without sufficient cause and differs from the common opinion of legal experts commits a sin. So if there are no other sufficient indications which would warrant torture, the judge who uses this water-test to establish someone's guilt will be committing a sin.]

Question 6: Certain other proofs in common use

There is the proof by weights and plate. In Germany they hang witches (*sagae*) and say they cannot sink beyond a certain weight however tall or fat they may be. Even Reckius condemns this.[49] My opinion on this is the same as it is about other common tests. It undoubtedly rests on a pact with an evil spirit, it is superstitious; and it is the same kind of thing as trying to test God. This method is not expressly forbidden by the canons because it is clearly a recent invention.

[Another method is testing by means of a cross. It is mentioned in the *Constitutions* of Charlemagne and is practised by the Frisians. Del Rio quotes the relevant article from their legal code. He then mentions another divinatory method used in Imperial Constantinople and concludes with references to Mediaeval literature.]

---

[49] Possibly Johann Reckius, one of the respondents to Arumaeus Dominicus (1579–1673), a commentator on both canon and civil law.

BOOK 5

The duty of judges in dealing with workers of harmful magic: or, the judicial process in relation to the crime of magic

[Del Rio begins with a few personal remarks and lists the main sources he has used for the legal discussions which follow: Clarus, Bossius, Simanca, and (as he says) especially Prospero Farinacci.] [1]

Section 1: Is the usual practice and method of procedure sufficient to try this crime?

Interpreters of the law are agreed that officially there is a difference between an 'offence', a 'crime', and a 'malefice', but this differentiation is not particularly appropriate for my purposes. In common with what other jurisconsults have said, in this case I take it as given that the crime of witchcraft (*sortilegium*) or malefice is a crime which is public, of mixed jurisdiction (i.e. if it is committed by a lay person, the case can be heard by an ecclesiastical or a lay judge), and is one which affects everybody. It is an ordinary, specific crime, in the sense that it belongs to a specific category of crime and carries a fixed penalty set by law. But it is also an extraordinary and exceptional crime, in that it has certain peculiar features and belongs to that class of offence which the law terms treason or heresy. So general legal opinion quite rightly says that malefice belongs to this category and that it is a crime of great enormity, great seriousness, and great wickedness because in it are combined the particular circumstances of outrageous crimes – apostasy, heresy, sacrilege, blasphemy, murder, and not infrequently parricide, unnatural sexual intercourse with a spiritual creature, and hatred of God; and there can be no offences more dreadful than these.

---

[1] Julio Claro [originally Chiaro] (1525–1575), Italian jurisconsult much in favour with Philip II and Philip III of Spain. Egidio Bossi (1487–1546), Italian jurisconsult who published several treatises on criminal law. Diego Simancas (died 1583), Spanish theologian and canon lawyer. Prospero Farinacci (1554–1618), Italian jurisconsult who published *Praxis et theoricae criminalis libri duo* (Two Books on Criminal Theory and Practice) in Frankfurt in 1606.

[Del Rio now lists points made by Farinacci concerning the discretion judges may use in cases of malefice when the attendant circumstances are taken into account. These are: (a) it spreads a bad example; (b) it takes place at night when people are off their guard; (c) it takes place in secret, like the more serious kinds of murder; (d) it harms those who are bound by close relationships; (e) its perpetrators commit sin deliberately, constantly stimulated thereto by the Devil; (f) this crime is punished very severely by burning; (g) those who commit this crime do so in full knowledge of what they are doing.

But Del Rio observes that in punishing this kind of criminal, a judge should not without a very good reason exceed the penalty laid down by law. Nor should he hand down a milder punishment, but rather apply the letter of the law. Farinacci, however, says that given a sufficient reason, a judge may lessen or increase the legal penalties at his discretion. In this sense, all penalties these days depend on the judge's discretion. But he may decide to lessen or increase them, says Del Rio, only before he passes sentence. After he has passed sentence, he may alter them only in accordance with the decree of his Prince – the exception being heresy when the penalty may be lightened should the guilty person return to the faith. 'I think this is true in the case of malefice, as well, and practice confirms this. Often judges who have condemned women to be burned give instructions that they be strangled or decapitated (as was done some years ago at Stavelot in the case of Jean del Vaulx).' Only certain judges may do this, however, and they cannot do so arbitrarily.

Del Rio ends the section by quoting a Mediaeval poem on the duties of judges and comments that a judge may depart from standard practice in dealing with this crime in as much as it is a crime with certain peculiar attendant features.]

Section 2: How should investigation of this crime be set in motion?

[A judge's investigation is either general (when he tries to find out who committed the crime and who were his associates), or specific (when he makes inquiries into a particular individual who has been accused, denounced, or brought to the attention of the authorities in some other way.) Witchcraft is a hard crime to pin down. Nevertheless, an investigation should be held even if there is no agreement about the identity of those involved, 'and the women[2] should be found guilty even if they simply say they were taken to a meeting'.[3] (References.)]

---

[2] Del Rio here uses the feminine form of the gerundive, *condemnandae*, even though there has been no direct indication hitherto in this section that he is thinking specifically of female accused.

[3] *Conventus* = witches' convention, or sabbat.

2) According to canon law it is preferable that some kind of accusation come before the investigation. But these days it is the general custom not to require this because the investigation is considered to be the ordinary means of dealing with the situation, and in all offences a judge can, of his own authority, institute an inquiry without the need for any accusation. However, there must always be something else in place of the accusation, such as denunciation, reputation, or indications (about which more in a moment).

3) As far as the form of the investigation is concerned, it must be indisputable, specific, and clear, and take into account the characteristics and circumstances of the offence in such a way that the accused may not erect a defence on its uncertainty, generality, or obscurity. [Del Rio now discusses what he means by the particularities of the offence. These details are required in a specific but not in a general investigation; nor are they required in crimes such as treason, heresy, and magic.]

4) [Indications must precede the investigation. This is generally considered to be fair, although there are those who think it dangerous and very unfair, even if the judge is exercising his own free will and operating on the orders of his Prince. Princes must be careful how they issue orders to have someone investigated, since accusers can often take advantage of Princes' natural goodness and credulity.]

5) The accused must be notorious or the object of common gossip – a charge which should be brought, not by the defendant's accusers, but by other people who are worthy of belief. But here there arises a great difficulty in connection with this fifth requirement. Is it always necessary that the bad reputation come first, even when other indications are available in support of the accusation? [Del Rio thinks that if the other indications are sufficient, notoriety is not a necessary prerequisite; but if they are lacking, notoriety is essential. He then goes on to discuss how this is to be handled in a specific and a general investigation, but adds, 'The accusation of having a bad character must come from reliable, not unreliable or malevolent sources. The accused must be extremely disreputable, and his or her bad name the subject of general gossip. Witnesses must agree on this matter, and at least two to whom no one can take exception admitted and examined, particularly on the subject of the ill-repute, as is the normal practice when any other crime is involved'. Some people say this is not necessary in crimes of heresy and treason, but Del Rio disagrees. He also says that investigation of bad character can be undertaken on the strength of denunciation by a single reputable man, and should bad character be established one can proceed to investigate the crime involved.]

6) The person under investigation must not have been acquitted of the same crime elsewhere by a judge in a foreign court, pardoned of the offence by the

Prince, or even sentenced by him to an appropriate punishment (although this should not be a lighter punishment). [Del Rio now goes into detail on the legal niceties involved in these points.]

7) As in every legal action, this type of investigation must be carried out by a competent judge: and in this matter it is generally agreed he should be equally learned in canon and civil law. The same goes for inquisitors of the faith. Simancas explains this very well in relation to particular cases, and it was especially because those who provide magical potions (*venefici*) and witches (*striges*) are accustomed to deny the Catholic faith, or at least to say and do things which smack of heresy, that this particular business was entrusted to inquisitors by Innocent VIII, Julius II, Leo X, and Hadrian VI.

In the case of *sortilegia* properly called (i.e. illicit divinations),[4] the investigation should not be conducted by inquisitors of the faith unless it is clear that the *sortilegia* savour of heresy, i.e. if something which is self-evidently impious and heretical is mixed up in it, or if the diviner (*sortilegus*) believes that his divination has something to do with God. The same may be said of all the other suspect prognosticators who fall easily into loss of faith, or worship the evil spirit, or make a pact with him, or believe he has certain knowledge about future possibilities, or abuse sacramentals.

In the cases of other superstitious people, the inquisitors do not ask whether what they have done is shocking or just irresponsible unless they detect something which is openly heretical, such as baptising someone the accused knows has been baptised already, or baptising an image.

In the case of superstitious magicians (*magi*), it scarcely ever happens that these people do not believe something which is heretical, or that they do not knowingly do something which is heretical because, as Saint Cyprian says in his *Book of Twofold Martyrdom*, 'Those who use magical arts tacitly deny Christ and at the same time make a pact with evil spirits'. So there will be scarcely any person of this kind against whom inquisitors cannot institute proceedings; and the inquisitors will be able to compel any judges to send to them any cases against heretical magicians of this kind.

All judges also agree upon this point: that the accused should come under the jurisdiction of the person carrying out the investigation either because of the type of offence he has committed, or the fact that he lives within the investigator's jurisdiction, or the fact that he was born there, or even because of his close association with some place within that jurisdiction for a period of not less than ten years. (This refers only to crimes committed outwith the jurisdiction during the ten-year period, since there must be a good reason for

---

[4] *Sortilegium* = prediction of the future by casting lots. The word later came to be used as one of the terms for witchcraft.

his choosing to live in a particular place for such a long time.) This cannot apply, however, to offences committed before that time.

[There are many other considerations relating to jurisdiction, says Del Rio, but he is not going to spend time on them. Witches/diviners (*sortiariae*) are almost always involved with heresy and heretics can be tried anywhere by different kinds of judges.]

8) In cases of divining/witchcraft (*sortilegia*) and malefices which are not heretical or outrageous, an investigation must be started within twenty years of the crime's having ceased because after a twenty year period the accused may claim that the process should lapse because people generally have a more accurate opinion about him. But when the malefice or divination/witchcraft involves heresy, no lapse of time can help the accused and an investigation of heresy can be instituted even after his death. Whenever the malefice or divinatory superstition[5] is so great that it should be considered an exceptional or horrendous crime, the accused will be subject to repeated investigation as long as he lives.

[These crimes are so serious that there can be no statute of limitation upon their being pursued.]

9) According to common law, a person cannot be investigated in his absence. But this rule lapses in exceptional crimes, and in general practice an investigation can be started even in other crimes against those who are present and those who are absent, whether they are contumacious or not.

Section 3: The best indications whereby a judge may proceed safely to try this crime

[There is general agreement (a) that the indications required at each stage of a judicial process which is particularly serious for the accused must be clearer, more plausible, and more relevant than for the preceding stage; and (b) that the indications may be slight, serious, or very serious. Slight indications give rise merely to suspicion or simple presumption; serious give rise to more than suspicion but less than proof; and very serious are half-way to proof. It is also agreed (c) that it is usually the judge who decides the status of the indications. He must also weigh in the balance persons and circumstances by giving due attention to the law, customary practice, and received opinion of his own country.

A general investigation can sometimes be instituted on other grounds, such as extrajudicial notification or information. These sources must be examined

---

[5] *Sortilegia superstitio.* Because of the ambiguity attendant on the word *sortilegium* and its variants, this may also refer to superstitious practices involving witchcraft.

and if they name an individual a specific investigation may be started against him. But a specific investigation cannot be started in the absence of any indications at all, and if a judge does start such an investigation the accused has the right to challenge him.]

Slight indications are enough to warrant taking unofficial information about the offence, but serious indications are required before the accused can be told he is being investigated or be cited for the offence. Slight indications are enough to have him arrested, if this is done simply so that the accused may not escape while an investigation takes place, but to institute a specific investigation against him, serious indications are required. In my opinion, indications more than just 'serious' are sufficient to allow one to proceed to torture, and I think Claro designates as 'serious' those indications which are normally held to be 'very serious'. As Farinacci sensibly observes, the indications should be compelling, certain, and clearer than light at noon so that the judge may come to a more or less definite view of the defendant, and so that he may lack nothing other than a confession by the accused. (It should be understood that we are talking here in terms of indication, not of proof: that is, about those things which are suitable for persuading the judge fully, but not for proving guilt beyond any doubt.) This determines that the judge has been persuaded that the accused is to blame and is guilty, even if his guilt has not been fully proved because a confession or some other proof is lacking. So when the judge thinks he has a complete set of indications, he can proceed to torture. If, however, he has a full set of proofs, he should proceed to pass sentence.

[Del Rio now discusses further the legal technicalities of how many witnesses are required for the admissibility of what kind of indication, and then passes on to review specific types of indication. First, a single witness is sufficient to start a specific investigation. Secondly, being denounced by a fellow criminal is also an indication.]

It is common legal opinion that workers of harmful magic (*malefici*) and astrologers (*mathematici*) can be questioned under torture about their associates. It is approved under civil law and accepted as a universal practice that a judge is bound to interrogate, and the accused is bound in conscience to denounce associates he knows (or rather presumes) have not reformed themselves and have not desisted from crime. It is the opinion of theologians that the judge who does not do this commits a serious sin because he is not confronting and impeding the subsequent harm to the state and to individuals, which flows therefrom, as he is bound to do. Consequently, he is obliged to give every satisfaction redounding thence to private individuals as well as to the state. Such is the general opinion of theologians, as it is of Binsfeld who adds (relying on

Soto and Navarre)[6] that a confessor is bound to advise those accused of this crime to denounce unregenerate associates, and that if they are unwilling to do so he should not absolve them of this obligation, even if he absolves them of their sins. But if the accused knew that one of his associates had come back to the faith and there was no danger that he would return to his vomit, or was going to do so, he could not, under these circumstances, name him and neither could his confessor give him leave to do so, even though the accused might wish to name his associate.

[There are, however, problems attendant upon believing denunciations or nominations made by an associate, since he or she is bound, by the nature of this crime, to be disreputable. Their evidence is admissible because 'workers of harmful magic usually commit this crime in front of their accomplices and reveal it only to them'. The normal rules about what constitutes admissible evidence, then, can justly be suspended in this case. According to Simancas, Claro, and others, denunciations of this kind should be made under torture because without that the evidence of disreputable witnesses can scarcely command belief. Binsfeld has reservations about this, however, and Del Rio proceeds to discuss the various points of view, with references to the relevant legal texts. Certain requirements emerge. (1) The person who names another should have no anger, rancour, or hatred against the person he names. (2) The judge must not interrogate a worker of venomous magic/witch (*veneficus*) about individual associates, but only about associates in general. (3) The person who names another must be questioned carefully about all relevant circumstances – who, what, when, where, with whom, how? One cannot proceed to torture the accused as a result of such a nomination unless this has been done first. (4) Trustworthy neighbours must be asked if the person named has ever been suspected of a crime such as this, or has ever had a bad reputation because of it. (5) There must be no wavering or hesitation when someone is named, and the person naming another must persevere steadily even under severe torture; and (6) the person who names another must swear an oath that he is telling the truth.

Two conditions are enough to warrant torturing someone who has been denounced or named by a single accomplice: (a) if other confessions from several accused persons are in agreement, or (b) if other indications give weight to the charge. (Some lawyers think that being named by one associate, without any other supporting evidence, is enough to lead to torture, but Del Rio says this has been very well refuted by others.)

<hr>

[6] Peter Binsfeld (1545/6–1598), German theologian. He published *Tractatus de confessionibus maleficorum et sagarum* (Treatise on Workers of Harmful Magic and Witches) in Trier in 1579. Pedro de Soto (died 1563), Spanish Dominican theologian. Francisco de Navarre (died 1563), Spanish bishop.

Del Rio, relying upon Farinacci, now mentions other points which he thinks need to be taken into account. (1) if there is a single eye-witness, the judge will be able to proceed with severe torture since this would provide more than half proof. (2) A minimum of two aural witnesses furnish some presumption of guilt. (3) Was there hostility between the person named and someone who has been executed or condemned to death? (4) Does the person named have a bad reputation, and if so, does it arise from trustworthy sources, and did it begin after he or she was imprisoned or accused? (5) After the accomplice gave his or her name, did the accused run away out of justified fear? When did he or she run away? (6) Is there a close friendship and constant association between the person named and the person who did the naming? (7) Did the two of them have any secret conversation before the crime was committed? (8) Did the person named make use of any superstitious practices?]

For example, did he try to teach other people the art of magic? Was a jar of magic ointment found in his house: or a jar of toads, or other pieces of equipment used in this treacherous art? In particular, was a book of magic found in his house and was it to be used for a purpose other than good? Did one person threaten another with malefice and did something result from this? In particular, did the person threatened usually answer with threats of his own? (Certain points must be in agreement here, but I shall come back to this later.) Was the named person found in someone's stable or house? Was he there at a time when he should not have been? Was he in a place where he should not have been? Did malefice follow? Did someone wound an animal, and was the person defamed found a short time afterwards with a wound in the same place, as often happens in cases of lycanthropy?

Not long ago here, in Belgium, Wanderburcht who is Dean of the church in Mechelen and a man of noble and noteworthy faith, told me about an extraordinary thing which had taken place there. A citizen wearing a gun was taking a walk outwith the town and a large number of birds of ill omen began screaming in a tree near the road. He levelled his arquebus at them, fired, and thought he had scored a direct hit on one of them which fell off its branch. But he found only an iron key which had dropped off a woman's belt. He picked it up, went home, and said to a friend of his. 'You don't recognise this key, do you?' he asked. His friend replied that he did. It belonged to his neighbour, N. So they went to the house and found the door shut. Inserting the key in the lock, they turned it and went inside, presuming on their close friendship with the owner of the house; and when they entered, they found the mistress of the house who had been struck in the side by a bullet.

Here is another example, Reader, and one which is quite beyond dispute. In 1587 I was staying in Calais which had had the good fortune to be captured by His Most Serene Highness, the Archduke Albert and was being held by troops of the Catholic King.[7] Near the Nuletum Bridge two signs had been put up to mark the boundary against the people of Boulogne who were the enemy at that time, and these markers were being guarded by a garrison of Walloons. Just before evening, two sentries saw a dark cloud flying towards them in a clear sky and thought they could hear the voices of many people jumbled together inside it, although neither man actually saw anyone. The one sentry, more daring than the other, said, 'What is all this? Do you think we're safe? If you like, I'll aim my gun at that cloud'. His companion agreed. There was a thunder-clap and a woman fell down from the cloud at their feet. She was drunk, naked, very fat, middle-aged, and her thigh had been shot through twice. They arrested her, but she began to pretend she was deranged and said scarcely anything in reply to their questions except, 'Are you friend or foe?'

[Del Rio follows this with two anecdotes from Rémy and further references. He then goes on to say that if a reliable witness depones that he saw a witch (*saga*) giving a potion to a horse which died soon afterwards; or two witnesses depone that the person named performed some act which workers of harmful magic (*malefici*) usually perform with a view to malefice, 'for example, if he stands in water and throws water behind his back into the air; or someone saw him strike a stone with a stick just before a hailstorm; or he picked flowers from various trees and throws them into a jar; or he strikes an animal with a stick or wipes it with his hand and the animal dies not long after' – these, according to Binsfeld, are absolutely compelling indications and any one of them by itself is sufficient to warrant torture. Del Rio, however, has his doubts about this.

Del Rio now returns to his list of points to be considered with regard to indications pointing at someone who has been named or denounced by an associate, which may be sufficient to lead to torture. (9) When they are arrested, do they do or say anything which signifies they are afraid they will not escape alive from the hands of the judges?[8] (10) An extrajudicial confession by the defendant, proved by two witnesses, unless it is shown there has been a mistake. All these, he says, are reliable and legitimate indications which amount to a half proof, provided they are detailed and consistent.

But there are yet further points to be considered. In cases of denunciation by

---

[7] There is something odd about this information. Archduke Cardinal Albert was not appointed Spain's Governor-General in the Netherlands until after the death of his brother, Archduke Ernest Rudolf, in February 1595. He came to the Netherlands on 29 January 1596 and seized Calais from the French on 17 April that year. During all this, Henri de Navarre was in Boulogne. The Pons Nuletum may have been part of the Calais fortifications, or some defensive barrier between Calais and Boulogne.

[8] The grammar here indicates that 'they' are women.

an accomplice, torture may be allowable under the following conditions. (1) The naming by an accomplice must carry such conviction that the judge (bearing in mind all relevant attendant circumstances) believes the deponent is telling the truth. (2) The accomplice who names his associates should not also be guilty of some other offence (such as gambling), because if he is, even in exceptional cases this is not enough to warrant a specific investigation, still less torture, regardless of whether he would have confirmed his nomination under torture. (3) Some lawyers argue that the naming by a single individual of someone of good reputation is not sufficient for torture, even if it is supported by other evidence. But it is sufficient if it weakens indications to the contrary. So the number and quality of the supporting pieces of evidence must be considered; and legal opinion says that if these destroy his good reputation, then the person named should not escape torture. (4) Spontaneous nomination by a defendant is not sufficient for torture without other supporting evidence. According to Farinacci, however, if there is supporting evidence, then torture may be applied. General legal opinion says that if a defendant, without any preceding interrogation, names accomplices, this does not amount to an indication – a point which Del Rio follows with a detailed discussion of legal technicalities. (5) Supporting evidence is of no value when the torture during which the associate was named was not legally carried out or legally ordered. Some people think that a statement by an accomplice is not a valid reason for torture if the truth could have been obtained by some other means; but this opinion, says Del Rio, has been deservedly refuted by Menochius[9] and Farinacci.]

A fourth indication is that of reputation. Now, I have to inform you that for reputation to be suitable as an indication, it must originate with men unless it concerns something which is better (or at least equally well) understood by women – that is, unless the deed in question touches women to a greater degree, or at least in equal measure – for example, a malefice of abortion or sterility, a malefice involving infanticide, and so forth. In offences involving witches (*strigae*), reputation can originate equally with women and men. At the same time, the reputation must be one which is substantial, not insignificant, and it must not be vague, fluctuating, in decline, or contradictory, but constant and growing; and everyone must be agreed on all its particulars.

[Contradictory reputations indicate that there is not total agreement by everyone, and this causes difficulties in assessing which aspect of the reputation should be believed.

---

[9] Giacomo Menochio (1532–1607), Italian jurisconsult. Del Rio is probably referring to his *De praesumptionibus, coniecturis, signis, et indiciis commentaria* (Commentaries on Presumptions, Conjectures, Signs, and Indications) which was published in Geneva in 1586.

Del Rio now goes on to make further points. (a) The reputation should have arisen at the time the offence was committed or immediately afterwards, not long after the event, and certainly not after accusation, investigation, or imprisonment, unless the reason for the reputation began a long time after the commission of the offence. (b) The reputation must occur in the place where the offence was committed, not elsewhere, although 'place' (according to the nature of the offence) may refer simply to a neighbourhood, or part of a town, the whole town, or a whole district. (c) The reputation must not be one which the person has sought to acquire or pretended to have, because this is not reputation but hypocrisy. (d) An evil reputation must not have been wiped out by a good one, because, all things being equal, a judge ought to heed the good reputation rather than the bad, and preference is given to a few witnesses to the good reputation over a larger number testifying to the bad. But a good reputation may have its effect weakened by an indication which supports the bad.]

A bad reputation in the case of some particular deed creates the presumption of an offence as long as the bad reputation concerns the same kind of offence as the one under investigation; and if there is other corroborative evidence, this will be sufficient warrant for torture, whether the person is of inferior rank or not, and whether the offence is difficult to prove or not. [Farinacci is right when he contradicts lawyers who have different opinions about this.] Proving a reputation with scrupulous accuracy is as necessary as it is rare in judicial procedures. Grammatico, the Neapolitan Senator, has written that he has never seen a trial in which a public reputation was proved in legal terms – something which Claro, Vulpellus, and other notable judges and advocates have said as well.[10]

[To prove reputation, the following points are required. (1) There must be at least two witnesses, and these ought to be conspicuous for their unblemished morals and hold absolutely correct opinions on the faith; and one should be able to define and prove these qualities in court. Those judges who commonly fail to do this when it comes to a specific investigation or torture are wrong. (2) Even witnesses who have not been interrogated must explain how the reputation started, along with the attendant indications and conjectures. It is not sufficient for them to say they heard it from many people or that it was public knowledge, unless they also add other causes and indications. (3) The witnesses must be able to give enough details of the reputation to satisfy the judge that they know what they are talking about. So if a witness cannot do so, or simply repeats what several people say, his evidence should be rejected. (4) He must

---

[10] Tommaso Grammatico (1473–1558), Italian jurisconsult. Octavianus Vulpellus (floruit 16th century), Italian grammarian and jurisconsult. He published a legal commentary in Venice in 1581.

be specific about the details. (5) The originators of the reputation must be named, and those named must be people other than the co-witnesses. If the witness names some of the people involved but says he does not remember the names of the others, that will be sufficient even if the reputation arose from probable conjectures and probable causes. (6) The witnesses must say that they heard the reputation from a majority of the people, or that a majority of the people spoke in this way – whether the witnesses add 'majority of people in this city' or not does not matter: their meaning is clear – and were talking about it either in public or in private. ('Majority' here means 'majority: not 'a thousand', or 'various', or 'many', or 'a growing number'.) If the witnesses say that the reputation was a matter of public gossip, one needs to make a distinction. In criminal cases, where evidence leading to torture is involved, such a statement would be sufficient, provided the witnesses added likely causes and conjectures. This would not be sufficient, however, in civil cases. (7) There is legal disagreement over whether reputation can be proved on the basis of testimony by individual witnesses or by co-witnesses who are in agreement on the principal points. Del Rio favours the latter view. (8) Reputation is proved by ten witnesses even if their testimony is not uniformly consistent, as long as they agree about the causes and originators of the reputation. This is not sufficient for torture, however, unless there is supporting evidence. (9) Reputation can be proved by written evidence, such as letters written by good men, but there cannot be fewer than two such pieces of written evidence and they must come from different people.

A general rule for proving a good reputation: each individual is presumed to be good (even an executioner), unless he is proved to be bad. This is particularly true if he comes from a good country or good parentage, and if he is noble and rich, or well-educated, unless there is some specific presumption of crime, in which case the specific presumption overrides the general. Exceptions to this rule are given by Menochius.]

The fifth indication is that of running away. The first point to make is that flight before an investigation has been instituted or an accusation has been levelled usually arouses suspicion against the fugitive and not a light presumption that there is intention to deceive and that an offence has been committed. Without other supporting evidence, however, this does not make a half proof, and there it is not sufficient, by itself, for torture, whatever many people have said.

Now, when I say 'running away', I am talking about the person engaged in flight, because I do not think that the flight of an associate ever constitutes an indication against someone who is free from blame, i.e. someone against whom there are no other indications. By 'fugitive' I mean (a) someone who lies hidden away in the city or the place where he lives; (b) someone who by general consent gives obvious signs that he is preparing to run away (even more so if he has wilfully disobeyed a judicial summons), whether he has fled through places without tracks, where people do not usually go – for example, a region of woodland interspersed with glades and passes, which is not the kind of place one usually goes through to get from one place to another – or if he has been discovered in the process of committing an offence, or preparing to do so, and rendered a fugitive by popular hue and cry. In this last case, arguments for the defence are denied a hearing and the person can be tortured, provided the hue and cry arose from a probable and likely cause – that it might be thought he wished to commit an offence but was prevented from doing so by the outcry. If he was afraid he would be thrown into prison suddenly, without warning, and fled or concealed himself before he could be arrested, this does not furnish an indication which warrants torture: even less if, once arrested, and in spite of his having been arrested legally and in conformity with the due process of law, he escapes from the hands of the sergeants and officers of justice.

[Sometimes people allow themselves to be recaptured: sometimes they are captured against their will. The latter applies especially to people who fled because they could not stand conditions in gaol, or because they would be ashamed to be imprisoned, on account of their family, their rank, or their profession. Someone is said to return 'of his own free will' when he could run away again but allows himself to be arrested, or turns up in answer to a summons. Such a spontaneous action weakens all indications against him and a judge may not have him tortured.]

After accusation or interrogation, in criminal cases, when the infliction of corporal punishment is involved, a flight does not yet furnish a sufficient indication to warrant torture, even if there is supporting evidence, because this supporting evidence is operative only before an investigation, not after the investigation has been started. Once an investigation has been started, flight does not provide any indication, and therefore other corroborative evidence cannot offer support to an indication which does not exist. If there are a good many other serious, compelling indications, they will have influence, but not with regard to lending support to a non-indication.

I think what I have just been saying is relevant even if a judge does not have a reputation for cruelty and has not threatened to conduct the trial badly. The reason is that the distress caused by judges and the very serious discomforts of criminal trials are actually a just cause of fear and flight, and so when either of these two things happens, everyone says that the flight furnishes no indication.

No matter how many corroborative indications there are, flight is not sufficient to condemn someone to corporal punishment or slight torture. But if it was conjoined with evidence from a single eye-witness to whom no objection can be made, then that can be regarded as sufficient to condemn the person to monetary punishment and severe torture.

A probable cause of flight is proved by the oath of the fugitive when there is general agreement about the probable cause, even if it can be presumed from other sources that he went way, not for this reason but because of an offence: e.g. someone says he went away because he was afraid of being accused or imprisoned. If there is general agreement that either of these had been threatened or prepared, it may be determined by oath that he went away for that reason.

The sixth indication is that of threats. Note that there is a difference between bragging and making threats. Someone can be said to be bragging when he says he can take revenge, do harm to someone, do someone wrong, etc. if he wishes. A person is said to be making threats when he says he wants to undertake an action, or that he will do so. Many people mistakenly confuse these two things.

[Del Rio now proceeds to discuss points raised under this heading. If a brag or a threat is followed by financial loss, loss of property, or some other offence, that is an indication sufficient to lead to torture when the person doing the threatening or the bragging is someone powerful, of evil life, and accustomed to follow up his threats. Del Rio thinks that the man's confessor must find out whether the man has been boasting or uttering genuine threats, because the man who boasts or threatens with the intention of following up what he says he will do is committing a serious sin. Such a man may be heard in court when there is no other corroborative evidence, but there are limits (which Del Rio specifies), and thus he ends the section.]

Section 4: Other less compelling and less certain indications

1) When someone could have hindered a malefice and did not do so.

[Under certain circumstances, this makes a compelling presumption of a secret (*occulta*) association between that person and the offender, and there may be sufficient warrant for the use of torture. If this person has not subsequently associated with the offender, however, there is no justification for torture. (References to legal texts.)]

2) It is just idle nonsense when someone speaks up in defence of workers of harmful magic (*malefici*) and tries to lessen the enormity of their offence by maintaining that one should not believe what is confidently said about them, as the heretic Wier has done, and as one of my contemporaries, the theologian Calidius Loseus[11] (whose soul may God not condemn!), has done as well. While

---

[11]   A printing error for 'Looseus' = Cornelis Loos (1546–1595), Dutch Catholic theologian

Loseus was alive, he was suspected of wavering in his faith and was expelled from Trier and imprisoned in Brussels because he had produced a short book and was trying to publish it secretly in Cologne – and here I add the observation that if by chance that unhappy final child of his (a menace to the public) has seen the light, or if written copies were distributed secretly, as is the custom with works of darkness, then each person must beware lest he inhale impiety disguised as piety – Loseus (let me repeat) had prepared and was trying to publish a small volume expressing this opinion. But he was compelled, quite rightly, to abjure sayings and writings of this kind.

[One generally finds that those who defend workers of harmful magic ally themselves secretly with the defendant and so everyone, especially officers of justice, must avoid believing what they say. Del Rio now quotes a variety of both Mediaeval and modern sources in support of this contention, showing that the Devil tries to persuade people that magic is not as harmful as is usually maintained.]

3) Since diviners (*sortiarii*) are, for the most part, heretics, those who knowingly defend them are worse than they are and should be considered as their associates; but those who do not know they are diviners should not be punished as such, unless their defence impedes the judge from carrying out his duty. Those who know they are diviners and defend the person and not the error, render themselves highly suspect and can be investigated in great detail. They should also be punished because of the defence they have undertaken. As for advocates and notaries, if they knowingly and deliberately act for the defence in court without first having sought the court's indulgence or without having been assigned by the court to perform this function; if they knowingly make themselves tools of the accused; and if judges or landowners defend these people within their own jurisdictions or territories: they should first be excommunicated and then, if they persist in their conduct, should be deprived of their offices, titles, and property and sent into exile, as happens quite justifiably according to the royal constitutions of Spain and Sicily. (None of this applies if the diviners are not heretics.)

4) What I have said about defenders of *malefici* also obtains in the case of those who promote their interests and assist them with words, deeds, advice, or money.

5) Those who conceal or receive workers of harmful magic put themselves under a greater presumption [of collusive guilt] if they have concealed or received

with controversially sceptical views on the reality of evil spirits. The work to which Del Rio takes exception is his *De vera et falsa magia* (True and False Magic), part of which was published in Cologne in 1592, the rest remaining in manuscript.

them knowingly and without compulsion. If there happens to be some other presumption against the concealer, it is incumbent upon him to prove he acted under compulsion or out of ignorance. He might, for example, be a friend or a relation. This relationship does not excuse him from punishment completely, but it is a reason for much lighter punishment, especially if the demands made by the relationship are particularly compelling, as those between a married couple or children or brothers. This is equally true when the malefice is conjoined with heresy.

6) Everyone is obliged, if malefice is conjoined with heresy, to denounce the malefice and to alert the judges to this additional fact. Anyone who does not do this is properly presumed to be an associate [of the defendant].

[But should brotherly monition be given beforehand in this case? Yes, provided the malefice is not conjoined with heresy. But in the case of witches (*strigae*), diviners (*sortiariae*),[12] and real magicians who work with evil spirits (*veri magi demoniaci*), they should be treated as though they were heretics. Lawyers give these reasons: (a) if the heresy is a question of doctrine, judges should refer themselves to *Deuteronomy* 13 and 17 and Saint Paul 2. *Timothy* 2. The implication is that these people will not renounce their errors and so they should be denounced for the good of society; (b) if someone errs out of ignorance and one believes he is likely to mend his ways after admonition, then admonition should be given in advance; (c) if there is doubt whether correction will be effective and whether the person is sinning from malice or ignorance and the doubt arises from his or her stubbornness, then the whole matter is in doubt. Some people think he should receive legal admonition rather than be denounced. The state, however, sees things differently and in this case especially it should defer to the Church. Del Rio's personal opinion follows.]

Because witches (*lamiae*) are always very stubborn, and it can hardly be that they sin through ignorance, and delay always tends to other people's ruin, in a crime of magic each living person is always obliged, under pain of mortal sin, to denounce them at once, even if their crime is not conjoined with heresy. Those who do not reveal this crime outwith the sacrament of confession provide what is generally accepted as an indication against themselves and one which calls, at all events, for special investigation. I am astonished that lawyers have not paid attention to this, although I think they have failed to do so because they have been accustomed to include this in the crime of heresy, as the Holy Inquisition does in Spain. Moreover, witches (*sagae*) ought be revealed because their offence is not one they have committed but one which they intend to

---

[12] Here Del Rio uses the feminine form of the word. Hitherto it has been masculine, in the generalised sense of 'male and female'.

commit, and their punishment depends upon their neighbour and the state. So no one, in conscience, can remain silent.

7) If the defendant lies, this provides an indication which is always sufficient warrant for an investigation. It is not enough for torture unless supported by other presumptions.

[These include the following points: concurrence of qualities and circumstances, or details closely affecting the defendant, such as those relating to time and place; anything he may have said prejudicial to his case; the absence of some other indications of the defendant's innocence, such as a witness, a good reputation, etc.]

8) This concerns inconsistency abetted by some other prejudicial point concerning qualities and circumstances most relevant to the defendant, and whatever is of immediate important to the defence. A defendant is inconsistent if he says one thing on one occasion and something else on another. This inconsistency creates an indication warranting torture when it arises before torture or during exam-ination, further torture if it takes place during torture, and fresh torture when it happens after preceding torture, provided the torture has been applied because of indications which are recognised in law and the torture has not been sufficient to explain the preceding indications satisfactorily. If they have been explained satisfactorily, the defendant cannot be interrogated further about the offence. The inconsistency would not impair his case, however, if it arose from forget-fulness or some other probable cause, e.g. if the defendant were inconsistent in the sense of correcting himself. In such cases, there is no reason to suspect trickery.

9) This concerns vacillation and hesitancy when someone trembles and quivers while he speaks, exhibits fear, turns pale, or sweats in an agony of fright, and the notary has made a note of this indication.

[Some legal texts say this is sufficient warrant for torture because the eye and the face are indicators of the state of mind. Del Rio, however, does not agree with their opinion.]

10) If the defendant was seen running away, pale-faced, with an instrument of harmful magic from a place in which a person who had been hurt is found, or something which has been bewitched (res maleficiata), then I definitely think that this is a relevant indication and sufficient by itself for torture. Compare a similar case in which everyone says he saw the defendant, fearful, pale-faced, and carrying a blood-stained sword, leaving a house in which a murdered man has been found. The common and well-founded opinion is that this is sufficient warrant for condemnation, especially if there are other attendant indications.

[Del Rio, however, follows lawyers who take the opposite point of view and expresses surprise that Farinacci is not one of their number.]

11) [This concerns the defendant's familiarity with evil people who are notorious for the same kind of crime, especially if the familiarity is intimate and continuous. This indication, however, is not a very strong one.]

12) [Once a malefice has been committed, if someone comes to court to urge that the malefactor be investigated or prosecuted, one should be suspicious if the complainant is too keen to press his charges, especially if he is denouncing someone who is not generally considered to be associated with this type of offence. But this is only a slight indication and needs to be corroborated by other firm presumptions if it is to warrant the use of torture. On the other hand, someone who should denounce another and does not do so, or is slow to do so, is also behaving suspiciously.]

13) According to learned opinion relating to the discovery of a dead body in someone's house, if someone has been found in a lodging or a private house, killed or injured by a poisonous substance (*veneficium*),[13] this could be an indication against the landlord or the master of the house, because it is presumed that such an offence committed has been committed by those living in the house. Therefore one will be able to have them tortured as witnesses (unless it is proved that they were not in the house when the crime was committed), and this can be done even without any other supporting indication.

[They cannot be tortured as prime suspects, however, if they are of good life and reputation, unless they have sought to conceal the body, or it is generally agreed that the murder could not have been committed by anyone else.]

14) An even slighter indication is if a dead person is found in the street near someone's house, because then there is the same suspicion about the master and the lodger. This is sufficient to warrant torture if the body was found right next to the house and if the master or the inhabitants of the household were at enmity with the deceased, or there were in any other way evil rumours springing from similar circumstances, or if other strong presumptions gave support to the suspicion. [Reference to Farinacci.] I remember the trial of a notorious prostitute in Madrid in 1573. They found a young donkey near her house. Its brains had been removed, and the woman confessed under torture that she had used them for a magic philtre. She was flogged and sent into exile.

15) It is a 'neighbourhood indication' that in the aforesaid cases there is also a presumption against the neighbours. This operates in the same way as the

---

[13] This word may have overtones of magical practice, as indeed its inclusion here seems to suggest. But there is no warrant for its being translated as 'witchcraft' *tout court*.

preceding, and even nullifies it if the neighbours are of good reputation, or the dead person had enemies outwith the neighbourhood, who could have killed him. [Reference to Farinacci.]

16) If, at the time of the malefice or immediately afterwards, someone is found where the offence took place or somewhere very near by connected with it in some way, and if he is carrying weapons or instruments of malefice: then, because there are two supporting indications (time and place), even if otherwise he is of good reputation he can be subjected to torture without any other corroborative evidence, because in this case the indication touches him very closely. If, however, he was found without instruments, other presumptions must concur if torture is to be applied. [Reference to Farinacci.]

17) It is an indication when someone haunts a place or street where a malefice has been committed, or if he was seen walking there immediately beforehand. If he has a bad reputation derived from similar circumstances, it will be possible to have him tortured at once, but if he is of good reputation, he cannot be tortured in the absence of other additional elements prejudicial to him. One must bear in mind that it should not have been his custom otherwise to frequent that place or street, and that he did not have some other good reason for passing that way, e.g. he wanted to get to his own home, or a church, or something else. [Reference to Farinacci.]

18) [Someone who has, or thinks he has, a serious reason for committing the offence is presumed to have done so.]

19) [If people cry out from a house that they are being hurt, and someone is seen coming out of the house or running away from it, this is a 'remote' indication.] [14]

20) Because it is the common opinion of academics and judges, some people regard it as an important indication if a corpse is placed in the presence of a defendant and begins to bleed from a wound or the mouth or the nostrils. I have disputed this elsewhere in this treatise. It is my opinion that this indication is never sufficient to warrant torture, whatever grave academics have said to the contrary, and I am prompted to say so because really it is a remote indication and smacks of the marvellous.

[What is more, no one agrees about what causes it, and it has not been proved juridically by any court of law. So unless there is a concurrence of reputation, threats, hostilities, or some other corroborative evidence, a judge, if he fears God, should never proceed to torture on this strength of this indication. (References to legal texts.)]

---

[14] I.e. one which does not indicate immediately and conclusively that the person under suspicion must be guilty.

21) Some people derive an indication from an evil physiognomy (e.g. if the person fixes his eyes on the ground), or from an evil name. The latter is the opinion of Marsilio Ficino, Giordano Bruno, and many others, but I think this is a ridiculous presumption, since a name is given to a child by its parents. If it was a nickname which had been given to a man or a youth (in the same way as workers of harmful magic are accustomed to change their name for another), then I should consider it a proper indication to prove that he was, in general, a wicked man. It is not sufficient, however, to prove some particular offence (unless the name itself were to signify that offence), and is not sufficient by itself to warrant torture. As for fixing the eyes on the ground, this is an even slighter indication, because such behaviour can arise from modesty. It is not a definite indication when it comes to one particular offence and is not even a sufficient argument in general. Neither are evil physiognomies. So the wise judge will take very little notice of any of these indications.

[We are told, for example, that heretic necromancers and heretic magicians usually have a grim, sidelong way of looking because they have been looking at evil spirits who appear before them and converse with them. These, however, are not indications sufficient to warrant torture, but general points to help one recognise such people.]

22) [It is an equally slight indication is if someone was born in a country where there are many criminals who commit this kind of offence. This may give rise to a general suspicion and Del Rio thinks the same is true if the defendant was born of evil parents. He adds that the parents present a greater danger than the native country, as experience bears out, especially when the mother is a worker of harmful magic (*malefica*), and very much so if the grandmother was, as well. But Catholic authors, he says, and those who have written more recently reject this indication as uncertain, unless it is accompanied by very strong presumptions.]
23) [Some people cite Binsfeld in support of the proposition that it is a proper indication if someone, who has been charged by his enemies or rebuked by his friends escapes into what looks like a contemptuous silence. They are, however, mistaken. This, without the addition of other corroborative evidence, is too slight and uncertain an indication even to institute a specific investigation.]
24) It is an indication if someone has been in the habit of giving vent to wicked oaths or blasphemies, or using very obscene language, or naming the evil spirit often and devoting other people to him, as – 'I give you to the evil spirit', 'May the Devil carry you off', etc. [This indication, however, is essentially one of bad reputation and is sufficient merely for investigation, not for torture, unless other presumptions corroborate it.]
25) It is an indication if they shed no tears while they are being tortured. Some

lawyers think they cannot weep even if they want to and therefore Sprenger, Grillando, and Bodin take this as an indication. But others quite rightly regard this as a useless, frivolous sign, because if the lawyers are talking about tears of repentance or devotion, those are not spontaneous but are given by God to anyone he pleases. If they mean tears on account of their feeling pain, it can happen that these women [15] are so physically constituted that they do not cry. I have known children you could flog until they bled, but you could still not shake a single tear out of them. On the other hand, there is a tribe of heretic Picards in Bohemia called 'Weepers' [16] and people say they cry copiously whenever they please. So are we saying that these heretics are witches (*striges*)?

26) It is an indication if they are nomadic and frequently change habitation and place of abode, especially after notice has been given of their bad reputation or after the arrest of their associates. This indication is a good one but in common with all criminal cases it has sufficient force to lead to torture when other indications are added. It is useless as an indication if the person is of good reputation because the one fact purges the other; and the same is true should it prove they have a proper reason for wandering about.

27) [It is an indication if people display some individual impiety, or ostentatious religiosity such as hanging around in church every day, etc., but Del Rio thinks that the latter may be a sign of hypocrisy rather than of sorcery.] [17]

29) A far more certain indication is the following. In the town of Halle in the diocese of Utrecht, a wretched woman one day put her feet in a basin and then jumped out of it, saying, 'Here I jump from the power of God into the power of the Devil'. The Devil snatched her away and bore her up in the air in the sight of many people who were in and outwith the house, carrying her over the tops of forests; and to this very day no one has caught even a glimpse of her. Caesarius [18] clearly showed that this was done by magic arts. Certainly I should think that a word or deed of this kind would be a most compelling indication and one which touched the suspect very closely.

Section 5: Denunciation and witnesses

[Del Rio says he has discussed these points already but here intends merely to add certain details of practice which are common in crimes of heresy and

---

[15] *Quarundam*: specifically female at this point.
[16] Picards were communities of heretics found in Bohemia from the late fourteenth century onwards. Their beliefs were highly unorthodox, including a denial of transubstantiation and the need for a priesthood.
[17] The next item deals with the sign of baptismal oil on the forehead, and appears in *The Occult in Early Modern Europe*, 187–8.
[18] Johann Caesarius (*c.* 1468–1550), German Humanist.

therefore relevant in the trials of witches 'because witches (*lamiae*) are always suspect of heresy and rarely is this suspicion wrong, for the things they do smack of manifest heresy'. The additional points he makes are these. (a) Judges or inquisitors must hear witnesses themselves and not delegate the task to others. (b) In cases of magic or witchcraft, judges (especially ecclesiastical judges such as inquisitors) can compel any persons of note and any blood-relatives of the accused to appear before them to give evidence. (c) No matter how many pieces of evidence are given by persons of ill repute or by accomplices of the accused, the judge cannot pass sentence on the strength of these alone. (d) If accomplices name names during the course of torture or any other part of the legal procedure, and confirm their testimony before sentence is passed, and then after sentence is passed retract their statements and proclaim the prisoner's innocence, the common opinion is that the judge should not take any particular notice. (e) When the workers of harmful magic themselves betray their accomplices and then after a while change their story, Del Rio thinks that if each testimony is confirmed by an oath and supported in equal measure by probable conjectures and reasons, the earlier testimony should stand, whether it makes revelations or not.]

Section 6: The usual alternatives to accusation in this crime. The accusation itself

[An *accusation* is more serious than a *denunciation*, but in practice people make a *complaint* rather than an accusation. A judge needs a complaint before he can proceed against anyone judicially, and in most cases an *investigation* usually takes the place of an accusation.]

With regard to the person: in this crime anyone who would otherwise be disqualified is admitted because this is an exempted crime.[19] Therefore in this crime a lay person will be able to accuse a cleric. Someone under the age of twenty is admissible even if he is not pressing injury to himself or to his family. A woman is admissible. So are those of bad reputation, criminals – even an accomplice – and excommunicates. The only people prevented from making an accusation are mortal enemies and this is because it is contrary to natural justice.

[Del Rio develops his remark about excommunicates with references to Claro and Farinacci, and then says that the accuser must set out his accusation to a judge and be careful to remember the penalties for calumny.]

---

[19] *Crimen exceptum*, i.e. a crime to which the usual rules do not apply.

Section 7: Arrest and imprisonment

No one is permitted under any circumstances to kill workers of harmful magic on his own authority. Anyone, however, is permitted to arrest and bring before a judge those who have been caught clearly committing a crime. [Reference to Binsfeld. Del Rio, however, is worried in case this opens the way to wrongful arrest and wrongful imprisonment.] The diviner/sorcerer (*sortilegus*) can be arrested anywhere at any time and imprisoned no matter where, because he has been stripped of every privilege. Even in the case of the most atrocious crimes the suspect is not treated as people are in this one: for in this case they can be detained in fetters, manacles, and stocks and held, by way of punishment, in a dark, noisesome prison where they may die within a few days, although you must understand that this happens after the person has confessed to the crime (one which merits death), and has been convicted and sentenced.

They cannot be arrested unless information has been laid against them beforehand at the conclusion of legal judicial proceedings. [Del Rio now enters into a technical discussion of legal opinion on this matter.] I do not think it is permissible for them to be arrested simply as a result of extrajudicial information which has not been put in writing, or which is not in the written records of the court (whatever some people's opinion), unless two conditions made by Claro concur: (a) the offence is very serious (and the crime of harmful magic is just such an offence), and (b) there is a danger that the defendant will run away while the information is being recorded. Since there is almost always such a danger in cases of malefice which renders persons, usually of the lowest rank in society, prone to flight, it scarcely ever happens that a judge is not permitted after unaccompanied extrajudicial information of this kind, or after a complaint such as I have already described, to have them imprisoned. [References to legal texts.]

In the case of noble persons and those who count as respectable because of their family or rank (including wives in respect of their husbands), Godelmann thought that they should be released on sureties and sworn bail.

[Del Rio objects that neither Godelmann nor the other lawyers who support him were speaking about workers of magic, and goes on to make further technical points.]

I think, for a variety of reasons, that diviners (*sortiarii*) or workers of harmful magic (*malefici*) can be arrested even in church. Their crime is appalling; they are sacrilegious, they are blasphemers, they are magical poisoners (*venefici*), and deliberate, traitorous murderers, and for the most part, they are heretics and apostates.

[Therefore they do not deserve the privilege of sanctuary. Del Rio, however, emphasises that secular authorities must not act in this question of arrest in church without permission from the local bishop, in accordance with the Bull of Gregory XIV; and in those places where the writ of the Bull does not run, the arresting authorities should behave in a seemly and proper fashion.]

Those workers of harmful magic who have been imprisoned unduly, even if they break out of prison, should not be punished for doing so, nor be considered to have confessed their guilt by doing so, nor be expected to return to prison even if they have promised to return. They will not be liable to the standard punishment or sureties if they have given any. They cannot be subjected to torture because of a flight of this kind (as they could be if their imprisonment had been just), even if they ran away without any intention of returning. [Further discussion, with references to relevant literature.]

The judge should observe certain things with regard to the arrest itself. First, all the floors and corners of the house must be searched thoroughly at once in case there should be found little boxes, ointments, powders, and other instruments of malefice. Defendants ought not to be allowed to return to the house in case they take drugs which will assist them to remain silent. [Reference given.] But the requirement by certain people that the officers of the law should take care to remove the most important people from the house so that they may not touch the ground before they are thrust into prison is superstitious. I believe they are afraid such people may be like Antaeus of Libya whose strength, according to legend, used to be restored by contact with the earth.[20] It is similarly superstitious to remove all their clothing and dress them[21] only in a shift which has been spun, woven, and sewn in a single day, although it would not be so much superstitious as useful to strip them of all their garments and dress them in others in case, for example, there is some malefice hidden in their own.

These women must certainly be searched and probed with care and attention. I find it very suspicious when certain important authors write that judges should be advised not to let workers of harmful magic touch them on their uncovered wrists or elbows. Why? If it is so that they do not smear the judges with poison [*venenum*], surely the judges can also be smeared by being touched on other parts of their body in such a way that the workers of harmful magic may not bewitch them (*fascinent*)? As far as I am concerned, there is no poison and consequently no bewitchment of those parts of the body.

---

[20] Antaeus was a giant who compelled all strangers passing through Libya to wrestle with him. Each time he was thrown he derived fresh strength from the touch of his mother, Earth, and so proved invincible. The story is told by the Greek mythographer Apollodorus.

[21] *Eas*: specifically female at this point.

The same writers say something similar when they add that witches (*maleficae*) [22] should be produced before a judge with their backs turned towards him, because they think that if the witches appear before judges and look at them, the judges, much more than other men, can be bewitched by a look and become more lenient and more ready to find the women not guilty. Isn't this childish drivel? What power does the glance of a witch have simply because she has looked at a judge once or twice? How does this story hang together? Witches who have been brought before a judicial inquiry immediately lose the power to work malefices, as these same authors tell us. Are we being told that these women bewitch at all in the ways I mentioned before, or are we being told that they really did bewitch before their trial began and after their imprisonment, but that once their trial has begun they can do so no longer? If the authors want us to believe them, let them demonstrate the reason for this anomaly.

Now, it is commonly said that as soon as witches have been imprisoned they can no longer do any harm. There has been no lack of people who have looked carefully into why this should be and two of them, who are not Catholics,[23] have produced the two following reasons. (1) The witches cannot have their poisons in prison (as if the Devil could not bring these to them, and they could not receive them from him except via the hand of a secretary, as the authors falsely suppose.) (2) Do they wish to communicate with their little master? They do not dare to do so, and are especially afraid to be caught by the judge in conversation with him (as if they could not be available to him for much of the night for this purpose, and could not speak secretly to the evil spirit, even with other people present. Satan is, I believe, rather hard of hearing and needs to be shouted at!) These authors are refuted by experience, for it is agreed that witches are often seriously injured by Satan in prison. [Reference to Rémy.] It is agreed that even in prison sometimes they have sex with him and that they can damage fields with hail; and since they do this damage by means of the evil spirit himself, they can merely by nodding give him a sign and he, since they are in chains, carries out the task by himself. In 1597, while Oranus and other inquisitors were making the journey to Stavelot from Liège, their carriage was suddenly overturned on a level stretch of road and broke in two in the most extraordinary way. No one was hurt, however, and so those who did not have horses finished the rest of the journey on foot. At Stavelot they visited in prison Jean del Vaulx whose trial they had started there. He said to them at once, 'You certainly turned pale on the road here. Everything did not go as well as it should have done for you'. They pretended they did not know

---

[22] Literally 'female workers of harmful magic'. In practice, this refers principally to witches.
[23] According to his marginal references, Del Rio means Lambert Daneau and Johann Godelmann.

what he was talking about, so he told them about the accident and added that he had obtained this information from his evil spirit. But their problem, he said, had been caused by another evil spirit who was not under his command. That evil spirit had wanted to do more harm, but he (Del Vaulx) had not allowed him to do it.

So here you have the reason. Harm can be done by an evil spirit if God permits, but God rarely gives permission lest the execution of justice against workers of harmful magic be hindered.

A more useful piece of advice is that judges do not keep these people long in prison, but that prisoners either receive a swift execution of their punishment if they are guilty or that they be set free at the earliest opportunity, if they are found to be innocent. They should be watched, too, lest they bring with them, or others bring to them, anything with which they can commit suicide. For the same reason they should not be left alone [24] for a lengthy period, because the Devil makes every effort to persuade them to kill themselves.

But why does he not rescue them from prison? Grillando in his *Question 9* writes that certain judges have often tested whether magicians (*magi*) under arrest smear themselves with ointment according to their usual practice and are carried off by an evil spirit, but says that no one has ever managed this by using sorcery (*sortilegia*). In consequence, he says, many people have maintained that women under arrest cannot be carried off by the evil spirit, for which he gives two reasons. (1) The Devil prefers that they die at once while they are still in his service. (2) God does not allow evil spirits to exercise their power in case it becomes a scandal to the judges themselves and a disgrace to God, for in this case the Devil would seem to have more power over his servants, the witches (*striges*) than God has over his, the judges. The first reason is that given by Saint Thomas Aquinas. It is confirmed that at Pompey there was an inquisitor who allowed a worker of harmful magic (*maleficus*) who had been arrested to anoint himself, and gave the man permission to fly if he could. Straight away, the man was lifted up into the air. I read this story while I was serving with the army in Spain, in a letter which had been given to a Doctor of Canon Law.

[Del Rio says he would urge judges not to try out these experiments, and he ends the section with references to Crespet [25] and Saint Thomas Aquinas.]

---

[24] Here again the Latin changes from masculine to feminine to emphasise the point that these people are predominantly women.

[25] Pierre Crespet (1543–1594), French Celestine. Del Rio refers to his book *De odio Sathanae daemonumque adversus homines* (The Hatred of Satan and his Evil Spirits For Humanity) which was published in Paris in 1590.

Section 8: Accusation after imprisonment

[Del Rio points out that he has dealt with this already but adds further references to Farinacci and Claro.]

Section 9: Torture

[Del Rio says he has already discussed this, but that there are other points which need to be made. What kind of torture should be used? When should it be repeated? When should it be decreed? What are the superstitious practices to be avoided in this matter? Grillando provides a list of questions which a judge can ask.] [26]

'What profession do they make to the evil spirit? How do they usually come to make that profession and what ceremonies and rituals do they use therein? What do they swear to the evil spirit they will do? What form of words is used in this oath? What observances are they to keep and to which are they bound? What rewards do they have and what rewards do they hope to have from their [27] prince, the Evil Spirit? From which simple or compound mixtures do they make the ointments with which they plaster their bodies when they go to the assemblies? [28] With what do they make other venomous malefices (*venefica maleficia*)? What system of ranking do they observe when they are about to go to the aforesaid assemblies? Is it true that they go in body, or do they have some illusion or vision in a form perceptible to their senses or in their mind and intellect? In the case where they go in body, do they walk on their own feet or are they carried in some other fashion? How, and by whom? What kind of sacrifices do they make and how are these celebrated? Do they offer prayers and gifts to the evil spirit? Do they pray for things during a special ceremony while they make their aforesaid profession of loyalty?'

[The judge should refrain from using torture if by doing so he can get the truth, since the application of torture often produces unreliable results. The type of torture used is left to the judge's discretion, but he should temper it with careful consideration and equity. For example, the judge should not have a defendant tortured until at least five or six hours after the defendant last ate or drank in case he vomits; and even in the case of an appalling crime, the defendant should not be injured during the course of torture – or at least, not much. Del Rio acknowledges, however, that 'laceration of the flesh, breakage of bones and muscles, and a not inconsiderable dislocation or rupture of joints

---

[26] Del Rio gives the references as Question 7, number 7.
[27] *Earum*: specifically feminine.
[28] *Ludi*, literally 'games'. This word is often used as a technical term for witches' sabbats.

and bones are scarcely avoidable during torture'. The judge should not use novel forms of torture, but should keep to the application of those normally used for this crime: 'for example, the rope; pouring a thin stream of cold water on to the back of someone who has been suspended; adding weights to his feet; inserting a stick between his feet so that he cannot bring them together; or (the best and safest method) keeping him awake'.

With regard to repetition of torture: the defendant should never be tortured more than three times, for any reason. The torture must not be repeated on the same day, and at least one day should intervene between sessions. It should not be repeated unless new indications have appeared, and the defendant must be strong enough to endure the torture. If the defendant confesses under torture but refuses to ratify what he has said when he comes to court next day, on the grounds that he confessed only because of the pain, he can be tortured again even without fresh indications. If he denies his confession once more during the second torture, this wipes out his confession and he cannot be tortured a third time. Del Rio now discusses further variant possibilities on this theme and refers the reader to a number of legal texts. He himself does not approve of the practice of continuing the torture after an interval on the same day. This, he says, is not really a continuity but a renewal of torture.

Once the defendant has been convicted, the judge will do better not to subject him to further torture. Del Rio gives various reasons for this opinion although, he says, the recommendation will not apply in every case: for example, the defendant may be tortured to reveal the names of accomplices, admirers, clients, etc.

People accused of the crime of magic, however, have been stripped of their rights and cannot claim exemption from torture. Such people may include those of high rank, clerics, monks, and youngsters, although Del Rio thinks that children under the age of fourteen should not be tortured but simply frightened by being stripped, tied up, and brought to look at the rack. They should not be put on it. If they are aged between fourteen and twenty-five, they may be tortured, but less harshly than their elders would be. This applies to old people, too. Always exempt from torture are pregnant women until such time as they have given birth and are out of danger. Other women, however, may be tortured unless they are respectable or virgins or nuns.]

Many workers of harmful magic endure their tortures in a most obdurate fashion, fortified with what they themselves call the 'remedy' or 'malefice of maintaining silence'. They say this remedy is composed of the powdered heart or of other parts of the body of an unbaptised infant who has been killed violently. When the accused have scattered these ashes over their own body, or concealed them about their person they acquire the power of silence. It is certain that many of them remain silent during their torments, as a majority of authors testify and as everyday experience tells us. But this cunning device of the Devil works in many ways and Binsfeld remarks on some of them.

There are several reasons for this silence. Either they are silent because they do not feel the pain; or because they are unable to speak even if they do feel it; or because they can neither feel the pain nor speak, as when they are overcome by a very deep sleep – the evil spirit causes this sleep by using natural means such as soporific drugs and suchlike – or because in spite of the fact that they feel the pain and are able to speak, they are sturdy and strong enough to resist everything and obstinately despise the torture and all their interrogations. So that they may not feel the pain, the evil spirit is accustomed to manufacture certain things which have the natural power of stupefying the senses, and these either enable them not to feel the pain or make it seem lighter and more bearable. (See above, Book 2, Question 21.)

Sometimes he lifts the weights which have been attached to them and holds their body up. He loosens the ropes with which they have been bound and stretched. Sometimes he uses some other object to turn aside the things which appear to be inflicting wounds on the body or pouring liquid on it; or he removes their power before they come into contact with the body; or he interposes something fairly thick and solid which, at the same time, he makes sure is not obvious to those who are standing at a distance. Sometimes he raises the body of the worker of harmful magic from the rack and replaces it with another. As long as God gives his permission, all this is very easy for the evil spirit. But I do not think such a switch of bodies happens very often. More often, in my opinion, the evil spirit distracts people's attention and turns it to other things while he interferes in the process of torture.

Either I am very much mistaken, or that is what clearly happened in the case of the Westphalian lycanthrope some years ago. (His Most Serene Highness, the Elector Ernst, Duke of Bavaria, described the incident to Karl Billheus who then told it to me.) A man was subjected to savage torture twenty times (now there's a merciful decision by the judges, according to which someone in those Northern regions can be racked!) He said nothing but bore all the tortures with a beaming face and a smile. Finally, the executioner prepared a drugged drink for him and one of pure, unadulterated wine for himself. This he drank, then he showed the other to the accused and made him drink it. Immediately, the accused gave an account of all his crimes, among which was the admission that for several years he had been a lycanthrope and that under this guise he had done all kinds of things. They asked him why there had been such a transformation in him. He answered that he had made a pact with an evil spirit who had promised him insensibility to pain and the ability to remain silent in the midst of his torment, saying that he would take upon himself all the tortures the executioner might inflict. (Here is an example of the way the evil spirit distracted people and interfered with the torture, for it would be silly to suppose that the spirit could have been tortured in place of the lycanthrope.) But as soon as the man had drunk the potion, whatever it was, the evil spirit vanished, either unwillingly or out of contempt for the pact. So the man did not want to be tortured any more and preferred to speak out of his own free will and accord.

The Devil is also accustomed to induce silence by occupying the body of the worker of harmful magic and blocking his throat and mouth from within. By these means the Devil controls him so that he does not suffocate but cannot speak. Sometimes he obstructs the organ of hearing so that the accused cannot hear the words spoken by the judge or the questions he is asking. (Examples of all these points are given by Nicholas Rémy.) Sometimes, however, he stands nearby and discourages the accused from making a confession, urging him to bear these brief torments in the hope of a longer life in this world and an eternity of blessedness with him; and then, if the accused reveals anything, the spirit adds threats and draws the attention of the accused to things which are even more painful.

Finally, he usually furnishes them with pieces of parchment and other instruments of magic, on which are written various characters. These are concealed in the most private parts of the body and, in accordance with the pact, remove the sense of pain.

[Judges make use of a good many methods to overcome all this, some proper, some improper. Pouring cold unblessed water into the defendant's mouth merely adds to the torture. Using holy water for the same purpose smacks of superstition, but if it achieves its purpose Del Rio is not prepared to condemn it. He now lists and discusses briefly eleven points made by Sprenger and his supporters.

1) The defendant is persuaded to confess by being told he will not be condemned to death if he confesses. The shock of imprisonment and the persuasions of trustworthy men usually dispose him to reveal the truth.

2) While the torturers are preparing themselves for their work, others should strip the defendant in case he has any malefices hidden in his clothing. A woman should be stripped by other women before being brought to the torture-chamber.

3) The defendant should have his head and cheeks shaved, along with the rest of his body – even the private parts. Men should shave men and women women.

4) The investigators should try to find out whether the accused has surrounded herself[29] with a malefice to help her maintain silence, or whether she can shed

---

[29] *Inviolata*, specifically feminine.

tears. Del Rio quotes from the *Malleus Maleficarum* and goes on to criticise this indication of tears as superstitious and fallacious, repeating the arguments he has used in an earlier section.

5) Once the head has been shaved, the malefice of silence can be removed by invoking the Holy Trinity, and making the accused drink a cup of holy water in which has been placed a drop of blessed wax. This must be done thirty times. Del Rio worries about possible superstitious elements in this.

6) Other malefices are used to lift this particular malefice. Del Rio points out in some detail, however, that this is not an approved way of going about things.

7) Prayers to God, allied with fasts and good works, are preferable.

8) Female workers of harmful magic (*maleficae*) should be interrogated during the time of Mass on particular days. Salt or other blessed objects may be bound to the defendant's neck, along with the seven words spoken by Christ from the cross. A piece of cord the same length as Christ may be tied to the accused's naked body. Del Rio does not feel at all easy with these suggestions. He himself has hung relics round the neck of the accused, or blessed objects such as an Agnus Dei.

9) While the defendant is being tortured, she[30] can be told the names of those who have witnessed against her. Del Rio does not see the point of this if one wishes to keep such information from the accused, or if one wants her to reveal it.

10) The defendant should be asked whether he wishes to undergo the test by red-hot iron to find out who is the real worker of harmful magic. Again, Del Rio does not approve.

11) Those who confess nothing under torture should be transferred from prison to somewhere less unpleasant, although they should not be released from their sworn caution. Del Rio does not think this a particularly good idea.

He ends the section with scathing comments on other notions he regards as frivolous and nonsensical.]

Section 10: Other methods of investigating the truth

[Is it permissible for a judge to get to the truth by telling lies and making false promises? Bodin thinks it is. Del Rio disagrees, but distinguishes between lying and equivocation.]

First conclusion: *so that he may induce the accused to tell the truth, and so that he may discover the author of the crime which has been committed, the judge can use equivocation and deceitful words which do not amount to actual lying and give an ambiguous promise that the accused will be set at liberty.*

---

[30] Again, the Latin uses specifically feminine pronouns in this point.

[What about the judge who expressly promises that the accused will not be punished? Del Rio thinks this is not permissible unless the judge has the power to fulfil what he has promised. If a lesser judge does this, he may be committing a sin. Del Rio now gives examples, drawn from Sprenger, of equivocal promises made to a defendant.]

Second conclusion: *if a judge has used dishonest trickery of the kind I have just illustrated, and extorted a confession by telling lies, he cannot condemn the accused on the basis of this confession alone unless the accused repeats it of his own free will later on when it is clear there has been a fraud; or there are other sufficiently pregnant indications and pieces of evidence; or, on discovery of the fraud, he does not retract what he said under the inducement of dishonest trickery.*

[If the accused neither ratifies nor retracts his confession and there are no additional indications, he should be given a lighter punishment than he would have been given otherwise.]

Third conclusion: *if the judge thinks he is allowed to do this, and if by means of deceitful trickery he has elicited a confession from the accused, and if the accused neither ratifies nor retracts it after the fraud has been discovered, and therefore the judge condemns him to the usual punishment, I would not venture to accuse the judge of committing a mortal sin.*

[If, however, the accused were expressly to retract his confession and there were no other pieces of evidence against him, then Del Rio thinks the judge might well be guilty of a mortal sin in passing sentence on such a defendant.
Sprenger and Krämer make certain recommendations. (a) The judge should consider carefully what is said by accomplices and should put this to the accused. If ointments, small boxes, toads, bits of dead bodies, etc. are found in his house, he should be questioned about them. (b) If the accused has accomplices who have offered evidence against him, they should be allowed to visit the accused, eat and drink with him, and discuss their crimes while people are concealed nearby to note down what is said. If there are no accomplices, the same should be done with people who are friendly with the accused. (c) When the accused starts to tell the truth, the judge should not interrupt but should make sure he gets the principal points at least, even if the interrogation goes on until midnight and he has to postpone his meals. (d) If none of the foregoing is successful, the accused should be taken to another castle and left there for a few days. The warder should then pretend he is about to leave on a long journey, and trustworthy men or women (depending on the gender of the accused) be allowed to visit to gather information using, if necessary, equivocal words and promises. Del Rio adds here a quotation from the *Malleus*. He notes, however, that there are occasions

for sin in the passage he has quoted and says that the judge must not lie or induce others, including the female worker of harmful magic (*malefica*), to lie.

Judges may also confront the accused with those who have denounced him. Such confrontation, he says, is either 'spontaneous', meaning that the accused is ready to argue his case with friends of his who have not yet been arrested: and 'violent', meaning that the accomplices are contradicting one another's testimony.

Section 11: Confessions

[In the case of those who have confessed, the judge's duty is to pass sentence, provided the confession is 'clear, certain, likely to be true, unwavering, and legally made'. If it is obscure and uncertain, it should be interpreted favourably to the accused and this will not lead to the passing of a sentence. It must be likely because an unlikely confession does not provide sufficient warrant for condemnation. Del Rio, however, thinks that the confessions of witches (*lamiae*) are notoriously full of falsehoods and improbabilities. It must be made legally. One must not presume it has been made. It must not be a legal fiction. It should not have been made by chance, or in fear of torture, nor outwith the court, nor in a court which is not valid, nor in the absence of the accused. A confession illegally obtained, however, will be valid in the case of witches (*lamiae*) and heretics.

A confession will be said to have been made in fear of torture not only if the accused has been tortured severely but even if he has been tortured lightly, shown the rack, stripped, or threatened with torture beforehand. It must not have been extorted, and it must be corroborated by sufficient indications because otherwise it will be invalid. It is likewise invalid if the only other thing against him is a bad reputation, no matter how often he ratifies his confession, and Del Rio lists a variety of circumstances which will negate a defendant's confession. None of this, he says, applies in the case of someone who is dumb and deaf by nature. Such a person, however, can be condemned on the testimony of witnesses and proof. What of someone who has confessed to malefice but says he did not do it with a bad intention? Presumption is against him, but the judge can make him swear to his good intention and then put him to further test.]

Section 12: Abjuration

As in other types of heresy, so also in the crime of witches (*lamiae*) there is a place for abjuration when a judgement rests only on suspicions, and here I take abjuration to mean a curse or execration made [as the result of Satan's failure to keep his promise] [31] and confirmed with an oath.

---

[31] *Execratio* and *anathematizatio*. I have brought out the meaning inherent in *execratio* and referred it specifically to this particular context.

[Del Rio now elaborates certain points. When a suspicion arises from a mild presumption of evil, proceeds from slight indications, and leaves some doubt in the judge's mind, it is properly called a *suspicion*. A suspicion may be slight, strong (or likely), or very strong. A strong suspicion arises from convincing indications which have every appearance of being true and so sway the judge's mind to one side of the argument while still leaving a little room for doubt. Such a suspicion is called a *belief*. The very strong suspicion eliminates all doubt and is properly known as a *presumption*, a *judgement*, or an *opinion*. Examples of further subdivisions are then discussed, along with the motives which will cause someone to make an abjuration, and an illustrative anecdote taken from a Mediaeval chronicle.]

Section 13: Canonical purgation

[This means that the accused demonstrates his or her innocence of this crime according to the rules laid down by the Church. Del Rio discusses various opinions about when and under what circumstances this may be done.]

Section 14: Acquittal

Acquittal should be granted either when the defendant has purged himself of the crimes of which he is accused or when the accuser has not proved them.

[Sometimes it will seem appropriate to acquit the defendant of the whole accusation, sometimes of the impending sentence, and sometimes of the surety attached to his or her sentence. A 'definitive acquittal' means that the accused has been found completely innocent because he did not commit the crime. 'Provisional acquittal' means he has not been found innocent but has been found not guilty on that occasion because (for example) of insufficient evidence to convict him. Unless further evidence turns up, he cannot be tried again for that crime after ten years if he lives within the jurisdiction of the court, or twenty if he lives elsewhere. Del Rio then discusses how to distinguish between a definitive and a provisional acquittal and observes that a judge who grants an innocent defendant only a provisional acquittal does a great wrong and commits a mortal sin.]

Section 15: Different types of sorcery (*sortilegia*). Which are heretical and which are not

[Del Rio says he must now discuss certain types of sorcery which are less dreadful than witchcraft, a crime always conjoined with heresy.]

First axiom: *everything an evil spirit is invoked to do, and those things he is invoked to reveal which a person either cannot do or cannot know himself – all this is known as heretical sorcery.* This is certain because it is heretical for someone to believe he can do or know anything he cannot do or know, since these things are reserved to God. I said 'heretical' and not 'leading to heresy', because 'leading to heresy' signifies as much what smacks of heresy as what is actually heretical. Many people do not distinguish between these two meanings. [Del Rio now develops this point.]

To rebaptise someone is an heretical act because the person who believes it is really possible to be rebaptised is a heretic. Being aware of the fact is what supplies the heresy. So the person who asserts that what he does *can* be done is making a proposition which may accurately be called one which smacks of heresy. It could not, however, accurately be called an heretical proposition. For example, if someone were to use sacramentals for profane purposes in order to make an express pact with an evil spirit, or for the express purpose of invoking an evil spirit, that would constitute an action smacking of heresy because if one were to say that this must happen or is allowed to happen, such an assertion would smack of heresy.

[Del Rio now gives consideration to an argument on these points between Barbatia[32] and other jurisconsults, and delivers his own opinion.]

Provided there is no express invocation of an evil spirit, I think it is not an heretical crime and that it does not smack of open heresy, unless something happens to make it otherwise. However, I should have thought it does smack of covert heresy when an evil spirit or a malefic diviner is consulted about things which have been lost because, although the evil spirit knows the answer to the question, it smacks of heresy to consult him, in secret anyway. The same can be said of philtres to which are added magical characters and other superstitious things which depend for their efficacy on a secret pact with an evil spirit. But in as far as they are furnished for love-spells to accompany philtres which are made from entirely natural ingredients, and do not involve superstition, I should have thought that they do not smack of heresy. A judge, therefore, must look carefully at these points and give them consideration. But the people I do not doubt smack of heresy (unless we are dealing with a case of genuine heretics), are those magicians (*magi*) who believe they are in the habit of projecting themselves into unity with a spirit (*spiritus*); or who think they have been possessed by some superior, powerful spirit by whose agency they are able to know the thoughts of others and divine secrets – something which is reserved to God alone – and who believe, along with other extraordinary things, that they can force another person to imagine something they want him to imagine.

---

[32] Andreas Barbatia (*c.* 1400–1479), Italian jurisconsult, author of a legal work, *De testibus* (Witnesses), for which no date of publication is available.

Even if they say they cannot do so, fact is either they are unable to do any of this and simply fake it, or they really are magicians such as I have described and have a pact with an evil spirit.

[Del Rio now discusses further those magicians who claim to work with astrological spirits (*spiritus influentiales*) in order to be able to produce all kinds of marvels. These magicians, says Del Rio, are bound to malignant spirits (*maligni spiritus*) by a treaty and pact of unity and offer them worship which is owed to God alone.

He then records further axioms, each accompanied by a brief comment. Second axiom: whatever sorceries (*sortilegia*) are done by sorcerers who have an express pact with an evil spirit smack of heresy as far as the sorcerer himself is concerned. Third axiom: if people deny God by practising sorcery, or make use of sacred Hosts in sorcery, or any other sacrament or even sacramentals, or relics, or Agnus Dei, or any other things blessed and consecrated by a rite of the Church, they are very strongly suspect of heresy. Fourth axiom: those who baptise images made from any material, or rebaptise children, are by this very fact heretics if they think the shape or matter of the thing or person baptised can become anything other than that which Christ instituted; and they are extremely suspect even if they deny they believe this. Fifth axiom: if someone uses things which are not sacred (e.g. an unconsecrated Host), in order to consult an evil spirit, even if a priest says Mass over such an object, provided that person does not have an express pact this is probably not a piece of sorcery which leads to heresy. Sixth axiom: whenever an evil spirit is invoked with sacrifice or worship, the act smacks of open heresy. This cannot be said, of course, when he is simply commanded to appear.]

Section 16: The penalty and punishment of those who work harmful magic

Let us leave these lesser points and proceed with our argument. First, however, it should be noted that certain excessively credulous people believe the heretic doctor Wier when he says it is important to distinguish between the names given to workers of harmful magic – (*venefici*) users of substances which may be poisonous for magical purposes (*malefici*) workers of harmful magic (*incantatores*) those who use incantations (*striges*) witches who fly through the air like birds of ill omen, and (*lamiae*) witches who devour children[33] – as if one should come to an opinion about them from their names and not from what they have done and the crimes they have committed. So let it be agreed that a judge will take no notice of names, because writers on this subject, either in ancient

[33] I have expanded each Latin word to take into account its particular associations, or the meaning it has in Classical Latin.

times or recently, have subordinated the name to the deed and taken *venefici*, *malefici*, *incantatores*, wise women (*sagae*), *striges*, and *lamiae* to refer to the same thing. Facts are more important than names, not the other way round.

[Now that that tiresome necessity is out of the way, says Del Rio, let us consider the facts. Both canon and civil law agree that sorcery may be punished by decision of a judge, although the judge should make his decision accord with both types of law. Under canon law, sorcerers, whether they are lay or clerics, are not usually considered to be people liable to become heretics and their punishment may be that of public penance, although this can be foregone. A lay person who is neither heretic nor tainted with heresy should be excommunicated the first time, although if he persists after being warned he should either make public penance or be sentenced to perpetual imprisonment. The same considerations apply whether the intention of the magic was good or bad. If the sorcerer is a cleric, he should be suspended from carrying out his office for a year. If his offence was a grave one, he may be defrocked and confined in perpetuity in a monastery. Priests who refuse to celebrate funerals in the customary way in order to inflict pain or gratify feelings of revenge are defrocked. If they celebrate Requiem Mass for the living to make someone die the faster, they are sent into perpetual exile together with the person who asked them to celebrate such a Mass, unless they confess their fault to a bishop. Grillando is mistaken to think such sorcery does not smack of heresy. It does. So does trampling underfoot a crucifix or a statue of the Blessed Virgin or of a saint. Further examples.]

A priest who celebrates Mass over profane objects which are popularly thought suitable for use in sorcery, such as unconsecrated Hosts which have certain marks and characters written round them in blood taken from a ring-finger; uncooked bread either in a rough lump or compressed into a flat cake or a stone commonly known as a 'lodestone', should be deprived of his benefices and thrown into prison. The same should happen if he has misused sacred vessels or vestments: for example, an altar cloth, a chalice, a paten, a purificator,[34] the tabernacle or a reliquary, the consecrated stone or its enclosed relic,[35] a corporal, maniple, stole, alb,[36] the cloth which covers a sacred object, etc. Let these people bear

---

[34] A cloth used by the priest after communion to wipe the chalice and paten, and his own lips and fingers.

[35] The altar should contain relics enclosed within a stone so that Mass can be said over them.

[36] The corporal is a cloth spread under the consecrated elements (wafer and wine) during the celebration of Mass. The maniple is a piece of cloth worn suspended from the left arm of the priest, deacon, and subdeacon while Mass is being celebrated. The stole is a narrow strip of cloth worn by the celebrant priest over his shoulders. The alb is a long white garment reaching to the feet, with enclosed sleeves, worn by the celebrant priest.

in mind the example of King Balthasar who did not misuse these things for sorcery but for profane domestic use, which is a lesser offence.[37] The priest who offers prayers during the solemn sacrifice of the Mass, which tend not to the worship of God or the salvation of his own soul, but rather to sin (like the priest whose frenzied love affair is described at length by Grillando), should be punished in the same way as the preceding.

Common to all are the following punishments. Those who consult diviners or seek remedies from workers of harmful magic incur the same ecclesiastical punishments as the diviners and *malefici* themselves. They are also, ipso facto, excommunicate with no time-limit to the excommunication.

If they are clerics they can be deposed; and clerics as well as lay people once upon a time used to undergo a five-year term of penance. Under civil law those who learn and those who teach incur the same penalty. Those who summon magicians (*magi*) to their home to have them exercise their art should be deprived of their property and deported to an island. Those who consult magicians are executed, according to a sanction of Charles V and the customary usage of the Empire, even if they asked their questions with a good purpose in view or if they used magical arts and remedies. They are condemned to exile or to some penalty short of death at the discretion of the judge. [References given.]

If snake-charmers make use of a magical chant and then merely implore God's help with simplicity and devotion, free from any superstition other than the preliminary chanting, they do not incur any fault. But if they invoke the Devil, either tacitly or expressly, they are to be punished as I said earlier in relation to sorcerers (*sortilegi*). In order to distinguish between these two cases, one must pay attention to the words they use, the method, the ritual, and the form of the incantation: because if they use any foreign words, or unknown names or characters, or other things which are not of themselves concerned with the intended effect, the whole thing should be considered superstitious and a work of the Devil. The same may be said of any other remedy against harmful magic (*maleficium*).

Judicial astrologers, chiromancers, and diviners of that kind should not be punished as sorcerers provided they merely predict an event as possible if one makes certain presumptions, or if there appear to be tendencies that way. If, however, they make a prediction as though it were infallible and must come true, they are heretic sorcerers. (See the Bull of Sixtus V against astrologers, published in 1585.)

Those who provide a natural draught to procure abortion should be punished as poisoners (*venefici*), not as sorcerers, unless they involve sorcery in it.

---

[37] Del Rio directs the reader to the story of Belshazzar's feast in *Daniel* 5.

[When a bishop holds prisoner a heretic sorcerer who is prepared to abjure and undergo penance, the bishop cannot hand him over to the secular arm without committing a canonical irregularity. But there are cases in which such people can be handed over: (a) if they are learned men and traitors; (b) if they are relapsed heretics; (c) if they are impenitent. Farinacci extends this to sorcerers who have killed someone or have done anything which the civil law would punish with death. When sorcerers are heretics or are tainted with heresy, they should be treated as heretics. Otherwise they may be punished short of execution.

If someone dies as a result of some act of malefice, the lex Cornelia [38] says that the sorcerer should be burned. It says the same of necromancers, other magicians and workers of harmful magic, with the single exception of witches (*lamiae*) and those who protect witches. But the common opinion of theologians and lawyers is that modern witches should not be so omitted. The arguments of Godelmann and others are as follows.]

(1) *Witches (lamiae) claim impossibilities — that they fly to assemblies, have sexual intercourse with an evil spirit, raise storms, and so forth.* But in Book 2 I have shown that none of this is impossible for an evil spirit and therefore Catholics generally think that the confessions of these women should be trusted.

(2) *The sins of witches are the sins of the mind or of unrealistic expectation [39] rather than of fact and performance, and therefore should not be punished by the Church or by any other judges.* I say this is a false presupposition. Witches progress from thought to actual deed and resort to even more atrocious crimes; and it is generally agreed that attempted deeds should sometimes be punished.

(3) *Their advanced years and the weakness of their sex should render their punishment lighter.* I say that old age is not a suitable reason for diminishing punishment in the more atrocious offences, as Julio Claro quite rightly maintains from the practice of the courts. Secondly, it is false to suppose that only old people fall into this sin, as it is also false to suppose that only foolish women [40] offend in this fashion, even though their sex does not excuse them either in heresy or in similar atrocious offences.

(4) *Witches should be thought of as being like sleepers, for they confess that their crimes*

---

[38] The *lex Cornelia de sicariis et veneficis* (Sulla's Law Against Assassins and Poisoners) passed into Roman law in 81 BC and thenceforth provided the fundamental piece of legislation which could be used in cases of magic brought before the courts. Its principal concern was with malevolent intention rather than with the particular rituals which might be used in any given magical practice.

[39] *Nudus conatus*, an attempt which is devoid of any substance or ground for hope that it will be successful.

[40] *Mulierculae*. This diminutive is commonly used in Latin as a term of patronising condescension.

are committed while their mind has departed or while they are deep in sleep. I say that witches (*sagae*) do almost everything while they are awake and in consequence should be punished: for example, because of their pact with an evil spirit, their sexual intercourse with him, their infanticides, the damage they inflict on crops and farm animals. As for what they do in sleep, they are not free of blame because they premeditated these things before going to sleep and after waking up consider that they have done them and approve of what they have done. (5) *Pacts of this kind are the fantasies of deluded minds. Sexual intercourse with an evil spirit, too, is an impossible fiction. What they tell people about storms and doing damage is more than they have power to do and what they say about being carried bodily from one place to another is merely twaddle.* I say first that the confession they make against themselves should be believed, just as in the case of other defendants; and secondly, that the testimonies given by all of them agree and that the experience of people everywhere in every age confirms them.

[Del Rio now provides a long list of authorities who have written about these various points and quotes a letter sent to him from Philip Numann, the Town Clerk of Brussels.]

'It is obvious that learned men who write on the subject of witches (*sagae*) agree to a man that the silly women [41] are often deluded and deceived by the evil spirit in such a way that they think through their imagination, and certainly believe that they really have carried out and done things they have seen merely in their fantasy, caused by the Devil's clouding over their mind. So judges must beware placing faith in witches' confessions (whether made voluntarily or extorted by force) and considering these as sufficient proofs: and of handing over to torture those wretched and perhaps innocent women who (since they have been deceived are in no position to deny the charges against them) think they really are guilty of these things. In consequence any judge must make sure he is absolutely scrupulous, because a confession in this matter should not be held as sufficient proof since it may be proceeding from a mind which has been deceived and is in error. Therefore the judge must distinguish whether, in any given case, the defendant standing in front of him has been deluded by his or her imagination, or has really committed the things to which he or she is confessing.'

[This stimulates Del Rio to observe that Calidius Looseus has spread ideas such as this, derived from Johann Wier, through Germany and especially through Belgium. These, he says, must be counteracted, and so he enters upon a long recapitulation of many of the points he has made already in Book 2 and Book 4. The things to which witches confess are neither impossible nor improbable:

[41] *Mulierculae.*

228

merely remarkable. Judges cannot set aside a witch's confession, although this must always be corroborated by indications, and if the confessions of thieves, adulterers, murderers, and so on can be accepted by the courts, why not those made by witches? Obviously one cannot demand a greater certitude than that which the nature of the crime will afford, and magic is such that it gives little more than indications and presumptions to accompany the confession since magic is a crime committed in secret and often leaves no trace afterwards. These confederates of evil spirits should certainly be counted as heretics and surely no one will deny that a confession legally obtained is enough to condemn heretics. So Del Rio thinks that a witch's confession should not be ignored and that he or she should be held guilty of a mortal sin. Witches (*sagae*) are dangerous to the state and try to draw large numbers of other people into their society. A judge cannot absolve them from the proper procedures demanded by law, although some people say he could if privately he knew the accused was not guilty.

Only writers such as Wier, Ponzinibio,[42] and Looseus dare to claim they are sure these women are deluded and innocent and that therefore a judge should hesitate before condemning them. Del Rio says he takes the opposite point of view and proceeds to argue that if a judge knows a woman is not deluded he will condemn her, so why should he not be obliged to condemn a woman who has confessed and whom he does not know is deluded? Delusion must be proved.

Del Rio now turns to the question of delusion and re-quotes the first part of Numann's letter upon which he offers lengthy comment. He has read the works of Wier, Ponzinibio, and the others quite carefully and they all agree that the women are deceived. Men, too, are often deceived but, says Del Rio, what exactly are these people deceived about, and are they always deceived, or are they deceived only some of the time? The general opinion of theologians, jurisconsults, philosophers, and ecclesiastical courts seems to be that the deception extends to a few specific things such as transportation to sabbats, changing shape, and sexual congress with evil spirits. So Wier and the rest are wrong. Del Rio quotes another section of Numann's letter relating to judges' handling of witches' confessions, and argues against it. The judge who does not believe a witch's confession is mistaken more often than the judge who does believe it. Sometimes the woman is deluded, in which case the judge can make a mistake. For the most part, however, the women are perfectly sane and in consequence the judge

---

[42] Giovanni Francesco Ponzinibio (floruit 16th century), Italian jurisconsult. His *Subtilis et utilis tractatus de lamiis* (A Subtle and Useful Treatise On Witches) appeared in a juridical compilation, *Tractatus Universi Iuris* dedicated to Pope Gregory XIII. This was published in Venice in 1584.

will very rarely be led into error, especially if the confession has been obtained legally. Moreover, if the confession is legal, the judge does no wrong in assigning the person who made it to legal torture, because he is acting in accordance with the demands of the law and of public and private conscience, and is taking into account supporting evidence and things which have already been proved.

This argument, if it holds good in this instance, holds good also in similar circumstances. If a woman confesses because of the pain of her torture, and if witnesses have been bribed, it is still possible for the judge to deliver a secure condemnation. The *reason* for a judge's being deceived is beside the point. If he has been deceived and passes judgement on the basis of that deception, he is not to blame, and it makes no difference whether the deception arose from torture, testimony, or the defendant's spontaneous confession. Del Rio adds that in all this he is supposing that every procedure has been followed properly.

It is possible, of course, that evil spirits may deceive people who commit other crimes, such as murder or adultery or forgery, but no one has ever suggested that the defendants should be let off because of such a deception. People have all kinds of illusions while they are asleep, some of which may be criminal. Suppose this leads to a real crime such as murder. What is a judge to do? Declare the offender innocent?

Now, says Del Rio, he will see if there is any rule whereby a judge may know whether a witch's confession is real or just idle and illusory. First, one should note that sometimes the thing a person dreams may actually happen or be seen by someone else. This point is illustrated by references to Holy Scripture. Secondly, someone is usually deluded because his mind is playing tricks, but this is not the case with witches. He may also be deluded because of trickery, as when a human being appears to be a wolf or a cat; or he can be deluded by an apparition manufactured and sent by the Devil, as when Satan makes for himself a body out of air and appears to a witch in the form of a man or a woman or a goat. But if the woman acts as a *succuba* to this 'man', or worships this 'goat', or is carried by this 'goat' to a meeting, it is not a deception as far as the accused is concerned, nor in respect of his or her wicked character and conduct.

One must distinguish between (a) delusion relating to the belief that someone has about something, and (b) delusion relating to the thing about which he has an opinion. (a) Witches are deceived by their senses and by trickery into a belief that they ride on a goat to one of their meetings, or that they really have sexual intercourse with an evil spirit, or that they are actually transformed into cats, and so forth. These days, many of them suffer from delusions sometimes, but it is for the judge to examine the facts and ask if any of these claims they make are actually true. They hold a mistaken opinion when they think that the evil spirit is a divinity, and their senses are deceived when they see or touch something which the Devil has brought to their attention. (b) Delusion relating to the thing about which they have an opinion is a complex issue. Sometimes the witches think something has happened to them while they were awake whereas they merely dreamed it happened. For example, one thinks she has been taken to a meeting while in fact she is asleep at home, although before she went to sleep she did everything which witches usually do to prepare for the 'witch-transport' (*stringiportium*); or she thought she had sexual intercourse with an evil spirit while she was awake, when in fact she was asleep and so has been deluded. Yet she was seeking out the evil spirit's embraces and was giving mental consent to the wicked crime. Her evil conduct, her attempt, the pact into which she has entered, her deceitful stubbornness that she was actually awake are sufficient. None of it excuses her from either the punishment or the incurrence of sin. Sometimes they think they have done something which was actually done by the evil spirit, such as raising a storm, damaging the fields, or killing livestock and small children. What about the very rare case in which the witches (*striges*) do not appear to have tried to do any of this? Individual circumstances will have to be taken into account by the judge, and this brings Del Rio to his rules for the guidance of judges.

(1) Judgement should be based on a consideration of the effect which followed the offence. Suppose one wants to decide whether Iphigenia in the Greek myth really was sacrificed by her father, or whether it was a piece of trickery. The fact that Iphigenia was found to be alive a long time later proves that she was not actually sacrificed, but that some other animal was substituted for her by the cunning device of an evil spirit. Now, it is clear to most people that what witches (*striges*) confess is the truth, not an illusion. Their infanticides are proved because the parents of children the witches say they have killed find that they have been suffocated or that the life has been sucked out of them. That they dig up bodies – a sacrilegious violation of the grave – is proved because bodies unearthed from their tombs are found in places where they should not be; a scrap of clothing which the witches said they gave to the evil spirit as a pledge has been found separate from the rest of the clothing, just as the witches said. People and farm animals are injured by malefices, and sometimes the witches let them loose when they have the chance.

(2) One must consider whether an evil spirit has the power to do what the witches claim is done.

(3) The third rule is taken from Saint Augustine. Consider the number of witnesses and whether their testimonies are likely to be true and agree with one another. There is a universal consensus among authorities on the subject, which precludes all idea of their being deceived in this matter. Del Rio lists

them. From Italy, Grillando, Albertini, Silvestri, Spina, etc.; from Spain, Cirvelo, Castro, Simancas, Tostado; from France, Jacquier, Michaëlis, Crespet; from Germany, Sprenger, Nider, Moller; from Lotharingia, Rémy and Grégoire; and from Trier, Binsfeld.] [43]

Witches themselves say the same in Italy as they do in Spain and Germany; an equal number in France echoes them in both word and deed; and one year after another for the past eighty years without a break they have been freely confessing the same kind of thing both on the rack and outwith the torture-chamber. What is more, they do this in so apposite a way that silly women (*mulierculae*) and children in other respects illiterate give the appearance of having read, understood, and committed to memory whatever has been written and translated by learned men from all the various languages of Europe on this subject. Isn't this universal agreement more than enough to convince us that these things have not happened to the witches in their sleep? For if they dreamed these things, by what pact did they all always dream the same thing – that the same thing happened to them in the same place at the same time, day or hour? As physicians tell us, the quantity and quality of food, a diversity of ages, the various balances of the humours in the body, generate different dreams. But in this case they dream exactly the same thing – that they (people who are poorer and more needy than Irus!) [44] are dazzlingly rich and clad in generous swathes of samite. Men, women, old people, children, the bilious, the phlegmatic, the sanguinary, the melancholy [45] – can all these people, of such a diversity of age, race, characteristics, at one time or another be said always to have eaten food of a similar quantity and quality, and to have been in the same physical condition, because their dreams have always been the same? Perhaps (it will be said) these dreams did not arise from a natural cause but were sent to the witches by an evil spirit, which is why they are so similar, and therefore these things are stronger than human nature and are caused by evil spirits. Why should critics

---

[43] Arnaldo Albertini (1480–1545), Bishop of Patti, whose *De agnoscendis assertionibus Catholicis et haereticis tractatus* (Treatise on How to Recognise Catholic Propositions from those of Heretics) appeared in Rome in 1572. Alfonso de Castro (1495–1558), author of *De justa haereticorum punitione* (The Proper Punishment of Heretics) which was published in Salamanca in 1547. Sebastien Michaëlis (1543–1618) was a reforming Dominican prior who presided over more than one trial for witchcraft. His *Pneumologie, ou Discours des esprits* was published in Paris in 1587. Martin Moller (1547–1606), German theologian whose *Handbook On How To Prepare For Death* and *Proof of the Gospels* both ran through several editions after his death. Pierre Grégoire (1540–c. 1597) published *De republica* (The State) in Pont-à-Mousson in 1596.

[44] The name of a beggar in Homer's *Odyssey*.

[45] These refer to categories of people in whom the humour yellow bile, phlegm, blood, or black bile is predominant.

not concede (a) that these things really do happen as the result of an evil spirit and not because of an illusion during a dream, and (b) that this is how these manufacturers of evil abuse people while they are awake, a perfectly easy thing for evil spirits to do, and not contrary to Holy Scripture, the opinion of the Church Fathers, or to reason?

[(4) All circumstances relevant to the case should be investigated thoroughly because from these one will be able clearly to ascertain if the person confessing to the deed is deluded. In so esoteric (*occulta*) a matter, rigorous proof is not required, and it is the person who says the confessing party is deluded who needs to prove his assertion, not the person who says the party is not deluded. The same may be said of attendant circumstances as may be said about witnesses: two affirmatives outweigh ten negatives.

[Del Rio now enters upon a discussion of seven such circumstances.

(1) Who? This refers to the person who confesses. Is he rational? Does he speak to the point? Are the reasons he gives for his actions probable or improbable? Does he say he can distinguish between things he does in his dreams and what he does while awake? Is he an idiot? Age, wealth, or poverty are not particularly relevant. Sometimes witches (*sagae*) say they are possessed. Be suspicious and exorcise them. If they have a clear memory of what they have done during their possession, they are not deluded. Del Rio says he himself would rarely believe a witch's claim that she was possessed.

(2) What? This refers to the confession. Is the offence therein confessed possible for an evil spirit, or for a human being with the aid of an evil spirit? Is a learned man likely to find it incredible, extraordinary, dreadful, abhorrent? Whether it is incredible or impossible is a question which should be decided by theologians. Lawyers and physicians are not suitable judges of such a thing. Neither, to say the least, are sceptics, atheists, or turncoat politicians [46] who neglect piety, public safety, and the Catholic religion in favour of their own ambition and the acquisition of riches. What abomination do they confess which is not done elsewhere and at other times? Unchastity, sodomy, parricide, apostasy, sacrilege? In our own day, surely it is the sabbat. [47] Cannibalism, says Del Rio, is loathsome and he offers several examples from modern times. This is the most cruel and most appalling crime to which witches (*sagae*) confess, and Del Rio quotes from a letter written to him by a fellow Jesuit from Munich to the effect that several people were executed there on 27 November, having confessed among other things to that very crime. So a judge should not consider

---

[46] Del Rio calls them *politici trochi*, 'political hoops', referring to circles of metal used for games or exercise.

[47] Del Rio calls it *ludus*, 'the game'.

the magnitude or otherwise of the offence, but whether the person confessing to having committed it has actually done so. No sin committed by witches (*striges*), however, is more difficult to prove or more likely to be delusion than that of having sexual intercourse with evil spirits, and Del Rio directs the reader to Rémy and other authorities for relevant advice.

(3) Why? Did the accused have a reason to enter into a pact with an evil spirit at the time he or she did so? Consider the motives of insatiable lust, simple-mindedness, desperation, a desire for vengeance, curiosity, sudden or severe poverty, and so forth.

(4) How? This is not particularly important, since what matters is *whether* they committed the offence or not. Do they admit to using powders, ointments, bits they have cut from dead bodies, toads, etc.? Were such things seen or found in their possession?

(5) With what help? This means, was the offence committed by the aid of an evil spirit? Who were their accomplices?

(6) Where? This is of very little importance.

(7) When? Again, this is not very important. Is it possible that more than one witness can testify to someone's presence at a sabbat, when in fact he or she was not there? Del Rio replies that either God does not allow this to happen or, if he does, he does not allow the innocent party to be condemned. His or her innocence is quickly brought to light. Del Rio now returns to the arguments of Godelmann and others, which he has been contesting.]

[They say that] workers of harmful magic should not be killed because they have denied the faith. All human beings commit a mortal sin when they deny the faith, abandon God, and adhere to an evil spirit, but they should not be killed on that account. Saint Peter denied Christ three times, but he was not killed for it. [Del Rio replies], sinners withdraw from God simply through disobedience and in consequence it is not correct to call them infidels or to say that they are denying the faith. Workers of harmful magic, or witches (*lamiae*), however, withdraw from God by an express denial of God and of the faith. This is apostasy, properly called a type of infidelity, and it constitutes a sin specifically distinct from the other mortal sins. (See Binsfeld.) As for Saint Peter, he sinned only against the precept of confession of faith and in no way actually lost his faith. Workers of harmful magic cast it away from their breasts as well as in their words, and do so of their own accord, not out of pressing fear. Peter repented at once. Witches (*sagae*) remain constant in their desertion of God.

[Godelmann and the others say that God allows malefices to happen and permits workers of harmful magic to live, and that therefore they should not be killed by other human beings. Del Rio replies that this is ridiculous because it is an argument for not executing any criminals. What is more, the notion is heresy because the magistrate is a sword given by God to punish the wicked. (*Romans* 13.1 *Peter* 2.)]

Conclusion: *Witches (lamiae) should be killed whether they have murdered anyone with a magical herb/poison or not,*[48] *and whether they have done harm to crops or living creatures or not. Even if they have not practised necromancy, the very fact that they allied themselves with an evil spirit by means of a pact, that they were accustomed to take part in a sabbat, and are responsible for what they do there, is sufficient reason.*

[Del Rio now sets out to prove this conclusion. He offers three proofs based on divine law, human law, and reason. In addition, he says, there are three further reasons why workers of harmful magic should be punished with death: (1) lest they inflict further damage on their immediate community and the state, should they be left alive; (2) lest they harm others by their example – and witches (*lamiae*) are increasing in numbers every day and spreading like a cancer; and (3) lest tolerance of their evil-doing bring down worse torments. All three reasons apply in the case of witches, even if they have not killed a single animal. It is objected that the Imperial Code does not support this, since it says, 'if they have hurt anyone by means of malefice or poison,[49] let them suffer punishment by burning. If they have not hurt anyone, let them suffer punishment in direct proportion to their offence'. Del Rio replies that if the offence has involved a pact with an evil spirit and attendance at sabbats, putting the guilty to death by burning is certainly in direct proportion to the offence; and he adds, users of poisons/magical herbs[50] should always be burned: the rest, as long as they are not users of poisons/magical herbs should sometimes be burned, sometimes punished in another way. He now appends a long anecdote dealing with a trial for witchcraft, which took place at Avignon in 1582.[51]

The next part of this section deals with the problem of what to do with

---

[48] *Venenum.* The double meaning is important here.

[49] *Veneficium.* The element of poisoning rather than magic seems to be at the fore of the legal thinking here. If someone administers a drink consisting of herbs chosen according to magical criteria, and the administration of it is accompanied by magical words, chanting, or even simple magical intention, and death occurs as a result of the drink's being ingested, it is more likely that the dead person was poisoned than that he was bewitched to death, even though magic was involved in one stage or more of the drink's being prepared and taken. Such a case cannot be regarded as simple murder by magic nor, because of the magical element, as a straightforward poisoning. Hence the ambiguity of *veneficium* and the importance of the context in which the word is used.

[50] *Venenarii.*

[51] It is taken from Sebastien Michaëlis, *Pneumalogie* (Paris 1587).

clerics, nuns, and monks who are to be handed over to the secular arm for punishment. Clerics are degraded from their clerical status and thus deprived of clerical privilege, and Del Rio thinks this should apply in the case of nuns and monks, too. He also remarks on those cases in which three other offences have accompanied the heresy and practice of magic – apostasy, sodomy, and murder – and comes to the conclusion that in any one of these cases, or any combination of the three, a worker of magic, who is also a monk or a priest, be he called magician (*magus*), diviner (*sortiarius*), worker of harmful magic (*maleficus*), enchanter (*incantator*), or any other name, should be degraded and then handed over to the secular arm for punishment.

Del Rio now discusses objections which may be raised and points out, for example, that divination such as is practised by astrologers does not fall foul of the law only when it remains strictly within accepted bounds and is not accompanied by an express pact of apostasy. But incantations, even when used with medicines in an attempt to cure harm which has been done to the patient, are, according to Saint Augustine, sufficient cause for clerical degradation. What happens if the accused gives clear signs of penitence? Under certain circumstances the guilty cleric may be sentenced to perpetual imprisonment in an ecclesiastical gaol. Death by fire is the generally accepted punishment throughout Europe for all magicians, workers of harmful magic, diviners, and witches (*lamiae*) because they are apostates, heretics, and sinners against nature.

Is it permissible for a judge to reduce this customary punishment? Del Rio now enters into a long disquisition on historical legal opinion and comments in detail on the *Canon Episcopi* which says that (a) bishops must do all they can to remove divination (*sortilega*) and malefice from their parishes, disgrace those who work such magic, and expel them from the diocese; (b) certain wicked women who have been perverted by the Devil claim that at night they ride with the pagan goddess Diana and obey her as their mistress; (c) they draw along with them large numbers of other people who begin to attribute power to divinities other than God; (d) and that therefore priests should take care to preach the falsity of all this. (e) Satan deludes women into thinking that the things they see in the illusions he creates for them are real. (f) People dream, but are they foolish enough to account real the things they see in their dreams? (g) Ezechiel and Saint John saw their visions in the spirit, not in the body; (h) therefore everyone must be told that whoever believes in the Devil's fantasies loses his or her faith and believes, instead, in the Devil. (i) Whoever believes that anyone but God can effect fundamental changes in people is an infidel and worse than a pagan.

Del Rio asks: Is this canon relevant at all to modern witches (*striges*)? Should it be extended to them? Certain writers such as Ponzinibio and Wier (whom

Del Rio regards as supporters of witches) say it should, but Del Rio disagrees. The opinion of those who extend this canon to modern witches (*lamiae*) is, first of all, unprofitable to the witches themselves; secondly, deadly to both Church and state; thirdly, dangerous to those who protect witches; and fourthly, scarcely consistent with reason and truth. It is of no use to the witches because they do not escape punishment thereby. They should be considered heretics and apostates and punished as such. It is deadly to Church and state because defenders of witches (*striges*) try to use the *Canon* as an argument for not killing them (*lamiae*), as may be seen from the writings of Ponzinibio, Wier, and others. Del Rio notes, from Sebastien Michaëlis, that the Genevans punish magicians (*magi*) only when they have harmed people or animals, and otherwise consider their detestable crimes as illusions. Apparently the Genevans do not care about idolatry, blasphemy, or sodomy, which is why they are now awash with atheism and idolatry. Brabant, which used to be free of this crime, now sees it increasing on power and violence as a result of many people's reading Wier and paying heed to Loos.

The opinion of the *Canon* is very dangerous to the witches' defenders because, as Isaiah shows, those who imitate the crime of Babylon incur the fate of Babylon, ignore the opinions and declarations of theologians and Popes, and so become subject to excommunication and render themselves suspect of all kinds of crimes. Finally, its opinion is not consistent with truth or right reason because it does not accord with the judgement of the Church and the declaration of the Popes. Catholic opinion as a whole, then, is against extending the opinion of the *Canon Episcopi* to modern witches. Thus, with one or two thrusts at those who would argue the opposite, Del Rio closes the section.]

Section 17: Books of magic

[They cannot be left to one's heirs, nor read, nor kept. They should be burned. Such books have been placed on the *Index*. Reading them is reserved to the Pope who may permit certain others to read them, too, namely inquisitors and their officers for the time being, and bishops. Bishops, however, should not burn these books on their own authority but hand them over to the inquisitors. Those people who keep them and are not prepared to hand them over should not receive absolution. In any case, the power to absolve them is reserved to specific individuals and any other absolution is invalid. Those who keep such books come under grave suspicion of heresy, and if they wrote them, may be condemned as heretical magicians (*magi*).]

Section 18: Offering the Eucharist to those about to die

In many places it is customary to deny the sacrament of the Body of God to workers of harmful magic who have been condemned to death, and this custom may be tolerated out of respect for the sacrament in those places where the defendant is executed immediately after sentencing. Navarre thinks that this custom should also be observed even in other places where the sentence is pronounced one day and the defendant is executed the next. But I am firmly of the opinion that under these circumstances the defendants ought to be given the sacrament, especially when they are Catholics and truly penitent, unless there is some impediment why this should not be done. [This is in accord with Pontifical and civil law and with reason. The defendant must fast before receiving it.] Care must be taken, however, that after receiving the sacrament, or after confession, the defendant does not (as frequently happens here in Belgium and Upper Germany) have visitors or become drunk, or do anything else which may get in the way of a pious death and a sober penitence.

Section 19: Should the corpse receive burial?

The custom of the region should be followed in the case of those who have been put to death by the public executioner in accordance with the details of the sentence passed against them. In the case of those who die before their execution, however, the nature of this exempted crime is like that of heresy: death does not finish the business and one may proceed against the dead. In places where their goods are confiscated, for example, one may take steps to confiscate the dead person's goods; and where there is no such custom one can at the very least dishonour the dead person's memory, exhume his corpse, and burn his bones. Those who commit suicide before their trial is over should not be buried according to the rites of the Church. The body must be condemned to the gallows by the judges. To the quite common contrary objection regarding such a body's final treatment – that the judges cannot behave cruelly to the corpse of someone who has died in prison, either by hanging it up or burning it, because death has brought the punishment to an end – I answer that this reason has no force in a case where the manner of the person's dying constitutes a fresh crime, and that neither the crime nor the punishment for that crime can be expiated by another crime.

[Most people have quite rightly thought that in the more atrocious crimes it is right and proper for the corpse to be punished, since the defendant has tried to escape his due punishment by committing a very serious crime. Relatives and friends who have provided the accused in prison with poison or a noose or a knife to assist his or her suicide should be punished.]

However, in a case where the defendant has not committed suicide but has died of sickness, weakness, or the conditions in prison before his sentence has been carried out, I follow the common opinion that if he has not confessed and has not been convicted, the judge who maltreats the body and does not hand it over for Church burial commits a mortal sin and by his action can be sued by the close relatives of the deceased.

[But Del Rio thinks that one should not be able to act against the dead after a space of forty years.]

BOOK 6

The duty of a confessor

Since the confessor acts in the dual role of judge and doctor, it is easy to appreciate that he must fulfil the duties of both. He plays the part of judge when he simply hears confessions, for then in binding and loosing he acts in the place of God; and he acts in the place of a doctor not only here but also outwith the tribunal of Heaven when he is consulted by those who are guilty of crimes, those who have suffered harm, officers and ministers of justice, or (in fine) anyone at all. So now I must deal with this dual office.

Chapter 1: The duty of the confessor as judge

A judge must find out about criminal acts and pass judgement on them in his court, and to help him recognise what these are I shall put before him, as it were in note form or summary, those sins or crimes I have discussed in the previous five Books. Our judge should look carefully at these and examine them in detail so that when necessary he can help the accused person by asking questions.

[Del Rio now summarises the subjects he has covered by indicating the kind of detail the confessor should seek to obtain from his penitent. For example, the following questions, based on Book 2, may be asked.]

1. Who do they think is the originator of the art of superstition and magic, and why do they think it works?
2. Which books do they possess?
3. About the pact – to which ceremonies do they have recourse? Have they been re-baptised?
4. About the results – are they intended to deceive? (Because this is a lie.)
5. Do they think the Devil can produce real miracles? (Because this is an error.)
6. Do they dishonour sacred images by spitting on them, or beating them, dragging them about, or drowning them?
7. Have they caused another person to be poor? Have they damaged his property?

8. Have they sought wealth by means of the art of magic? Have they in some other way asked an evil spirit for riches, honours, or victory?

9. Have they enchanted animals? How have they done so?

10. Have they had sexual dealings with animals?

11. Have they had sexual intercourse with an evil spirit? In what way?

12. Have they attended sabbats and there done those things which people say they usually do? (Let it be noted where, and on what occasions the light has been extinguished and they have lain, not with evil spirits, but promiscuously with whoever might be next to them, man or woman.)

13. To what extent do those being examined consider themselves to be werewolves? To what extent are they thought to be such by other people? (Because in the second case there is always a pact.)

14. Have they used anything to deal with wounds or extreme pain? What have they used?

15. Have they tried to evoke spirits? Have they tried to raise the dead?

16. Have they conjured up ghosts?

17. Have they shown any kind of veneration to ghosts? What kind of veneration? To what kind of ghosts? Did they make a pact with them? Did they have intimate and frequent converse with them?

18. Have they procured the appearance of ghosts?

19. Has the defendant made an evocation? What power did he think was possessed by the thing he evoked? Did he have an evil spirit locked away somewhere? Did he try to lock one away, or did he have one at his beck and call? Under what sort of pact? For how long? For what purpose? Etc.

Section 2: The seal of confession in this matter

I add this section because of the naivety of certain confessors and the malicious temerity of certain judges who do the best they can, either directly or indirectly, before or after the death of the accused, to worm out of confessors an admission that the accused must have known that what he or she was doing was sinful. This is so much the case that I have heard that in one place abroad it has been the custom to interrogate the accused after the judge has passed sentence, asking him whether he has been justly condemned or not. I have also heard that certain monks have spoken out strongly against this unfair badgering by the judges, calling it sacrilege, and have stopped coming out in answer to calls to hear the confessions of those accused of crimes.

First, then, one should note that the seal of confession has equal force in every crime, even the worst, such as treason and heresy. So the popular saying, 'Heresy is a crime which confession does not keep secret', is false and wrong. Secondly, common opinion says that the seal should be preserved after the death of the accused just as much as before it, because he did not lose his right to reputation by dying and neither did his confession become of less importance after his death than it had been before. Thirdly, when learned men grant that something which has been heard in confession may be revealed or told, they mean that the offence must not be described in detail nor anyone's name be given, but that everyone should aim simply at a general revelation of the offence made in such a way that people cannot be identified as a result of what is said. Fourthly, the case of a crime which is going to be committed is different from that of a crime which has been committed already.

[Del Rio now discusses various legal opinions on whether a priest can reveal either of these two offences for certain reasons, such as the public good. Most lawyers and theologians say that if someone subjects him or herself to the seal of the confessional, then it is illegal to reveal what has been confessed, even if that be treason. They add certain conditions, however: (a) the priest should make every effort to get the penitent to abstain from the intended offence and can then reveal it to the magistrates and bishop; (b) if the penitent has accomplices who may commit the offence, even if the penitent no longer plays a part in it, the priest can reveal the intended crime, even if the penitent does not agree to its being revealed; (c) if the penitent prefers to persist in his intention to commit the offence, the priest is not bound by silence because the confession is not genuine. Del Rio disagrees and says that these reservations could open the door for wicked priests to make secrets known. If the confession is genuine, the priest is bound to keep silent.]

With regard to the second restriction, both it and the first depend on the question, 'Can a priest sometimes use knowledge gained from a confession at least for the good of the government and to avert impending ills?' For example, a worker of harmful magic confesses that he or someone else has put powder or something else under a threshold and unless it be removed the house will burn down, the Prince will die, and anyone who enters or leaves the city will come into great ruin or danger. With scarcely any exceptions nearly all lawyers agree that in this case very great care must be taken so that neither directly nor indirectly shall anyone fall under suspicion of confessing to the sin. But the opposite opinion[1] is more worthy of approval and more consonant with religion and the reverence one owes this sacrament.

[Del Rio offers reasons for his contrary opinion, and then says there are only two cases in which a priest may reveal what he has heard in confession: (1) when the penitent gives the priest permission to do so (although Del Rio warns

---

[1] I.e. maintaining absolute secrecy.

that a priest who claims to have such permission should not necessarily be believed unless he has a good reputation, confirms his claim on oath, and is not contradicted by the penitent); and (2) if the priest has heard the same information elsewhere or by some route other than the confessional. The priest should take care not to use permission from the penitent save in the most serious matter, and a priest who claims to have heard the business outwith confession must be able to prove it under threat of punishment. Apart from these two cases, a priest who breaks the seal of confession should be defrocked and condemned to perpetual imprisonment.]

Section 3: The method of confession

[There are certain points a confessor needs to observe. Some relate to his questioning of the penitent; some to preparation of the mind for confession; some to the obligation of making reparation; and some to the giving of absolution. These are discussed in some detail, and Del Rio supports his observations with references to a wide range of relevant literature, most of it modern.]

Chapter 2: The duty of a confessor as physician.

A doctor must know the causes, types, and cures of diseases. The diseases of the mind are sins whose types and causes the preceding five Books have discussed. This Book will discuss how to use remedies. These are licit or illicit. The latter are illicit if they are dangerous and superstitious. All the licit remedies are completely uncontroversial and emanate from the Church or from God. Sometimes natural remedies are illicit because of their attendant danger. Superstitious remedies, or those originating with evil spirits, are always illicit. So now let me discuss each in turn, starting with the last one I mentioned.

Section 1: Superstitious or illicit remedies

I can divide my comments about those remedies I call 'demonic' into three: (a) certain general propositions (b) a discussion about whether remedies can really be sought from workers of harmful magic, and (c) whether it is legal for workers of harmful magic to destroy and remove malefices.

Question 1: Examples of superstitious cures or magical remedies

[This section consists largely of references to magical cures and remedies, taken from a very wide range of literature. After a preliminary survey of ancient examples, Del Rio turns his attention to those from more recent times.]

1) Cures by means of making images of wax into which magicians (*magi*) think

they divert the disease. Paracelsus describes them thus. 'The doctor makes a wax image in the likeness of the patient and in the patient's name. He shapes a small piece of wax so that it looks like the affected part and with unwavering faith and a strong imagination believes he can restore health to the sick person by these means. At length, after he has said some short magical prayers, he throws the small wax image on the fire. But if by chance he fears that the patient's life is in danger because of the severity of the pain or because of the way part of the body has been affected, the doctor murmurs certain words and burns the whole image and the sick person is set free from the illness'. Elsewhere, however, Paracelsus has a different opinion and wants the image made in the shape and likeness of the female worker of harmful magic (*malefica*) who has caused the disease. But this whole art of making images to remove diseases well as to cause them is an invention of the Devil with whom it originates. [References to Plato, Ficino, Philastrius,[2] and Saint Jerome.]

[No. 2 is also taken from Paracelsus.
No. 3 describes a cure in which the sick had hung round their body pieces of parchment bearing magical characters and the names of certain evil spirits.
No. 4 refers to insulting and injurious terms designed to drive out evil spirits. Luther took extraordinary pleasure in assembling lavatorial collections of foetid insults, by means of which he thought he could expel the temptations of evil spirits. The man was as excremental as he was vain, and I shall not soil the page with examples of his work.
No. 5 is taken again from Paracelsus.
No. 6 is a cure described by Grillando.]

In Sabina there lived an advocate. He was married but impotent because of a malefice, and no doctor had had the skill to help him. He consulted a magician (*magus*) who told him that when he was going to sleep with his wife he should drink a certain potion before he lay down in bed, only he must take great care that neither he nor his wife make the sign of the cross on themselves that night and they should not be afraid if they heard or saw anything strange. The advocate did as he was told and observed every instruction to the letter. At about the fifth hour of the night, there came rain, a violent gale, thunder, and great flashes of lightning, and all this was quickly followed by such a dreadful earthquake that the battered house rocked on its foundations, like a tree almost uprooted by winds.

Then came loud human cries and lamentations and when the husband turned his eyes in their direction (and here I quote directly from Grillando), 'he saw in the room nearly a thousand people, or so it seemed, struggling with one

---

[2] Saint Philastrius (died 397), Italian theologian, Bishop of Brescia.

another and fighting like savages with their nails, fists, and heels, tearing each other's faces and ripping each other's clothes to shreds. Among them he saw a woman who came from a neighbouring town and was said to be a female worker of harmful magic (*malefica*). The husband suspected she had bewitched him. She more than anyone else was rent by groans and shrieks, and tore her hair and her whole face with her nails. Because of this the bewitched man said that from the start he was rather afraid something evil might happen to him. Then he remembered the master's words of warning, pulled himself together, and held his wife who had hidden under the bedclothes in case she saw any of these sights.

After the fight had continued for half an hour or so, the master came into the bedroom (it was then about midnight), and at his entry all those who were fighting, together with the woman, suddenly and completely disappeared. Then the master came to the bewitched man touched his shoulders and rubbed them a little and said he had no doubt at all that the man was now free from the malefice'.

[No. 7 notes various anecdotes taken mainly from Classical literature, although Del Rio includes, by way of comparison, an account of a Japanese practice, which he takes from Luis Froes.][3] When someone has been possessed by an evil spirit, the Japanese say that a wolf has jumped into him, 'wolf' being their term for an evil spirit. To get rid of the evil spirit, they use exotic and outlandish ceremonies along with a thousand superstitious procedures, one of which I saw. It was absolutely ridiculous. They ordered all the dogs in the city of Ozanaco to be slaughtered in order to create terror in the 'wolf' enclosed in the possessed lady's stomach.

[Nos 8–12 include washing one's hands in the morning to ward off malefice that day; various uses of urine; divination by clouds; the story of a shepherd's use of the name of Saint Blaise; amulets described by Pliny the Elder, and the planetary images discussed by Marsilio Ficino; and instances of superstitious practice noted by George Pictorius,[4] including the following.]

There are those who do not throw away any locks they have pulled out while they are combing their hair unless they first spit on them three times; and if they have eaten eggs, they do not throw the shells into a basin unless they first dig through them three times with a knife, for fear that if they neglect

[3] Jesuit Portuguese missionary (1528–1597). He wrote extensively on Japan. Del Rio gives no reference to the title of the book from which he has taken his anecdote.

[4] George von Villingen Pictorius (1500–*c.* 1569), German physician. He published *De illorum daemonum qui sub lunari collimitio versantur* (Those Evil Spirits Who Live Beneath the Sphere of the Moon) in Basel in 1563.

to do either of these things, they will furnish workers of venomous magic (*venefici*) with an opportunity to do them harm.

[No. 14 says that in spite of what Rémy maintains, Del Rio is of the opinion that evil spirits do not hate unblessed salt.

Nos. 15–25 tell us that changing words in Kabbalistic fashion is superstitious, as is the notion that if you can enter the house of a worker of harmful magic, either by asking him a favour or without his or her knowing it, the malefice will stop. Neither dogs, nor horses, nor the twanging of a drawn sword do any good against ghosts. Some people think their remedies against a malefice will be rendered invalid if they have consulted their doctor or their confessor first. This is what made me very suspicious of a document made public this year, 1597, in Louvain by an itinerant woman doctorette (*muliercula medica*), because one of its paragraphs contained this particular condition. It is superstitious to think that a female worker of harmful magic (*malefica*) cannot remove her own malefice before she has been set free from prison; or that she stops someone coming out of a house by putting sprigs of broom in the doorway; or that by throwing sandals or locks of her hair or needles into boiling oil, she compels someone to rush to her aid. It may be less of a superstition to believe that one can compel workers of harmful magic (*malefici*) to lift a malefice provided (a) one knows the author of the malefice (b) no superstition is involved thereby, and (c) there is no danger of bringing in another disease to fill the gap created. Remedies against the magical use of wax figures are superstitious, as is the use of a malefice of hatred to remove a malefice of love. For example, they employ a certain ritual to consecrate (or rather execrate) a black dove, then cut the bird in half and give it to the lovers to eat. Similarly, they may use a malefice of love to remove a malefice of hatred: for example, they keep the sacred Host in their mouths and kiss the woman they want to induce to love them, or they do the same thing after smearing their lips with holy oil. If they want to lift a malefice of sterility from their fields, they reduce a sacred Host to powder and scatter it over their garden or field.

[Del Rio then completes his list with anecdotes and information taken from Battista Codronchi.]

'Outwith a certain castle in Sweden, a merchant accompanied by two servants was taking a walk for his own pleasure through a meadow. A female worker of harmful magic (*malefica*), who was known to one of his servants, urged the merchant to sign himself with the cross because a more powerful worker of venomous magic (*venefica*) than herself who knew how to inflict malefice by thought alone, was coming towards them. The merchant, however, made light of the warning, maintaining that such things had never before struck fear into him.

But scarcely had he said these words than he experienced such a pang in his left foot that he could not move it from the spot and was racked with pain. They brought him back to the castle on a horse and there, for three days, his pains increased. A man from the village came to him, claiming he could cure evils of this kind. He made a magical test-piece [5] from molten lead, threw it over the foot into some water, and said that the affliction originated from a malefice. Then he pronounced certain words, touched the foot, and in another three days the merchant was cured.' This comes from Book 2 of his *De morbis veneficis*.

A common method of testing is as follows. They set up a jar full of water over the affected part of the body and pour into it liquefied lead while whispering certain words. From the different configurations of the drops of hardened lead they judge, first whether the trouble is a malefice or not and secondly, what kind of a malefice it is. Codronchi makes quite an accurate observation on this whole matter when he says, 'Since the method is superstitious, one must believe it is done with the aid of an evil spirit. Nevertheless, there is no shortage of people who think that this power in the lead comes from Saturn precisely so that he may reveal the existence of malefices – a notion far removed from the truth'.

They ought to offer proof of what they say. As it is, they merely assume it and attribute a power to the planet, which is not his at all by nature; for it is absolutely no part of the work of the natural world to harden drops into this or that shape in accordance with the nature of a disease. Codronchi continues: 'I cannot applaud another test which I learned from a certain person. The patient is washed with a decoction of verbena (popularly known as "the herb of Saint John"). If nothing is found during this ablution or the decoction does not change colour, it means that the patient has not been subjected to venomous magic (*veneficium*). If a large number of hairs, especially the patient's own, is discovered, it is a valid argument not only for the presence of venomous magic but also for the magic's being extremely serious. It also indicates that there is little hope of a cure. If there are not many hairs it means the disease is not so serious and can be cured. If the decoction turns black it is a sign that an evil spirit is present. If it changes to some other colour it has another meaning. Is there anyone who cannot see that this method, too, is superstitious, since those hairs cannot be drawn forth nor created by the power of the verbena or of the ablution?'

[Del Rio adds further comment of his own and similar remarks by Codronchi. He notes that all the examples he has given have one thing in common: it is the evil spirit who actually gets the benefit. Del Rio finishes the section by

---

[5] *Periculum*. This is (a) a test or trial; (b) danger, and (c) responsibility for damage.

illustrating from relevant literature the further points that evil spirits may seduce many people into fraud when they try to cure the sick by such means; or they may try to make the sick despair; and that workers of harmful magic may transfer disease from one person to another.]

Question 2: Is it permissible to seek a remedy from workers of harmful magic?

[The question is one which many people have discussed. Unfortunately their discussions contain somewhat dangerous mistakes. Del Rio makes five points. (1) Those lawyers who think it permissible in civil law to use workers of harmful magic for a good end are wrong. (2) Both the God-given and man-made laws of the Church have always forbidden the use of malefic arts and consultation of workers of harmful magic, even for a good end. Consequently, those judges who force witches to remove a malefice by giving a malefic blessing commit a sin. The saying of Paracelsus, that it does not matter whether God, the Devil, angels, or unclean spirits assist in curing a disease is both impious and heretical. The opinion of Rémy, too, that whereas it is illicit to entreat help from workers of harmful magic, it is permissible to beat it out of them is both wrong and dangerous. (3) It is not permissible to ask a worker of harmful magic to remove a malefice either by improvising a method or by using means which have been prepared in advance. (4) There is no doubt that a worker of harmful magic can be induced to remove a malefice by some licit method. (5) It is permissible to ask a worker of harmful magic to remove a malefice, and permissible to compel him to do so by threats and light blows, whenever one believes it is likely he or she can do so by using some licit method which does not involve malefice. Del Rio concludes this section by explaining, with references to relevant literature, the reasons for his fifth assertion.]

Question 3: Is it permissible to destroy a sign of malefice so that the Devil stops doing harm?

I draw to your attention first of all those things which are called 'signs of malefice' – jars, ligatures, keys, feathers, snake-skins, and suchlike which, through the pact he has made with an evil spirit, the magician (*magus*) uses to harm someone by means of a malefice. There is usually a pact that as long as the knot remains tied, or something stays buried under the threshold, or a bar remains across a door, the person will stay bewitched, or that death will come to those who are going to be in a particular place, or enter or leave it.

[References to relevant literature. Del Rio says that a contemporary of his,

Jan Hessels in Louvain,[6] maintains that destruction of such signs is in no way permissible and he spends most of the rest of the section refuting Hessels's arguments. But first, he tells us what these are.]

(1) When the sign is removed, one does not expect to recover one's health from God or the saints through a miracle, or from an act of human will, or from a natural cause. Therefore one expects to receive it from the Devil. This, however, is superstitious. Therefore it is not permissible to remove the sign.

(2) Whoever removes the sign in the hope that the harm may cease is associating himself with a pact which exists between a worker of harmful magic (*maleficus*) and the Devil, because the Devil has made a pact with the worker of harmful magic saying that the *maleficus* may do harm once the sign has been put in place, but must desist once it has been removed. Therefore the person who removes it enters into a kind of association with the Devil, is at one with him, and shares in the pact the Devil has arranged.

(3) To remove the sign is to worship the Devil because it is to bear witness that he can harm whom he likes, when he likes, as if he were an independent entity. Now, although a person who keeps an agreement with his own people is both loyal and trustworthy, he is not allowed to honour or worship the Devil. Therefore it will not be permissible to remove the sign.

(4) It is not permissible to visit magicians (*magi*), as the Scriptures tell us. But the person who removes the sign does visit magicians. Therefore my point is proved because he is asking the worker of harmful magic to remove the signs, or he is pointing out to him the signs he wants removed.

(5) The person who removes the signs shows that he is afraid of the workers of harmful magic and of the evil spirit. But the Scriptures tell us to fear God alone.

(6) It is not only the thing which is put in place or removed which is a sign of the Devil; so also is what is done with it – placing it for the purpose of doing harm, leaving it in place so that it may continue to do harm, moving it so that the harm will cease. Compare water: this is used not only as a sign of Christ, but also for washing something. Therefore the person who places the sign administers a sacrament of the Devil, and so does the person who removes it, because each person performs the action with a consequent effect in mind, and this has no power other than that which comes from its origin with the Devil.

(7) The Devil will never cease doing harm to the body unless he can do more

---

[6] 1522–1566, Belgian theologian. Del Rio is referring to the preface to his *De officio pii et Christianae pacis vere amantis viri* (The Duty of a Pious Man Who Truly Loves Christian Peace), published in Louvain in 1566.

serious damage to the soul, since he is our deadly enemy and always wants to do as much harm as possible. Therefore, as Saint Leo says, 'His good deeds do everyone more harm than wounds'. Therefore although one harm ceases when the sign is removed, a greater harm takes its place, either to the person who does the removing, or to the person bewitched, or both.

(8) If it is permissible to remove the signs of malefice or to ask for the help of a worker of harmful magic for that purpose, the person who is suffering the malefice will be bound to seek a removal of the sign as long as he has no other remedy to help him, just as a sick person is bound to seek a licit and effective cure so that he may be restored to health. For he would commit a sin if he waited for health from God and in the meantime rejected the advice of his doctor. Yet none of those who think differently say this, i.e. that sometimes a person is obliged *in conscience* to remove or destroy a sign of malefice.

(9) If it is permissible to remove a sign of malefice, then those who shave all the body hairs of those workers of harmful magic summoned to the torture chamber, in case there is some sign of malefice sticking to their body, which will render them insensible to pain and thus make it impossible for anyone to compel them to confess, are doing the right thing. Yet this is manifestly superstitious. As Francisco di Vittoria says in his *Relectiones* 12, 'On the art of magic', 'if they shave hair from the body and the head in order to expel evil spirits, or do anything similar, it is manifest magic'.[7] The true saints, who possess the grace of God, never use such rites or ceremonies.

[10–12: references to sayings in the Gospel, Jerome's *Life of Hilarion*, and Gratian.]

(13) The Devil is not bound by signs. He can do harm without them and even when the signs have been put in position he is still free not to do any harm, just as he is free to do harm and not desist from it once they have been removed. Therefore removing the signs does no good unless it interferes with the pact between the worker of harmful magic and the Devil. Therefore removing them gives consent to this pact.

(14) The Devil cannot afflict a person longer, nor more strongly, nor more briefly, nor more lightly than the extent which is permitted by God who is not bound by such a pact. Therefore it is ridiculous to await a remedy by removing such a sign or to worry about this kind of pact with the Devil. But one should have recourse to God in whose power the Devil rests.

These are the arguments used by Hessels and his adherents, and I have reported them verbatim in case I be suspected of acting in less than good faith.

---

[7] *Relectiones theologiae* (Fresh Readings in Theology), published in Lyons in 1587.

Nevertheless, one's conclusion must be that it is permissible to seek out the signs of malefice and, once they have been discovered, remove and uplift them in the hope of making the disease or the evil cease.

[Del Rio now gives his reasons for coming to this conclusion. (a) once the sign has been put in place, so is the evil spirit who causes the evil. So if the sign is removed, so is the evil spirit. (b) It is one thing to use someone else's sin for a good end, another to co-operate with that sin. (c) The sign is removed either by the person who put it there or by someone else who did not. In the first case, the person has entered either into two pacts with the evil spirit or only one. There are two if it is agreed that the evil spirit may do harm as long as the sign remains in place and cease to do harm once it has been removed. There is only one pact if it is agreed merely that the spirit will do harm while the sign is in position. If there are two pacts, one must consider the motives of the worker of harmful magic in wanting to remove the sign. Has he repented of his pact, or does he wish to reserve its power to himself? If there is one pact, when the *maleficus* removes the sign he breaks the pact and does not enter into another. (d) If scandal should follow, the sign cannot be removed.

Thus, says Del Rio, his conclusion is proved, and he goes on to show that large numbers of other writers have come to the same conclusion.[8] One is Battista Codronchi who quotes a story from Vincenzo Carrari's book *De medico et eius officio* (The Doctor and his Duty).][9]

'I remember a certain person's sister who was afflicted by a malefice and got better after the numerous magical signs (*signis veneficis*)[10] of the malefice had been found and burned. Jerome Mengus[11] writes of a most noble widow who had been afflicted with a fatal and incurable disease by venomous magic (*veneficium*). While she was being given extreme unction, the instruments of the malefice were burned and spiritual remedies applied and quite suddenly, to

---

[8] One of his illustrative anecdotes, a story from 1589 relayed to him in a letter by a fellow Jesuit, Francisco Bencius, is translated in *The Occult in Early Modern Europe*, 45.

[9] His book was published in Ravenna in 1581. I have transposed Carrari's narrative from the third to the first person.

[10] There was something poisonous and something magical about these signs, as the adjective indicates. They may have consisted of herbs known to do harm, or of other objects associated with illness magically induced.

[11] I.e. Girolamo Menghi (died 1610), Italian exorcist. Three of his books on exorcism went into several editions: (1) *Compendio dell'arte essorcistica* (A Compendium of the Exorcist's Art), Bologna 1576; (2) *Flagellum daemonum* (A Scourge for Evil Spirits), Bonn 1584; (3) *Fustis daemonum* (A Cudgel for Evil Spirits), Bonn 1584. These last two are companion tracts.

everyone's astonishment, she recovered her health. Mengus also tells the story of a priest who was very badly affected by a malefice and for several months was confined to his bed. His doctors' innumerable remedies did no good but a large number of signs of venomous magic (*signa venefica*) was found in his bed and then burned. Another month went by and they kept finding other different instruments of malefice and throwing them on the fire to be burned. At last, by the help of God and the remedies of the Church, the priest regained his former health.

A few years before that, my daughter Francisca who was ten months old grew extremely thin. According to what her nurse told me Francisca would give great sighs with ever increasing frequency, and when her swaddling was taken off she always used to cry. So she rarely gave indications of wanting to be unswaddled – unlike boys who may be in great discomfort or suffering some pain but relax when the swaddling is taken off and then enjoy themselves. We found no preternatural reason for her behaviour, but changed her nurse when she started to deteriorate. Then my wife started to suspect that because Francisca was very attractive the cause lay in envy or the venomous magical hatred (*odium veneficium*) of some old woman. So a skilled exorcist looked in the child's bedding and found several signs of venomous magic – chick-peas, coriander seeds, a piece of charcoal – and brought out a compacted lump which I could not identify. It was made out of bones from a corpse and certain other things these shameless women had bound together with menstrual blood. There were also some feathers with threads attached to them, so that they could easily be sewn to a cap in the usual way. We burned everything in a fire which had been blessed and exorcisms were carried out for three days, along with a number of other holy remedies.

My daughter began to feel better and started to eat meat, so we thought she was cured. But after a few days she became very hard to please and started to cry a lot. We searched her bed again and found several more instruments of malefice and after these had been burned she seemed to recover her health. But at the time of the full moon she was awake the whole night, crying. In the morning her complexion had turned ash-grey and this change was so marked from the way she had looked the previous evening that we were more ready to weep than feel astonished. We searched her bedding again and found two small pieces of dried nut and bone in different places, nine or ten fish-bones shaped like the combs one uses on one's hair, and certain miniature garlands made with extraordinary skill out of various things. These we threw on the fire. Then we re-arranged the furniture and much else besides, and a skilled exorcist afforded us his more powerful aid, and by God's kindness rather than any natural remedy, the child recovered her health'.

[Del Rio now says his conclusion is also proved by what is everywhere common practice, and he quotes a lengthy anecdote from a book by the Belgian physician Baudouin van Ronss [12] in support of this contention. Then he says his conclusion is proved by reason, and discusses this point at length.]

The conclusion is proved fourthly because a worker of harmful magic does ill in placing the sign and therefore does well in removing it. Hessels and the others reply that this does not follow because there is also superstition in removing it on account of the tacit pact which they think is then initiated with the Devil, especially when the sign is removed in the hope that the harm caused by the malefice will stop. But on the contrary, without that hope the pact is not brought to an end. For example, if a peasant or a boy out of complete ignorance removes something which magicians have put in place in order to cause harm, it is obvious there will not be any tacit pact. But the evil spirit would cease from doing harm. So this hope is not (as I have proved) superstitious or illicit.

The conclusion is proved fifthly because it is permissible to turn away from a place where someone has put a sign, in the hope that one will thereby avoid the evil. It is also permissible for someone to avoid persons he fears may harm him by malefice. Therefore it is permissible to remove the sign with that same hope. [Del Rio now discusses this point at greater length.]

It is permissible for workers of harmful magic to remove themselves from society in the hope and desire that they may do no further harm to human beings through the agency of the Devil who uses them as his living instruments. Therefore it is also permissible for someone to remove signs of malefices so that these mute, unnatural instruments of the Devil's code of behaviour may no longer do harm through his agency; and just as trumpets, drums, and standards during war are the instruments of the army's code of behaviour, so signs of malefice are the instruments of the iniquity and premeditated malice of the Devil – not operative in themselves but able to rouse the inherent malice into action. [This argument has not yet received an answer from those who think the contrary.]

Did the worker of harmful magic put the sign in place? What is he going to do now? According to you, Hessels, if he removes it he commits a sin. But if he does not remove it, does he actually commit a more serious sin, since by staying it where it is, the sign remains as a cause of harm to those who come close to it?

[12] Died 1596. The book in question is *Venatio medica* (A Medical Hunt), published in Leiden in 1589.

[Del Rio now discusses Hessel's objection to this point and finds it invalid. He then produces the following illustration. Two kings help each other in warfare against a third and raise a monument as a sign of their mutual pact. The third king knows they have made this pact and destroys the monument in an effort to make them stop fighting against him. No one, says Del Rio, will argue that the third king thereby gives his consent to the pact which was formed between the other two. Therefore it cannot be said that because someone who has been bewitched (*maleficiatus*) destroys the sign with a view to forcing the evil spirit to cease from doing harm, he thereby forms an association either with the worker of harmful magic or with the evil spirit. The same point may be made if someone hangs out a sign on a city wall to help an enemy capture the city and a third party removes the sign. That third person cannot be said by his removal of the sign to be giving his consent to treason.]

Finally, it is permissible to hinder all such attempts by an evil spirit. Let us suppose someone uses incantations to invite an evil spirit to do harm. The person who shoved his fist in the enchanter's mouth to stop his whispering would be doing the right thing. Let us suppose someone tries to work magic via written words and characters. The person who scattered the pages and ripped them to shreds would be worthy of praise. So why should one not have the right to do the same thing with signs which have been put in position to attract an evil spirit and get him to do harm? Just as I can stop a magician from trying to achieve an effect through an evil spirit by using words or characters, so I shall be able to get rid of such an effect by destroying the sign which someone else has put in position.

[The rest of the section is devoted to further rebuttal of objections to this proposition, answering the various points made by Hessels and others. For example, in reply to point 9 which asserts that if removal of a sign of malefice is permissible, shaving workers of harmful magic prior to torture to ascertain whether they have any magical protection about their persons or not is a legitimate thing to do, Del Rio says the following.]

If the shaving is done under the particular circumstances I demanded in Book 5, it is not done superstitiously or imprudently, but wisely and honourably by judges who have the highest reverence for God. Francisco di Vittoria misses the point about the expulsion of the evil spirit from the person possessed. Depilation is not the same as washing away the sign, because the hairs are not the signs of a malefice but hiding-places for it.

Section 2: Natural remedies against malefices

[Del Rio begins with a large number of references in both modern and ancient literature to herbs and other natural substances which expel evil spirits. He then gives more detailed accounts drawn from modern authors.]

There may be some natural, indirect power in human blood. Columella tells us that the Dardanians thought that harmful vermin are killed when a menstruating woman walks round their fields;[13] and Ludovicus Banairolus writes in chapter 2 of his *Enneades Muliebres* (Poems About Women) that if the doorposts of a house are smeared with menstrual blood, the demonish arts and traps of magicians (*magi*) are stopped from entering therein. In Michael Isselt (1586)[14] we read that in Livonia there was a place where the local spirits (*daemonia*) used to roam about violently and aggressively, accompanied by cloud-bursts, thunders, and lightnings unless the peasants poured the innocent blood of young children into a certain lake. In later times this was obviously a Satanic practice, but in earlier times it could have had some natural effect, although one which would have acted indirectly.

But now it will give me great pleasure to quote a few verses from Baudouin Ronss's poem on hunting, which may delight the inquisitive reader either because of the elegance of the verse or the unusual nature of its subject; and if the Spirit of Nature is well-disposed, it may also assist someone who is ill. In the section entitled 'The Wolf', he writes:

'Its muzzle is not without power because, by means of a certain secret gift of nature, it repels dire magical glances (*fascina*),[15] provided it has first been dried. For this reason in ancient times it was affixed to the doorways of houses. Why? Because when the neck has been stripped of its skin, one may say that it can drive away pitiless, grim magical glances. There remains the rich, soft fat which Saturnian Juno has made famous, since she looks after the bonds of marriage and smears the front door-posts with this ointment before the groom comes to the threshold of his much-desired bride. Hence, once upon a time, young men and unmarried girls began festive sports and yearly festivities. It also gave all kinds of witches (*lamiae strigesque*) an opportunity to stir up new trouble for the bridal couple and do them harm. So by name and deed it turns out that the goddess is called "Unctuous Juno".

[13] *De re rustica* (Country Matters) 11.3.64, quoting a lost book on antipathies by Democritus.

[14] Michael von Isselt (died 1597), German historian. He published a continuation of a modern history by the Carthusian Laurentius Surius (1522–1578) at Cologne in 1586. It is to this work that Del Rio refers his readers.

[15] *Fascinatio* was the power to bewitch other people by looking at them – the peculiar attribute of the evil eye.

What can I tell you about slaughter or about wounds caused by swords? Or what shall I say about new poisons (*toxica*) mixed with other things which can be eaten? One human being is an evil spirit to another, and so uncontrolled lust arouses us and is always dragging us towards every type of evil. Thus, the dread witch (*strix*) in her madness casts a spell over our eyes and all our limbs and causes a sluggish viscous fluid consisting of putrid matter to eat away our bodies. It is an absolutely appalling crime. But witches do not fear such a thing and thrust meritorious people upon violent death and strip them of their belongings.

The ruler of great Olympus, however, has taught humanity antidotes. For they say the skin of the night-wandering hyaena, when worn upon the forehead or preserved in secret, repels frightening magical glances. His droppings protect one from a violent death and his bones are believed to repel the deceitful mischiefs of magic. Smearing the blood of a black cat over the inside of a house confers a benefit; so does daubing the walls with a scarlet layer or smearing the beams on high. Cut off the swollen lumps[16] of a swift dromedary, dry them, and keep them in the large beds of the house. These are an aid to us because they drive away the deceits and magical glances of witches (*striges*). Enclose the right eye of a weasel in gold and wear it at the back of the tender fingers, for it is said to keep them safe from the binding spells of all kinds of frightful witches (*lamiae strigesque*). Many people believe that preserving part of the tail of a grim lion helps men who are troubled by magical glances; and it is said that the nail of a leopard exerts a similar power.'

[After referring to one of Ronss's letters which discusses the same kind of power resident in the nail of an onager, Del Rio offers brief quotations from several ancient and Mediaeval poets, gives a number of references to authors who have dealt with the expulsion of malefices in food and drink, and then turns to what theologians think. Their opinion, he says, is that stones, herbs, bits of living creatures, and other medicines have no direct or even proximate effect upon evil spirits, but that they may help indirectly via some other medium against attempts at bewitchment by removing physical, astrological, or psychological conditions which an evil spirit is able to use to his own advantage. Ricardus de Mediavilla[17] thinks that malefice can sometimes be overcome entirely by natural remedies. Del Rio, however, disagrees and notes that most scholars

---

[16] *Lichines*. This word refers to (a) lichen or (b) the scabs and excrescences of skin disease. But it may also refer to a hard lump on the skin of a horse's foreleg, the 'chestnut', and it is this I have taken as a guide to its meaning in this context.

[17] I.e. Richard of Middleton or Moyenneville (*c.* 1249–*c.* 1308), a French or English theologian and a Franciscan, who spent most of his life in France and may have been born there.

say this is not possible and that one malefice is cured by means of another. When using natural remedies, he says, one must consider whether they operate against those conditions which the evil spirit is accustomed to use in order to cause human beings harm and distress.

Natural remedies can be classed under two headings: (a) those which track down the cause of an illness (is it malefice or not?), and (b) those which cure the illness. The former heading may be called 'signs' or 'indications', and the latter, 'remedies'. With regard to the first, Del Rio says that exorcists and more especially doctors have discussed them and refers his readers to the exorcist, Zacharias Visconti,[18] and the physician, Battista Codronchi. From the former, Del Rio quotes passages to indicate some of the physical signs an exorcist may expect to encounter.]

'Some of those who have been subjected to malefice (*maleficiati*) have complexions the colour of cedar wood. In other cases, the eyes are contracted, all parts of their body seem to be stiff, and their shoulders are dry to the touch. But there are two very powerful signs: constriction of the heart and constriction of the entrance to the stomach, especially when they imagine they have an affliction[19] above the stomach. Some have stabbing pains in the heart, as though it had been pierced with pins. Some imagine their heart is being gnawed away. Some have great pain in the heart or in the kidneys and think that dogs are tearing at these parts of their body. Some imagine there is a bolus rising and falling in their throat. Certain of them think their channel of generation has been tied off. Some have their stomach so disposed that they vomit whatever they eat or drink'.[20]

[Codronchi has recorded all these signs and many others, too. He says there are some signs which are common to all cases of malefice and others which are peculiar to certain cases, and he is careful to ask what caused the illness – an intense love for someone? an irrational or unjust hatred of someone? did workers of harmful magic utter curses or threats? have instruments of malefice been found? From the answers to these he deduces the stage the illness has reached and the remedies he should apply or avoid.]

[18] Italian exorcist, floruit 16th century. His book, *Complementum artis exorcistae* (A Complete Account of the Art of Exorcism) was published in Venice in 1600.
[19] *Bonum*. Strictly speaking, this should refer to a kind of eye disease, but here we are obviously meant to think of some kind of cyst or ulcer in the upper part of the chest.
[20] A further list of symptoms described by Zacharias and quoted by Del Rio may be found in *The Occult in Early Modern Europe*, 46–8.

The signs common to all are as follows:

1) Illnesses brought on by malefice are very difficult to recognise and when doctors are faced by them, they hesitate and are in two minds what to do, uncertain about what advice they should offer.

2) When medical remedies have been employed, the illness does not get better. On the contrary, it is aggravated and increased.

3) The illness does not grow little by little as is the way with natural illnesses, but frequently reveals itself, right from the start, in very severe symptoms and pains, even though there is no reason it should appear since there is no problem with any of the humours.

4) The illness is very unstable and although it has the appearance of being one of the intermittent illnesses, it rarely observes their usual periods; and although it seems like one of the natural illnesses, it differs from them in many ways.

5) Often the patient may be in great pain, but he or she cannot say where the pain is located.

6) Sometimes, for no apparent reason, patients emit deep sighs (which are known as 'distressing').

7) Some people lose their appetite; others vomit up what they have eaten and their stomach is so badly affected that they frequently suffer from constipation; or they notice there is something bulky in their stomach and, in addition to that, something which comes up along the gullet and then goes down again. If they try to swallow down whatever has been brought up into the throat, however, they are simply wasting their time, because the stuff soon plunges down of its own accord.

8) They notice a stabbing pain in the region of the heart. This pain is so severe that sometimes they say their heart is being ripped to shreds.

9) In certain people one finds the arteries round the neck obviously pulsating and, as it were, trembling.

10) Some patients are tortured by a savage pain in the neck or in the kidneys; or they notice very sharp pains round the lower stomach; or they remark that frequently they suffer from a very cold, persistent wind round their stomach and that this wind is quick to come back; or that they are troubled in more or less the same way by a vapour like a very hot flame.

11) Some people are rendered impotent.

12) Some people have been seized by light sweats without warning, especially at night and when there is a rather cold draught.

13) Some people seem to have had small pieces of their body torn away, as though they had suffered a series of injuries.

14) The illnesses which trouble those who have been harmed by poison/venomous magic (*veneficium*) are principally (i) a thinning and wasting of the whole

body, (ii) a wasting away of one's strength accompanied by immense tiredness, (iii) stupidity of mind, (iv) various melancholic deliria, (v) various kinds of fever which give the doctors a lot of work, (vi) certain convulsive movements which make them seem like epileptics, and (vii) a rigidity of the limbs preceded by a type of convulsion. Sometimes all parts of the head swell; or the patients notice such a lassitude throughout their whole body that they can scarcely be induced to move. Very often the whole skin, especially of the face, is suffused with a tawny or ashen colour. Some people's eyebrows become so knotted that they can hardly open their eyes. The eyes are very bright and light shines through them, like the eyes of long-tailed monkeys. On occasion, the eyes look as though they contain ghostly images, or there is a film over them; and several patients have their eyes fixed in a grim stare.

15) People suffering from this kind of illness can be recognised by certain experiments. Those who have been affected by venomous magic scarcely have the power to look at a priest's face, or at any eye which is in any way fixed upon them; and the white of the eye is changed in various ways. When the instruments of magic are burned, the sick usually change for the worse and, depending on whether the venomous magic is weaker or more severe, will suffer somewhat less or more; and if the harm they suffer increases, they may be compelled to utter dreadful cries, or low like cattle. If, however, there is no perceptible change or damage, there is a good chance the patient will recover and be restored to good health with little difficulty.

One may add that if by chance the worker of venomous magic (*veneficus*) comes to see the patient, the sick person is immediately affected by immense discomfort and seized by some terror or trembling. If the patient is a child, he or she at once bursts into tears. The sick person's eyes are changed to a dusky shade, or some other change worthy of note is observable. Finally, when a priest places holy strips of cloth on the eyes, ears, forehead, and other parts of the body in order to cure the illness, if sweat appears on those parts, or if there is any other change, it is a sign of venomous magic.

[Those are the signs common to all malefices. They may not necessarily all appear in a patient at the same time. Signs peculiar to certain acts of malefice are more difficult to recognise. The evil spirit may mingle himself with the substance introduced into the patient and damage the natural functioning of specific parts of the body. But in most people he produces depraved imaginings, especially by way of dreams. These alone are not sufficient indication of possession, however, since they often appear in melancholics, too. Del Rio gives a further list of physical symptoms which indicate possession. These include a feeling that ants are crawling under the skin, stabbing pains, the sudden appearance and disappearance of a blister on the tongue and sensations of very cold water running down the back. More reliable signs are the patient's speaking an unknown language; the ability of an uneducated person to answer abstruse and difficult questions; the patient's revelation of secret information; or the manifestation of such frenzied rage that several strong men cannot hold the patient down. Some of the possessed become quiet and say they feel that an evil spirit is speaking through them but that they do not understand what he is saying. Others have no recollection of what has happened to them. There are those who maintain it is a particular sign of possession if the patient cannot bear holy water or listen to talk of God; and they say that if they are forced to undergo church ceremonies, something inside them continues to torment them, even though they themselves may want to benefit from the Church's assistance. Some of them occasionally give way to such despair that they lay violent hands on themselves. Finally, Del Rio says he will not dwell on the more spectacular manifestations of possession noted in Holy Scripture in which the sick become mad, dumb, deaf, blind, grind their teeth, dash themselves to the ground, shrivel away, run round naked, tear at themselves and others, live in graveyards, hurl themselves into water or fire, and endure other very severe, incurable afflictions.]

To find out whether the sick person is a demoniac, the following is usually done. They spread out over the patient a small sheet on which are written the sacred words of God, or relics of the saints, or a blessed Agnus Dei made of wax, or some other sacred object. The priest puts his hand and stole on the demoniac's forehead and utters sacred words. At these, the patient begins to tremble and shudder, and under the pressure of pain, starts to perform many ungainly movements and to say and do a great deal else which is strange. If the evil spirit has gone for the head, the patient is afflicted and pierced more sharply in the head, or his head and face are suffused with redness and fiery heat. If he has gone for the eyes, the sick person twists them this way and that; and if he has gone for the back, he makes person's the limbs contort themselves forwards and backwards. Sometimes he makes the whole body so rigid and inflexible that there is no way it can be bent. Sometimes the afflicted fall down as if they were dead and suffering from the third degree of epilepsy. When a breeze rushes through their head, at the priest's command, they are lifted up and the breeze returns whence it came. If the spirit goes for the pharynx, this area is so constricted that the patient thinks he is being strangled. If the spirit is borne into the more noble parts of the body, such as the area near the heart or the lungs, he causes shortness of breath, palpitations, and syncope. If he makes his way towards the belly, he precipitates convulsive catching of the breath and vomiting so that sometimes the patient cannot take food or retain what he has eaten. There may also be the movement of something like a small ball round the entrance to the stomach; and the spirit causes the sick person to bellow and make other discordant sounds. These are accompanied by searing pains[21] and gusts of air round the lower chest. Sometimes the possessed can be recognised with the help of certain fumigations of sulphur or other things with a strong smell, which I shall discuss later. Some people write that demoniacs are so offended by the smell of roses that they cannot be made to go anywhere near a rose-garden.

[Del Rio now tells us how Satan invades human beings, and quotes from Andrea Cesalpino on drugs and amulets. He refers to Codronchi on the use of purgatives, baths, suffumigations, and ointments, and notes with approval four observations made by him. (1) Even if substances such as herbs cannot cure the distress caused by an evil spirit, they can ameliorate the condition. (2) Evil spirits regard whatever is done to the body of the afflicted, such as the use of blows or foul and bitter substances, as something done either to mock or harm *them*, and since they do not wish to be harmed by these, they prefer to run away. (3) Evil spirits hate signs of the pains and punishments they themselves are suffering – for example, sulphur accompanied by fire, which is the sign of their imprisonment in Hell. So they run away from these things. (4) Similarly, things associated with God and his divine justice operate against evil spirits.

Next, Del Rio quotes at length from a letter sent to him in reply to one of his own by Federico Iametius, according to Del Rio a well-known musician, poet, and doctor. The reply is dated 1 August 1600. After describing the actions of various natural remedies discussed by older authorities such as the herbalist Dioscorides, Pliny the Elder, Orpheus, Nicander, and Marbodius, Del Rio's correspondent recommends the medical principle of treating symptoms by their opposites and the careful use of bleeding, purgatives, and baths, the object of which is to remove the harmful humours which the evil spirit or the worker of harmful magic has introduced into the sufferer's principal organs.

Finally, Del Rio (following Codronchi) turns to what he calls 'the most frequent malefice of our times', sterility and impotence.]

Wives should make confession of their sins and reverently receive the most holy body of Christ, especially on the more important feast days. Let them give one another the kiss of peace. Let the priest bless them and then, according to the example of Tobias, let them abstain from sexual intercourse for three days before fulfilling their conjugal duty. If, because of some hidden purpose of God or some fault in the married couple, the venomous magic is not untied, they should find time for diligent prayer, fasting, and other pious works, go more frequently to Mass, go on pilgrimage and visit the shrines of the most holy Virgin or other saints, make frequent confession to a priest, take the holy

---

[21] Reading *tortiones* for *torsiones*.

Eucharist, and devoutly avail themselves of the exorcisms ordained by the Church especially for this situation. As for natural remedies, Codronchi writes that if some manifest characteristic appears in the malefice, one can safely and advantageously make use of drugs which are effective against it and have been strengthened by being blessed.

Section 3: Supernatural remedies which come from God or from the Church

These alone are free from all sin and danger, having been instituted by Christ or the Apostles and their successors, and people should be instructed and advised to use them in preference to all others. These always benefit the soul and never harm the body, and on many occasions they free or save people from illness and other harm brought by malefices.

[A list of doctors and Catholic sympathisers who agree with this is followed by an anecdote from a Jesuit, Fr Bencius, dated to 1591, which is intended to illustrate the point that often God compels an evil spirit to acknowledge the force of ecclesiastical remedies. Del Rio then devotes the rest of the section to describing twelve of these, and illustrating them with suitable anecdotes and references.

1) A true and lively faith. References to Scripture, the Church Fathers, and Mediaeval literature, including a quotation from Cornelis Kempis's book on Frisia.[22]

2) Legitimate use of the Catholic sacraments. Del Rio spends most time on baptism and records several anecdotes to illustrate its power. They include a long story from Petrus Chieza de Leon's *History of Peru*,[23] and quotations from Luis Froes's *Letters from Japan*. The latter include the two following.]

'In Bungum in 1596, there was a pagan woman who was possessed by an evil spirit, and she was told she could not be freed from it unless she became a Christian. After a year had passed she started to get herself ready to be baptised, but the very next night the evil spirit urged her not to become a Christian, saying, 'After we have been such close friends for such a long time, you are married to me, and yet you are now deserting me? Be sure you will not leave unscathed!' So while she was asleep and not able to feel what he was doing, he cut off her hair, leaving one tuft behind. Very early next morning she discovered that her hair had been removed and wound round a reed which

---

[22] Cornelis Kempis (*c.* 1516–1587), Dutch historian. His *De origine, situ, qualitate et quantitate Frisiae* (The Origin, Geographical Position, Character, and Extent of Frisia) was published in Cologne in 1588.

[23] Pedro de Cieza de León (1518–1560), Spanish historian. He published *La crónica de Perú* in Sevilla in 1553.

had been placed in front of the bed. But she regarded this, added to the spirit's deception of her, as a spur to get herself baptised that much more quickly, as an antidote; and indeed after receiving the sacrament she remained immune from all the harassments of the evil spirit.

On the island of Ciazzurana, a pagan lad aged eighteen frequently thought that a huge, dreadful dog with red hair would appear to him. The dog used to speak to him and lead him through the mountains into places completely hidden from view, and keep him there for two or three days, forcing him to lift up his hands and worship him and do other things too shocking for me to write down. The wretched youth, seeing that it was the deadly enemy of the human race who was causing him such distress, finally ran away to the Church where he heard and learned the teaching of Christ, and bound himself to Christ by the sacrament of baptism; and from that point onwards he was never troubled by the hound of Hell'.

[The evil spirit is driven away, however, only by one's reception of the *true* faith, as the following anecdote from Germany reveals.]

'In 1583 in Würzburg, there was a house in a parish not far from the city, which was infested either with an evil spirit or with some form of trickery (*praestigia*). The parish priest and those who lived in the houses next door used to say that whatever was in the house would be dashed to the ground with great force, especially lighted torches, very many of which used to be extinguished with a single breath in the lavatory after the door had been closed and where there was no draught. Beds were dragged very violently from under those who were sleeping in them, and the pillows plucked from beneath their necks. Most of the servants had their throats so obstructed that they thought they were being suffocated, and it was common in that house to see and hear much that was foul. The unhappy parish priest, not knowing what to do, came to us,[24] told us about the assaults people were suffering and demanded that the Rector send him a priest who could help protect them. The business was entrusted to one who fasted and then directed his attention to it as soon as evening fell. Scarcely had he set foot over the threshold when he witnessed the things he had been told about. A dish was dashed violently against a wall while he and his companion were watching, and with such force and such violence that those who were present more or less fainted with fear. The Jesuit father told everyone to be of good cheer and urged the parish priest to prepare himself to take confession. He himself put on a surplice and stole and went upstairs to that part of the house where the evil spirit was most accustomed to make a disturbance. Here he conducted the usual rites of the Church for the expulsion of evil spirits,

---

[24] I.e. the Jesuits.

and when he received no reply and no one answered his summons, he came back downstairs to encourage the servants make sure they cast away heresy and expiated their sins through confession. Then he sprinkled the house with holy water and returned to the college, leaving behind him a great deal of satisfaction; for it was agreed that many had been rescued from heresy and restored to the Church, and that the house had been set free (as the parish priest bore witness), from all its former molestation'.

[There follow quotations from Prudentius and Thomas of Cantimpré; the relation of an incident from 1591, taken from a letter from the Jesuit, Fr Bencius; a quotation from Hector Boethius [25] and references to several other Mediaeval authors; two anecdotes from Austria and Bavaria, dated 1591; a further mixture of incidents from Mediaeval sources, interspersed with modern references; a quotation from Pico della Mirandola; incidents from 1370 and 1599; references to the virtues of the Mass and unction of the sick; and finally further references to Mediaeval literature. All bear upon the same general point, that evil spirits can be dealt with effectively by ecclesiastical rites and ceremonies; after which Del Rio returns to his list of twelve such remedies.]

3) The third remedy is to go to seek the help of those saintly men who, by general agreement, have the power to work miracles. (Such a gift can also be found, if somewhat infrequently, in those whose life is not one of good repute, provided they have the correct faith.) This remedy is scarcely used these days because there are hardly any such men in existence, especially in this part of Europe. [Once there were many of them, and Del Rio gives relevant references.]

[4] The fourth remedy is that of ecclesiastical exorcism. Del Rio points out that the Church has had exorcists for a long time and quotes two Mediaeval anecdotes to show that exorcism can be a dangerous business. The first is taken from Nider's *Formicarius* (The Ant Heap).]

'I have seen', says Nider, 'in a monastery in Cologne a brother who is very famous for having the gift of expelling evil spirits, although he himself makes jokes about it. On this occasion, he had an evil spirit "bottled up" (to use the terminology of that particular monastery) in the body of the person it had possessed, and the spirit asked him for a place to which it could retire. This made the brother very pleased and he said by way of a joke, "Go into my lavatory". So the evil spirit went away, but at night when the brother wanted

---

[25] Hector Boethius or Boece (*c.* 1465–*c.* 1536), Scottish historian. His *Scotorum historiae a prima gentis origine* (A History of the Scottish People from their Beginning) was published in Paris in 1526.

to purge his stomach, the evil spirit tortured him so dreadfully upon the lavatory that he scarcely escaped with his life'.

[Del Rio now recounts a lengthy exorcism undertaken by Jesuits in Graz in 1600, a written account of which, he says, is in front of him as he writes.][26] [5] The fifth remedy is to be found in atoning works of compassion such as fasting, charity, and prayer. Del Rio gives references to Scripture, followed by a mixture of modern and Mediaeval illustrative anecdotes. The first comes from a private letter written by a trustworthy witness.]

In 1549, a certain person made a particular confession to our Jesuit brothers and, about the middle of the night, while he was performing the penance demanded of him for his offences, suddenly he saw cats, mice, and other creatures black in colour and dreadful to look at. There were so many of them that they seemed to fill the whole bedroom. At this sight he was filled with fear and began to be frightened that these animals would tear him alive. Anxious and fearful, he ran to the image of our Lord and in a loud voice implored his aid, and at this, the spectres of all the animals suddenly vanished with such a great rush, racket, and crashing that the house seemed to be falling down.

[There follows another incident from Japan in 1555, involving a man and his sister, both possessed by evil spirits. They are released by the efforts of Jesuit brethren, conversion to Christianity, and prayers to Saint Michael.]

In 1588 At Brno in Moravia there was a woman in Nosocomium so overwhelmed by a particularly vigorous assault of the Devil that on one occasion she had to be prevented forcibly by everyone else in the hospital from drowning herself, and on another from harming herself with a knife she had in her hand. For three years she had sustained this affliction and then she was seized by an apoplexy, became tongue-tied, and had her ability to speak taken away. Our Jesuit brothers were sent for so that they might pray earnestly at a gathering of the local community; and it appears that after they had prayed to God, first the knot of the woman's tongue was untied and then, after she had been to confession, the knot of her soul.

[There follow two extracts from Book 8 of Hector Boethius's *History of the Scots*, and two anecdotes from Japan, dated 1569 and 1596, along with references to relevant Patristic and modern literature. Del Rio continues by complaining about attacks on the Jesuits, made by an anonymous poet, and then recommends the *Ave Maria*, *Salve Regina*, and Litany as prayers effective in warding off magical assaults.]

---

[26] A version of this appears in *The Occult in Early Modern Europe*, 52–7.

6) The sixth remedy is that of invoking Christ, the Virgin Mary, and one's guardian angel, for all of which Del Rio gives relevant references.]

What stops me from recalling the memory and veneration of the Blessed Virgin Mother of God in another completely reliable anecdote, so that my readers may understand how efficacious invocation of her always is against the tyranny of Hell? Orazio Torsellino, in his *History of Loreto*, tells the story with elegance and honesty.[27]

'The Virgin's protection preserved another young man from Loreto. Insane lust had propelled him to a point of precipitous descent and at this moment, overtaken by the recklessness of his desire, he had plunged himself into forbidden pleasures. Having battered down the modesty of a good many married women, he started to burn with immoderate love for a particular woman and when neither prayer nor bribe nor force nor trick could win him control of her, he decided to attempt the ultimate means. So he attracted the favour of an evil spirit by magical incantations and begged him to grant his prayer, making clear to the spirit that there was nothing he was not prepared to do if only he might enjoy the sexual fruits he was trying to obtain. By order of the Devil, therefore, he abandoned Christ and gave himself over completely to the spirit, confirmed this with an oath which the spirit dictated to him, and bound himself thereto with his signature. (This is how far people go when love of pleasure blinds their befouled minds!) Apart from this, however, he did what he had wanted to do – to the point of satiety, as it turned out.

But at this point the light of Heaven suddenly arose and the youth gave belated thought to the magnitude of his crime and as a result, penitence came to assist his mind which was distressed by cares. Intent on hope of pardon, he began to look for heavenly aid and pray to God and the Mother of God. During this he remembered the Virgin of Loreto and the priests of the church there, who had been given complete authority to absolve sins. Forthwith under God's inspiration and guidance, he went to Loreto where he had no doubt he would find a remedy for those afflictions of his. Nor was he deceived in that hope; for he came to Loreto, got hold of a suitable priest, told him everything, and asked him, "Have I any hope of salvation?" At first the priest hesitated a little, scared by the atrociousness of the crime. Then he pointed out its enormity and said that the young man did have a hope of salvation if he set about making every effort to please God by prayers, fasts, and voluntary corporal hardship. Since the man did not baulk at doing any penance, the priest promised that if

---

[27] (1545–1599), Italian Jesuit, historian, Professor of Literature at the Roman College. A Tuscan translation of his *De l'historia Lauretana* (The History of Loreto) appeared in Milan in 1600.

he did as he was told, he would listen to him with indulgence and, with God's blessing, absolve his great sin unreservedly. As they parted company, he advised the youth to mortify his body for three days by abstaining from food, wearing a hair-shirt, and whipping himself while imploring the aid of the Blessed Virgin. Through her he should seek God's favour; and he said that he himself during that same period of three days would say Mass with the intention that the young man be set free.

Each man's faith made itself clear and when the three days were over, the priest thought it best before he absolved the young man of his sins that the youth extract from the evil spirit the paper he had signed in case it should have any legal validity to the young man's detriment. He advised the youth accordingly and sent him away to enter the most venerable shrine and assail the Mother of God with prayers and tears until he had twisted his signature out of the Devil. The young man did as he was bid, eager to be saved and set free from anxiety, in full hope that he would prevail upon the Virgin Mother of God by his entreaty. Therefore he prostrated himself in front of the Virgin and, weeping, earnestly prayed that, once he had got back his wicked signature, she might be willing to be an advocate for his salvation and peace of mind and grant an answer to his prayer with a great miracle. He repeated these verses from memory: "Show that you are a mother. Let him who was born for us and acknowledges himself to be your son receive my prayers through you".

Having prayed thus, suddenly he saw that the paper he had signed had fallen down into his hands and, scarcely believing his unexpected happiness, he wept again and assiduously gave thanks to the Virgin. Then he came out of the shrine and ran, leaping with joy, to the priest and showed him the manuscript he had received through the kindness of the Mother of God. This manuscript was crammed with so many great, dreadful curses against Christ and against the man who had signed it that it was obvious [28] it had been dictated by the eternal enemy of the human race. This is how the power of God proved to be greater than all the Devil's deceitfulness, and released from such a great pact the man who had so devoted himself to Hell, setting him free through the kindness of the Mother of God into the liberty of the children of God. So do not let anyone at all, however criminal and lost, despair of salvation, if he does not wish to perish; and do not let anyone doubt the clemency of God whereby he has given sinners his Mother to be an advocate for their salvation'.

[Del Rio now gives further references to miracles of the Blessed Virgin, and quotes from a hymn by Prudentius.]

[7] The seventh remedy is the sign of the cross and Del Rio gives a large number

---

[28] Reading *facile* for *facilem*.

of references to Patristic and Mediaeval literature by way of illustration, ending with an elevating story taken from a letter by his fellow Jesuit, Fr Bencius.

8) The eighth remedy is invocation of the saints, discussion of which is again supported by references, mainly to Mediaeval literature.

9) The ninth remedy is the use of holy water. Here Del Rio gives not only Patristic and Mediaeval references, but records four short modern anecdotes.]

At "Riga in 1583, a man from Rüthen was advised on more than one occasion to return to the grace of the Roman Church, but always used to turn a deaf ear. Then he died impenitent. From that day onwards, various spectres appeared in his house to the servants. Tables were moved away from those who were sitting at them and yet no one was to be seen. The doors of bedrooms, which had not only been bolted but barred as well, swung open on every pivot. Huge stones smeared in pitch were thrown from the roof of the house. A Jesuit priest stopped people from picking these up but a Pole who, according to the Jesuit, saw the whole thing, was so seriously wounded on top of his head that for several days he lay half-dead. In the same house there was a lot of straw: it was all torn into tiny pieces. In sum, the people in the house saw all kinds of other terrifying things, which plainly indicated to them how much control Satan had assumed over it. But along came the priest I have just mentioned, with a companion, and purified it with holy water and incense; and after this exorcism the whole tumult of evil spirits fell quiet, something which was later acknowledged with much gratitude by the whole local church". (From a letter from the college at Riga in that year.)

In the province of Mexico, our Society established a house at Pascuara in the year 1587. According to a letter I received from there, the son of an Indian woman felt something was seizing hold of his side every night when he went to bed, and then letting him rest again. His mother did not know what was possessing him, and meanwhile the boy himself was having his vital spirit extracted from him day after day, and was slowly wasting to death. He was saved, however, by being taken into the church and asperged with holy water to the accompaniment of prayers.

In the following year, 1588, a peasant woman from Trier offered a man some eggs. His manservant put them in his cap and then put the cap with the eggs inside back on his head. At once there began such a pain that he almost went out of his mind and, not knowing what to do, he took refuge in a church. There he thrust his burning head into a vessel of holy water and recovered. The sorceress (*maga*) was arrested and during torture said that the eggs had been bewitched by venomous magic (*fuisse venenata*) in such a way that anyone who tasted them would die, and anyone who touched them would develop a tumour. (Letter from Trier, 1588.)

At Pont-à-Mousson in 1593, a virgin of advanced years was troubled by so many tormenting spirits (*furiae*) that it might be said she was under siege. One of our Jesuit priests recited the litanies. A second woman afflicted by malefices swallowed holy water. Another troubled by a malign spirit (*malignus spiritus*) hung round her neck a holy Agnus Dei made of wax. All were restored to themselves and, soon after, made their confession and died in the midst of their prayers. (This comes from a letter from the Province of France for that year.)

[Del Rio adds once more reference from Francisco Lopez Gomara's *History of the Conquest of Mexico*,[29] and then goes on to remedy number ten.

10) Del Rio recommends the Agnus Dei and provides a sequence of modern anecdotes to support his recommendation. They are drawn from Jesuit documents, official reports from Trapani, Trier, Freiburg, Tours, and Avignon in 1585, 1586, 1589, and 1590. Typical is the following from Trier where, says Del Rio, there was a very large number of witches (*sagae*).]

'One of them made it her habit to entrap a boy about eight years old with her tricks and her incantations and carry him off to the city. Here, under licence of night and darkness, the witches could take pleasure in their wicked sports and here, too, the boy would be given his particular task. So, while the women joined hands and led each other through their dances, he would accompany their leaping on a drum. Nor was he a spectator merely of their games and dancing but often of their tricks, too, whereby they harm the bodies and lives of human beings. The Archbishop ordered the boy to be brought under guard to his palace so that he could instruct him in the catechism, of which the boy was plainly ignorant. One of our Jesuit priests hung an image of the heavenly lamb around the boy's neck and at night an evil spirit came to him and upbraided the child forcefully because he had allowed himself to be deceived so easily. The spirit told him to throw away the wax image unless he wanted to be thrashed and so the terrified boy did as he was told. Once he had removed it out of fear, the evil spirit immediately bore him off to the city walls on the back of a black goat and in an instant carried him away to the filthy regions of the witches. There the boy remained hidden for a while among these workers of venomous magic (*veneficae*), but once the cord from which the wax image had been suspended (which was tied in a series of intricate knots) had been snapped off, he was returned to the Archbishop's palace'.

[11] The eleventh remedy consists of devout writings or holy medals (*amuleta*) hung round the neck. Examples of the practice are given.

---

[29] 1510–c. 1560, Spanish historian. *Historia de la conquista de Mexico* was published in Anvers in 1554.

12) Ringing the bells of a Catholic church. Again, suitable examples are given.]

Finally, it should be noted that these ecclesiastical remedies are always effective, but do not always liberate people from malefices. There seem to be two particular reasons for this: (a) the sin of the person damaged by the malefice, or the medicine prescribed for it, especially if this is not free from superstition, or the patient has only a moderate hope of cure, or is lukewarm in the faith. Both of these will show that the patient is unworthy of obtaining a favourable outcome. (b) The second reason is, I think, the greater good of the person who is sick or has been harmed, because affliction and sickness usually draw people away from their sins, or serve as expiation for former sins, or increase the patient's merit and provide a display of patience and other virtues to other people.

Chapter 3: A defence of certain of the Church's remedies against the false accusations of heretics

[Del Rio begins by observing that 'those featherless chickens who fly away from the bosom of Mother Church, and from her learning and piety, are always raging insanely against traditional ceremonies', and goes on to deal with certain assertions in Godelmann's treatise De lamiis (Witches).]

First he objects to Papal exorcisms and says that Papal exorcists should be counted as enchanters. Why? 'To begin with', he says, 'because Aretius [30] writes that for the most part they are magicians (magi)'. Aretius writes! Ha! How much belief in God does he have? As much as that of any enemy of Papists, presumably. A Swiss heretic! A suitable witness you may trust without Bible oath! What kind of a courtroom is this which produces such witnesses? I see I must add many others (whom he names, in my opinion, simply honoris causa): Chemnitz, Lavater, Peucer, Bodin, and Wier.[31] But that is fine, because they are made from the same flour. That is fine, because they too are overt heretics, each one of them either a heretic or someone of no fixed faith, all of them inadmissible as witnesses, names one can score out with a single line, men one can reject with a single phrase: *a sworn opponent is not believed in the face of an enemy.*

---

[30] Benedict Aretius (1505–1574), Swiss Calvinist Greek scholar, theologian, and botanist.
[31] Ludwig Lavater (1527–1586), Swiss theologian. His best-known work, De spectris, lemuribus, et magnis atque insolitis fragoribus et praesagationibus quae obitum hominum, clades, mutationesque imperiorum praecedunt (The Apparitions, Malevolent Ghosts, Loud Unusual Cracking Noises, and Presages of the Future Which Precede the Death of Human Beings, Disasters, and the Change of Empires) was published in Zurich in 1570. Kaspar Peucer (1525–1602), German scholar. He published Commentarius de praecipuis divinationum generibus (An Essay on the Best-Known Types of Divination) in Wittenberg in 1553.

Godelmann adds a second 'proof'. 'Enchanters (*incantatores*) evoke devils from Hell by means of divine evocations, and in similar fashion exorcists try to drive out malign spirits (*maligni spiritus*) from human beings and living creatures by reciting certain prayers and performing ceremonies to which they add characters, curses, and frequent repetition of the names of God, Mary, and the saints'.

Look at the comparison and laugh! Enchanters evoke evil spirits (*daemones*) from Hell with dreadful chants, etc. First falsity, that the enchanters have summoned evil spirits from Hell. Such spirits existed only in the air and had not yet been rounded up and driven into the wicked mansion of Hell. There is no way out for any of them from there to respond to magicians' chants, since this power of sending them forth belongs to God alone. But you must excuse him, this specialist in legal technicalities, for making a mistake – a man who has read bits and pieces of Chemnitz, Aretius, and Lavater en passant, and has suddenly turned into a theologian. Someone who tries to expel an evil spirit from people's bodies is not a magician (*magus*) because he makes the attempt. He is a magician only if he tries to do so by means of a magic ritual. 'That is why' (Godelmann will tell us), 'I said it was those who try to do so by means of certain prayers, characters, and curses, etc.' What Godelmann says about characters is a lie. Papal exorcists do not use them, and to his remark about prayers I reply that those which are prescribed in the *Pontificale Romanum* are holy and pious and contain nothing which smacks of superstition.

So what else do we have? Curses. These are heaped on the Devil not merely as insults to an enemy – and this in itself would not be a piece of magic – but as a punishment for the Devil's crime and as a commemoration of that punishment inflicted by God: and they are heaped on him by people who are employing the authority granted to them by God, and by the Apostles and their successors. What is magical about this? The names of God are repeated because by these is declared the power of God and such a declaration is very hateful to the evil spirit and shows a great deal of honour to God, for the exorcist hopes to expel the evil spirit by the power of God, and this is how he makes his claim to do so. But when the names of the Blessed Virgin and the saints are joined thereto (and this does not often happen), they are there to take a bite out of the evil spirit who is thereby reminded that he has often been conquered and that others have often triumphed over him. The use of such names causes him exquisite torture. Moreover, these saints and especially the Virgin Mary, Mother of God (whom Godelmann's dog-like mouth contemptuously names 'Mary', *tout court*), by their intercession obtain from God freedom for the demoniac. What sort of a person (you insane individual) can ascribe this to enchantment? Many of you heretics oppose invocation of the saints even as I write these words, and you employ equal amounts of pettifogging misrepresentation, lame ineptitude, and want of judgement. Nevertheless, you are not so driven by insanity as to argue that there is any magic in this kind of invocation.

Next, Godelmann goes on to say, 'In the early Church it was a particular gift to drive out the Devil from the bodies of demoniacs or confine him within them by means of the human voice and the power of God. "The people who did this", he says, "were called exorcists because they laid their hands on those troubled by the evil demon (cacodaemon) and expelled evil spirits (daemones) by means of certain solemn curses and appeals".'

So you yourself, my fine fellow, are a witness that there were exorcists in the early Church. We call such people by the same name today and they discharge their office for the same reason as did the ancients, with the same ritual and by means of the same gift. So what do you find wrong with out exorcists? Do you criticise the ancients for doing the same thing? Do you turn them into enchanters? I think not, and since you do not, I have to ask what difference do you see between exorcists then and now? Why are our exorcists 'enchanters' and those who used to do what ours do now are not? If you cannot demonstrate any difference, shall I not correctly state as a fact that you are the most inept of slanderers? Ah, but here is your point about difference. 'In the early Church', he says, 'this was once a particular gift. But when this gift of expelling evils spirits disappeared from the Church, a poor imitation took its place and changed to superstitious exorcisms and enchantments more accurately called magical, as Chemnitz says' – and he proceeds to fetch up his oracle from Chemnitz's tripod.[32]

Now, I maintain that there is one clear thing about this particular contribution to the rest of the lies with which his book is filled: that it is not a simple lie, but several lies in one. First, he lies when he says that this gift of expelling evil spirits has disappeared from the Church. At what point did it disappear, when every day we see it flourishing throughout the whole of Europe where the Catholic Church flourishes, and it has extended itself to both the Indias? Read histories of the Indies; go to Catholic churches anywhere in Italy, Germany, France, or Spain. You will find nothing more common than absolutely true stories of the expulsion of evil spirits. I do say that this gift is lacking in Protestant assemblies. But those have ceased to be parts of the Church because of their wicked schism.

Secondly, he lies when he calls this Catholic observance 'a poor imitation'. Our exorcists are complying with an instruction from God and retaining a rite received from the Apostles by laying on of hands. They know it has been promised to them: 'In my name they shall cast out evil spirits'. They know that

[32] The allusion is to the ancient oracle at Delphi where the resident priestess uttered the words of the god while seated upon a three-legged stool.

this promise of the faith which they preserve tenaciously cannot fail, and in this faith and for love of their neighbours who need help they are led to undertake battle with the evil spirit. Trusting in that promise, and with the grace of God's help, even now they expel the enemy from the places he has occupied.

Thirdly, he lies when he says that our exorcists have turned aside to superstitious exorcisms and magical incantations. Let him and his like produce in evidence a superstitious exorcism from the *Ceremonial of the Roman Church*, a work to which they refer by name. Let them produce one, I say, if they can. They have not done so because they cannot. In such a serious matter, such an important matter, they should not have used bald assertion and they would not have done so unless they had been lying.

[Del Rio now refers to a book by the exorcist Girolamo Menghi, and the use of the Virgin Mary's name. He adds that he himself does not defend every exorcism carried out by various exorcists, only those done according to the approved Catholic rite, since these are completely free from superstition. He then turns to individual aspects of exorcism – the people involved, the situation, the words which are used and the intention informing use of the ritual – referring his readers to relevant literature, after which he returns to his attack on Godelmann. To the charge that Catholics exorcise salt as an apotropaic against the Devil, Del Rio answers, with relevant quotations, that this is legitimate. Godelmann's assertions that Catholics exorcise herbs for the same purpose, and that the Agnus Dei, like Christ's blood, breaks the bonds of sin, he condemns and dismisses as outright lies, and offers a wide range of authorities to support his condemnation. Godelmann objects to Catholics' exorcising oil: 'of balsam and oil they say, "I exorcise you" (you can hear the words used by magicians)'. Del Rio objects strongly to this parenthesis and again defends the practice by referring to Patristic literature.]

At the same time Godelmann adds another censorious paragraph. 'They use oil to anoint the limbs of the sick', he says, 'these being the organs of the external senses, so that through this anointing whatever wrong this person has done with his limbs or senses may be absolved. These created things do not have such a power either by nature, or by divine ordinance, or by any institution of God's word. Therefore this is pure, truly diabolical, impious, blasphemous magic, as the theologian Jakob Heerbrand, the Chancellor of the Academy at Tübingen, has correctly written. Lerchemer writes similarly about this Papist consecration in the German version of his *Tractate*, as does Dr Jakob Andreae in his *Disputations from Essen*, etc'.[33]

---

[33] Jakob Heerbrand (1521–1600), Augustin Lerchemer = Hermann Witekind (1522–1608), Jakob Andreae (1528–1590). All three were German Lutheran theologians.

Godelmann slips in the German versions of the two last mentioned so that scholars who do not know German may not be able to criticise, but I hope my distinguished readers will not imagine there is anything worthwhile secreted away in those words. Lerchemer calls all the blessings I am discussing an abuse of God's word and the work of imposters and monkeys. Schmidelin [34] says that the sacrament of confirmation is no more than a work of the Devil, but offers no other 'proof' than the form of words used in consecrating the holy oil, the sign of the cross made by the priest, and the exorcism which accompanies it. This exorcism, however, is not a work of the Devil but of God, the sign of the cross is not a work of the Devil but a sacred sign instituted by the Church from the time of the Apostles, and the ritual formula contains nothing which is not holy, pious, and in harmony with the Scripture. So it follows that this Dr Jakob Andreae from Tübingen was a slanderous, blasphemous buffoon and a mouthpiece for the Devil to speak through. The blessing of created things originated not in magic circles, nor on the platforms of juggling imposters or actors, but has always been used by the Catholic Church. So it follows that Lerchemer in his satyr's mask is playing the part of a comic actor with his insulting taunts.

[As for the Chancellor of the Tübingen Academy, Del Rio dismisses him as an impious, blasphemous critic of no value whatever and refers the reader to a large number of relevant sources by way of proof. He also proves the validity of blessing bread and salt, to which the same Protestants had objected, again pointing out that ceremonies of blessing and exorcism have long been instituted by the Church. They have no power to remit mortal sins, he says, but they may remit venial sins if they were instituted by the Church expressly for that purpose. The power of the Church's ceremonies and sacramentals to drive out evil spirits does not lie in their physical constitution or nature, but in their moral power to achieve that effect. So the evil spirit sees the signs, hears the words, and is forced to obey. Godelmann lies when he says that Catholics anoint the sick so that these people may be absolved thereby from their sins of the senses, as reference to the Greek and Latin Fathers demonstrates. Nor does Godelmann even understand Chrysostom and Clement and other Church Fathers when he tries to use them in his raving and ranting about Catholic ceremonies, as Del Rio proceeds to show. Then he turns to another of Godelmann's assertions.]

There remains one weapon Godelmann uses, not against us but against Christ himself. He calls it 'the crime of bread worship' [35] which he explains as follows:
'By uttering of these five words, "For this is my body", which are accompanied

---

[34] I.e. Jakob Andreae.
[35] Here Del Rio uses a Greek word. It seems to be an early modern coinage.

by a breath of air, Catholics persuade themselves and others that they change the substance of the bread, bring down the body of Christ from Heaven, and change the former into the latter. This is obviously a piece of magic'.

Now there is a tongue which should be torn out by its root, and a mouth which never stops vomiting forth filth and blasphemies! So when Christ said that the bread he was holding was his body, he was a magician? If it was flesh, it was not bread. If it was bread, what Christ said was not true. But, Godelmann, you will say that the bread exists alongside the flesh, slipping your breadification into the argument, o Creator of Bread, as though you were shutting Christ up in an earthenware pot or a purse. 'Creator of Bread' is just the name for you. You should be sewn up in a sack or enclosed in a pot and thrown into fast-flowing water.[36] But any number of Catholic theologians have refuted your remark, and I have no time here to deal with transubstantiation; nor is this the place for disputation. So let us see what magic there is here. It does not lie in uttering those five words which Christ himself uttered at the last supper, and which Saint Peter, Saint James, and Saint Andrew repeated in their liturgies or Masses, and which have always been embraced *in toto* by the Church. It does not lie in the breathing, to which we Catholics attribute no power and which we do not consider necessary – other than it is necessary for the person uttering the words to breathe. If we could speak without exhaling, the job of speaking would not need us to take a breath. If we did indeed believe that the character of the bread must depend upon our breathing out, then by attributing the power of transubstantiation to that breathing, we should certainly be superstitious, and we would rightly hear ourselves described as brainless and stupid. But we Catholics do not believe anything like that.

[Del Rio continues to denounce Godelmann as a liar. Transubstantiation is not a piece of magic. It is an article of faith which the Church has always held, as references to Scripture and Church liturgists demonstrate. But French Calvinists, and Scaliger in particular, are unwilling to acknowledge these authorities, and especially the authority of Dionysius the Areopagite whom Del Rio has just quoted. So Del Rio completes the chapter with a defence of Dionysius as a legitimate source of authority.]

[As a coda to Book 6, Del Rio then offers his readers a summary of twelve points which are intended to constitute an easy set of references for confessors.]

1) *Evil spirits do exist.* When it occurs to atheists to doubt whether there are evil spirits or not, suggest to them (a) that their existence is clearly taught by Holy Scripture in various places (b) that this has always been the Church's

---

[36] This is a reference to the ancient Roman way of dealing with parricides.

understanding, and (c) that it is heresy to defend the contrary opinion. These three points are proved by theologians in their work on angels. (d) Reason tells us evil spirits exist because we have experience of certain extraordinary effects. For example, a mountain suddenly moves from its place or animals talk or apparitions of the dead appear before our eyes, speaking in unknown languages. One can place on a table iron objects, silver plates, or things of a similar weight, and they jump about and move from one end of the table to the other without the help of a cord (or of a magnet in the case of the iron objects), or anything like that. Someone says he will accurately predict which playing card a person will select from a pack. The person pulls out the card, keeps it in his hand, and the figure on the face changes. It is made to change three times. Three or more people are made to think of one and the same thing. One person so works on the imagination of someone else that the second person can hardly think of anything except what he is compelled to think of by the first person. (I say 'hardly' because an evil spirit cannot entirely compel either the will or the intellect or drive someone to do this by any absolute necessity.) They make mirrors in which one can see things ten miles away. In three hours a genuine shrub a span high grows out of a table. They make certain lanterns in the light of whose flames any women who are present strip themselves naked, expose to view those parts which nature intends should be covered, and in this naked state do not hesitate to dance as long as the lantern placed in their midst (which is engraved with certain characters and other things such as that) burns brightly with hare's fat. These are the kinds of things itinerant performers palm off on us, according to Battista della Porta;[37] and since we are offered no proper natural or artificial explanations for these effects, we must attribute spiritual causes to them, namely angels and evil spirits.

[2] *It is not lawful to enter into any pact or friendship with evil spirits.* Del Rio points out that this is contrary to the First Commandment and further adduces passages from Scripture to underline his assertion.]

[3] *Judges must not fail to punish the practice of magic, nor must they turn a blind eye to it.*] When confessors come upon prelates, princes, or judges who are too lenient, remiss, and negligent in rooting out this sect, they should warn them that they have been ordained by God to punish the wicked, that they should not have taken up the sword without reason, and that they should eject with the greatest severity these evils which, through their negligence, are being sown in the world and the Church, and are increasing in power and violence.

---

[37] Giovanni Battista della Porta (*c.* 1535–1615), Italian natural philosopher. He published his major work, *Magia Naturalis* (Natural Magic) in Naples in 1558. It rapidly became very popular and ran into several editions.

[Del Rio then supplements his point with references to Scripture and Classical and Mediaeval literature.

4) *The use of superstitions is harmful and abhorrent.* Those who make light of learning superstitious ceremonies and practising them should be warned that the inventor of all superstitious and vain observances is the Devil who from the beginning of the world has seduced almost the entire human race into idolatry in an instant. But the Son of God destroyed his rule. 'The reason the Son of God appeared was to destroy the works of the Devil', and a few days before his Passion he said, 'Now is the judgement of this world, now shall the ruler of this world be cast out';[38] and this has been the rock of Apostolic preaching throughout the whole world. Nevertheless, Satan's ancient ambition to be worshipped as a god has not diminished along with his rule and to fill the place of that open, manifest idolatry which is almost extinct, he has introduced, under the guise of piety and personal advantage, a covert idolatry, namely a desire for and a cultivation of the superstitious arts. This is why he has invented this dire curiosity and spread it abroad, first in order to recover secretly and by means of a wicked trick that possession of souls of which the power of the cross had deprived him; secondly, so that by this pact people might become accustomed to violate the first and greatest commandment and the vow of religion whereby they bound themselves to God in baptism; thirdly, so that people may lose the hope they should have in God and put it in these useless things, and so become cursed by God who hates 'those who superstitiously observe vanities'.[39] Fourthly, once they have been drawn into mortal sin, the raging lion devours them and the snake filled with poison deceives the human being whom God has fashioned and so makes mock of him. These are the 'benefits' of superstitious observances, and those who employ them or love them demonstrate that they are disciples not of Christ but of the Devil, that they love his authority, and that they have been drawn into his assembly [40] and away from the teaching of the Catholic Church. [There follow references to and quotations from Classical, Mediaeval, and modern literature illustrative of Del Rio's argument.]

[5) *How the confessor can recognise whether an effect comes form an evil spirit, from nature, or from God.* Penitents are to be told not to do or say anything in the hope of producing an effect which their action clearly has no natural or supernatural power to achieve, such as sowing seeds in a river, or ploughing the sea-shore.]

[38] 1 *John* 3.8 and *John* 12.31.
[39] *Psalm* 30.7
[40] *Ludus*, the word meaning 'game' or 'school', which is also used as a technical term for the sabbat.

So, if someone wants to drive away a headache and ties strips of linen or scraps of white paper round the patient's skin, or leads him or her between split twigs, or measures the patient's belt with the palm of his hand, these actions are obviously useless and superstitious because they have no power to expel the harmful, distressing humour from the head. On the other hand, if one applies rose-water to it, or uses rhubarb to expel the bile, or eats white mustard to induce sneezing which will draw off phlegm from the head, that will not be a vain observance but a licit remedy, because nature has implanted a power in these things for that purpose.

[No words have power by nature to achieve physical effects, but certain words may have power to bring about a supernatural effect if they have been so instituted by God. Examples are the words of consecration from the Mass, and the words of absolution from confession. Misusing these is sacrilegious, useless, and superstitious.]

[6) *The safest remedies.* As Del Rio has pointed out before, these are the remedies offered by the Church.

7) *Those people who are curious about divination and secret things.* They should be warned that although the desire to know is entirely natural, it must be constrained by the laws of God. Certain mysteries are reserved to God and the wish to explore further than is permissible is one stimulated by the evil spirit.

8) *Those who strive to acquire knowledge effortlessly by means of certain rituals, etc.* They should be warned that curiosity to know things which are not necessary for us to know is usually not just useless but actually very harmful.

9) *Those who want physical health, or honour, or money, or the acquisition or recovery of favour, and for this purpose use suspect methods.* They should have it drummed into them that in every reversal of their good health or their fortune (reversals usually inflicted on people as a punishment for their sins) they should seek protection by doing two things: (a) finding out natural remedies, and (b) commending themselves, their households, and their goods to God and his saints.]

10) *People who profess to exorcise evil spirits from those who are possessed,*[41] *or who try to conjure them forth.*

In several areas many abuses have crept into legitimate Catholic exorcisms, which run contrary to the customary practice of the Apostolic Roman Church.

---

[41] *Exorcisatores.* The word is unusual and clearly does not refer to a regular exorcist (*exorcista*). Del Rio has based his usage on a Greek original, the root of which is *orkos* = 'oath' or 'the object by which one swears an oath'. Since this strongly suggests the demonic pact, Del Rio's use of the word immediately apprises the reader of the meaning he intends by it.

[Jesus gave power to the Church to expel evil spirits, but not to every cleric, only to bishops, priests, deacons, subdeacons, and exorcists.] So it follows that lay men or clerics not given the grade of exorcist are suspect of a pact with an evil spirit if they usurp this gift *ex officio*, so to speak, and use it other than as a particular grace or gift from God. Suspect also are those clerics and religious who claim this gift as peculiar to themselves, saying that they have more natural or supernatural power to exorcise than anyone else of the same grade or rank.

Some of these people are accustomed to have special formulae and ceremonies which they use in exorcism, which are different from those rites and formulae in common use by the Church. These should be carefully investigated by bishops and permission to use them should not be granted easily unless they have been approved by pious and learned men. There is a very strong suspicion that these are part of a pact with evil spirits and that by their use the spirits pretend they are being forced to come out of the person possessed. The evil spirits' reason for compliance is that while these conjurings are being conducted in front of a crowd, there is always money to be made from the throng of bystanders. Large numbers of people come to hear the sermons and the pseudo-exorcist and the Devil mingle with them, going back and forth, back and forth. The evil spirit is happy because he usually manages to sow some errors of faith and morals among them, or at any rate succeeds in making people do things which are superstitious, useless, or superfluous. He slanders the innocent and reveals the hidden crimes of wrong-doers, so that everyone else may have evil suspicions about them. He urges some people to carnality and others to avarice, and he pretends he is afraid of those who are good in order to push them into pride.

[The confessor must, therefore, advise his penitents to steer clear of unnecessary discussions on the subject, to steer clear of using novel formulae and mystic rites which are not approved by the Church and, like Christ, to exorcise only a few people in order to avoid giving occasion for public gossip. Lay people should be told to beware of pseudo-exorcists and to avoid going to their meetings, 'because God has forbidden us to listen to women who prophesy (*pythones*) and has done this in case we pay heed to the evil spirits who speak within the bodies of those they have possessed'. Evil spirits should not be questioned because association with them is forbidden, and in any case they lie.]

11) *Those who conjure clouds and insects.* It is easy to refute the boasts of those cloud-conjurors who put it about that they have the power to drive clouds away from certain places. (a) Ask them whether those clouds have their origins in nature, or arise from malefice and the operation of an evil spirit. If they say 'from nature', their exorcism is contrary to God, the creator of nature, and this is both blasphemous and sacrilegious. Their power to control clouds must be

either natural or supernatural, and since they have not received supernatural power from God (who is not in opposition to himself), and have not received it from good angels, this ability of theirs must have issued from the power of an evil spirit. If they say the cloud arises from malefice and is controlled by an evil spirit, how do they know this save from their pact with him? (b) Ask them, if they have the practical knowledge and power to drive away harmful clouds, why don't they know how to call up beneficial, life-giving clouds and make them appear over the fields in time of barrenness and drought? Why can't they do this? (c) Why don't they have the power to keep away or to extinguish lightning and fire falling from the sky, which burn up people's houses? (d) Why don't they know how to conjure whirlwinds and floods whereby plants and homes and trees are laid flat and uprooted? For just as the clouds we have been discussing are, with God's permission, sometimes formed and sent by wicked angels, so also are these other calamities, as we learn from the story of Job. So why, if this art or power has been given to these conjurors by God for the common *good* of humanity, do they restrict God's beneficence to this single thing? The conclusion must be that they achieve their effects because of their pact with an evil spirit.

[The confessor must warn his penitents to avoid having dealings with such people. If help is needed, one should use the methods furnished and recommended by the Church — prayer, emendation of life, fasting, and good works.]

There are others who lay claim to have the art or special power (granted to them, they say, by God) of driving away and killing caterpillars, locusts, beetles, and other insects and vermin which feed on fruit, roots, and seeds, and frustrate the farmers' hopes; and in many places it is the custom for the peasants to call upon these people every year at great cost. What they usually do is this. The imposter sets himself up as a judge and they bring before him two proctors. One discharges the procurator's office of pleading the people's case; the other acts in place of a bishop's vicar or a royal official. Each in turn speaks on the matter in hand — an infestation of locusts or some other insects — fights his case and observes all the usual tricks, time-wasting, and postponements of a law-suit. Finally the pleading is brought to an end and the wonderful judge passes sentence, ordering the insects in question to depart beyond the bounds of that territory within the space of so many days, under the penalty of excommunication, etc. The superstition in this is too obvious to be concealed.

[Cirvelo, from whom Del Rio says he has borrowed for this section, says that all the holy Doctors of the Church have condemned this. It is blasphemous to play this kind of game and none of these pseudo-judicial actions has any power, natural or supernatural, over insects. Again, the penitent should be advised to turn to natural or ecclesiastical remedies for his problems. Natural remedies are listed in the *Geoponica*.[42] Cirvelo gives an example of ecclesiastical remedies which include prayers, fasting, public processions, and the giving of alms.]

[12) *The vain observances in prayers and petitions, which one should treat with caution.*

The Devil is accustomed to violate the sanctity of prayers with many attendant superstitious practices. Penitents should therefore be advised to pay attention to the following points. (a) Sin in prayer lies in its subject matter, as when one prays for illicit or harmful things, or when one asks too persistently for things indifferent in themselves (such as wealth, honour, learning, etc.), or when one seeks something which it may not be right to ask for; or one wants to know the future. (b) Secondly, it lies in the form of the prayer, as when the words or their sense is mendacious or when one uses unknown or barbarous words. (c) Thirdly, it lies in the manner of praying or the ceremonies attached to the prayer, as when these do not conform to the normal practice of the Church, when one employs a certain posture, a certain way of looking, when one observes fixed hours or days, when one uses a certain number of candles of such and such a colour, etc. Penitents should be warned against these sins and told to avoid illicit superstitions, implore God's help, and submit themselves to him piously even if he does not grant their petition.]

[So Del Rio comes to the end of his work.]

Let these remarks be sufficient. They are poultices for the chief sources and causes of superstition and any others must be sought from what I have written in the rest of this work.

Whatever I have written in this work, I submit to the judgement of the Holy, Apostolic, and Catholic Roman Church, and to the censure of pious theologians. If I have inadvertently said anything which does not have the approval of the Church, I repudiate it and condemn it, and it is my wish that people regard it as though it had not been written.

Martín del Rio
A priest of the Society of Jesus

[42] A work which Del Rio has had occasion to cite before. It is a compilation of extracts from earlier manuals of husbandry and agriculture, probably compiled between 944 and 959.

Select bibliography

There is very little published on Del Rio himself, and not much more on the *Disquisitiones* and its relationship with other demonologies. On Del Rio's subject-matter, of course, the bibliography is vast. The following list, then, is intended merely to give a brief notice of some of the more relevant work which is available.

(a) *Biographical notices*

Biographie Nationale de Belgique, Vol. 5 (Brussels 1876), 476–91.
New Catholic Encyclopaedia, Vol. 4. p. 740.
Enciclopedia Universal Ilustrada, Vol. 17. p. 1540.
Robbins R. H., *Encyclopaedia of Witchcraft and Demonology* (London 1979), 121–3.
Rosweyde P., *Martini Antonii Del Rio ... Vita* (Antwerp 1609).
Sommervogel C., *Bibliothèque des Ecrivains de la Compagnie de Jésus*, s.v.

(b) *Secondary Published Literature*

Anderton, B., *A Stoic of Louvain: Justus Lipsius* (London 1915).
Baldwin, M., 'Alchemy and the Society of Jesus in the seventeenth century: strange bedfellows?' *Ambix* 40 (1993), 41–64.
Baroja, J. C., 'Martín del Rio y suas Disquisiciones mágicas', in *El señor Inquisidor y otras vidas per oficio* (Madrid, Alianza Editorial 1968), 171–96, 237–45.
Behringer, W., *Witchcraft Persecutions in Bavaria*, English translation (Cambridge University Press 1997).
Brann, N. L., 'The proto-Protestant assault upon Church magic: the 'Errores Bohemanorum' according to the Abbot Trithemius (1462–1516)', *Journal of Religious History* 12 (1982), 9–22.
Busson, H., 'Montaigne et son cousin', *Revue d'histoire de la France* 60 (1960), 481–99.
Clark, S., *Thinking With Demons* (Oxford University Press 1998).
Dell'Anna, G., 'L'interpretazione della stregoneria in Vanini e Del Rio', *Bollettino di storia della filosofia* 6 (1978), 79–118.
Delvigne, A. C. H., *Mémoires de Martin-Antoine Del Rio*, 3 vols (Brussels 1869–1871).
Fischer, E., Die *'Disquisitionum magicarum libri sex' von Martin Delrio als gegenreformatorische Exempel-Quelle* (Hanover 1975).
Fraikin, J., 'Un épisode de la sorcellerie en Ardenne et en région Mosellane: l'affaire du moine de Stavelot, Dom Jean del Vaulx, 1592–1597', *Revue d'histoire ecclésiastique* 85 (1990), 650–68.
Heiss, G., 'Konfessionelle Propaganda und kirchliche Magie: Berichte der Jesuiten über

den Teufel aus der Zeit der gegenreformation in den mittel europäischen Landern der Habsburger', *Römische Historische Mitteilungen* 32–3 (1990–1991), 231–46.

Hoensbroech, P. von, *Der Jesuitenorden*, 2 vols (Bern and Leipzig 1926), 1.615–30.

Labbeke, L., 'De Recrutering van de Jesuïeten in het Hertogdom Brabant, 1584–1640', *Trajecta* 5 (1996), 193–212.

Lea, H. C., *Materials Towards a History of Witchcraft*, 3 vols (New York 1957), 2.640–6.

Maxwell-Stuart, P. G., *The Occult in Early Modern Europe: a documentary study* (Macmillan 1998).

Menéndez y Pelayo, M., *Historia de los heterodoxos españoles*, 3 vols (Madrid 1880–1881), 3.655–9.

Pearl, J. L., *The Crime of Crimes: demonology and politics in France, 1560–1620* (Wilfrid Laurier University Press 1999).

Saunders, J. L., *J.Lipsius: The Philosophy of Renaissance Stoicism* (New York 1955).

Schnyder, A., 'Der "Malleus Maleficarum" Fragen und Beobachtungen zu seiner Druck-geschichte sowie zur Rezeption bei Bodin, Binsfeld, und Delrio', *Archiv für Kulturgeschichte* 74 (1992), 323–64.

Shumaker, W., *Natural Magic and Modern Science* (Binghamton, New York 1989).

Taylor, R., 'Architecture and magic: considerations on the *Idea* of the Escorial', in D. Fraser, H. Hibbard, M. J. Lewine (eds), *Essays in the History of Architecture, presented to Rudolf Wittkower* (London 1967), 81–109.

—— : 'Hermeticism and mystical architecture in the Society of Jesus', in R. Wittkower and I. B. Jaffe (eds), *Baroque Art, the Jesuit Contribution* (New York 1972), 63–91.

Walker, D. P., *Spiritual and Demonic Magic from Ficino to Campanella* (London 1958).

Webster, C., 'Paracelsus confronts the saints: miracles, healing, and the secularisation of magic', *Social History of Medicine* 8 (1995), 403–21.

Index

Abano, Pietro d' 37, 60
Abenezra 94
acquittal 222
Agnus Dei 19, 121, 219, 224, 260, 269, 273
Agrippa, Heinrich Cornelius 37, 69, 70, 72, 86, 113, 166
Albertini, Arnaldo 232
Albertus Magnus 72
alchemy 11, 22, 59–67
Alciati, Andrea 91, 92
Al-Kindi 40
Ambrose, Saint 143
Ammianus 170
amulet 11, 16, 58–9, 123, 147 n. 37, 245, 261, 269
Anabaptists 104
Anania, Giovanni Lorenzo d' 46 n. 36, 68 n. 2, 72 n. 12
Andreae, Jakob 273, 274
Anselm, Saint 143
Antichrist 17, 81
Apuleius 35
Aquinas, Saint Thomas 38, 41, 60, 73, 78, 90, 95, 114, 137, 142, 156, 180, 214
Aratus 165, 170
Aretius, Benedict 270, 271
Aristotle 13, 40, 61, 68, 167
Arnald of Villanova 63, 67
Arnobius 52
astrologers 145, 155, 164–8 passim, 172, 194, 226, 236
astrology 70, 159, 164–8
astronomy 164
Augurello, Aurelio 64–5
Augustine of Hippo, Saint 45, 73, 80, 86, 95, 132, 135, 142, 143, 156, 166, 188, 231, 236
Ausonius 168

Averroes 60, 68
Avicenna 40, 41

Barbatia, Andreas 223
Beauvais Vincent de 130
Bede, the Venerable 179
Beetz, Johann 126
Benci (Bencius), Francesco 21 n. 52, 262, 264, 268
Bernard of Siena, Saint 158
Bielski, Martin 83
Binsfeld, Pierre 95, 120, 126, 187, 194, 195, 197, 208, 211, 217, 232, 234
Bizzarri, Pietro 136
Bodin, Jean 21, 37, 53–4, 64, 130, 209, 219, 270
Boethius, Hector 264, 265
Bökel, Johann 41
books
    magic 15, 27, 70, 71, 74–5, 76, 196, 237
    requests 74
    superstitious 77
Bossi, Egidio 189
Bossius, Thomas 121
Brahe, Tycho 164
Bredenbach, Matthias 134, 136
Briand, Jean 180
Bruno, Giordano 208
Burchard, Johann 142
Bustamante de la Cámara, Juan 56

Caesarius, Johann 209
Cajetan, Tommaso de Vio 60, 67, 140, 166
Calcagnini, Celio 72
Camden, William 99
Canon Episcopi 92, 236–7
Cardano, Girolamo 37, 63, 126, 167, 168 n. 27

Carrari, Vincenzo 251
Cassiodorus 149
Castanheda, Fernão Lopes de 87
Castro, Alfonso de 232
Catholic Church 16–17, 51, 59, 77, 81,
    97, 115, 136, 138, 139, 163, 181,
    187, 204, 222, 227, 237, 252, 272,
    273, 274, 277, 278, 279, 281
Cattaneo, Andrea 40
Cedrenus, Georgius 64
Celsus 125
Cesalpino, Andrea 40, 41, 127, 131, 261
Chemnitz, Martin 185, 270, 271, 272
Chieza, Petrus 88, 262
chiromancy 13, 173–4
Cicero 51, 152, 165, 170
Cirvelo, Pedro 140, 232, 280–1
Claro, Julio 21, 189, 194, 195, 199, 210,
    215, 227
Claudian 3, 83
Cocles 174
Codronchi, Battista 20, 21, 38, 41, 49,
    131, 246–7, 251, 257, 261–2
Columella 255
comets 168–9
confession
  judicial 15, 97, 100, 194, 195, 197,
    206, 211, 212, 216, 218, 220, 221,
    227, 228, 229, 230, 232, 233, 234,
    238, 240, 241–3
  sacrament 16, 140, 169, 204, 238,
    261, 263, 265, 269, 278
confessor 177, 195, 202, 240–3, 246,
    275, 276, 277, 279, 280
Covarrubias y Horozco, Juan 173
Cranzius, see Kranz
Crespet, Pierre 214, 232

daemon 24, 25, 104, 115, 271, 272
Damiani, Pietro 136
Daneau, Lambert 28 n. 3, 213 n. 23
Della Porta, Giovanni Battista 37, 79, 276
Del Rio, Antonio 2
  Del Rio, Luis 2, 4, 44
  Del Rio, Martin 2–8
Del Vaulx, Jean 5–7, 190, 213–14
Democritus 68, 128
denunciation 191, 195, 197, 209–11, 221

Devil 6, 12, 14, 16, 53, 54, 74, 75, 76,
    78–9, 81–3, 84, 86, 88, 93, 94,
    99–100, 102, 104–5, 107, 108, 110,
    112, 113–14, 119, 121, 125, 130,
    134–7 passim, 141, 145, 150, 151,
    153–4, 157, 163, 169, 177, 179,
    183–4, 190, 203, 208, 209, 213,
    214, 215, 217, 218, 221, 226, 228,
    230, 231, 236, 240, 244, 248,
    249–50, 253, 261, 265–8 passim,
    271–4 passim, 277, 281
Dheure, Pierre 6,7
Dionysius the Areopagite 8, 78, 275
Dioscorides 48, 261
Disquisitiones Magicae 8–10, 17, 21, 23
  summary 10–16
divination 12, 13, 22, 33, 147, 148–9,
    152, 155–63, 172, 174, 187, 192,
    193, 236, 245, 278
Douai 3, 5
dreams 13, 97, 114, 149, 150, 167,
    174–9, 231, 232–3, 236, 259
Dubravius, Janus 79
Du Laurens, André 20, 39, 48

ecstasy 108
effects 78–9, 80–3, 138, 139, 162, 176,
    276, 277
Engel, Johann 65
Epicurus 128
Erasmus 131
Eusebius 166
exorcism 115, 116, 146, 147, 160, 182,
    233, 252, 262, 264–5, 268, 270,
    273, 274, 278, 279
exorcist 134, 252, 257, 264, 270, 271,
    272, 273, 279

Farinacci, Prospero 21, 189, 190, 194,
    196, 198, 199, 206, 207, 210, 215,
    227
fascinatio 12, 49, 122–5, 212, 255–6
Fernel, Jean 44
Ferrier, Oger 20, 41
Ficino, Marsilio 42, 208, 244, 245
Fracastoro, Girolamo 103
Froes, Luis 21, 181, 245, 262
Fulginas 40–1

Galen 168, 176
Gaufrido 127
Gemma, Cornelius 20, 126
Gentili, *see* Fulginas
Geoponica 147, 281
Germanicus 165
Gerson, Jean 149, 150, 151
ghosts 241, 246, 276
Giovio, Paolo 173
gipsies 174
Glycas, Michael 71
Godelmann, Johann 16, 97, 136, 183,
    186, 211, 213 n. 23, 227, 234,
    270–5
goetia 68 n. 2, 69, 71, 72, 141
Gomara, Francisco Lopez 269
Grammatico, Tommaso 199
Graz 7, 265
Grégoire, Pierre 232
Gregory of Valencia 60–1, 78
Grillando, Paolo 76, 95, 120, 122, 133,
    156, 209, 214, 215, 225, 226, 232,
    244
Guillaume de Paris 100

Haemmerlein, Felix 12, 145
Heerbrand, Jakob 273
Heliodorus 124
Hemminga, Sixtus van 166
heresy 14, 28–9, 135, 155, 174, 189–93
    passim, 204, 209–10, 222–5 *passim*,
    227, 235–8 *passim*, 241, 264, 276
heretic 29, 71, 76, 89, 97, 134, 135,
    147, 193, 203, 204, 209, 211, 221,
    223, 224, 226–7, 229, 236, 237, 270
Herodotus 99, 122
Hesiod 165, 170
Hessels, Jan 249–50, 253–4
Hincmar 35
Hippocrates 116, 125, 168, 172, 176
Homer 175
Host 93, 120, 146, 224, 225, 246
hydromancy 157–8

Iamblichus 69, 80
idolatry 18, 31, 32–3, 38, 76, 142, 152,
    154, 237, 277
Ignatius of Loyola, Saint 105, 151

imagination 38–45, 54, 97, 107, 114,
    121, 123, 127, 131, 176, 223, 228,
    257, 259, 276
incantations 52, 57–8, 72, 105, 119,
    120, 159, 224, 226, 236, 254, 266,
    269
incubus 89, 91, 110, 176
indications 14, 186, 187, 191, 193–5,
    197–202, 204–9, 216, 220–2, 229,
    257
Isidore of Seville 31
Isselt, Michael 255

Jacquier, Nicholas 125, 133, 232
Japan 21, 181, 245, 262–3, 265
John of Salisbury 70, 121
judges 13–14, 23, 125, 132–3, 182, 184,
    186–95 *passim*, 197–9, 201, 203–4,
    207–8, 210–24 *passim*, 227–31
    passim, 236, 238–43 *passim*, 248,
    276
Juvenal 160, 164

Kabbalah 22 n. 54, 69 n. 4, 246
Kempis, Cornelis 262
Koch, Konrad 168, 173
Kranz, Albert 162

Lactantius 31
Lambert von Hersfeld 136
lamia 15, 35, 36 n. 13, 89, 187, 204,
    210, 221, 224–5, 227, 234–7 *passim*,
    255, 256, 270
Lavater, Ludwig 21, 270, 271
Le Loyer, Pierre 150
Lerchemer, *see* Witekind
Libavius, Andreas 39
Liège 6, 213
Lipsius, Justus 1, 177–8
Llull, Ramón 63
Loos, Cornelis 202–3, 228, 229, 237
Louvain 3, 4, 8, 177, 246, 249
Luca, Costa ben 58
Lucan 83, 119
Lucretius 31, 49–50
Luther, Martin 84, 91, 97, 134, 135,
    185, 244
lycanthropy 20, 99, 196, 217–18, 241

maga 268
magic
    artificial 10–11, 51–4
    defined 32
    demonic 10, 19, 68–116
    harmful 12, 65
    natural 10, 36–7
    venomous 12
magician 11, 15, 46, 69, 70, 72–6 *passim*,
    78–86 *passim*, 94, 98, 99, 100, 102,
    108, 109, 113, 115, 117, 120, 129,
    130, 131, 134, 135, 136, 152, 158,
    169, 192, 204, 208, 214, 223, 224,
    226, 227, 236, 237, 243, 244, 248,
    249, 253, 254, 255, 270, 271, 273,
    275
magus 35, 46, 69, 99, 100, 108, 113,
    120, 130, 136, 152, 158, 169, 192,
    214, 223, 226, 236, 237, 243, 244,
    248, 249, 255, 270, 271
Maldonado, Juan de 2, 28
malefice 12, 13, 95, 117–18, 120–22,
    124, 125, 127, 129–31, 133, 134,
    137, 143, 154 n. 6, 174, 182, 186,
    187, 189, 190, 193, 196, 197, 198,
    202, 204, 206, 207, 211, 212, 213,
    215, 216, 218, 219, 221, 231, 234,
    235, 236, 243–8 *passim*, 250–9
    passim, 261, 262, 269, 270, 279, 280
maleficium 33, 65, 70, 117 n. 1, 118,
    182, 226
maleficus/a 15, 24, 33, 74, 89, 93, 94,
    103, 117, 122, 125, 128–31 *passim*,
    182, 185, 186, 187, 194, 197, 202,
    203, 208, 211, 213, 214, 219, 221,
    224–5, 226, 236, 244, 245, 246,
    249, 251
Malleolus, *see* Haemmerlein
Manzoli, Pietro Angelo 71
Mariana, Juan de 167
mark (diabolic) 75
Martial 172
Martin of Arles 142
Mass 93, 144, 145, 219, 224, 225, 226,
    261, 264, 267, 275, 278
Mattioli, Pierandrea 56, 104, 126
Medina, Miguel de 38, 41, 42
Mela, Pomponius 99

Melampus 172
Melanchthon 91, 97
Menghi, Girolamo 251–2, 273
Menochio, Giacomo 198, 200
Mercuriale, Girolamo 48
Metaphrastes, Symeon 151
Michaëlis, Sebastien 232, 235 n. 51, 237
Miedes, Gomez 64
miracle 13, 19–20, 32, 51, 69, 80–1,
    115, 116, 151, 154, 177, 180, 182,
    187, 188, 240, 249, 264, 267
Mocenigo, Marco Antonio 108
Molina, Luis de 83
Molitor, Ulrich 53, 91
Moller, Martin 232
More, Thomas 43
Muhammad 105
Münster, Sebastian 174

Navarre, Francisco de 195, 238
necromancer 71, 208, 227
necromancy 156, 157, 235
Netter, Thomas 136
Nicander 48, 261
Nicetas Choniates 153, 157
Nider, Johann 53, 104, 133, 136, 232,
    264–5
numbers 54–5

ointment 92, 94–5, 100, 103, 119, 127,
    196, 212, 214, 215, 220, 234, 255
Olaus Magnus 108, 126
Origen 166
Ovid 83, 119–20, 121, 124, 130, 142

pact 32, 49, 65, 72, 73–83, 86, 92, 95,
    100, 105, 106, 108, 113, 117, 118,
    121, 124, 127, 129, 131, 132, 137–
    40 *passim*, 144, 148, 149, 152,
    154–6 *passim*, 160, 167, 177, 187,
    188, 192, 217–18, 223, 224, 228,
    231, 232, 234–6 *passim*, 240, 241,
    248–51 *passim*, 253, 254, 267, 276,
    277 278 n. 41, 279, 280
Palladius 99
Paracelsus 37, 40, 244, 248
Paulinus, Fabius 55–6
Pereira, Benito 22 n. 54, 42, 60

Peru 21, 84, 150, 169, 262
Petronius 130
Peucer, Kaspar 270
philtres 120–2, 206, 223
physiognomy 13, 171–3, 208
Pico della Mirandola
   Francisco 37, 170
   Giovanni 65, 150, 166
Pictorius, George von Villingen 245
Plato 13, 244
Pliny the Elder 48, 124, 245, 261
Plotinus 69, 166
Plutarch 123, 124, 159
Pomponazzi, Pietro 40, 41, 50, 52
Ponzinibio, Giovanni Francesco 229,
   236, 237
Porphyrius 69, 80, 116, 166
possession 259–61, 262–3, 278
powder 94, 118, 216, 234, 242, 246
Proclus 69, 116, 170, 172
prognostication 148, 153–5, 157, 164,
   168–71, 179
prophecy 148–51, 152, 155, 157, 161
Psellus 86, 90, 110
purgation 180–3

rays 124
Reckius 188
Rémy, Nicholas 58, 77, 84, 85, 86, 89,
   90–1, 92, 94, 97, 113, 118, 120,
   127, 131, 137, 197, 213, 218, 232,
   234, 246, 248
reputation 191, 195, 198–200, 205–10
   passim, 221, 243
Rhodoginus, see Ricchieri
Ricardus Angelicus 124
Ricchieri, Lodovico 161, 162
Richard of Moyenville 256
Romano, Egidio 60
Rosweyde, Heribert 1

sabbat 92–4, 118, 190 n. 3, 215, 229,
   233, 234, 235, 241
sacramentals 19, 115, 121, 139, 192, 223, 274
saga 15, 16, 33, 74, 90–2 passim, 94, 95,
   108, 118, 133, 136, 178, 183, 184,
   187, 197, 204, 225, 228, 229, 233,
   234, 269

Salamanca 3, 7, 28, 68, 74 n. 18
salutatores 50, 144
Samuel 80
Sanders, Nicholas 151
Satan, see Devil
Scaliger 48, 275
Scribonius 183–5
Segni, Giovanni Battista 141
Seneca 49 n. 44, 68 n. 2, 83, 119, 131,
   157, 160, 161, 170 n. 30
Serenus, Quintus 119
signs (magical) 75, 76–7, 78, 81, 152,
   154, 156, 248–54
Silvestri of Ferrara 41, 232
Simancas, Diego 189, 192, 195, 232
Simplicius 68
Sirenius, Julius 166, 167
Solinus, Julius 3, 48
Sophronius 136
sorcery 15, 214, 222–4, 226
sortiarius 36 n. 13, 97 n. 50, 124, 193,
   203, 204, 211, 236
sortilegium 54, 65, 156, 189, 192, 214,
   222, 224
sortilegus/a 35, 36 n. 13, 96, 192, 211,
   226
Soto, Pedro de 195
Spina, Bartolommeo della 95, 97, 100,
   114–15, 232
spiritus
   astrological 224
   demons 177, 223, 224, 269, 271
   physical 69, 71, 76, 104, 124, 127, 130
   vision 151, 178
Sponde, Jean de 98
Sprenger, Jakob 15, 90, 119, 125 n. 14,
   126, 127, 130, 132, 209, 218, 220,
   232
Squarcialupi, Marcello 169
Stadius, Johann 3, 165
Stellatus, see Manzoli
Stitillius, Gaspar 84
strix/striges 15, 35, 36 n. 13, 75, 92, 94,
   98, 100, 114, 118, 119, 124, 125,
   129, 132, 183, 192, 198, 204, 209,
   214, 224, 231, 234, 236, 237, 255,
   256
succubus 35, 89, 90, 230

Suetonius 35, 142

superstition 10, 18, 22, 31–2, 66, 73, 77, 78, 81, 137, 139, 140–4 *passim*, 155, 156, 157, 160, 161, 163, 170, 174, 180, 193, 212, 218, 223, 226, 240, 246, 253, 270, 273, 277, 280, 281

swimming 13, 20, 183–8

Synesius 117

tarantula 56–7

Tertullian 35, 79, 150

theurgia 69–70, 72

Thomas of Cantimpré 47, 112, 136, 180, 264

Thyraeus, Petrus 72 n. 12

Tibullus 83

Tooker, William 51, 81

Torsellino, Orazio 266

torture 14–15, 103, 186–7, 194, 195–202, 205–9, 212, 215–19, 221, 228, 230, 250, 254, 268

Tostado, Alonso 60, 116, 124, 232

Trithemius, Johannes 72, 133

vain observance 22, 33, 137–47, 277, 278, 281

Vairo, Leonardo 38, 41, 46, 49

Valladolid 4, 173 n. 37

Valles, Francisco de 20, 41, 43, 124, 125, 127, 168 n. 27, 173

Van Ronss, Baudouin 20, 95, 253, 255

veneficium 24–5, 33, 127, 128, 206, 235 n. 49, 247, 251, 252, 258

veneficus/a 24–5, 35, 183, 195, 211, 224–5, 246, 259, 269

 poisoner 226

 potion 192

Verdier, Antoine de 173

Vergil 119, 121, 122, 161, 165, 170, 175

Visconti, Zacharias 257

Vitoria, Francisco de 32, 250, 254

Vitry, Jacques de 151

Vulpellus, Octavianus 199

werewolves, *see* lycanthropy

Wier, Johann 15, 19 n. 47, 58, 74, 97, 128, 202, 224, 228, 229, 236, 237, 270

Wimpina, *see* Koch

witchcraft 19, 54, 65, 75, 187, 189, 190, 210, 222, 235

witches 15, 33, 74–6 *passim*, 88–97 *passim*, 100–1, 108, 114, 118–20 *passim*, 125, 132, 133, 136, 178, 183–8, 192, 193, 197, 198, 204, 209, 210, 213, 214, 221, 224, 227–37 *passim*, 248, 255, 256, 269, 270

Witekind, Hermann 273, 274

witnesses 14, 191, 194, 197, 199–200, 202, 206, 221, 223 n. 32, 230, 231, 233, 234, 270

Zahuri 21, 48–9

SOCIAL AND CULTURAL VALUES
IN EARLY MODERN EUROPE

Series editor Paolo Rossi

MARTÍN DEL RIO
INVESTIGATIONS INTO MAGIC

P. G. Maxwell-Stuart

This is the first English translation of one of the most important, interesting and comprehensive discussions of the occult sciences ever published. Martín Del Rio's *Investigations into Magic* deals not only with magic in all its forms, from the manipulation of angelic and demonic powers to straightforward conjuring and illusion, but also with witchcraft, alchemy, astrology, divination, prophecy, and possession by evil spirits. In addition, Martín Del Rio offers judges and confessors practical advice on the most effective ways of dealing with people who are accused of practising magic, and enlivens his whole discussion with anecdotes drawn from a remarkable range of sources, including his own experience. Nothing so panoramic had ever appeared before, and for the next 150 years *Investigations into Magic* was the indispensable reference work on the subject.

Modern historians and students of the sixteenth century, as well as readers across many interdisciplinary fields, will find this translation an invaluable and fascinating guide to certain modes of early modern thought.

P. G. Maxwell-Stuart is a Research Fellow in the Department of History at the University of Aberdeen, and Honorary Lecturer in the Department of History at the University of St Andrews.

Cover illustration:
Anon: The Astrologer of the
Nineteenth Century,
(London 1825).

ISBN 978-0-7190-8053-1
90000

9 780719 080531